Springer Proceedings in Business and Economics

More information about this series at http://www.springer.com/series/11960

Aswini Kumar Mishra · Vairam Arunachalam
Debasis Patnaik
Editors

Current Issues in the Economy and Finance of India

ICEF 2018

Springer

Editors
Aswini Kumar Mishra
Department of Economics
Birla Institute of Technology and Science (BITS), Pilani
Goa, India

Debasis Patnaik
Department of Economics
Birla Institute of Technology and Science (BITS), Pilani
Goa, India

Vairam Arunachalam
Trulaske College of Business, School of Accountancy
University of Missouri
Columbia, MO, USA

ISSN 2198-7246 ISSN 2198-7254 (electronic)
Springer Proceedings in Business and Economics
ISBN 978-3-030-07610-8 ISBN 978-3-319-99555-7 (eBook)
https://doi.org/10.1007/978-3-319-99555-7

This Springer imprint is published by the registered company Springer Nature Switzerland AG
The registered company address is: Gewerbestrasse 11, 6330 Cham, Switzerland

Preface

This book includes papers presented at the International Conference on Economics and Finance (ICEF 2018) held at Goa, India. The 2-day event was organized by the Department of Economics, BITS Pilani, K.K. Birla Goa Campus during February 16–17, 2018. The event aimed at stimulating critical thinking and sharing knowledge across emerging themes toward sustainable development, economics, finance, and related fields. Through this event, it is being strived to provide a platform for researchers from academia, industry, and regulatory organizations to deliberate on empirical findings, advances in economic and finance theories, and policy implications related to emerging market economies, with special reference to India.

Eminent speakers like Dr. Viral Acharya (Deputy Governor, Reserve Bank of India); Prof. Chetan Ghate (Indian Statistical Institute, New Delhi), Mr. W. Andreas Bauer (Senior Resident Representative, International Monetary Fund, New Delhi), and Dr. Jose Antonio Pedrosa Garcia, Economic Affairs Officer, United Nations ESCAP) delivered distinguished lectures on this occasion. The event was supported by ICSSR and provided an avenue for disseminating information on contemporary research and future practices in economics and finance.

We have sought to assemble a set of studies addressing a broad spectrum of recent trends and issues in economics and finance, particularly those concerning India. The papers cover a wide range of contemporary issues in an ever-changing flow in services, finances, labor, and developmental hierarchies across industries in India under the influence of rising aspirations. The papers deal with monetary policy issues within a macroeconomic framework. The relationship between stock market, inflation, and stock indices is explored. Regional growth patterns, MSMEs, and the role of banks for financial inclusion of migrants have interesting treatments. Governmental responses find echo in the fulfillment of policy orientations while researchers seek innovative ways of possible optimums.

The chapters have been organized into four major fields and themes in economics and finance: Globalization, Macroeconomic Performance, and Monetary Policy; Financial Institutions, Instruments, and Markets; Regional Economic Development Issues; and Public Policy Economics and Analysis. The details of which have been clearly spelt out in the introductory chapter. An edited book such as this also required the cooperation and dedication of its many contributing authors. Apart from penning excellent chapters, the authors were always prompt in their responses. We are also indebted to the anonymous referees and members of scientific committee for providing insightful reviews with many useful comments and suggestions.

This book deserves mentioning of a few colleagues and research scholars, whose indefatigable efforts helped us in compiling this book. We would particularly like to thank (in no particular order) for the help and cooperation received from Dr. Rajorshi Sen Gupta, Dr. Sukumar Vellakkal, Prof. Rudra Prasad Pradhan, Abhishek Kumar Sinha, Manogna R. L., and King David Kweku Botchway. We would also like to acknowledge the support we received from Prof. Raghurama G., Director, BITS Pilani, K.K. Birla Goa Campus in organizing the above-mentioned event and this book is an outcome of it.

Finally, we would like to acknowledge the support and dedication of staff at Springer International Publishing AG, particularly David Bull, Eric Schmitt, Nitza Jones-Sepulveda, Allison DeVille, Susan Westendorf, Ravi Vengadachalam and Shobana Ramamurthy without whom the book would not have been finished.

Goa, India — Aswini Kumar Mishra
BITS Pilani, K.K. Birla Goa Campus

Columbia, USA — Vairam Arunachalam
University of Missouri

Goa, India — Debasis Patnaik
BITS Pilani, K.K. Birla Goa Campus

Contents

Editors and Contributors

About the Editors

Prof. Aswini Kumar Mishra is currently an Associate Professor and Head of the Department (HoD) of the Department of Economics at BITS Pilani, K.K. Birla Goa Campus, India. His current areas of research include economic inequality and economic mobility, industrial organization, price discovery in agricultural market and behavioral economics. He has published related articles in recognized international and national journals, such as *Journal of Quantitative Economics, International Economic Journal, The Economic and Political Weekly, Science, Technology and Society*, etc.

Prof. Vairam Arunachalam serves as Director of the School of Accountancy and PricewaterhouseCoopers Distinguished Professor at University of Missouri. His research and teaching interests relate to forensic accounting, data analytics, and information systems. He is a member of Accountancy Advisory Board at University of Illinois and Board of Regents of Institute of Certified Management Accountants, and has chaired several AACSB accounting accreditation review teams. His research has been published in several leading journals.

Prof. Debasis Patnaik is currently an Associate Professor in the Department of Economics at BITS Pilani, K.K. Birla Goa Campus, India, works in the area of Growth, Productivity, and Dispersal of Industries since 2005. His extended research interests are in the areas of Quality Health Care Assessment, Economic Analysis of Industrial Water Pollution, Port Logistics and Supply Chain Management and Risk Analysis of Financial and Non-financial Companies, Corporate Governance in Banks, etc., and has presented and published papers in National and International Conferences and Journals.

Contributors

Kshamanidhi Adabar Centre for Studies in Economics and Planning (CSEP), Central University of Gujarat, Gandhinagar, India

V. Suresh Babu Centre for Climate Change and Disaster Mitigation, National Institute of Rural Development and Panchayati Raj, Hyderabad, India

Rubina Barodawala Department of Economics, Faculty of Arts, The Maharaja Sayajirao University of Baroda, Vadodara, Gujarat, India

Alok Ranjan Behera Department of Analytical & Applied Economics, Utkal University, Bhubaneswar, Odisha, India

Nupur Moni Das Department of Commerce, Assam University, Silchar, India

Joyeeta Deb Department of Commerce, Assam University, Silchar, India

Mridula Goel Department of Economics, BITS Pilani, Goa, India

Sanjeev Gupta School of Business and Management Studies, Central University of Himachal Pradesh, Dharamshala, India

Matthew Hammill United Nations ESCAP, New Delhi, India

Ranu Jain SIMSREE, University of Mumbai, Mumbai, India

Parthajit Kayal Madras School of Economics, Kottur, Chennai, Tamil Nadu, India

Swati Khanna University School of Management Studies, GGSIP University, New Delhi, India

Ashish Kumar University School of Management Studies, GGSIP University, New Delhi, India

S. Maheswaran Institute for Financial Management and Research, Nungambakkam, Chennai, Tamil Nadu, India

Firdous Ahmad Malik Department of Economics, BBAU, Lucknow, Uttar Pradesh, India

Tomy Mathew Department of Commerce, CMS College (Autonomous), Kottayam, Kerala, India

Bishnu Prasad Mishra XIMB, Xavier University Bhubaneshwar, Bhubaneshwar, Odisha, India

Abha Mohan School of Contemporary Knowledge Systems, Chinmaya Vishwavidyapeeth, Ernakulam, Kerala, India

Saurabh Nayak BITS Pilani, Goa, India

Yadawananda Neog Department of Economics, Banaras Hindu University, Varanasi, India

Jose Antonio Pedrosa-Garcia United Nations ESCAP, Bangkok, Thailand

Diksha Ranawat Department of Economics, Faculty of Arts, The Maharaja Sayajirao University of Baroda, Vadodara, Gujarat, India

T. Prabhakara Reddy Satavahana Development Society, Hyderabad, India; SDS and Consultant (former) P P E, UNICEF, Patna, India

Abdul Rishad Department of Accounting and Finance, Central University of Himachal Pradesh, Dharamshala, India

Chinmayee Sahoo School of Humanities and Social Sciences, National Institute of Science Education and Research, Khorda, Odisha, India

Trupti Mayee Sahoo Centre for Studies in Economics and Planning (CSEP), Central University of Gujarat, Gandhinagar, India

Priyanka Sahu School of Economics, University of Hyderabad, Hyderabad, India

Seema Saini Department of Economics Sciences, IIT Kanpur, Kanpur, India

Akhil Sharma Department of Accounting and Finance, Central University of Himachal Pradesh, Dharamshala, India

Naresh Kumar Sharma School of Economics, University of Hyderabad, Hyderabad, India

Gyanendra Pratap Singh Govind Ballabh Pant Social Science Institute, University of Allahabad, Jhusi, Allahabad, India

K. Subramanian School of Contemporary Knowledge Systems, Chinmaya Vishwavidyapeeth, Ernakulam, Kerala, India

D. K. Yadav Department of Economics, BBAU, Lucknow, Uttar Pradesh, India

List of Figures

List of Tables

Introduction

Aswini Kumar Mishra, Vairam Arunachalam and Debasis Patnaik

This volume includes papers by leading academicians, scholars, and practitioners from Asia and the rest of the world that expand on contributions to contemporary economics and finance-related issues, providing in the process an insightful description and analysis with special reference to India. The Indian economy today is remarkable and, not surprisingly, it is growing very rapidly. It has emerged as the fastest growing major economy in the world as per the Central Statistical Organization (CSO) and International Monetary Fund (IMF) and it is expected to be one of the top three economic powers of the world over the next 10–15 years, backed by its strong democracy and partnership. The International Monetary Fund (IMF) projected the GDP growth in India to increase from 6.7% in 2017 to 7.4% in 2018 and 7.8% in 2019 lifted by strong private consumption as well as fading transitory effects of the currency exchange initiative and implementation of the national Goods and Services Tax (GST).

With the improvement in the economic scenario, there have been significant improvements in various sectors of the economy. India stands out this year as one of the ten economies that improved the most in the areas measured by doing business. It has improved its ranking by 30 spots over its 2017 ranking and is ranked 100 among 190 countries in the 2018 edition of the World Bank Group Flagship Report titled "*Doing Business 2018*". India has retained its position as the third largest startup base in the world just behind the UK and the US with over 4750 technology startups, with about 1400 new startups being founded in 2016, according to the NASSCOM-Zinnov report titled "Indian Startup Ecosystem Maturing—2016". The M&A activity in India increased 53.3% to US$ 77.6 billion in 2017 while Private Equity (PE) deals reached US$ 24.4 billion. Numerous foreign companies are setting up their facilities in India on the account of various government initiatives like Make in India and Digital India according to a report by India Brand Equity Foundation. Moreover, India is expected to be the third largest consumer economy as its consumption may triple to US$ 4 trillion by 2025, owing to a shift in consumer behavior and expenditure pattern, according to a Boston Consulting Group (BCG) report; and is estimated to surpass USA to become the second largest economy in terms of Purchasing Power Parity (PPP) by the year 2040, according to a report by PricewaterhouseCoopers.

Needless to mention, the experience of globalization and economic reform of many countries failed to pursue the twin objectives of both growth and development simultaneously. However, it is apparent that the development strategy does not give adequate attention to the distributional aspects of developmental outcome and hardly succeeds to achieve a balanced and sustained growth path. At the backdrop of the impressive progress of the Indian economy during the past two decades, the question that remains to be answered is does India still have a long way to go before it is functioning well as a market economy? This book critically examines the performance of the Indian economy at the national, state, and sectoral levels.

Each contribution also provides extensive references. There are 16 original papers in this book, authored or co-authored by 32 scholars. The contributors to this volume critically address and flesh out this simple but fundamentally important point of achieving a balanced and sustained growth path from diverse economics and finance perspectives, touching on a wide array of economic and social analyses. This volume is organized in a unique way. It goes deeper into the issues—both at the "policy" and at the "impact" levels. Of particular significance in this volume is the due importance to papers that are presently quite relevant in the field of Globalization, Macroeconomic Performance, and Monetary Policy; Financial Institutions, Instruments, and Markets; Regional Economic Development Issues; and Public Policy Economics and Analysis. Accordingly, this volume is categorized into four parts.

In the first part of this volume, "Globalization, Macroeconomic Performance, and Monetary Policy" there are five papers with contributions by Priyanka Sahu, Naresh Kumar Sharma; Abdul Rishad, Akhil Sharma, and Sanjeev Gupta; Gyanendra Pratap Singh; Abha Mohan, Dr. Tomy Mathew, and Dr. K. Subramanian; Diksha Ranawat, Rubina Barodawala. The first chapter of this part contributed by Sahu and Sharma empirically investigates the impact of macroeconomic variables on core inflation in India. First, it calculates core inflation through asymmetric trim mean approach and second autoregressive-distributed model is used to explain the dynamic effects of demand and supply shocks on core inflation. Results based on ARDL bound test confirm the existence of a long-run relationship between core inflation with other macroeconomic variables. Cumulative sum test (CUSUM and CUSUMSQ) validates the long-run relationship between variables and shows the stability of coefficients in the model. Overall, the response of core inflation to demand shock is high in case of real variables as compared to monetary variables, indicating higher impact of a non-monetary factor on core inflation in India. However, with respect to supply shock, the response of core inflation to skewness-based inflation is high as compared to food and fuel inflation. The study of Rishad, Sharma, and Gupta (Chap. 2) uses an ARDL Approach to empirically examine the broad money (M3) money demand function in the Indian economy by using a robust Autoregressive Distributed Lag (ARDL) model. It uses annual data on GDP per capita, exchange rate and inflation for a period of 41 years from 1975 onwards. The study found a strong co-integration relation between M3 and its determinants for long run but only the inflation was co-integrated for short term. It further found that the GDP elasticity and inflation elasticity of money was positive and the elasticity of exchange rate is negative. The result of CUSUM and CUSUMQ confirms a stable money demand in the Indian economy and using M3 as the policy yardstick is effective for monetary policy decisions. In Chap. 3, Singh highlights the case of global financial crisis of 2007–2008, that has been one of the most difficult financial and economic episodes for the world economy. His paper investigates changes in the impact of monetary policy on some key macroeconomic variables in pre-and post-global financial crisis of 2007–2008. The empirical evidence suggests that monetary policy shocks have expected effect on output and prices. However, the monetary policy transmission lags are significantly reduced in post-crisis period. The peak effect on output and prices are felt with a lag of 5 months and 12 months which were 13 months and 23 months, respectively, in pre-crisis periods. In the next Chapter, Mohan, Mathew, and Subramanian explore the relationship between select macro variables and stock prices. LR assessment in industry spent and inflation rates using four major indices BSE, FMCG, IT, and Healthcare. Their study examined a long-run association between industry-specific indices and inflation rate. Inflation rate measured in terms of CPI and four major sector indices of Bombay Stock Exchange such as S&P BSE Fast Moving Consumer Goods, S&P BSE Healthcare, S&P BSE Information Technology, and S&P BSE Bankex were taken for industry-specific analysis. In view of the fact that CPI numbers are measured monthly, the study makes use of monthly data of CPI and BSE Sectoral Indices, starting from January 2012 to October 2017. Econometric techniques such as Augmented Dickey–Fuller test, Johansen Cointegration test, VECM and VAR models are used to analyze the time series data. The results show that there is a negative long-run causality running from inflation rate toward FMCG and Banking indices, but no relationship was established with Pharmaceutical and IT indices. Finally, in Chap. 5 of this part, Ranawat and Barodawala pen the final chapter of this section. This paper while negating the normality of normality distribution of mean-variance portfolio model uses higher moments approach to access risk-return tradeoff to provide insights into dynamics of stock markets booms and busts. Skewness and kurtosis help investors think in terms of uncertainty, expectations, and magnitude of outcomes. The paper explains unexpected returns beyond Beta, size, book-to-market ratio. A negatively skewed significant amount experienced increased volume versus trend over the period 1981–2018. Further, the paper examines the relationship in stock market returns and selected macro variables using ARDL, which enhances investors' portfolio understanding and evaluating in terms of sensitivity of stock price to systemic effects of macro variables like GFD and call rate at various levels of significance.

In the second part, "Financial Institutions, Instruments and Markets", we have four papers written by Ashish Kumar and Swati Khanna; Joyeeta Deb and Nupur Moni Das; Seema Saini and Yadawananda Neog; Parthajit Kayal and S. Maheswaran. In Chap. 6, Kumar and Khanna investigate the lead–lag relationship in price discovery, volatility spillover, and leverage effect in stock exchanges of four Asian economies namely India, China, Hong Kong, and Japan. Data has been collected for a period from April 1, 2010 to October 31, 2016, which covers the period of post-US financial crisis of 2008. Data comprises of daily closing values of the indices Hang Seng Composite for Hong Kong, Nikkei for Japan, Shanghai Composite Index for China, and Sensex for India. Johansen Cointegration Test, VEC model, Granger Causality Test, ARCH LM test, and EGARCH model were used to examine and explore price discovery, volatility behavior, and leverage effect from one country to another. Multivariate GARCH model has been used extensively for analysis. Johansen Cointegration Test, and VEC model for price discovery and EGARCH model to analyze the leverage effect. In post-crisis period, India is co-integrated with China but is not integrated with Hong Kong and Japan. China is co-integrated with Hong Kong but not with Japan. Hong Kong and Japan are co-integrated with each other. India leads China in price discovery process. Hong Kong leads China and Japan in price discovery process. Volatility spillovers have been found among these Asian countries in post-recession era. Leverage effect is observed among all market pairs except for Hong Kong and China. The study further shows that good news information transmission generates less volatility for stock markets of India, Hong Kong, and Japan but on the contrary it generates more volatility for stock markets of China. Chapter 7 (by Deb and Das) analyzes the association of capital adequacy and insolvency risk of the Indian Commercial Banks, while controlling for various other bank-specific and macroeconomic factors which also affects the risk level of the banks. To find the interrelationship of Capital Adequacy Ratio (CAR) and insolvency risk, the data from 21 years (1991–2016) and 43 banks (25 Public Sector and 18 Private Sector Banks) have been taken into consideration and used Two-Stage Least Squares (2SLS) method to estimate the parameters of the Simultaneous Equations Model. The study employed Augmented Dicky–Fuller test, Multicollinearity test, Co-integration test, and Hausman Error Specification test in order to check for stationarity, multicollinearity, existence of long-run association and endogeneity, respectively. The results revealed that CAR and risk of the banks are positively associated. The association is bidirectional which implies nonachievement of the purpose of the Basel norms that aims to reduce the risk level of the banks. Saini and Neog (Chap. 8) examine long-run equilibrium and existence of causal relationship between financial development, energy consumption, economic growth, and FDI in India from 1978 to 2014. The Johansen–Juseling Maximum Likelihood Estimators (MLEs) in multivariate frame and Granger Causality in Vector Error Correction Model (VECM) frame are used to assess co-integration and causal assumption across variables. While long-run relationship across variables is seen, the long-run causality across variables is absent. However, bidirectional SR causality in Financial Development and Energy Consumption is seen in the Indian context. One of the policy suggestions was to develop energy infrastructure for development of the financial sector. The final chapter of this part, written by Kayal and Maheswaran, examines the leverage effect over a period by classifying days into positive-return and negative-return days. It examines the volatility asymmetry in leverage effect by decomposing the volatility into "up" and "down" volatilities. This paper makes use of extreme value estimators to examine 14 indices from different emerging economies and 10 indices from developed economies. There is evidence of a negative relationship between volatility and returns in developed markets. This study also observes a dominance of "down" volatility over "up" volatility during negative-return days.

In "Regional Economic Development Issues" part, there are three papers. In this part, chapters are contributed by Kshamanidhi Adabar and Trupti Mayee Sahoo; Chinmayee Sahoo and Alok Ranjan Behera; T. Prabhakara Reddy and V. Suresh Babu. Adabar and Sahoo in Chap. 10, examine the relationship between structural change and economic growth across 14 major Indian states from 1993–1994 to 2011–2012. Calculating income share for various economic activities and following Dietrich for NAV and MLI, McMillan, and Rodrik for within and static effects, de Vries et al. for within effect, static and dynamic effects. Increasing trend in patterns of structural change evidenced by NAV and MLI across sectors contribute to the growth process in per capita real income. However, since it is based on population instead of employment data for labor productivity, these estimates for McMillan, Rodrik, and de Vries et al. indices are examined for structural changes in per capita real income rather than labor productivity. Using catch up regression for absolute convergence, it finds evidence of absolute beta divergence meaning relatively richer states having grown faster than the poorer counterpart has. In Chap. 11, Sahoo and Behera raise the issues on Micro, Small and Medium enterprises (MSMEs) in the form of marketing, infrastructural, financial, and other constraints and challenges. These, ultimately, put a hindrance on the way to achieve a faster growth of this sector. The authors have taken the case of Bhubaneswar city, Odisha as the study area and through cluster sampling technique, 60 enterprises has been drawn randomly for the demand side analysis. Personal interview method is used by taking semi-structured questionnaire schedule for sample entrepreneurs. Factor analysis with rotate varimax normalization method is used to find out the major constraints faced by the MSMEs and to rank their problem. It identified six major factors among its interest rate is the number one constraint in the demand side which impedes the growth of MSMEs. Other problems identified are competition from well-running firm and lack of labor that is experienced by the sampled entrepreneurs. The results also show that manufacturing sector is rife with more financial issues. Chapter 12 (by Reddy and Babu), assesses the MGNREGS impact on rural labor employment via changes in land use, cropping pattern and micro irrigation. This paper is a useful contribution to study a public policy project via institutional intermediaries defining agricultural productivity parameters. A decentralized governance structure shows greater improvement in Betul though gender disparity decrease in both reflects socioeconomic urge beyond institutional outcomes. Data on agricultural wages from 2005 to 2010 shows the distributive and livelihood impacts possible with 'normal' years chosen within a comparative static framework wherein small and marginal farmers were placed in one group and medium and large farmers were placed in another group. However, migration continued showing lagged perception of institutional changes.

The final part, "Public Policy Economics and Analysis" contains four papers. The authors of this part—Matthew Hammill and Jose Antonio Pedrosa-Garcia;

Mridula Goel and Saurabh Nayak; Firdous Ahmad Malik, D. K.Yadav, and Ranu Jain; Bishnu Prasad Mishra—discuss direct policy relevance from the theory of economic policy. The paper by Hammill and Pedrosa-Garcia (Chap. 13) critically evaluates the case of South and Southwest Asia where tax systems face several challenges as reflected in terms of poor efficiency in trying to mobilize and manage public financial resources. The complexity of tax structures and the granting of exceptions undermine effectiveness, introduce regressiveness in tax systems, and hinder the social contract. Inefficiency in the tax system does not favor inclusion, which in turn lowers tax morale. Financial contributions by people and businesses to their Government depend on the perception of the public goods and services received, such as education, healthcare, basic utilities, or responsive government administration. Across South and Southwest Asia, the collection of personal income tax and property tax tends to be below potential, because of high thresholds and various exemptions. Increasing the tax base may require a carrot-and-stick approach, which also can be highly country-specific. Environmental and green taxes that internalize negative externalities are necessary in the subregion, but their design needs to accommodate two challenges. One of the challenges is to create adequate national and subregional markets for environmental taxation and emissions-type trading systems to allow enterprises to internalize costs for the first time. In Chap. 14, Goel and Nayak investigate the financial behavior of migrants that would have implications to reducing crime due to migrants. A tourism-driven economy demands perennial locational labor availability that is provided by migrants but adds the concomitant uncertainty in economic living that accompanies tourism sector. This paper starts by looking at migrant remittances in financial inclusion issues as tourism is a state subject but remittances go beyond the border. It goes on to look at demand side challenges for banking sector and willingness to look at shift to mobile-based platform for inclusion. The study focuses on access and usage of financial services like remittances and payment system, savings, credit, insurance availability to migrant. The survey also tries to capture mobile literacy and mobile usage of migrants among 15–55 years age group. It seeks to provide a methodology that can be used by financial institutions to gauge markets for financial inclusion via readiness of mobile remittances. The next chapter by Malik, Yadav, and Jain, based on survey observed that income and expenditure did not remain similar among households. In low-income households, there is a possibility of consumption without expenditure and earnings. This study examines the income and expenditure pattern of slums dwellers and their financial requirements among the key financial services (i.e., savings, credit, insurance, micro-leasing, and pension schemes) of Lucknow city. The findings suggest that poor people can and do save, particularly when institutional barriers to saving are cut off. The net mismatch position of slums in short run monthly is 70.55% and the short-run annual mismatch is 5.44% in medium run 91.84% of surplus, and in long run 94.62% of surplus. So, the slums are having surplus income in two of the three periods chosen. In case of slums, they have positive savings but they are compromising all their essential expenditures i.e., Housing, Education of Children, and other day-to-day things. The last chapter of this part by Mishra critically assesses the spectrum of financing infrastructure in India that ranged from complete budgetary support to extensive fund raising in the private space including frantic effort to internationalize the funding channels. He observed that, it is high time to strengthen the sources where considerable success has been achieved and reappraise the risk and potent deterrent/road blocks where the result has somewhat not up to the expected level. In short, the infrastructure funding space currently looks hazy and badly in need of a relook, if all the announced policy goals have the slender chance of meeting with success in days to come.

We wish to thank the authors for making their studies available for our volume. We hope that this volume lives up to their expectations. In spite of our intention to address a wide range of issues pertaining to economics and finance with special reference to India, we recognize that there are myriad issues that still need to be researched. We hope that the studies included in our volume will encourage further research and analyses in these related fields.

References

Boston Consulting Group (BCG)—Center for Customer Insight (CCI). 2017. *The New Indian: The Many Facets of a Changing Consumer.*

International Monetary Fund. 2018. *World Economic Outlook: Cyclical Upswing, Structural Change*. Washington, DC, April.

PricewaterhouseCoopers (PwC) LLP.2017. *The World in 2050: How will the global economic order change?* UK, February.

World Bank. 2018. *Doing Business 2018: Reforming to Create Jobs*. Washington, DC: World Bank.

Part I
Globalization, Macroeconomic Performance and Monetary Policy

Chapter 1
Core Inflation Dynamics and Impact of Demand and Supply Shocks: Evidence from India

Priyanka Sahu and Naresh Kumar Sharma

Abstract This paper attempts to investigate the impact of demand and supply side factors on core inflation in India. First, we empirically calculate core inflation through conventional exclusion based measure (excluding food, excluding energy and excluding both food and energy) as well as statistical measure (asymmetric trimmed mean approach). Next, we empirically try to observe the association of core inflation with macroeconomic variables through autoregressive-distributed lag model (ARDL) and bound test approach. Empirical findings based on ARDL bound test approach confirms the existence of short run and long run association of core inflation with macroeconomic variables. Overall, the response of core inflation to demand-side factors is high in case of real variables as compared to monetary variables and its response to skewness-based supply-side factor is high as compared to food and fuel inflation.

Keywords Core inflation · Demand shock · Supply shock · ARDL bound test approach

1.1 Introduction

Targeting inflation within the specific range has become the major objective of the monetary policy. Recently, there are two majors development in the macroeconomics management in India. First, announcement of a new monetary policy committee for the task of deciding the benchmark policy rates to target inflation at a specific level. Next, formal declaration of inflation targeting as a new monetary policy objective, where Consumer Price Index (CPI) acts a nominal anchor to target inflation at the rate 4% with a band of 2–6%.

P. Sahu (✉) · N. K. Sharma
School of Economics, University of Hyderabad, Hyderabad, India
e-mail: priyanka.7mar@gmail.com

A. K. Mishra et al. (eds.), *Current Issues in the Economy and Finance of India*,
Springer Proceedings in Business and Economics,
https://doi.org/10.1007/978-3-319-99555-7_1

Monetary policy works with influencing aggregate demand in an economy and therefore it is very essential for the central bank to know the underlying demand pressure prevailing in the economy. To understand the demand side pressure, most of the central banks, which consider inflation targeting as their one of the major objectives are more closely following the core inflation than the headline inflation or the overall inflation. Core inflation gives an indication about the prices rise due to demand side pressure in the economy.

However, both demand and supply side factors create large variations in the relative prices. Headline inflation consists of both transitory price changes and the permanent price changes. It takes the form as

$$(\pi_{ht}) = C + \beta(\pi_{ct}) + T_t \tag{1.1}$$

$$(T_t) = (\pi_{ht}) - C - \beta(\pi_{ct}) \tag{1.2}$$

where, (π_{ht}) = Headline inflation, (π_{ct}) = Core inflation and $(\mathrm{T_t})$ = Transitory price change.

Transitory price changes are mainly due to temporarily supply side pressure in the economy such as, temporarily food inflation due to monsoon failure and fuel inflation due to oil price hike in the external market. Lafleche and Armour (2006) has a view that monetary policy operates with lag; hence, price rise due to temporarily shocks will get correct by its own and does not require monetary policy action to deal such situation.

Therefore, the major challenges with the monetary policy is to understand the demand pressure, which persist in both short-run and the long-run. The most important challenge in front of the policy makers is to forecast inflation expectation accurately. Central banks of developed countries specially with the inflation targeting have given more attention to core inflation for forecasting inflation expectation.

However, measuring inflation expectation with headline inflation is difficult because it contain transitory noise, which, creates biasness and inaccurately observed in the long-term trend of inflation (Cecchetti 1996). In addition to this, headline inflation is highly volatile due to temporarily price changes mainly because of food and oil price shocks in the short-run, which makes ineffectiveness in the monetary policy decision making to forecast inflation expectation. Taking decision to set the benchmark policy rate through headline inflation can be misleading for the policy purpose. However, the policy decision can be effective, if one can forecast on core inflation, which eliminates all the volatile components from the headline inflation and can be considered as a good underlying trend for the headline inflation. Therefore, the study empirically examine core inflation through conventional exclusion based measure (excluding food, excluding energy and excluding both food and energy) as well as through statistical measure (asymmetric trimmed mean approach) for India by using CPI headline inflation. Further it analyse the impact of demand and supply side factors on core inflation through Autoregressive Distributed Lag Model (ARDL) Bound Test approach.

The study is organised as follows; introduction is followed by literature review in Sect. 1.2. Section 1.3 discusses the objectives of the study. Data description and methodology for constructing core inflation as well as econometric modelling is explained in Sect. 1.4. Sections 1.5 and 1.6 discuss the empirical findings and conclusion of the study.

1.2 Literature Survey

Otto Eckstein (1981) has first coined the concept of core inflation and defined it as "the trend increase in the cost of factors of production that originates in the long-term expectations of inflation in the minds of households and businesses."

The concept of core inflation is an attempt to measure the underlying trend in inflation as a monetary phenomenon under the assumption of long-run monetary neutrality (Byran and Ceechetti 1994). Empirical and theoretical works of Byran and Ceechetti (1994) and have given more strong arguments in support of using core inflation while making a policy decision as it can be used as a well-defined underlying trend for headline inflation that persists for a longer period and therefore useful for near and medium-term inflation forecasting.

At the global level, research has been conducted for the construction of core inflation based on both conventional exclusion based criteria and statistical measures by Bryan and Cecchetti (1994), Quah and Vahey (1995), Rich and Steindel (2005), Blinder and Reis (2005), Marques et al. (2003), Mishkin (2007), Bodenstein et al. (2008) and Gamber et al. (2015). In India Mohanty et al. (2000), Kar (2009), Raj and Mishra (2011), Ramachandran and Kumar (2017). Naresh and Motilal (2015) have worked on the measure of core inflation by using wholesale price index.

There are different methodologies for the construction of core inflation, namely the statistical measure and the conventional exclusion based measure. The Reserve Bank of India (RBI) mostly uses conventional exclusion-based measure (excluding food, excluding energy and excluding both food and energy) to calculate core inflation in India. It tries to remove the highly volatile elements from the headline or the total inflation such as food and fuel inflation. There is a pre-specific list of items, which is define to have transitory price movement and hence removed from the total headline inflation.

However, there are arguments put against of this approach is that the excluded item may consist of relevant information about the underlying inflation. Therefore, for the policy purpose, the conventional exclusion-based measure cannot be consider as the best measure for core inflation. On the other hand, the statistical measure such as trimmed mean, weighted median approach, moving average method, exponential smoothened series, HP Filter, common component method are more flexible and appropriate approach due to their statistical property to exclude the impact of different components each months, based on their extreme price movement at the specific point of time.

Bryan and Cecchetti (1994) have supported the significance of the statistical measure for core inflation through weighted median method, whereas Clark (2001) has favored the approach of trimmed mean method for the calculation of core inflation. According to them, both weighted median and trimmed approach removes the highly volatile components, which arises due to temporarily supply shocks. Such shocks create large movement in the prices of the components, making the overall inflation highly volatile. In this aspect, Bernanke (2007) stated that monetary policy works with lag and therefore policymakers must focus on the economic outlook. The total inflation or the headline inflation is highly volatile due to temporarily shocks, which arises because of short-run price fluctuations in food and energy components; therefore, core inflation (which exclude the highly volatile components) can acts as a better gauge for a forward-looking approach for the policy forecasting. In Addition to this Mishkin (2007), Bodenstein et al. (2008), Kiley (2008) study have suggested optimal monetary policy with distinct core and headline inflation rates. Mishkin has examined how shock to headline inflation feedback into core inflation and whether the existence and strength of shock differ across different measures of core inflation, while Kiley has examined both Consumer Price Index (CPI) and the Personal Consumption Expenditure deflator (PCE) and considered less food and energy (LFE) measures as core inflation. Alkhareif and Barnett (2015) have analyzed core inflation indicators for Saudi Arabia for the period of March 2012 to May 2014 using two alternative approaches, i.e. the exclusion method (ex-food and housing/rent) and the statistical method. The findings suggest that excluding food and housing/rent inflation is more volatile and weakly correlated with headline inflation. In contrast, the statistical core inflation is relatively more stable, less volatile and exhibits a stronger correlation. This combination of lower volatility and higher correlation with headline inflation makes the statistical method a much better choice for policymakers. Similarly, Gamber et al. (2015) have analyzed the dynamic relationship between headline and core inflation across monetary policy regimes for both Consumer Price Index and Personal Consumption Expenditure deflator by using a series of bivariate vector autoregressions model (VAR). The findings suggest that the shock to headline inflation would have a more persistence response in core inflation. On the other hand, when the monetary policy is not accommodative, headline shocks will transfer the small persistent effect on core inflation. Edward and Saeed (2017) have proposed a model for nowcasting headline and core inflation in the U.S. consumer price index and the price index for personal consumption expenditures that relies on small data series. Simple univariate and multivariate regressions were used to forecast the inflation.

Empirical studies to capture the dynamic effects of macroeconomic indicators on Inflation

This section of literature survey has mainly focused on the impact of macroeconomic variables on overall inflation i.e. headline inflation. There are literature that have mainly focused on the impact assessment of headline inflation both in India and internationally due to its theoretical understanding as well as easy availability of the data by the central bank.

In India, Bhattacharya and Patnaik (2014) have studied the monetary policy analysis for inflation targeting framework by applying a semi-structural New Keynesian open economy model for anchoring inflation expectation. The underlying framework is a standard New-Keynesian model with rational expectations, nominal and real rigidities with aggregate demand having a role in output determination. The framework blends to a reduced form version of the forward-looking general equilibrium model with New-Keynesian features. The findings suggest that the positive domestic aggregate demand shocks coupled with accommodative monetary policy and supply-side pressure have resulted in unanchored monetary policy. Similarly Rina (2013) empirically understand the overview of inflation dynamics and monetary policy transmission in Vietnam. The study has considered CPI inflation as the weighted function of the changes in the prices of tradable and non-tradable goods. The rate of changes in the prices of tradable goods is the function of the nominal exchange rate and the international price of the tradable goods. The inflation model is empirically analyze by using VAR model. The short and medium-term elasticities of inflation were estimated from the impulse responses based on a Cholesky decomposition. The findings based on impulse response function suggest that inflation is responsive to nominal effective exchange rate in the short-run, whereas in the medium run GDP growth and money supply are the principal drivers of inflation.

Moses (2013) study applied the P-star model of inflation to examine the performance of Kenyan economy over the time of 1960–2011. The empirically tested results show that past inflation contributes significantly to current inflation suggesting a high level of persistence of inflation. Domestic price gap are more significant in predicting Kenya's rate of inflation when compared with the foreign price gap.

Darbha and Patel (2012) study inflation dynamics by using the novel measure of inflation known as Pure Inflation Guages (PIG) by decomposing the price movement into (i) aggregate shocks that have equal proportional effects on all sector prices (ii) aggregated relative price effects; and (iii) sector-specific and idiosyncratic shocks. The findings show that Wholesale Price Index (WPI) inflation by the end of 2008–09 had declined to about 1% from about 8% in 2007–08. The decline in the level of headline inflation in 2008–09 have conveyed the authorities to adopt the more tightening policy to look at inflation measures corrected for sectoral and idiosyncratic shocks.

1.3 Objective of the Study

3.1 Empirically estimate the core inflation, which can be considered as the best measure for the underlying trend in the headline inflation

3.2. Empirically analyze the short run and long run effects of demand side and supply side factors on core inflation in India

1.4 Data Description and Methodology

1.4.1 Data Description

The empirical study has carried out by using monthly time series macroeconomic data covering the sample period of January 2012 to December 2017 with (2011–12) as base year price. Combined Consumer Price Index (CPI) Y-o-Y inflation data is used to calculate core inflation.

For the proxy of demand-side factors influencing core inflation, macroeconomic variables such as output gap, money growth, interest rate, effective exchange rate are taken into consideration. On the other hand, fuel inflation, food inflation and skewness-based inflation are three alternatives supply-side factors influencing core inflation.

In the present study, the output gap is defined as the difference between the actual outputs of an economy from its potential output. Potential output is the maximum amount of goods and services that an economy can turn out when it is at the most efficient. The deviation from the real GDP from its long-term trend is calculated from Hodrick–Prescott (HP) decomposition. Due to unavailability of monthly data on real GDP in India, index of industrial production (IIP) is used as a proxy for GDP. Before calculating the output gap, we filtered the seasonality components using the Census X12 method.

To reflect the demand side effects on core inflation through monetary factors, monetary variables such as, weighted average call money rate is considered as a proxy for the short-term interest rate and money growth is calculated from money stock (M3). For the external demand shock on core inflation, NEER (trade-weighted—36 currency) is used as a proxy for the effective exchange rate. Fuel and food inflation is the monthly percentage change in the fuel and energy component as well as the food component of the CPI basket of commodity, while skewness-based inflation is the deviation of core inflation from headline inflation.

The time series data is taken from Ministry of Statistics and Programme Implementation (MoSPI) and Reserve Bank of India, Database on Indian economy.

1.4.2 Methodology

This section has two parts. First, it calculates core inflation through asymmetric trimmed weighted mean approach and conventional exclusion based approach (excluding the volatile components from the overall headline inflation). Next, it discusses the methodology to capture the dynamic effects of demand and supply side factors on core inflation through Autoregressive Distributed Model and Bound Test approach.

1.4.2.1 Calculation of Core Inflation

Let, p_{it} is the price index of individual items (i) in period (t) and w_i is the weight[1] for each commodity in the CPI basket such that $\sum_{i=1}^{n} w_i = 1$. Therefore the aggregate price index (P_t) takes the form as;

$$P_t = \sum_{i=1}^{n} P_{i,t} \times w_i \tag{1.3}$$

Here, {n} represents the number of a basic commodity in the CPI basket.

Now, for calculating time-varying weights w_{it}, we multiply the price index of each commodity with their respective weights w_i such that;

$$w_{i,t} = w_i \times \frac{P_{i,t-12}}{P_{t-12}} \tag{1.4}$$

For calculating aggregate Y-o-Y inflation rate (π_t)

$$\pi_{i,t} = \frac{P_{i,t} - P_{i,t-12}}{p_{t-12}} \tag{1.5}$$

$$\pi_t = \sum_{i=1}^{n} \pi_{i,t} \times w_{i,t} \tag{1.6}$$

where π_t represents the aggregate Y-o-Y inflation rate of all items in the CPI basket of commodity.

1.4.2.2 Distribution of Inflation Data

To know the distribution of the inflation data, we have calculated the skewness and kurtosis. It is calculated through the Kth weighted central moments (m) of the cross-sectional distribution of inflation data at time (t). It is define as;

$$m_{kt} = \sum_{i=1}^{n} \frac{w_{i,t}(\pi_{i,t} - \pi_t)^k}{N} \tag{1.7}$$

Next, Karl Pearson moments coefficient of skewness (SK_t) and kurtosis (KU_t) can be expressed as;

---

[1]Weight for each component of CPI is collected from Ministry of Statistics and Programme Implementation

$$(SK_t) = (m_{3t})^2/(m_{2t})^3$$
$$(KU_t) = (m_{4t})/(m_{2t})^2$$

The coefficient of the skewness (SK_t) measures the lack of symmetric distribution of an inflation data around its mean, whereas the coefficient of kurtosis (KU_t) measure the excess kurtosis relative to the normal distribution of a data.

Figures 1.1 and 1.2 show the distribution of data. It indicates that the price distribution is more right skewed, indicating that the price distribution is positive. The average value of the coefficient of skewness is 1.145. Similarly, the average value of the coefficient of kurtosis is 6.183, indicating positive price distribution of CPI headline inflation data in India. However, data distribution is highly skewed and therefore, the asymmetric trimmed weighted mean approach is the suitable measure to calculate core inflation.

1.4.2.3 Asymmetric Trimmed Weighted Mean Method

We can use symmetric trimmed mean when the data is normally distributed. In this, the right and the left side of the distribution of data is equally trimmed. On the other

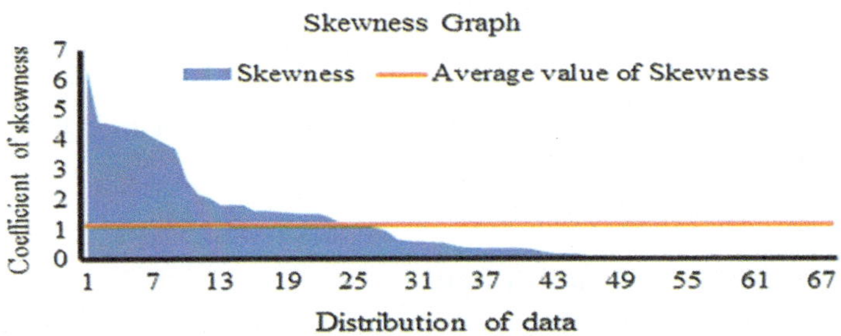

Fig. 1.1 Distribution of inflation data (Skewness graph)

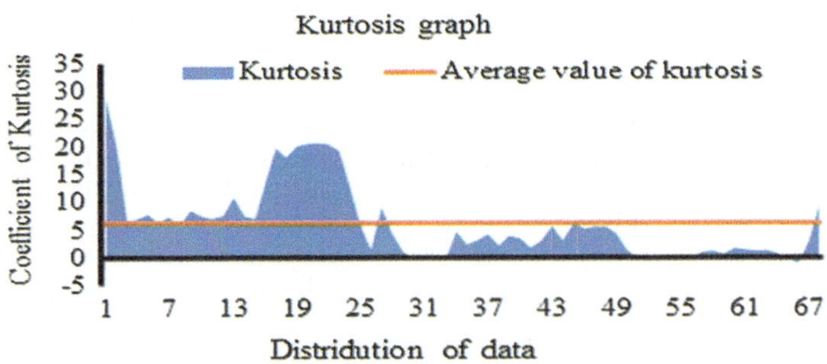

Fig. 1.2 Distribution of inflation data (Kurtosis graph)

hand, when the data is not normally distributed, asymmetric trimmed mean is consider by choosing the percentage of left trim and the right trim of the given distribution of data. Before trimming the data, it is convenient to arrange the data in ascending or descending order with their respective weights and express the data in percentile score ranging from 1 to 100. Now, for trimming, we need to define the centre (c) and the percentage of trim (p). For a symmetric distribution of data, the centre should be defined as 50, whereas for the asymmetric distribution, the centre should be greater or less than 50.

The percentage of left trim and the right trim is defined as (L, R), where L = {(c + p − 50) and R = (c − p + 50)}. Here, c denotes centre and p denotes percentage of trim. Suppose if the centre is fixed as 54 and the percentage of trim is fixed as 10, then it gives the percentile interval (L, R) as (14, 94) which is obtained by asymmetrically trimming the value of the price distribution, which is less than 14th percentile and more than 94th percentile. The percentage of a trim mean is obtain by trimming 14% of the smallest and 6% of the largest price changes. Similarly, if the centre is fixed as 50 and the percentage of trim is fixed as 10, then it gives the percentile interval (L, R) as (10, 90) which is obtained by symmetrically trimming the value of the price distribution less than 10th percentile and more than 90th percentile. In this case, the percentage of a trim mean is calculated by symmetrically trimming 10% of the smallest and the largest price distribution.

Now, Core inflation $\pi_{c,t}$ for the period (t) is defined as the weighted average of the commodity prices after trimming. It takes the form as;

$$\pi_{c,t} = \sum_{j=1}^{n} (w'_{j,t}\pi'_{j,t}) \Big/ \sum w'_{j,t} \tag{1.8}$$

Here, j represents the number of items in the CPI basket of commodity after trimming.

In the present study, the percentage of trim mean (p) is set at an interval of 5 starting from 5 to 45% and the centre (c) is chosen between 40th percentile to 60th percentile at an interval of 0.50 percentile point. Thus, a total (369 time series of trimmed means) are computed over the sample period of January 2012 to December 2017. The computational and calculation of 369 trimmed means time series is performed through R-Studio package.

1.4.2.4 Selection of the Best Measure of Core Inflation

To identify the best measure of core inflation, one can rely on the three properties of core inflation i.e. (i) it should be stable and less volatile than the headline inflation (ii) it should able to track the trend of the headline inflation and (iii) it should able to predict the future headline inflation. To test these properties of core inflation, we have formulated three condition.

First Condition—Property of Unbiasedness

For a good forecasting, it is necessary that the residual should normally distributed. It should be stationary at level with zero mean, constant variance and uncorrelated.

$$[(\pi_{ht}) = C + \beta(\pi_{ct}) + U_t] \tag{1.9}$$

where, (π_{ht}) is the headline inflation, (π_{ct}) is the core inflation and U_t is the white noise error term.

In the present study, headline and core inflation is non-stationary at level and become stationary at first difference, therefore the residual obtain after regressing headline inflation on core inflation should be stationary at level. After regressing headline inflation on each 369 trimmed mean time series or core inflation, the residual of 141-time series is found be stationary at a level I (0) with one percent level of significance.

Second Condition—Core inflation as an attractor of headline inflation

Core inflation is derived from trimming skewed prices from the headline inflation; therefore, there exists a long-run relationship between the two. However, in the present study both headline and core inflation is non-stationary at the level and become stationary at first difference, therefore, the long-run cointegrating relationship is explained through Error Correction Mechanism (ECM) model, which takes the form as;

$$\Delta\pi_{ht} = \sum_{i=1}^{n} \alpha_i \Delta\pi_{h_{t-i}} + \sum_{j=1}^{m} \beta_j \Delta\pi_{c_{t-j}} - \varepsilon_{t-1} + u_t \tag{1.10}$$

Here, ε_{t-1} is the Error Correction Term $((ECT)\, or\, \varepsilon_{t-1} = y(\pi_{h_{t-1}} - \pi_{c_{t-1}})$ and (n and m) represents the number of lags of the headline and the core inflation. In order to prove the attractor property, it assumes the null hypothesis of no attraction $(y = 0)$ against the alternative hypothesis.

As an attractor property, the ECT should exhibit the long-run relationship between the headline and the core inflation. Therefore, a negative and significant coefficient of the ECT (y) exhibits the attraction property and describe the long-run causality between the headline and the core inflation.

However, before proceeding, it is necessary to calculate the rank of a cointegrating equation. Johansen cointegration test (1991, 1995) using T-Statistics and Maximum Eigen Value is used to identify the number of cointegrating equation. Out of the 141 trimmed mean series, 111-time series passes the Johansen cointegration test. Next, the ECM model is estimated for the 111 trimmed time series. Out of 111-time series, 74-time series pass with the second condition. In this, the error correction term of each trimmed mean time series is negative and significant and therefore we cannot accept the null hypothesis of no attraction at one percent level of significance. For selecting the optimum number of lags values, Akaike information criterion (AIC) is used in the model and the maximum lag value is taken as three.

Third Condition—Property of Exogeneity

In order to show the exogenous property of core inflation, we have run the Error Correction Model on 74 trimmed mean time series, which takes the form as;

$$\Delta\pi_{ct} = \sum_{k=1}^{o} e_k \Delta\pi_{c_{t-k}} + \sum_{l=1}^{p} d_l \Delta\pi_{h_{t-l}} - \delta_{t-1} + v_t \tag{1.11}$$

Here, δ_{t-1} is the Error Correction Term $(ECT)\ or\ \delta_{t-1} = x(\pi_{c_{t-1}} - \pi_{h_{t-1}})$ and (o and p) represents the maximum number of lags of core and headline inflation.

To test the exogeneity of core inflation, we have applied (i) weak exogeneity test as well as (ii) strong exogeneity test.

1. *Weak Exogeneity test*

First Null Hypothesis = $H1_0 = (x = 0)$—It implies there is no long-run association. It is tested through T-Statistics.

Second Null Hypothesis = $H2_0 = (d_1 \ldots d_p = 0)$—It indicates the lag values of headline inflation has no effect on core inflation. The joint effects of the lag values of the headline inflation is tested through block exogeneity Wald Test.

2. *Strong Exogeneity test*

Third Null Hypothesis = $H3_0 = (x = d_1 = \cdots = d_p = 0)$—Acceptance of the null hypothesis implies that core inflation is exogenously determine by its own lag values. To perform the strong exogeneity test, we use Wald Statistic, which indicates joint effects of regressors on the dependent variable. Wald statistics assume the null hypothesis of no effect.

Out of 74 trimmed series, 67 series pass the weak exogeneity test. Out of 67-time series trimmed mean, we have selected those trimmed means series, which strongly accept the null hypothesis, i.e. whose p-value is 0.9 or approximately one. Based on the first and second null hypothesis, the p-values of [(47, 10); (48, 20); (48.5, 20); (51.5, 10); (52, 10); (52.5, 10); (53, 10)] trimmed mean time series is approximately near to one. Therefore, the strong exogeneity test is applied to these seven trimmed mean time series.

Table 1.1 represents the strong exogeneity test. Wald Statistics based on F-Test is used to test the joint effect of the regressors. The null hypothesis i.e. $H3_0 = (x = d_1 = \cdots = d_p = 0)$ has to be accepted. Hence, the insignificant F-statistics suggests that there is no joint effect of the regressors on core inflation. Core inflation is only affected by its own past values.

Table 1.1 Strong exogeneity test (Wald statistics)

Trimmed mean	F-statistic	(DF)	*P*-value
(47_10)	0.056	(3, 59)	0.938
(48_20)	0.236	(3, 59)	0.947
(48.5_20)	0.136	(3, 59)	0.938
(51.5_10)	0.196	(3, 59)	0.899
(52_10)	0.250	(3, 59)	0.861
(52.5_10)	0.058	(3, 59)	0.982
(53_10)	0.058	(3, 59)	0.982

1.4.2.5 Variance and the Relative Variance of Core Inflation

To select the best core inflation among the selected seven alternatives core inflation, which passes all the three condition, we have chosen the variance and the relative variance criteria. Among the seven alternatives of core inflation, the one that indicates the smallest variance and the relative variance is considered as the best measure of core inflation and therefore could be considered as a good trend for headline inflation. The least variance and the relative variance indicates the small volatility between core inflation and headline inflation.

Table 1.2 represents the variance and the relative variance of the seven best measure of core inflation, which passes the above given three condition. Among seven alternatives, the variance and relative variance of (48.5_20) trimmed series is the smallest and optimal measure of core inflation in the class of all trimmed mean time series.

1.4.2.6 Alternatives Measure of Core Inflation

Further, the study has also calculated core inflation through conventional exclusion based measure i.e. excluding food, excluding energy and excluding food and energy along with the symmetric trimmed mean measure of core inflation. The purpose of calculating core inflation through different method is to understand,

Table 1.2 Variance and relative variance of core inflation

CPI inflation	Variance	Relative variance
Headline inflation	3.91	1
(47_10)	3.75	0.96
(48_20)	2.88	0.74
(48.5_20)	2.70	0.69*
(51.5_10)	3.79	0.97
(52_10)	3.79	0.97
(52.5_10)	3.35	0.86
(53_10)	3.35	0.86

Note Relative variance = variance of core inflation/variance of headline inflation

* Denotes (48.5_20) trimmed series as a best measure of core inflation

which measure of core inflation can give a good trend for the underlying headline inflation. All thc measure of core inflation has shown the long run association with the headline inflation. The error correction term (ECT) is negative and significant except for CPI _ excluding food and energy measure.

Next, we have to estimate how well the core measure predicts the underlying trend of inflation. To construct the trend measure of inflation, we have applied Baxter and King (1999) band-pass filter to the headline inflation data (Dolmas 2005; Clark 2001; Cogley 2002; Bryan and Cecchetti 1994) and then calculated the Root Mean Square Error Test (RMSE). It is the difference between the trend inflation and the core inflation. The value of (RMSE) lies between zeros to one. Lower the value of (RMSE) indicates the better predictive ability of core inflation.

$$\mathrm{RMSE} = \frac{\sqrt{\sum[\pi_t(Trend\ inflation) - \pi_t(Core\ inflation)]^2}}{T}, \quad \text{where } \mathrm{t} = 1,\ T$$

The estimated (RMSE) for the conventional exclusion based measures i.e. (CPI_excluding food, CPI_excluding energy and CPI_excluding food and energy) are greater than one, indicating that these measures of core inflation are not good for predicting headline inflation. However, the (RMSE) of symmetric trimmed mean series i.e. [(50, 5) (50, 10) (50, 15) (50, 20)] have performed better, but the core inflation calculated from asymmetric trimmed mean approach i.e. (48.5, 20) trimmed series is observed to have the least (RMSE) indicating that it is good fit for predicting the headline inflation.

Table 1.3 represents that (48.5_20) trimmed series of core inflation is considered as the best series, which can also be considered as a good trend for headline inflation. Thus, 20% of trimming from the headline inflation performs better to explain the underlying trend in inflation in the present study. On the other hand, the conventional exclusion based measures of core inflation that is (CPI_excluding food, CPI_excluding energy and CPI_excluding food and energy) has not performed well (Figs. 1.3, 1.4 and 1.5).

Table 1.3 Alternatives measure of core inflation

Core inflation	ECT	Standard error	t-statistics	*p*-value	RMSE
CPI_Excluding food	−0.147	0.077	−1.905	0.061	1.401
CPI_Excluding energy	0.311	0.242	1.286	0.203	1.221
CPI_Excluding food and energy	−0.132	0.078	−1.687	0.097	1.463
CPI_(50,5)	−0.218	0.097	−2.251	0.028	0.303
CPI_(50,10)	−0.219	0.081	−2.461	0.017	0.288
CPI_(50,15)	−0.212	0.086	−2.474	0.026	0.271
CPI_(50,20)	−0.207	0.087	−2.366	0.021	0.222
CPI_(52.5,10)	−0.184	0.082	−2.241	0.029	0.252
CPI_(48,20)	−0.195	0.089	−2.192	0.032	0.284
CPI_(48.5,20)	−0.208	0.088	−2.379	0.021	0.219*

* Denotes (48.5,20) trimmed series as a best measure of core inflation

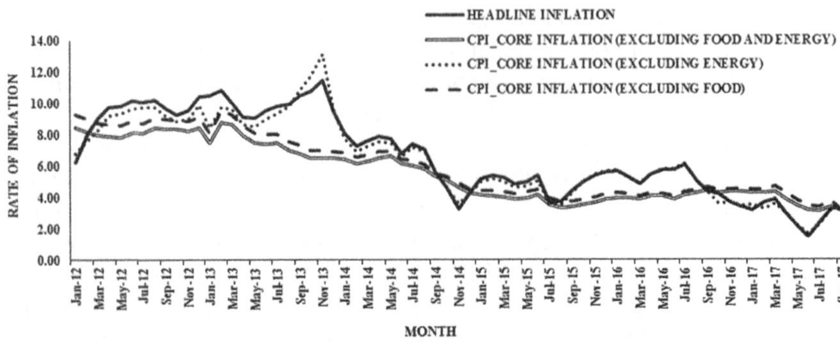

Fig. 1.3 CPI_Core inflation conventional exclusion based measure

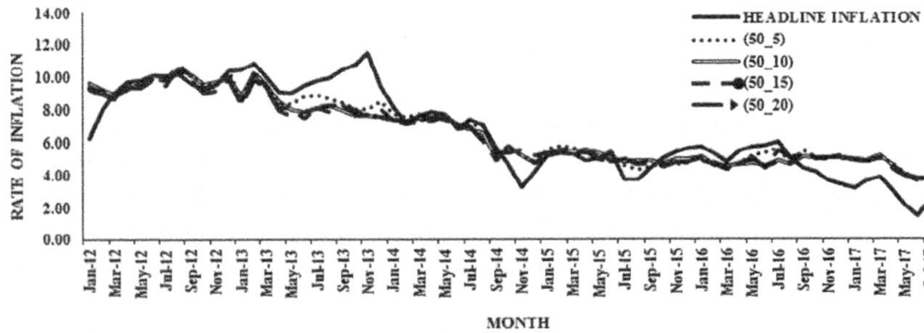

Fig. 1.4 CPI_Core inflation symmetric trimmed measure

Fig. 1.5 CPI_Core inflation asymmetric trimmed measure

1.4.3 Model Specification and Econometric Modelling

This section deals with econometric modelling to capture the dynamic effects of demand and supply side factors on core inflation[2]. Macroeconomics indicators such as output gap (o^g) money growth (m^g) short-term interest rate or call money rates (i) effective exchange rate (ex) are considered as demand side factors as because any changes in these indicators will directly affect the aggregated demand (AD) of an economy. On the other hand, fuel inflation (F_u) food inflation (F_O) and skewness-based inflation[3] (S_s) is considered as three alternatives supply shocks in the model.

The theoretical framework for modelling inflation can be understood from augmented Philips Curve, where the expectation is formed adaptively. Additionally, inflation and output gap is positively associated. A positive output gap i.e. when actual output is greater than the potential output can lead to inflationary pressure in an economy and vice versa. Similarly, the role of supply shocks has gained its importance in predicting inflation during the 1970s. Gordon (1977, 1982) study extended the expected augmented Philips Curve by incorporating the supply shocks and (Hallman et al. 1993, 1991) develop the P-star model of inflation based on the quantity theory of money, i.e., PY = MV. Considering the theoretical understanding, we have formulated three econometric modelling with respect to three different supply shock i.e. $(S_s)(F_O)$ and (F_u).

***MODEL 1*: (*Supply Shock—Skewness Based Inflation* (S_s))**

$$\pi_t^c = \partial + \sum_{i=1}^{n} \alpha_i \pi_{t-i}^c + \sum_{j=0}^{n} b_j o_{t-j}^g + \sum_{k=0}^{n} c_k m_{t-k}^g + \sum_{l=0}^{n} d_l I_{t-l} + \sum_{q=0}^{n} f_q ex_{t-q} + \sum_{r=0}^{n} g_r S_{st-r} + u_{1t} \quad (1.12)$$

***MODEL 2*: (*Supply Shock—Food Inflation* (F_o))**

$$\pi_t^c = \partial^* + \sum_{i=1}^{n} a_i^* \pi_{t-i}^c + \sum_{j=0}^{n} b^* o_{t-j}^g + \sum_{k=0}^{n} c_k^* m_{t-k}^g + \sum_{l=0}^{n} d_l^* I_{t-l} + \sum_{q=0}^{n} f_q^* ex_{t-q} + \sum_{r=0}^{n} g_r^* F_{O_{t-r}} + u_{2t} \quad (1.13)$$

[2]Estimated Trimmed mean (48.5_20) core inflation is used as a proxy for core inflation in the econometric modelling.

[3]Skewness based inflation or supply shock is calculated by differencing core inflation (calculated through asymmetric trim mean approach) from headline inflation.

***MODEL 3*: (*Supply Shock—Fuel Inflation* (F_u)**

$$\pi_t^c = \partial^{**} + \sum_{i=1}^{n} a_i^{**}\pi_{t-i}^c + \sum_{k=0}^{n} b_k^{**} o_{t-k}^g \sum_{k=0}^{n} c_k^{**} m_{t-k}^g + \sum_{l=0}^{n} d_l^{**} I_{t-l} + \sum_{q=0}^{n} f_q^{**} ex_{t-q} + \sum_{r=0}^{n} g_r^{**} F_{u_{t-r}} + u_{3t} \quad (1.14)$$

The study uses linear Autoregressive Distributed Lag (ARDL)[4] Bound test procedure, originally introduced by Pesaran and Shin (1999) and Pesaran et al. (2001) to estimate the impact of macroeconomic indicators on core inflation. Linear Autoregressive Distributed Lag (ARDL) takes the form as;

$$y_t = C + \sum_{i=1}^{p} a_i \Delta y_{t-i} + \sum_{j=0}^{q} b_j \Delta x_{t-j} + \rho y_{t-1} + \propto x_{t-1} + \varepsilon_{t-1} + U_t \quad (14)$$

where, y_t is the k × 1 vector of endogenous variables, x_t is the k × 1 vector of exogenous variables, ε_{t-1} is the error correction term, U_t is the white noise error term and a_i, b_j, ρ and $\propto$ are the parameters coefficients in the ARDL model. ARDL bound test is used to capture the dynamic effects of core inflation in the short run and long run. The bound test is based on F-statistics. It indicates the long run association among the macroeconomic variables only if the F-statistics is greater than the critical values of the upper bound i.e. I(0) in the ARDL bound test.

1.5 Empirical Analysis

1.5.1 Stationarity Test

The unit root test is performed by Augmented Dickey-Fuller procedure ADF test for each time series data. It takes the form as;

$$\Delta y_t = b0 + b1t + b2\Delta y_{t-1} + \cdots + bp\Delta y_{t-p+1} + u_t$$

where, b0 is a constant, b1 is the coefficient for a time trend, and bp is the coefficient for the lagged differences of y_t such that u_t corresponds to white noise. The unit root test is carried out using the hypothesis that a unit root is present, against the alternative hypothesis.

[4]ARDL bound test is convenient to use with a combination of stationary and non-stationary data (at level).

Table 1.4 Stationarity test

Variables	With intercept		With intercept and trend	
	At level	At first difference	At level	At first difference
Core inflation	0.711	0.000	0.098	0.000
Money growth	0.707	0.000	0.180	0.000
Output gap	0.159	0.040	0.409	0.036
Interest rate	0.001	–	0.008	–
Effective exchange rate	0.001	–	0.005	–
Skewness based inflation	0.090	0.000	0.081	0.000
Food inflation	0.254	0.000	0.058	0.000
Fuel inflation	0.391	0.000	0.047	0.000

Note Figures denotes the *p*-value
Source Author's calculation

Table 1.4 reports stationarity test. The entire macroeconomic variables except for the interest rate and effective exchange rate depreciation are stationary at level i.e. I(0), whereas all the other variables become stationary after first difference i.e. I(1).

1.5.2 Bound Testing Approach

ARDL model is best fitted with the combination of I(0) and I(1) variables. Before proceeding with the ARDL techniques, we have performed the Bound test based on F-statistic.

Table 1.5 reports the ARDL Bound test. In the entire three model, F-statistic is greater than the critical value of the upper bound, indicating the long-run association of core inflation with the regressors incorporated in the entire model.

Table 1.5 ARDL bound test

	Model 1		Model 2		Model 3	
F-statistics	15.969		12.477		16.531	
Level of significance (%)	10		5		1	
Critical value bounds	I(0) (2.26)	I(1) (3.45)	I(0) (2.62)	I(1) (3.79)	I(0) (3.41)	I(1) (4.68)

Source Author's calculation

1.5.3 Dynamic Effects of the Macroeconomic Variables on Core Inflation

Short-Run Dynamic Effects

The speed of adjustment coefficient, i.e. the Error Correction Term (ECT) reinstates equilibrium in the dynamic model has a negative sign and statistically significant ensuring long-run equilibrium can be attained. Akai Information Criteria (AIC) is used to select optimal lag length in the entire three model. In model 1, 2 and 3, we have taken two lag values of core inflation, whereas all other variables are taken without their lags, except in model 2, where only one lag value of food inflation is considered.

Table 1.6 represents the short-run dynamics of the macroeconomic variables on core inflation. It is empirically observed that the past values of core inflation have a positive and statistically significant effect on the present core inflation. Additionally, the demand side variables, i.e. output gap (o^g) and the money growth (m^g) show a positive and significant effect on core inflation, whereas effective exchange rate (ex) and interest rate (i) show a negative association with the core

Table 1.6 ARDL (short-run coefficients)

Variable	Model 1			Model 2			Model 3		
	ARDL model selection (2, 0, 0, 0, 0, 0)			ARDL model selection (2, 0, 0, 0, 0, 1)			ARDL model selection (2, 0, 0, 0, 0, 0)		
	Coeffi	S.E	T-stat	Coeffi	S.E	T-stat	Coeffi	S.E	T-stat
Constant	−0.087	0.045	−1.919	−0.105	0.050	−2.082	−0.123	0.052	−2.366
$(\ln)\Delta\pi^c_{t-1}$	0.297	0.099	2.992	0.389	0.120	3.251	0.416	0.114	3.637
$(\ln)\Delta\pi^c_{t-2}$	0.225	0.091	2.469	0.281	0.119	2.359	0.226	0.110	2.054
Δo^g_t	0.279	0.134	2.076	0.282	0.129	2.182	0.307	0.142	2.166
Δm^g_t	0.072	0.034	2.117	0.048	0.015	3.201	0.025	0.015	1.666
ΔI_t	−0.415	0.079	−5.225	−0.217	0.079	−2.750	−0.160	0.068	−2.364
Δex_t	−0.125	0.054	−2.314	−0.154	0.052	−2.961	−0.187	0.054	−3.462
ΔS_{st}	0.428	0.096	4.448						
ΔF_{Ot}				0.068	0.066	1.034			
ΔF_{Ot-1}				0.161	0.074	2.173			
ΔF_{Ut}							0.068	0.021	3.238
ECT (−1)	−0.552	0.161	−3.428	−0.670	0.197	−3.401	−0.642	0.188	−3.414
R-square	0.683			0.554			0.582		
Adjusted	0.590			0.437			0.448		
D–W stat	1.955			1.979			1.997		
F-statistics	7.329			4.708			4.345		
RMSE	0.312			0.384			0.388		

Note Variables are significant at 1 and 5% level of significance
Source Author's calculation

inflation in the short-run. Similarly, three supply-side factors i.e. fuel inflation (F_u) food inflation (F_O) and skewness-based inflation (S_s) have shown a positive and significant relationship with the core inflation in the short run. Moreover, while considering the magnitude of response of the demand side factors, such as, real variables (output gap) and monetary variables (money growth, interest rate and exchange rate) it is observed that real output gap has the higher impact on core inflation as compared to monetary variables in the entire three model. One percentage change in output gap will create an inflationary pressure by 27. 9% in model one, 28.2% in model two and 30.7% in model three respectively.

With respect to supply-side factors, the magnitude of response of core inflation to one percentage change in skewness based inflation (S_{st}) is (42.8%), fuel inflation (F_{ut}) is (6.8%) and food inflation $\{(F_{Ot}\ and\ F_{Ot-1})\}$ is (6.8 and 16.1%) respectively. The magnitude of response of the supply shock i.e. (S_{st}) is high as compared to (F_{ut}) and (F_{ot}).

Overall, it is observed from the short-run dynamics that both demand and supply side factors have significant effect on the core inflation. The F-statistics in the entire three model is significant at one percent level of significance. Similarly, the predictive ability of the entire three model is performed through Room Mean Square Error (RMSE) is lies between (0–0.5) for the entire three model.

Long-Run Dynamic Effects

Table 1.7 reports the long-run dynamic effects of the macroeconomic variables on core inflation. The impact of output gap on core inflation is negative in the long run indicating that the gap between actual output and the potential output get minimize

Table 1.7 ARDL (long-run coefficients)

	Model-1			Model-2			Model-3		
Variable	Coeffi	S.E	T-stat	Coeffi	S.E	T-Stat	Coeffi	S.E	T-stat
Constant	−0.057	0.028	−2.029 (0.048)	−0.063	0.029	−2.159 (0.035)	−0.075	0.030	−2.506 (0.016)
O_t^g	−1.012	0.944	−1.073 (0.289)	−1.049	0.428	−2.450 (0.018)	0.438	0.994	0.440 (0.662)
m_t^g	0.070	0.043	1.630 (0.109)	0.022	0.023	0.967 (0.338)	0.078	0.065	1.207 (0.233)
I_t	−0.273	0.067	−4.043 (0.000)	−0.208	0.071	−2.910 (0.005)	−0.098	0.045	−2.178 (0.034)
ex_t	−0.452	0.252	−1.793 (0.066)	−0.256	0.089	−2.876 (0.036)	−0.259	0.254	−1.019 (0.068)
S_{st}	0.281	0.076	3.704 (0.001)				0.041	0.054	0.763 (0.449)
F_{Ot}				0.055	0.068	0.820 (0.416)			
F_{Ut}							0.438	0.994	0.440 (0.662)

Note Figures in the parenthesis denotes the *P*-value
Source Author's calculation

in the long-run. However, money growth has a positive, but insignificant effect on the core inflation in the long indicating that there is no long-run effect of money growth. Similarly, interest rate also keeps inflation low in the long run. The monetary variables such as money growth and interest rate keep inflation low by targeting its policy rates, thus indicating the effectiveness of the monetary policy in India.

Additionally, it is also empirically observed that there persist a long-run impact of skewness based supply shock on the core inflation in India, where as food inflation and fuel inflation does not seem to affect core inflation in the long-run.

1.5.4 Residual Diagnostic

Table 1.8 reports the residual diagnostic test. For testing serial correlation in the error term, Breusch–Godfrey Serial Correlation LM test based on F-statistic is applied. It assumes the null hypothesis of no serial correlation in errors terms. The F-statistics indicates that there is no problem of serial correlation in the entire three model. Breusch-Pagan-Godfrey-Test is used to test heteroscedasticity in the data. The test results suggest that residuals are homoscedastic. To test the normal distribution of data Jarque–Bera test statistics is used. The results indicate that the residuals are normally distributed in the entire three model.

1.5.5 Stability of the Coefficient (CUSUM Square Test)

To test the stability of the parameters, we have estimated (CUSUMSQ) cumulative sum of square test.

Figures 1.6, 1.7 and 1.8 represent CUSUMSQ test for the three model. It suggests the stability of the parameters at 5 percent level of significance in the entire three model.

Table 1.8 Residual diagnostic

Test-statistics	Model 1	Model 2	Model 3
Jarque–Bera statistics Normality test	2.264 (0.322)[c]	0.058 (0.971)	5.004 (0.813)
Breusch-Godfrey Serial correlation[a]	0.334 (0.716)	0.106 (0.899)	0.049 (0.951)
Breusch-Pagan (BP) test Heteroscedasticity test[b]	0.707 (0.915)	0.376 (0.784)	0.528 (0.803)

[a]Breusch-Godfrey Serial Correlation LM Test is based on F-statistics
[b]Breusch-Pagan (BP) test of heteroscedasticity is based on Chi-square Test
[c]Figures in the parenthesis denotes the *p*-value
Source Author's calculation

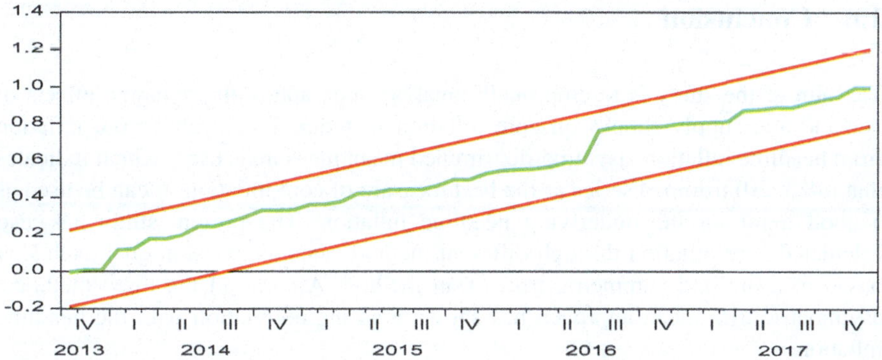

Fig. 1.6 CUSUM square test (model 1)

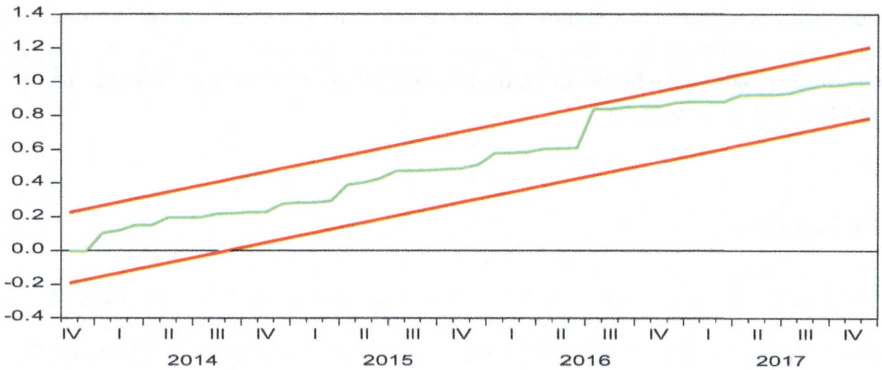

Fig. 1.7 CUSUM square test (model 2)

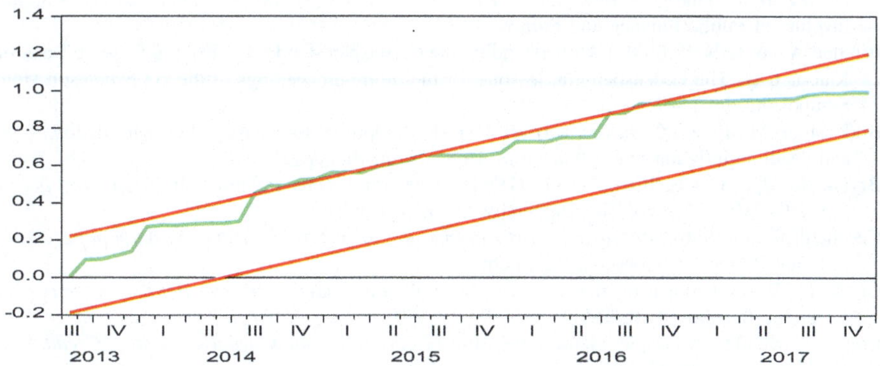

Fig. 1.8 CUSUM square test (model 3)

1.6 Conclusion

The aim of the study is to empirically analyse and capture the dynamic effects of demand and supply shocks on core inflation in India. To calculate core inflation from headline inflation, asymmetric trimmed mean measure is used, which indicates that (48.5_20) trimmed series as the best measure of core inflation. It can be used as a good trend for the underlying headline inflation. The present study has also calculated core inflation through different method, such as, conventional exclusion based measure and symmetric trim mean method. Among all the three methods, asymmetric trim mean approach has shown a strong correlation with the headline inflation.

Further, ARDL Bound testing approach is used to capture the dynamic behaviour of the macroeconomics variables towards the core inflation. The evidence from empirical investigation suggest that there is a significant impact of demand and supply side factors on core inflation. The response of core inflation to demand side factor is high in case output gap as compared to monetary variables, indicating the higher impact of non-monetary factor on core inflation in India. Similarly, the response of skewness-based inflation on core inflation is high as compare to food and fuel inflation in India.

References

Alkhareif, R. M., & Barnett, W. A. (2015). Core inflation indicators for Saudi Arabia. *Panoeconomicus, Savez ekonomista Vojvodine, Novi Sad, Serbia, 62*(3), 257–266.

Baxter, M., & King, R. G. (1999). Measuring business cycles: Approximate band-pass filters for economic time series. *Review of economics and statistics, 81*(4), 575–593.

Bernanke, B. S. (2007). Inflation Expectations and Inflation Forecasting. Monetary Economics Workshop of the National Bureau of Economic Research Summer Institute, Cambridge, Mass.

Bhattacharya, R., & Patnaik, I. (2014). Monetary policy analysis in an inflation targeting framework in emerging economies: The case of India. Working Papers 14/131, National Institute of Public Finance and Policy.

Blinder, A ., & Reis, R. (2005). Understanding the Greenspan standard in Federal Reserve Bank of Kansas City, The Greenspan era: lessons for the future.proceedings of the 2005 Jackson Hole Symposium, pp 11–96.

Bodenstein, M., Erceg, C. J., & Guerrieri, L. (2008). Optimal monetary policy with distinct core and headline inflation rates. *Journal of Monetary Economics, 55,* 18–33.

Bryan, M. F., & Cecchetti, S. G. (1994). Measuring core inflation. In *Monetary policy* (pp. 195–219). Chicago: The University of Chicago Press.

Cecchetti, S. G. (1996). *Measuring short-run inflation for central bankers. Working paper 5786.* National Bureau of Economic Research.

Clark, T. (2001). Comparing measures of core inflation. *Federal Reserve Bank of Kansas City Economic Review, 86*(2), 5–31.

Cogley, T. (2002). A simple adaptive measure of core inflation. *Journal of Money, Credit, and Banking, 34*(1), 94–113.

Darbha, G., & Patel, U.R. (2012). Dynamics of inflation "herding": Decoding India's Inflationary Process: Brookings Report.

Dolmas, J. (2005). Trimmed mean PCE inflation. Working Papers 0506, Federal Reserve Bank of Dallas.

Eckstein, O. (1981). *Core Inflation*. Englewood Cliffs, N.J.: Prentice-Hall.

Edward, K., & Saeed, Z. (2017). Nowcasting US Headline and Core Inflation. *Journal of Money, Credit and Banking, 49*(5), 931–968.

Gamber, E. N., Smith, J. K., & Eftimoiu, R. (2015). The dynamic relationship between core and headline inflation. *Journal of Economics and Business, 81,* 38–53.

Gordon, R. J. (1977). The Theory of Domestic Inflation. *The American Economic Review, 67*(1): 128–134.

Gordon, R. J. (1982). Price Inertia and Policy Ineffectiveness in the United States, 1890–1980. *Journal of Political Economy, 90*(6): 1087–1117.

Hallman, J. J., & Anderson, R. G. (1993). Has the long-run velocity of M2 shifted? Evidence from the P* model. *Economic Review, 29*(1), 14.

Hallman, J. J., Porter, R. D., & Small, D. H. (1991). Is the price level tied to the M2 monetary aggregate in the long run? *The American Economic Review*, 841–858.

Johansen, S. (1991). Estimation and Hypothesis Testing of Cointegration Vectors in Gaussian Vector Autoregressive Models. *Econometrica, 59*(6), 1551–1580.

Johansen, S. (1995). A stastistical analysis of cointegration for I (2) variables. *Econometric Theory, 11*(1), 25–59.

Kar, S. (2009). Statistical tools as measures of core inflation for India. *Indian Economic Review,* 225–245.

Kiley, M. T. (2008). *Estimating the common trend rate of inflation for consumer prices and consumer prices excluding food and energy prices*. Divisions of Research & Statistics and Monetary Affairs, Federal Reserve Board.

Moses, C. K. (2013). The P-star model of inflation and its performance for the Kenyan economy. *International Journal of Economics and Finance, 5*(9), 82.

Laflèche, T., & Armour, J. (2006). Evaluating measures of core inflation. *BoC Review, 19*, 29.

Marques, C. R., Neves, P. D., & Sarmento, L. M. (2003). Evaluating core inflation indicators. *Economic Modelling, 20*(4), 765–775.

Mishkin, F. S. (2007). Headline versus core inflation in the conduct of monetary policy. In: *Business Cycles, International Transmission and Macroeconomic Policies Conference, HEC Montreal, Montreal,* Canada.

Mohanty, D., Rath, D. P., & Ramaiah, M. (2000). Measures of core inflation for India. *Economic and Political Weekly, 35*(5), 273–282.

Naresh, S., & Motilal, B. (2015). Measuring core inflation in India: An asymmetric trimmed mean approach. *Cogent Economics & Finance, 3*(1), 1014252, 1–15.

Pesaran, M.H., Shin, Y. (1999). An autoregressive distributed lag modelling approach to cointegration analysis. In: Strom, S. (Ed.), *Econometrics and Economic Theory in 20th Century: The Ragnar Frisch Centennial Symposium.* Cambridge University Press, Cambridge Chapter 11.

Pesaran, M. H., Shin, Y., & Smith, R. J. (2001). Bounds testing approaches to the analysis of level relationships. *Journal of applied Econometrics, 16*(3), 289–326.

Quah, D., & Vahey, S. P. (1995). Measuring core inflation. *The Economic Journal, 105*(432), 1130–1144.

Raj, J., & Misra, S. (2011). Measures of core inflation in India–an empirical evaluation. Reserve Bank of India Department of Economic and Policy Research Working Paper 16.

Ramachandran, M., & Kumar, R. (2017). *Inflation and shocks*. Development research Group, Reserve Bank of India.

Rich, R. W., & Steindel, C. (2005). A review of core inflation and an evaluation of its measures. Federal Reserve Bank of New York Staff Reports, no. 236

Rina, B. (2013). Inflation dynamics and monetary policy transmission in Vietnam and emerging Asia. *Journal of Asian Economics, 34,* 16–26.

Chapter 2
Demand for Money in India: An ARDL Approach

Abdul Rishad, Akhil Sharma and Sanjeev Gupta

Abstract Understanding the stability of monetary aggregates and different determinants of money demand in an economy is necessary for the planning and implementation of monetary policy because of the sensitivity and importance of money in an economy. This study empirically examines the broad money (M3) money demand function in Indian economy by using a robust Autoregressive Distributed Lag (ARDL) model suggested by Pesaran et al. (J Appl Econom 16:289–326, 2001). It uses annual data on GDP per-capita, exchange rate and inflation for a period of 41 years from 1975 onwards. The study found a strong co-integration relation between M3 and its determinants for long-run but only the inflation was co-integrated for short-run. It further found that the GDP elasticity & inflation elasticity of money was positive and the elasticity of exchange rate is negative. The result of CUSUM and CUSUMQ confirm a stable money demand in Indian economy and using M3 as the policy yardstick is effective for monetary policy decisions.

Keywords Broad money · ARDL · India · Determinants · CUSUM
CUSUMQ

A. Rishad (✉) · A. Sharma
Department of Accounting and Finance,
Central University of Himachal Pradesh, Dharamshala, India
e-mail: ktdahsir@gmail.com

A. Sharma
e-mail: 1990akhilsharma@gmail.com

S. Gupta
School of Business and Management Studies,
Central University of Himachal Pradesh, Dharamshala, India
e-mail: sanjeeveco@hotmail.com

A. K. Mishra et al. (eds.), *Current Issues in the Economy and Finance of India*,
Springer Proceedings in Business and Economics,
https://doi.org/10.1007/978-3-319-99555-7_2

2.1 Introduction

Understanding money demand function is useful to assess the effectiveness of monetary policies, as it is a central issue in the macroeconomic stability of an economy. As a crucial economic growth indicator, increase in money demand indicates the progress in economic activities, and a drop in money demand usually is a sign of worsening economic climate (Maravic and Palic 2010). Many monetary economists have highlighted the role of money supply in national production, especially for short-term periods. Similarly, its role in affecting inflation for long-term also has been noted by academicians. These perspectives have highlighted the importance of monetary authority in managing money supply by targeting rate of changes in an economy. Since the inflation is a monetary phenomenon, central banks should maintain supply and demand of money at an equilibrium point (Friedman 1970)

During the 1980s, a number of monetary authorities considered monetary targets as a parameter for monetary policy actions. They used to estimate the optimal money stock to achieve the desired economic objectives. But during the 1990s, monetary authorizes switched their priority from monetary target to inflation target in the climate of globalised economies. This drastic shift in policy was visible among Emerging Market Economies (EMEs) also. This shift indicates the failure of the previous policy in the new scenario. Moreover, researchers like (Oluwole and Olugbenga 2007) argued that since the money demand function is used for managing liquidity and controlling inflation in the economies, it also indicates the failure of the stability assumption of money demand function for planning and implementing monetary policy.

Since the stable money demand function is the precondition for planning and implementation of monetary policy, examining the money demand function is necessary for understanding specific condition in the economy. Moreover, it will help to understand the liquidity conditions in an economy (Handa 2009). So it is very important to understand the different factors which influence the money demand functions and the long-run relationship between money stock and its determinants. There are some studies which analysed the same issue in the Indian context, but these studies have their own limitations in terms of data used and the methodological approaches (Moosa 1992; Singh and Pandey 2009; Inoue and Hamori 2008). Considering this fact, the present study tries to fill the gap with an ARDL approach by using updated data for Indian economy. Since RBI using M3 for its monetary policy decisions (Bhattacharya 2006; Mohanty 2012), including broad money give clear picture than using narrow money for money demand function.

A radical shift in the development and implementation of monetary policy occurred in India during 1990s when RBI governed policies were deregulated to give way to a market-driven policy regime. Economic and political crises, currency issues, global recession, dominance of informal sector and hyperinflation complicated Indian economy's transition to a market-oriented system. So it is not easy for the central bank to choose a suitable instrument, intermediate target and policy plans for the effective implementation of monetary policy. However, RBI still follows monetary target as an intermediate target for monetary policy despite the implementation of multiple indicator approaches in the 1990s (Padhan 2011).

Framing and implementing a strong monetary policy requires a strong linkage between the determinants of money demand like output, prices, interest rate, exchange rate and income are included in money demand function (Singh and Pandey 2009; Halicioglu and Ugur 2005; Akinlo 2006; Baharumshah et al. 2009). This study found such a strong co-integration relation between the broad money and its determinants for long-run. But the study failed to found any short-run co-integrating relationship with M3 and its determinants except inflation. The theoretical arguments on positive relationship between GDP and inflation with money demand are confirmed in this study. Substitution effect of money demand on foreign exchange indicated by the negative coefficient of exchange rate in the model.

Economic reforms and money market innovations in the last few decades might have affected the behaviour of money demand. Assessing the stability and predictability of money demand function in the light of these reforms is necessary for understanding the monetary policy of the country. This paper tries to analyse the characteristics of money demand function in an Emerging Market Economy (EME) like India, which has undergone different phases of reforms since 1980s. An Autoregressive Distributed Lag (ARDL) model is used for filling the gap in the literature caused by methodological limitations and the use of time-specific variables to an extent as it assesses the money demand function and its stability in India.

Further, this paper is divided into separate sections which deal with the review of empirical studies, data and methodology, econometric analysis of determinants of money demand and next section deal with empirical result and its interpretation respectively.

2.2 Literature Review

The academic debate about the factors which determine money demand in long-term and short-term is still inconclusive. This inconclusiveness is related to the continual and ongoing nature of economic and financial innovations in economies to achieve broader economic goals. Another debatable point in the literature is about the stability of money demand, mainly in terms of the definition of money used for analysis. Researchers like Dornbusch and Fischer (2001) argued that money demand will adjust to the changes in income and interest rate with a lag.

Even though there is no intrinsic value for money, people still hold their wealth in the form of cash in most of the economies. It may be because of the transaction, speculative and precautionary motives. The transaction and precautionary motives are derived from income only (Keynes 1930, 1936). Similarly, interest rate also influences the money demand because it is the opportunity cost of holding money

(Gujarati 1968). An increase in the interest rate decreases the money demand because it increases the opportunity cost of holding money. Numerous factors influence the demand for money in an economy, especially financial innovations and reforms (Nchor and Adamec 2016).

The increased academic interest about the innovative fiscal and monetary policy changes during different periods has resulted in bringing out a large corpus of academic studies on stability and determinants of money demand in industrialized countries. For instance, Hafer and Jansen (1991), McNown and Wallace (1992), Mehra (1993) in USA, Drake and Chrystal (1994), Haug and Lucas (1996), Lim (1993), Orden and Fisher (1993) for UK, Australia, Canada and New Zealand respectively. Similarly, Arize and Shwiff (1993), Bahmani-Oskooee (2001) analysed money demand in Japan also. But the drastic change in the financial and economic climate in EMEs contributed to the recent growth in literature. Financial liberalization, economic globalization and adoption of the floating exchange rate also contributed to such a drastic change in few decades.

In case of EMEs, there is a large corpus of literature which highlights some key variables of money demand function. In addition to the key variables (Income and interest rate), studies identified exchange rate, foreign interest rate and inflation as other variables which influence the money holdings. Among such studies, there are only limited ones which used ARDL model for examining the co-integration relationship between those variables. Most of them show stable money demand with a co-integrative relationship between money demand (both narrow and broad) and its determinants. For instance, Halicioglu and Ugur (2005) who analysed the money demand function (M1) in Turkey with annual data found stable money demand. Akinlo (2006) found a co-integrated relationship between M2 and exchange rate, interest rate and income but criticized the conventional money stability concept. Study on money demand in Chinese economy by Baharumshah et al. (2009) also found strong relationship between broad money (M2) with foreign interest rate, inflation, real income and stock price. Samreth (2008) also found the same result in Cambodia with M1, industrial production index, consumer price index, and nominal exchange rate. The CUSUM and CUSUMQ roughly support the stability of money demand. Long and Samreth (2008) also supported the same. Researchers like Achsani (2010) from Indonesia also found similar results and argue that ARDL approach is more appropriate over other conventional models for predicting the stable money demand.

There are several studies which examined the stability of money demand function and its determinants in Indian scenario. Most of the studies used narrow money (M1) or broad money (M3) for measuring the monetary aggregates. The results of these studies are mixed especially when it comes to the stability of the money demand function. Researchers like Moosa (1992) who analysed the relationship between money supply and real interest rate, real money balance and industrial production for a period between 1972 and1990 established a co-integration relationship between monetary aggregates (cash, M1 and M2) and determinant variables like output and interest rate. Based on the findings, the study argues that narrow definition of money is the suitable variable for formulating RBI monetary policy. Similarly, Bhattacharya (1995) also found cointegrative relationship between narrow money (M1) and real money balance, long-term and short-term interest rates and real GNP. He failed to detect such relationship with M2 and M3. It further found that short-term interest rate is least sensitive to money demand than of long-term interest rates. The study argues that the narrow definitions of the money is best for framing monetary policy because it is stable for long-term and the error correction term is significant and negative too. Inoue and Hamori (2008) also supported the stability narrow definition of money (M1 and M2) and rejected the concept of broader money (M3). They found co-integrative relationship between narrow money and real money balance, interest rate and output. Bahmani-Oskooee and Rehman (2005) also supported the findings of previous studies on stability of narrow money.

Studies by Arif (1996), Joshi and Saggar (1995), Das and Mandal (2000), Mohanty and Mitra (1999) supported the idea of stability of money demand in Indian context. Rao and Singh (2006) also supported the findings after studying the Indian money demand for 50 year period from 1953 to 2003. Studies which contradict this view are also prominent, like Bhoi (1995), Pradhan and Subramanian (2003) noticed that economic liberalization of 1990s and financial deregulations destabilized the broad money demand. Time-specific instability was also mentioned by Singh and Pandey (2009) arguing that demand for money was unstable during 1975–1998 and stabilised after the few years of economic reforms. This instability may be because of the policy reforms, balance of payment crisis, currency devaluation, fiscal expansion and other reforms in monetary policy.

By assessing medium to long-term impact of a monetary aggregate to price stability, many researchers argue that a monetary aggregate should fulfil two conditions for using it as a yardstick for monetary policy. First, the existence of a long-run stable relationship between monetary aggregates and its determinants (Bruggeman et al. 2003; Carstensen 2004; Coenen and Vega 2001). Second, monetary aggregate should be a leading indicator of inflation (Altimari 2001; Trecroci and Vega 2002). If the monetary aggregate fulfils these two fundamental conditions, it can be considered as the best aggregate for policy purpose.

Development of the financial market and emergence of innovative financial instruments questioned the use of M3 for monetary policy (Drake and Mills 2002; Lim and Khun 2014). But in some EMEs, researchers failed to find clear evidence supporting the use of narrow money for policy target. But M3 (total liquidity in domestic currency) was found to be an information variable, because it is the only money which is able to forecast inflation (Lahura 2010). In the post-reform period, RBI gives more emphasis on indirect instruments like Open Market Operations (OMO), repo, bank rate, etc. mainly because of the emergence of the interest rate as a more resourceful variable for policy actions (Kanagasabapathy 2001). Mohanty and Mitra (1999) noticed that in the post-reform period, there is an inconsistency in the M3 and reserve money as the actual growth rate of M3 deviates from targeted growth. In this backdrop, this study aims to find the reliability of M3 as an indicator for money in money demand function.

Even though all types of definitions of money provide unique information, there are few reasons for selecting M3 in our money demand function. It is one of the good monetary aggregates in Indian context because it includes assets which are considered as a short-term investment with moderate liquidity in which financial institutions including banks, business organizations temporarily stockpiles fund. Thus it can be used for forecasting inflation. Similarly, under the multiple indicator approach, RBI use M3 for its policy purposes (Padhan 2011). In addition to that, literature on Indian context is inconclusive about the use ofbest monetary aggregates for policy actions. For instance, Moosa (1992) found the existence of cointegration relationship between three types of money (cash, M1 and M2), and argued that narrow definition of money is best for policy purpose. Bhattacharya (1995) used co-integration approach for money demand function and strongly supported that stability of money demand is only possible if money is narrowly defined (M1). Contrary to that, Das and Mandal (2000), Ramachandran (2004) only considered broad money (M3) and found cointegrating relationship between M3 and other determinants. Further, Ramachandran (2004) found that M3 can be used for inflation forecasting. The notable point is that even after financial reforms, the stability of money demand sustains.

However, it is clear from the literature that determinants other than the fundamental ones increase with time, even though the fundamental factors stay unchanged. Generally, it can be seen that more recent studies recommend broader definition of money for the monetary policy formulation. Only few studies have considered broad definition of money for model building. Similarly, there is scarcity of studies which use real exchange rate, inflation and other variables along with fundamental determinants. In this backdrop, the present study is the first to use an ARDL co-integration approach to understand the different determinants of money demand in India.

2.3 Data and Model Specification

In order to assess the factor determining the broad money demand (M3), a three-factor ARDL model is formulated, which apart from the M3 includes Inflation, nominal exchange rate (INR/USD) and gross domestic product per capita. The dataset consists of time series annual data over the period of 1975–2016 and is retrieved from the Federal Bank of St. Louis. The dependent variable in our study is broad monetary aggregates (M3) and independent variables are inflation rate for macroeconomic stability, which is measured through the consumer price index (CPI) in case of India, nominal exchange rate (INR/USD) and gross domestic product per capita for market size. All the independent variables are carefully chosen, based on the previous literature. For consistency reasons, all variables are converted into the natural log form.[1] So the log-log model is used in this paper which is as follow as:

$$\mathrm{LM3_t} = \alpha_0 + \beta_1\mathrm{LCPI_t} + \beta_2\mathrm{LEXC_t} + \beta_3\mathrm{LGDP_t} + \mu_t\ldots \quad (2.1)$$

where, LM3 is the log of monetary aggregates (M3), not seasonally adjusted, converted into USD, LCPI is the log of consumer price index, index 2010 = 100, not seasonally adjusted as a measure of inflation, LEXC is the nominal exchange rate (INR/USD), LGDP is the log of gross domestic product per capita, not seasonally adjusted, measured in USD, μ_t is the white noise error term.

We apply the robust Autoregressive Distribution Lag (ARDL) co-integration approach developed by Pesaran et al. (2001) for realistic and efficient estimates. Co-integration is concerned with the analysis of long-run association between the integrated variables and re-parameterizing the relationship between the considered variables into an Error Correction Mechanism (ECM). The reason behind chosen of this model is:

(a) This test is based on single ARDL equation, rather than on a VAR as in Johansen, thus it reduces the number of parameters to be estimated.
(b) This test is relatively more efficient in small and finite sample data sizes as is the case in our study (Ghatak and Siddiki 2001).
(c) This test can be applied irrespective of whether the regressors in the model are purely I(0), purely I(1) or mutually co-integrated.
(d) ARDL representation does not require symmetry of lag length; each length can have a different number of lag lengths.
(e) This approach provides a method of assessing short run and the long run effect of one variable on the other simultaneously and it also separate the short run and long run effects (Bentzen and Engsted 2001).

In order to implement the bound testing procedure Eq. (2.1), transformed into an unrestricted error correction model (UECM). The unrestricted error correction model (UECM) of ARDL approach can be written as:

$$\begin{aligned}\Delta LM3_t = {} & a_1 + \sum_{i=1}^{p} a_2\Delta LM3_{t-i} + \sum_{i=0}^{p} a_3\Delta LCPI_{t-i} + \sum_{i=0}^{p} a_4\Delta LEXC_{t-i} + \sum_{i=0}^{p} a_5\Delta LGDP_{t-i} \\ & + \lambda_1 LM3_{t-1} + \lambda_2 LCPI_{t-1} + \lambda_3 LEXC_{t-1} + \lambda_4 LGDP_{t-1} + \mu_t\end{aligned} \quad (2.2)$$

where, α_1 is the drift component, $a_2 - a_5$ represent short run dynamics, $\lambda_1 - \lambda_4$ represent long run dynamics, Δ denote the first difference operator, μ_t is the white noise error term.

[1]The log-linear specification provides the efficient results as compared to simple specification (Layson 1983; Shahbaz 2010)

The existence of cointegration relationship between the variables from Eq. (2.2) is examined by testing the significance of the lagged level of variables using bound testing procedure provided by Pesaran et al. (2001). This bound testing procedure is based on F-statistics computed through a Wald test. This F-statistics is actually a test of the null hypothesis (H_0) of no cointegration between the variables against the alternate hypothesis (H_1) of co-integration among the variables. Two critical values are provided by the Pesaran et al. (2001) for cointegration test, i.e. lower critical value I(0) and upper critical value I(1). When the computed F-statistics is greater than the upper bound value, then the null hypothesis is rejected (concluding there is co-integration among variables). If in case F-statistics is less than the lower bound value, we don't reject the null hypothesis (there is no co-integration among the variables). When computed F-statistics fall under I(0) and I(1), the results are inconclusive. However, it is advisable to follow (Narayan 2005) critical value table instead of Pesaran et al. (2001) for small sample sizes, ranging from 30 to 80 observations

After estimation the long run association between the variables, we use the following equation to estimate the short-run coefficients:

$$\Delta LM3_t = a_1 + \sum_{i=1}^{\rho} a_2 \Delta LM3_{t-i} + \sum_{i=0}^{\rho} a_3 \Delta LCPI_{t-i} + \sum_{i=0}^{\rho} a_4 \Delta LEXC_{t-i} + \sum_{i=0}^{\rho} a_5 \Delta LGDP_{t-i} + \varphi EC_{t-1} \quad (2.3)$$

φ is the parameter of error correction term (EC_{t-1}) in the model which can be described as how the time-series adjust to disequilibrium. A positive coefficient indicates a divergence and negative coefficient indicates convergence. ECT can also be explained as the speed at which dependent variable returns to equilibrium from the changes in the independent variables. Thus, it shows that the deviation of the current situation will be fitted into its short-run relationship from long-run relationship. Lastly, parameter stability is important, since unstable parameter can result in model misspecification (Narayan and Smyth 2004). Therefore, CUSUM and CUSUMQ test suggested by (Brown et al. 1975) is employed for stability of parameters.

2.4 Estimated Results

a. **Testing of the Unit Root Hypothesis**

Although this co-integration technique does not require pre-testing for unit roots, to avoid ARDL model crash in the presence of integrated stochastic trend of I(2), we are of the view the unit root test should be carried out to know the number of unit roots in the series under consideration. Therefore, we have adopted the most

Table 2.1 Unit root testing

Variables		ADF			PP		
		Intercept	Intercept and trend	None	Intercept	Intercept and trend	None
LM3	Level	−0.742	−1.998	2.706	−0.791	−1.873	5.486
	Δ	−3.704***	−3.681***	−2.277***	−3.614***	−3.602**	−2.140**
LCPI	Level	−1.488	−1.557	3.844	0.028	−2.185	6.959
	Δ	−6.585***	−6.534***	−1.619*	−6.354***	−6.359***	−1.617*
LEXC	Level	−0.692	−1.508	1.970	−0.714	−1.371	2.751
	Δ	−3.956***	−3.915**	−3.093***	−3.934***	−3.888**	−3.070***
LGDP	Level	0.362	−1.002	4.817	0.214	−1.256	4.204
	Δ	−5.785***	−5.753***	−2.312**	−5.875***	−5.837***	−4.242***

***, **, * shows significant at 1% level, 5 and 10%
Source Authors calculation

popular strategy for testing the stationarity property of a single time series using the Augmented Dickey-Fuller (ADF) and Phillip and Perron (PP) unit root test respectively (Dickey and Fuller 1979; Phillips and Perron 1988). A summary of results is given below in Table 2.1.

From the above result, it is apparent that none of the variables are able to reject the null hypothesis of a unit root at the level. However, all the variables become stationary after first differencing, indicating these variables have integrated of order one I(1). It is also noted that none of the variables are stationary at I(2) so as to avoid spurious results. According to Ouattara (2004) in the presence of integrated stochastic trend of I(2) variables, the computed F-statistics provided by Pesaran et al. (2001) are not valid because the bound test is based on the assumption that the variables are I(0) or I(1). So, in the next step, we proceed to apply ARDL Model.

b. **Autoregressive Distributed Lag Model (ARDL) Lag Selection**

The first step in the ARDL bound testing approach is to estimate the Eq. (2.2) by OLS in order to test the presence of long-run association between the variables and it is first done through by selecting the optimum lag order of the ARDL model. Table 2.2 reports the different information criteria for all lags up to three.

The optimum lags are those which minimize the absolute values of above information criteria as presented in the Table 2.2. Keeping in mind the assumption of serially uncorrelated errors for the validity of the bounds test, the lag $p = 2$ has been selected [2]. We then calculate the co-integration between the variables. For this purpose Wald test is used with the null hypothesis H_0: $\lambda_1 = \lambda_2 = \lambda_3 = \lambda_4 = 0$ against H_A: $\lambda_1 \neq \lambda_2 \neq \lambda_3 \neq \lambda_4 \neq 0$ and the calculated F-statistics is 13.411 which

[2]Narayan (2004) and Pesaran and Shin (1999) argued that the SBC-based ARDL model performs better than the AIC-based model in case of small samples.

Table 2.2 Information criteria for selecting the lag order

Lag	LogL	LR	FPE	AIC	SC	HQ
0	60.38313	NA	6.52e−07	−2.891442	−2.720821	−2.830225
1	323.2149	458.2707	2.09e−12	−15.54948	−14.69637*	−15.24339
2	345.2927	33.96594*	1.57e−12*	−15.86117*	−14.32557	−15.31021*
3	361.0901	21.06322	1.71e−12	−15.85078	−13.63269	−15.05495

* Indicates lag order selected by the criterion (each test at 5% level)
LR sequentially modified LR test statistic; *FPE* final prediction error; *AIC* akaike information criterion; *SC* Schwarz information criterion; *HQ* Hannan-Quinn information criterion
Source Authors calculation

Table 2.3 Co-integration bound test result

	Bound test F-statistics computed value	Bound test F critical value at 5% level		Decision
		I(0)	I(1)	
$LM3_t = f(LCPI_t, LEXC_t, LGDP_t)$	13.411***	5.01	6.61	Cointegrated

Notes
(1) The bound test F-statistics results are obtained from Narayan critical value Table (2005) Case III-unrestricted intercept and no trend
(2) *** denotes significant at 1% alpha level
Source Authors calculation

is compared with the lower bound value I(0) and upper bound value I(1) of Narayan (2005) critical value table.

The value of the F-statistics is greater than the upper bound value I(1) of bound table as shown in Table 2.3. Thus, the null hypothesis of no co-integration is rejected, and therefore we conclude that all the variables are significantly different from zero and there is a long-run association between the variables. The results of the long run coefficient are shown in Table 2.4.

The coefficient of determination, R^2, is acceptable, explaining 98% of the variation in the LM3 is explained by the independent variables. The Durbin-Watson value is greater than 2 indicates the residuals are not serially correlated with their lagged values. All the long run variables are statistically significant except GDP per capita. The estimated coefficients of the Inflation (LCPI) and GDP per capita (LGDP) have positive sign showing that 1% increase in Inflation and GDP per capita will increase the money demand (LM3) by 20 and 8%, however, GDP per capita is not statistically significant. This kind of phenomena is the general feature of the developing economies. An increase in GDP and inflation increase the money demand because people need money for their transactions. For exchange rate it is showing the negative effect showing 1% depreciation of INR/USD exchange rate will reduce the money demand (LM3) by 93%. It shows the substitution effect of exchange rate on money demand. When rupee starts depreciating people start

Table 2.4 Estimated long run coefficients using the ARDL approach dependent variable: DLM3

Variable	Coefficient	Std. error	t-statistic	Prob.
Constant	23.58	3.571	6.601	0.000***
LM3	−0.937	0.136	−6.887	0.000***
LCPI	0.202	0.094	2.122	0.046**
LEXC	−0.936	0.187	−4.993	0.000***
LGDP	0.088	0.094	0.938	0.359
Long-run diagnostic results				
Serial correlation (LM test) = 4.522(0.10)			R-square = 0.987	
Heteroscedasticity test = 8.412 (0.81)			Adjusted R-squared = 0.979	
Normality (J-B test) = 0.862(0.64)			Durbin-Watson stat = 2.328	
F-statistic = 121.439			Prob (F-statistic) = 0.000	

***, **, * denotes significant at 1, 5 and 10% significance level
Source Authors calculation

demanding less money and increases their investment, especially in foreign currency to protect the value of their assets.

Based on the long run estimation results, we can conclude that inflation rate, exchange rate and gross domestic product are the major determining factors of the money demand in India. After obtaining long-run coefficients, we move to the unrestricted error correction version of ARDL model shown in Table 2.5

The sign of the estimated one period lagged error correction term ECT_{t-1} is negative and also highly significant at the 1% significance level and indicates that the system is getting adjusted towards long-run equilibrium at a slow speed of 9.9%. (Banerjee et al. 1998), states that a significant ECT is further proof of the existence of a stable long-run relationship in his study. The variety of diagnostic tests has also been applied for goodness of fit of ARDL specification. These tests indicate that the short run estimates are free from serial correlation, non-normality of error term, misspecification of short-run model and Heteroscedasticity. In the short-run, exchange rate and GDP per capita do not significantly affect the money demand in India. However, the estimated coefficient of consumer price index (LCPI) significantly affects the money demand in the short run at 1% significance level.

Next, the CUSUM mean plot and CUSUMQ variance plot in Figs. 2.1 and 2.2 are employed to find out the structural break in the data set and to test the stability of the model with SBC based error correction term. The results indicate the absence of any instability of the coefficients because the plot of the CUSUM and CUSUMQ statistic fall inside the critical boundary lines at 5% level of significance. These findings are not in consensus with the earlier findings of Inoue and Hamori (2008),

Table 2.5 Error correction representation of ARDL model (lag order: 2, 0, 2, 1 and 1)

Variable	Coefficient	Std. error	t-eatistic	Prob.	Results
C	0.120264	0.013420	8.961611	0.0000	Significant
$\Delta LM3_{t-1}$	0.234664	0.119792	1.958933	0.0618	Significant
$\Delta LM3_{t-2}$	−0.007568	0.074221	−0.101966	0.9196	Insignificant
$\Delta LCPI$	0.267235	0.072711	3.675322	0.0012	Significant
$\Delta LEXC$	−1.163247	0.068902	−16.88258	0.0000	Significant
$\Delta LEXC_{t-1}$	0.248803	0.165162	1.506418	0.1450	Insignificant
$\Delta LEXC_{t-2}$	−0.067093	0.100336	−0.668681	0.5101	Insignificant
$\Delta LGDP$	−0.075679	0.065909	−1.148241	0.2622	Insignificant
$\Delta LGDP_{t-1}$	−0.024014	0.064744	−0.370915	0.7140	Insignificant
ECT_{t-1}	−0.099771	0.019908	−5.011498	0.0000	Significant
Short-run diagnostic results					
Serial correlation (LM test) = 4.400(0.11)				R-tquare = 0.957	
Heteroscedasticity test = 10.380(0.32)				Adjusted R-tquared = 0.941	
Normality (J-B test) = 0.789(0.67)				Durbin-Watson stat = 1.981	
F-statistic = 59.680				Prob (F-statistic) = 0.000	

Notes
(1) The value in the parenthesis represents the probability value of F-statistics
Source Authors calculation

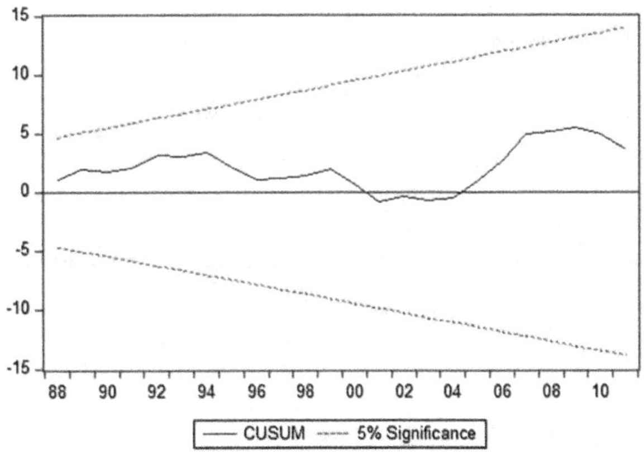

Fig. 2.1 CUSUM. *Source* Authors calculation

Bhattacharya (1995). However, this result could be a signal of the fact that M3 must be the monetary aggregate that RBI should control, as it fulfils two conditions for using it as a suitable monetary aggregate for policy action.

Fig. 2.2 CUSUMQ. *Source* Authors calculation

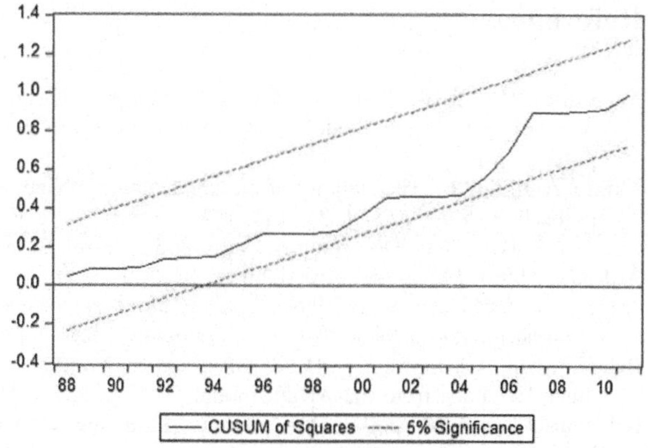

2.5 Conclusion

This study has examined demand for money in India, by using an ARDL co-integration approach developed by Pesaran et al. (2001). Generally, this model does not require information about the order of integration of variables. This makes this model an effective and appropriate one to examine the co-integration among money demand and its determinants. The empirical results indicate that all variables except GDP per-capita are statistically significant and consistent with the theory of money demand only for long-term. However, only CPI is found to be significant and consistent for short-term.

The Empirical analysis based on bound testing approach support long-run stable money demand (M3) for India. It can only be decisively established when exchange rate, inflation and GDP are included in the model. The result reveals that GDP and inflation are positively associated with M3 and the exchange rate negatively affects M3. The positive coefficient of GDP per-capita indicates that GDP growth enhances money demand in the economy as suggested by economic theories. Similarly, positive coefficient of inflation support the theoretical idea of positive relationship between money demand and inflation, i.e. raise in inflation reduces the real value of money and people keep more money in their hand for fulfilling their needs. The cointegration relation between price and money (M3) for both long run and short run shows that M3 is the leading indicator of inflation. Similarly, depreciation of the domestic currency also decreases the money demand because of the substitution effect. The study further found a stable money demand by using CUSUM and CUSUMQ test. Inclusion of determinants like GDP, exchange rate and inflation makes the model of M3 stable. Thus the study concludes that M3 is also the best monetary aggregate for RBI's monetary policy actions.

References

Achsani, N. A. (2010). Stability of money demand in an emerging market economy: An error correction and ARDL model for Indonesia. *Research Journal of International Studies, 13,* 54–62.
Akinlo, A. E. (2006). The stability of money demand in Nigeria: An autoregressive distributed lag approach. *J Policy Model, 28,* 445–452.
Altimari, S. N. (2001). Does money lead inflation in the Euro area?
Arif RR. (1996). Money demand stability: Myth or reality—An econometric analysis.
Arize, A. C., & Shwiff, S. S. (1993). Cointegration, real exchange rate and modelling the demand for broad money in Japan. *Applied Economics, 25,* 717–726.
Baharumshah, A. Z., Mohd, S. H., & Masih, A. M. M. (2009). The stability of money demand in China: Evidence from the ARDL model. *Econ Syst, 33,* 231–244.
Bahmani-Oskooee, M. (2001). How stable is M2 money demand function in Japan? *Japan and the World Economy, 13,* 455–461.
Bahmani-Oskooee, M., & Rehman, H. (2005). Stability of the money demand function in Asian developing countries. *Applied Economics, 37,* 773–792. https://doi.org/10.1080/0003684042000337424.
Banerjee, A., Dolado, J., & Mestre, R. (1998). Error-correction mechanism tests for cointegration in a single-equation framework. *Journal of Time Series Analysis, 19,* 267–283. https://doi.org/10.1111/1467-9892.00091.
Bentzen, I., & Engsted, T. (2001). A revival of the autoregressive distributed lag model in estimating energy demand relationship. *Energy, 26,* 45–55.
Bhattacharya, R. (1995). Cointegrating relationships in the demand for money in India. *Indian Economic Journal, 43,* 69–75.
Bhattacharya, K. (2006). Monetary policy in Asia: Approaches and implementation.
Bhoi, B. K. (1995). Modeling buffer stock money: An Indian experience. RBI Occasional Paper 16.
Brown, R. L., Durbin, J., & Evans, J. M. (1975). Techniques for testing the constancy of regression relationships over time. *Journal of the Royal Statistical Society* 149–192.
Bruggeman A, Donati P, Warne A (2003) Is The Demand For Euro Area M3 Stable?
Carstensen, K. (2004). Is European money demand still stable?
Coenen, G., & Vega, J.-L. (2001). The demand for M3 in the euro area. *Journal of Applied Economics, 16,* 727–748. https://doi.org/10.1002/jae.629.
Das, S., & Mandal, K. (2000). Modeling money demand in India: Testing weak, strong & super exogeneity. *Indian Economic Review, 35,* 1–19.
Dickey, D. A., & Fuller, W. A. (1979). Distribution of the estimators for autoregressive time series with a unit root. *Journal of American Statistical Association, 79,* 427–431.
Dornbusch, R., & Fischer, S. (2001). *Macroeconomics* (8th ed.). New York: McGraw-Hill.
Drake, L., & Chrystal, K. A. (1994). Company-sector money demand: New evidence on the existence of a stable long-un relationship for the UK. *J Money, Credit Bank, 26,* 479–494.
Drake, L. M., & Mills, T. C. (2002). Is M3 an appropriate aggregate for guiding ECB monetary policy?
Friedman, M. (1970). A theoretical framework for monetary analysis. *Journal of Political Economy, 78,* 193–238.
Ghatak, S., & Siddiki, J. U. (2001). The use of the ARDL approach in estimating virtual exchange rates in India. *Journal of Applied Statistics, 28,* 573–583.
Gujarati, D. (1968). The demand for money in India. *Journal of Development Stud, 5,* 59–64.
Hafer, R. W., & Jansen, D. W. (1991). the demand for money in the united States: Evidence from cointegration test. *J Money, Credit Bank, 23,* 155–168.
Halicioglu, F., & Ugur, M. (2005). On stability of the demand for money in a developing OECD country: the case of Turkey. *Global Business and Economics Review, 7,* 203–213.
Handa J (2009) Monetary Economics ., 2 ndEditi. Routledge Taylor & Francis Group, New York.

Haug, A. A., & Lucas, R. F. (1996). Long-term money demand in Canada. In search of stability. *Review of Economics and Statistics, 78,* 345–348.
Inoue, T., & Hamori, S. (2008). An empirical analysis of the money demand function in India.
Joshi, H., & Saggar, M. (1995). The demand for money in India: stability revisited. *Reserve Bank India Occasional Paper, 16,* 79–100.
Kanagasabapathy, K. (2001). Monetary policy underpinnings: A perspective. *Economic and Political Weekly, 36,* 303–310.
Keynes, J. M. (1930). *A treatise on money*. London: Macmillan.
Keynes, J. M. (1936). *The general theory of employment, interest and money*. Basingstoke: Palgrave Macmillan.
Lahura, E. (2010). Monetary aggregates and monetary policy: An empirical assessment for Peru.
Layson, S. (1983). Homicide and deterrence: Another view of the Canadian time-series evidence. *Canadian Journal of Economics, 16,* 52–73.
Lim, G. C. (1993). The demand for the components of broad money: Error correction and generalized asset adjustment system. *Applied Economics, 25,* 995–1004.
Lim, S., & Khun, C. (2014). Money demand in Australia: Which monetary aggregate matters? *Economic Papers: A Journal of Applied Economics and Policy Banner, 33,* 95–103. https://doi.org/10.1111/1759-3441.12062.
Long, D., & Samreth, S. (2008). The monetary model of exchange rate: Evidence from the Philippines using ARDL approach. *Economic Bulletin* 1–12.
Maravic, J., & Palic, M. (2010). Econometric analysis of money demand in Serbia.
McNown, R., & Wallace, M. S. (1992). Cointegration test of a long-run relation between money demand and effective exchange rate. *Journal of International Money and Finance, 11,* 107–114.
Mehra, Y. P. (1993). The stability of the M2 money demand function: Evidence from an error-correction model. *Journal of Money, Credit and Banking, 25,* 455–460.
Mohanty, D. (2012). Evidence of interest rate channel of monetary policy transmission in India.
Mohanty, D., & Mitra, A. K. (1999). Experience with monetary targeting in India. *Economic and Political Weekly, 34,* 123–132.
Moosa, I. (1992). The demand for money in India: A cointegration approach. *Indian Economic Journal, 40,* 110–115.
Narayan, P. K. (2004). New Zealand's trade balance: Evidence of the J-curve and granger causality. *Applied Economics Letters, 11,* 351–354.
Narayan, P. K. (2005). The saving and investment nexus for China: Evidence from cointegration tests. *Applied Economics, 37,* 1979–1990.
Narayan, P. K., & Smyth, R. (2004). The relationship between the real exchange rate and balance of payments: Empirical evidence for China from cointegration and causality testing. *Applied Economics Letters, 11,* 287–291.
Nchor, D., & Adamec, V. (2016). influences the demand for money in an economy. *Procedia—Social and Behavioral Sciences, 220,* 288–293.
Oluwole, O., & Olugbenga, A. O. (2007). M2 targeting, money demand, and real GDP growth in Nigeria: Do rules apply? *Journal of Business and Public Affairs, 1,* 1–20.
Orden, D., & Fisher, L. A. (1993). Financial deregulation and the dynamics of money, prices and output in New Zealand and Australia. *Journal of Money, Credit and Banking, 25,* 273–292.
Ouattara, B. (2004). Modelling the long run determinants of private investment in Senegal. *Center for Research in Economic Development and International Trade, 44,* 37. https://doi.org/10.5539/ass.v8n13p139.
Padhan, P. C. (2011). Stability of demand for money in India: Evidence from monetary and liquidity aggregates. *International Journal of Economic and Finance, 3,* 271–282.
Pesaran, M. H., & Shin, Y. (1999). An autoregressive distributed lag modeling approach to cointegration analysis in Strom. In S. Strom (Ed.), *Econometrics and Economic Theory in the 20th Century: The Ragnar Frisch* (pp. 371–413). Cambridge: Cambridge University Press.
Pesaran, M. H., Shin, Y., & Smith, R. J. (2001). Bounds testing approaches to the analysis of level relationships. *Journal of Applied Economics, 16,* 289–326. https://doi.org/10.1002/jae.616.

Phillips, P. C., & Perron, P. (1988). Testing for a unit root in time series regression. *Biometrika, 75,* 335–346.

Pradhan, B. K., & Subramanian, A. (2003). On tthe stabiliy of demand for money in a developing economy some empirical issues. *Journal of Development Economics, 72,* 335–351.

Ramachandran, M. (2004). Do broad money, output, and prices stand for a stable relationship in India? *Journal of Policy Modelling, 26,* 983–1001.

Rao, B. B., & Singh, R. (2006). Demand for money in India: 1953–2003. *Applied Economics, 38,* 1319–1326.

Samreth, S. (2008). Estimating money demand function in Cambodia. *ARDL Approach.* doi: https://mpra.ub.uni-muenchen.de/16274/1/MPRA_paper_16274.pdf.

Shahbaz, M. (2010). Income inequality—Economic growth and non-linearity: A case of Pakistan. *Int J Soc Econ, 37,* 613–636.

Singh, P., & Pandey, M. K. (2009). Structural break, stability and demand for money in India.

Trecroci, C., & Vega, J. L. (2002). The information content of M3 for future inflation in the Euro area. *Weltwirtschaftliches Archiv, 138,* 22–53. https://doi.org/10.1007/BF02707322.

Chapter 3
Some Empirical Evidence on the Effects of Monetary Policy in India: A Vector Autoregressive Based Analysis

Gyanendra Pratap Singh

Abstract The global financial crisis of 2007–08 has been one of the most difficult financial and economic episodes for the world economy. This chapter investigates changes in the impact of monetary policy on some key macroeconomic variables in pre-and post-global financial crisis of 2007–08. We estimate a reduced form Vector Autoregressive model of five variables: money, output, prices, interest rates and the exchange rates for pre-and post-crisis periods. The empirical evidence suggests that monetary policy shocks have expected effect on output and prices. However, the monetary policy transmission lags are significantly reduced in post crisis period. The peak effect on output and prices are felt with a lag of 5 and 12 months which were 13 and 23 months respectively in pre-crisis periods.

Keywords Monetary policy · Vector autoregressive model · Structural break Impulse responses

JEL Classification E43 · E51 · E52 · E58

3.1 Introduction

Monetary policy affects macroeconomic variables such as real gross domestic product (GDP) and inflation through a mechanism called monetary policy transmission mechanism (MPTM). MPTM entails the entire process through which monetary policy actions are transmitted into the ultimate objectives of monetary policy. The Reserve Bank's mandate for monetary policy is clearly enunciated in the Preamble of the Reserve Bank of India Act, 1934 as: "to regulate the issue of Bank notes and the keeping of reserves with a view to securing monetary stability in India and generally to operate the currency and credit system of the country to its

G. P. Singh (✉)
Govind Ballabh Pant Social Science Institute,
University of Allahabad, Jhusi, Allahabad, India
e-mail: shantanugbpant@gmail.com

A. K. Mishra et al. (eds.), *Current Issues in the Economy and Finance of India*,
Springer Proceedings in Business and Economics,
https://doi.org/10.1007/978-3-319-99555-7_3

advantage". Thus the primary goal of the RBI is to ensure monetary stability in terms of preserving the purchasing power of the rupee. Ultimately, this can only be ensured when the prices are low and stable.

With the amendment of the Reserve Bank of India Act, 2016 the primary objective of monetary policy is to maintain price stability while keeping in mind the objective of economic growth. For the Reserve Bank to achieve its mandate effectively, the Monetary Policy Committee (MPC) has been constituted under the amended RBI Act to determine the policy repo rate in order to achieve the specified medium-term inflation target of 4%, within a band of 2%. Since price stability alone not necessarily can ensure financial stability, the latter being another important objective of monetary policy. Most of the literature on the transmission of monetary policy has focused on four key channels: the interest rate channel, the credit channel, the exchange rate channel and the asset price channel. In most of the countries, central banks use a short-term interest rate as their primary instrument of monetary management. Given inflexibility of prices and wages in the short-run, a shift in monetary policy rate leads to changes in market interest rates which in turn affects households and firms saving and investment behavior and ultimately real activity and inflation.

It is however, increasingly realized that the impact of monetary policy shocks on the macroeconomic variables may vary both across country as well as within the same country over time. The global financial crisis of 2007–08 has been one of the most difficult financial and economic episodes for the world economy. In recent research work, Friedman and Kuttner (2010) have demonstrated that developments since the 2008 crisis have made it necessary to reassess the impact of monetary policy shocks on macroeconomic variables where the changes have been very significant. Furthermore, they argued that use of both quantity (size of balance sheets) and price instruments (policy rate) by the central banks represent a fundamental departure from decades thinking of the scope of central bank actions. Financial environment in which monetary policy is conducted in the emerging market economies (EMEs) has changed over the past decade in terms of increasing role of debt markets relative to banks, globalization of debt markets and behavior of long term interest rates (Mohanty and Kumar 2016). Against this backdrop, the objective of this chapter is to provide evidence on the effect of monetary policy on the key macroeconomic variables in India. The main focus of the study is to test the hypothesis whether the response of macroeconomic variables to unexpected monetary policy shocks have changed significantly in post crisis years in comparison to pre-crisis period. The chapter employs a Vector Autoregression (VAR) methodology for empirical investigation of the monetary policy effects on some key macroeconomic variables. Vector Autoregression (VAR) models have been extensively used in the empirical analysis of monetary policy issues.

The remainder of this chapter is organized as follows: Section 3.2 presents literature review on monetary policy analysis based on VAR models. Section 3.3 gives a brief account of monetary policy operating procedure of the RBI. Section 3.4 specifies the reduced form VAR model consisting of five variables and dataset. Section 3.5 reports the results of Chow structural break test. Section 3.6

provides empirical evidence of the effects of monetary policy on macroeconomic variables in pre-and post-crisis from impulse responses and variance decompositions. Section 3.7 presents the concluding remarks.

3.2 Review of Literature

VAR models have been used in standard literature for studying the dynamic relationship among macroeconomic variables. The use of VARs to estimate the impact of monetary policy on the real economic activity was pioneered by Sims (1972, 1980). Sims (1972) studied the role of money stock in explaining business cycles in the United States during inter-World War and post-World War. In another study (1980), he estimated the VAR model for different countries in order to examine the role of money as a good indicator of monetary policy. In most fascinating study, Bernanke and Blinder (1992) found the US federal funds rate as extremely informative about future movements of real macroeconomic variables. After estimating three variable VAR model with fund rate, log of CPI and prime age [25–54] male unemployment, they found inflation shocks drive up the fund rate with the peak effect coming 5–10 months and then decaying very slowly, while unemployment shocks push the fund rate in the opposite direction but with somewhat longer lags and smaller magnitude.

A number of studies have been conducted in India using VAR models especially after the structural and macroeconomic reforms of the early 1990s. Therefore, it appears that VAR assumptions throw light on theorization of monetary policy transmission effects in India. To examine the implications of structural reforms (April 1992 to March 1997) on monetary policy transmission, Ray et al. (1998) establish the importance of both interest rate and exchange rate channel in the monetary transmission in post liberalization era. They found that money, income, prices and exchange rates are cointegrated and interest rate and exchange rate which were exogenous in the pre-reforms period became endogenous variables in post reforms periods. This evidence suggests of shift in monetary policy transmission. Applying VAR models in the vector error correction form, Al-Mashat (2003) demonstrates that the interest rate channel and exchange rate channel are most important while bank lending channel is found weak reflecting low pass-through of changes in policy rate to lending rates.

In order to explore the channels of monetary transmission the RBI (2004) estimated a five variables recursive VAR model. These variables are log of index of industrial production (LIIP), log of WPI (LWPI), Bank rate (BRATE), log of broad money (LM3) and log of exchange rate (LEXCH). Empirical evidence of transmission channels shows that monetary policy shocks have the expected effect on output and prices. Interest rate and exchange rate as financial variables are found more effective than earlier. Bhattacharya and Ray (2007) present both narrative analysis of monetary policy stance as well as empirical evidence based on Vector autoregression model with three variables output, prices and "measure" of monetary policy stance. Their findings indicate that monetary policy had been more effective in controlling inflation vis-a-vis stimulating output growth. Moreover, the results are quite robust and remain consistent despite changing the ordering of variables. Using quarterly data from 1996 to 2007, Aleem (2010) examines monetary policy transmission channels. The VAR results support the importance of the bank lending channel in a bank based Indian economy. While both asset price channel and exchange rate channel are not found significant which, he argued, are consistent with lower market capitalization of listed companies and massive interventions by the Reserve bank of India in foreign exchange market respectively.

Based on structural vector autoregression (SVAR) model, Mohanty (2012) provides the empirical evidence of interest rate channel of monetary policy transmission in India. Using quarterly data, the results show that monetary contraction has a negative effect on output with a lag of two quarters while impact on inflation with a lag of three quarters. The overall impact persists through eight to ten quarters. After finding a structural break at a time ofLiquidity Adjustment Framework (LAF) introduction, Sengupta (2014) examines the changes in transmission channels of monetary policy in pre-LAF and post-LAF periods. Using vector autoregressionmodel with monthly data from April 1993 to March 2012, the study finds that the bank lending channel although has weakened still remains an important channel of monetary transmission. Moreover, the interest rate and asset price channels have become stronger while the exchange rate channel though weak, shows a mild improvement in the post-LAF period. Mishra et al. (2016) examine the empirical evidence of the strength of monetary transmission in India using the structural vector autoregression (SVAR) method. While the pass-through from the policy rate to bank lending rates is in right direction, it is not complete. The responses of real activity (IIP) and prices (WPI) are not found significant following monetary policy shocks. The estimated effect may reflect either weakness in monetary transmission or the limitations of empirical methodology. Overall, the empirical results do provide a mixed message on the effectiveness of monetary policy in India. Mohanty and Kumar (2016) reviewed the recent changes in financial intermediation in Emerging Market Economies (EMEs) and its implications on the monetary transmission.

3.3 Reserve Bank's Current Monetary Policy Operating Procedure

Based on the recommendations of the Committee on Banking Sector Reforms (Narasimham Committee II 1998), RBI had adopted an Interim Liquidity Adjustment Facility (ILAF) as its operating procedure in April 1999. The Interim LAF was transitioned towards full-fledged LAF in June 2000. The modified new operating framework (Reserve Bank of India 2011) has allowed banks to manage their daily liquidity more efficiently and reduced volatility in money market.

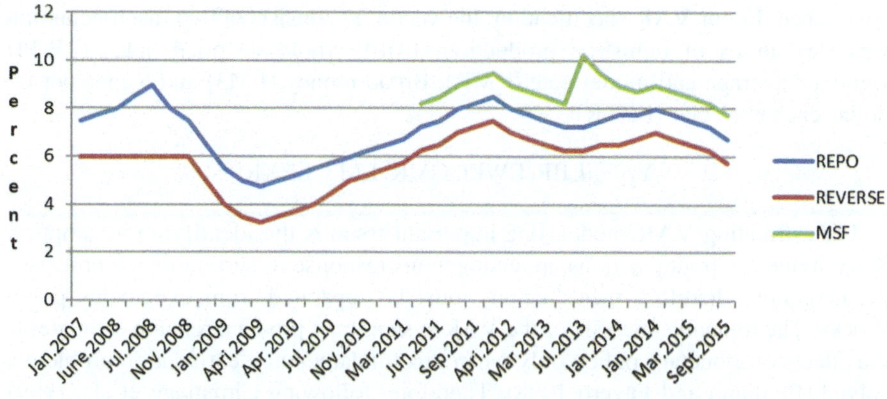

Fig. 3.1 Some key policy rates. *Source* Handbook of Statistics on the Indian Economy, 2015–16

According to which liquidity injections are done at the Marginal Standing Facility[1] (MSF) and liquidity absorptions are through fixed reverse repo rate. The fixed overnight repo rate is the single monetary policy rate and has been placed in the middle of the corridor, with the reverse repo rate 25 basis points below it and the MSF rate 25 basis points above it. The weighted average call money rate (WACMR) is the new operating target of monetary policy. The main objective of the liquidity management is to anchor the weighted average call money rate (WACMR) around the policy rate (Fig. 3.1).

3.4 Methodology and Data Set

We estimate a reduced-form vector autoregression (VAR), as proposed by Sims (1980), to examine the response of macroeconomic variables to unexpected monetary policy shocks. In a reduced form VAR, each variable is expressed as a linear function of its own lagged values, lagged values of all other variables and a serially uncorrelated error tem. Thus a reduced form VAR is a system of equations and can be written in matrix form as:

$$Y_t = A_0 + A(L)Y_{t-1} + u_t$$

where Y_t is vector of macroeconomic variables included in our model. A_0 is a vector of constants. A is the matrix of coefficients. L is lag operator. And u_t is a vector of serially uncorrelated disturbances that have zero mean and time invariant

[1]MSF is the rate at which scheduled commercial banks (SCBs) can borrow overnight without giving any collateral at their discretion up to 1% of their respective Net Demand and Time Liabilities (NDTL) at penal rate 25 basis points above the repo rate.

covariance. In our VAR specification, the vector Y_t consists of five macroeconomic variables: index of industrial production (LIIP), wholesale price index (LWPI), weighted average call money rate (CMR), Broad money (LM3) and Rupee per US dollar exchange rate (LEXR):

$$Y_t = [\text{LIIP}, \text{LWPI}, \text{CMR}, \text{LM3}, \text{LEXR}]$$

For estimating VAR model, one important issue is the identifying assumption. Since monetary policy actions are endogenous response to current developments in the economy; therefore these actions must be separated from exogenous policy shocks. The dynamic analysis of the VAR system may produce reliable estimates of the effects of monetary policy only when this fundamental identification problem is solved (Bagliano and Favero 1998). Therefore, following Christiano et al. (1999), we identify monetary policy shocks by a standard choleski-decomposition with the order of variables as given in the vector $Y_{t.}$ In other words, monetary policy reacts to development in real economy contemporaneously but does not affect output and prices contemporaneously (i.e. in the same period). Accordingly, real variables like output and prices have been placed before monetary policy instrument in the model. Given the monthly data, this identifying assumption seems reasonable.

We have used Index of Industrial Production as a proxy variable for GDP output data as the monthly data of GDP output is not available in India. Monetary policy rate is proxied by overnight weighted average call money rate (CMR) because it is also the operating target of the Reserve Bank. For price index, the headline wholesale price index (WPI) has been selected. For quantity variable, I have taken monthly data of broad money (M3) in real terms by deflating correspondingly monthly WPI index and rupee per US dollar for exchange rate. In general, estimation of any VAR model requires long time series data. Accordingly, the model has been estimated using monthly data running from 2000–01 April to 2015–16 March. The entire sample is divided into two sub-sample for pre-crisis (April, 2000–August, 2008) and post-crisis (October, 2008–March, 2015). The data set has been taken from the Reserve bank's site: http://dbie.rbi.org.in and also from Handbook of Statistics on Indian Economy: 2015–16. All the variables except the policy interest rate are seasonally adjusted using X–12 ARIMA and are transformed into natural logarithms. The Augmented Dickey-Fuller test results indicate that all the variables except call money rate are non-stationary. As differencing of series throws away important information and does not improve asymptotic efficiency, the VAR model has been estimated in levels (RBI 2004). The appropriate lag length in our VAR model has been decided on the basis of various information criteria: Akaike Information Criteria (AIC), Schwarz Criteria (SC), Hannan-Quinn (HQ), Final Prediction Error (FPE). All these information criteria except SC indicate the appropriate lag length of two (Appendix table). Thus our VAR model includes only two lags of variables (Fig. 3.2).

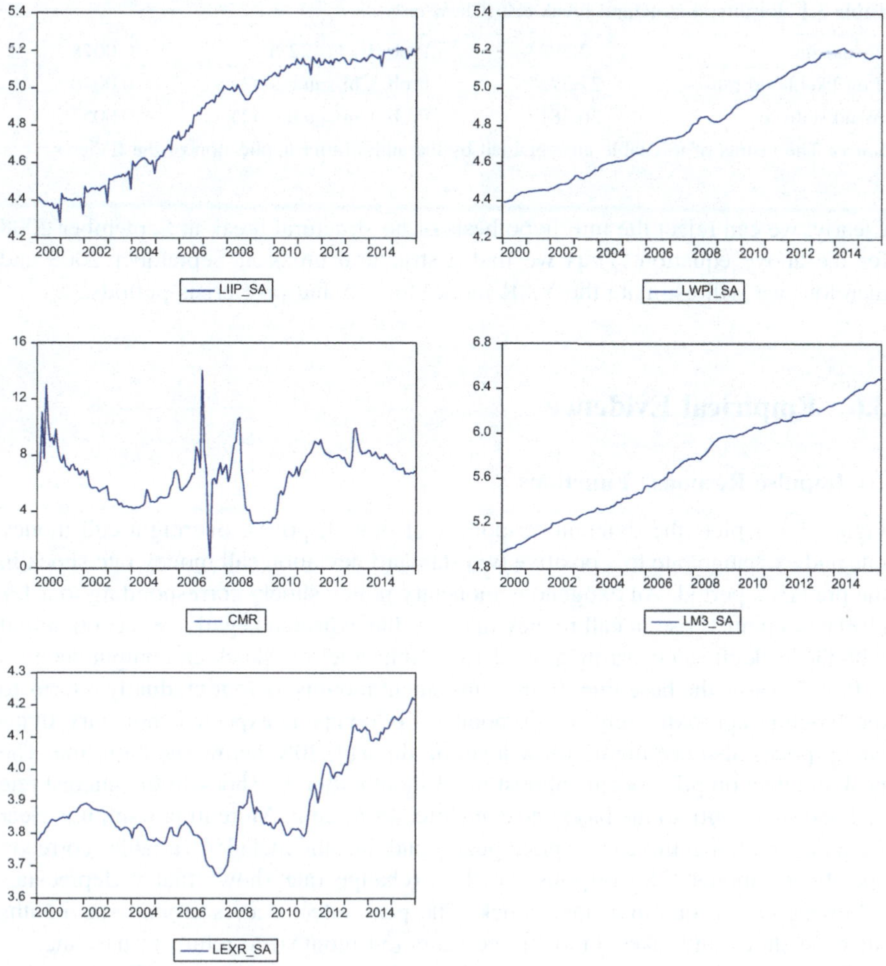

Fig. 3.2 The time series variables included in VAR analysis (for all the graphs X axis shows months and Y axis units)

3.5 Test of Structural Break: Chow Test

To check the presence of structural break in the sample, we estimate one of the VAR equations of broad money in terms of output, prices, interest rate and exchange rates. In a span of eight months from September 2008 and April 2009, the Reserve Bank followed unprecedented policy activism. Therefore it does make sense to check whether there is a structural break between this period. Table 3.1 shows the results of Chow test when we choose September 2008 as break point.

Table 3.1 Results of structural break test (Chow test)

F-statistic	2.3983	Prob. F (11, 228)	0.0078
Log likelihood ratio	27.3725	Prob. Chi-square (11)	0.0040
Wald statistic	26.3817	Prob. Chi-square (11)	0.0057

Source The results of this table are obtained by the author after application of the EViews

Clearly, we can reject the null hypothesis of no structural break at September 2008 for the above equation. Thus we find a structural break at September 2008 and therefore we will estimate the VAR model for pre and post crisis periods.

3.6 Empirical Evidence

(i) **Impulse Response Functions**[2]:

Figure 3.3 depicts the dynamic responses of output, prices, overnight call money rate and exchange rate to a positive two standard deviation call money rate shock in the pre-crisis period. An exogenous monetary policy shock- corresponding to a 1% (100 basis points) rise in call money rate- has the expected negative effect on output with the peak effect occurring around 13 months after the shock and output declines to 0.35% below the base line. In the subsequent months, output gradually returns to the baseline approximately in 40 months. Following unexpected monetary tightening, prices also decline to a low level of almost 0.20% below the base line. The peak of effect on price occurs almost in 23 month after the shock to the interest rate and does not return to the base line even after 45 months. More important, it is clear from the graph that there is no price puzzle and thus the included variables correctly specify the model. The response of the exchange rate shows that it depreciates following exogenous monetary shock. The peak effect occurs around six months after the shock and takes almost three years (34 months) to return to baseline.

We now repeat the interpretation of impulse response functions for post-crisis period. From Figure 3.4, it is clear that a positive shock to call money rate (0.8% rise in CMR) leads output to decline to a low level of 0.24% below the baseline after five months. In almost 22 months, output gradually returns to the baseline. The maximum negative effect on prices (0.28%) occurs in almost 12 months and remains below the baseline even after three years. The response of the exchange rate shows that it depreciates following monetary tightening shock with the maximum effect at 5 months.

(ii) **Variance Decomposition analysis**:

Variance decomposition analysis examines the variance of output and prices that can be explained by monetary policy and other shocks in the economy.

[2]For all the figures X axis shows months and Y axis units.

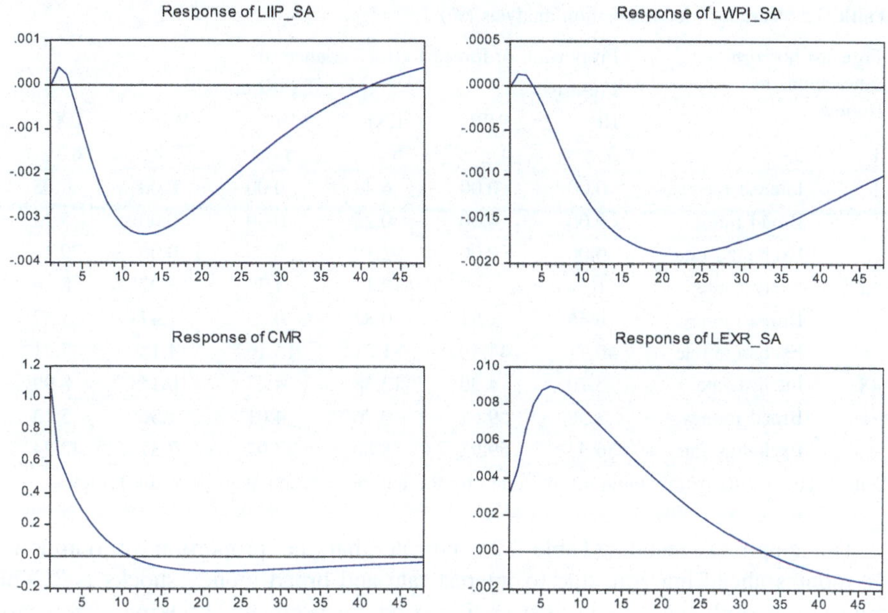

Fig. 3.3 Impulse responses of output, prices and exchange rate to interest rate shock (pre-crisis)

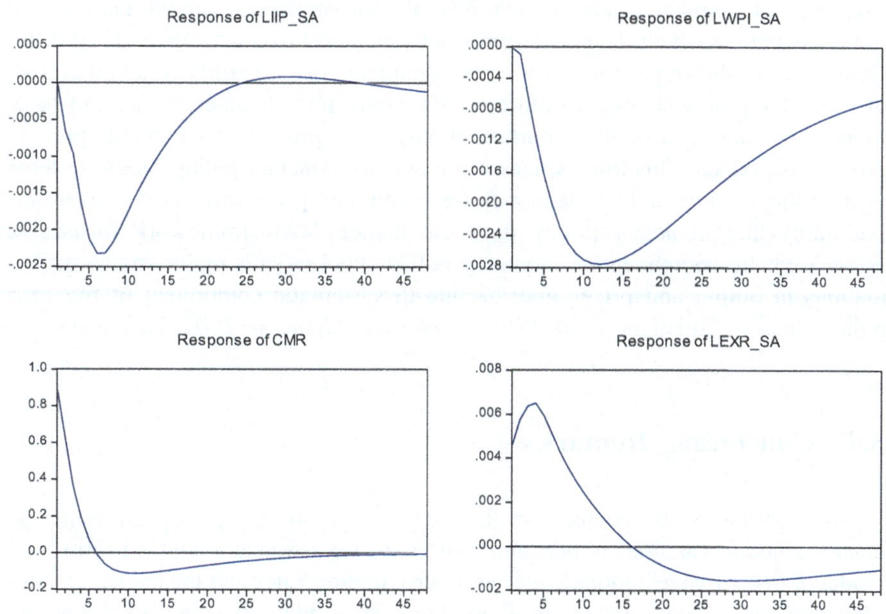

Fig. 3.4 Impulse responses of output, prices and exchange rate to interest rate shock (post-crisis)

Table 3.2 Variance decomposition analysis (%)

Forecast horizon (months)	innovations to	Proportion of forecast error variance in					
		Pre-crisis			Post-crisis		
		IIP	WPI	EXR	IIP	WPI	EXR
1	2	3	4	5	6	7	8
1	Interest rate	0.00	0.00	6.42	0.00	0.00	6.85
	Broad money	0.00	0.00	0.25	0.00	0.00	5.13
	Exchange rate	0.00	0.00	92.19	0.00	0.00	79.46
12	Interest rate	1.74	3.99	12.15	4.79	5.97	8.66
	Broad money	0.46	2.81	0.82	0.29	1.47	5.57
	Exchange rate	40.71	44.40	81.21	18.16	4.15	47.71
48	Interest rate	3.70	4.30	12.38	4.77	10.15	8.99
	Broad money	3.38	9.61	0.76	4.01	1.36	5.13
	Exchange rate	56.33	59.92	78.80	17.02	7.37	42.24

Source The results of this table are obtained by the author after application of the EViews

The empirical results (Table 3.2) indicate that the proportion of output at 48 months ahead horizon, due to interest rate and broad money shocks is 3% in pre-crisis periods and 4% in post crisis periods respectively. Looking at forecast error variance of prices, shocks to interest rate and broad money explain almost 4 and 9% of volatility in prices in pre-crisis periods and 10 and 1% in post crisis periods respectively. Similarly, interest rate and broad money shocks explain only a small proportion of variance in exchange rate. Moreover, the innovations to exchange rate explain almost 56 and 59% of total variance in output and prices in pre-crisis period which declined significantly in post crisis periods to 17 and 7%. Overall, a significant proportion of both output and price volatility is not on account of monetary policy shocks. In other words, innovations to interest rate and broad money explain only a small proportion of output and price variance in both pre- and post-crisis periods. This low explanatory power of monetary policy shocks in terms of both interest rate and broad money for output and price variance however does not imply that monetary policy does not matter. VAR framework focuses on non-systematic component of monetary policy shocks. Thus major source of fluctuations in output and prices may be due to systematic component of monetary policy shocks (Christiano et al. 1999; Boivin and Giannoni 2002; RBI 2004).

3.7 Concluding Remarks

In order to assess the changes in the impact of monetary policy on some key macroeconomic variables in pre- and post-crisis, we estimate a reduced form VAR model of five variables: money, output, prices, interest rates and the exchange rates. The empirical results are analyzed in terms of impulse response functions and variance decomposition. The empirical evidence shows that both output and prices respond negatively to unexpected monetary policy shock- in terms of two standard deviation shock to overnight call money rate. More importantly, we can notice that in response to monetary policy shock the decline in output precedes the decline in prices in both pre- and post-crisis periods. But the response of output and prices to monetary policy shock is sooner in post-crisis in comparison to pre-crisis periods. In other words, the monetary policy transmission lags are significantly reduced in post crisis period. The peak effect on output and prices are felt with a lag of 5 and 12 months which were 13 and 23 months respectively in pre-crisis periods. The response of exchange rate is however is not in right direction (a monetary tightening leads the exchange rate to depreciate) and which might be consistent with the finding of weak exchange rate channel (Mishra et al. 2016). Variance decomposition results show that innovations to interest rate and broad money explain only a small proportion of output and price variance in both pre- and post-crisis periods. For sensitivity of results, alternative ordering of variables has been undertaken but the impulse responses remain broadly unchanged.

Acknowledgements The author is very grateful to Prof. Chetan Ghate and Dr. Jose Antonio Pedrosa Garcia for valuable comments and discussions in the International Conference on Economics and Finance, organized by BITS Pilani, KK Birla Goa Campus. Further, the author expresses sincere gratitude to Prof. U. Kalpagam (DPhil Supervisor) for extremely useful suggestions and encouragement all the time.

Appendix

VAR lag order selection criteria

Lag	Log L	LR	FPE	AIC	SC	HQ
0	416.2659	NA	9.49e−09	−4.284019	−4.199189	−4.249662
1	2073.012	3209.945	3.94e−16	-21.28137	−20.77239[a]	−21.07523
2	2131.920	111.0672[a]	2.77e−16[a]	−21.63458[a]	−20.70145	−21.25666[a]
3	2147.914	29.32199	3.04e−16	−21.54077	−20.18348	−20.99106
4	2158.157	18.24530	3.56e−16	−21.38705	−19.60561	−20.66555
5	2173.813	27.07228	3.94e−16	−21.28972	−19.08412	−20.39644

[a]Indicates lag order selected by the criterion
Source Same as for Table 3.1

References

Aleem, A. (2010). Transmission mechanism of monetary policy in India. *Journal of Asian Economics, 21,* 186–197.

Al-Mashat, R. (2003). Monetary policy transmission in India: Selected issues and statistical appendix. *Country Report No. 03/261, International Monetary Fund.*

Bagliano, F. C., & Favero, C. A. (1998). Measuring monetary policy with VAR models: An evaluation. *European Economic Review, 42,* 1069–1112.

Bernanke, B. S., & Blinder, A. S. (1992). The federal funds rate and the channels of monetary transmission. *The American Economic Review, 82*(4), 901–921.

Bhattacharya, I., & Ray, P. (2007). How do we assess monetary policy stance? *Economic and Political Weekly, 42*(13), 1201–1210.

Boivin, J., & Giannoni, M. (2002). Assessing changes in the monetary transmission mechanism: A VAR approach. *Federal Reserve Bank of New York Economic Policy Review, 8*(1), 97–111.

Christiano, L. J., Eichenbaum, M., & Evans, C. L. (1999). Monetary policy shocks: What have we learned and to what end? In J. B. Taylor & M. Woodford (Eds.), *Handbook of macroeconomics* (Vol. 1A). Amsterdam: North-Hlland.

Friedman, B. M., & Kuttner, K. N. (2010). Implementation of monetary policy: How do central banks set interest rates? In: B. M. Friedman & M. Woodford (Eds.), *Handbook of monetary economics* (Vol. 3B). Amsterdam: North-Holland.

Khundrakpam, J. K., & Jain, R. (2012, June). Monetary policy transmission in India: A peep inside the black box. *Reserve Bank of India Working paper Series WPS (DEPR): 11/2012.*

Mishra, P., & Montiel, P. (2013). How effective is monetay transmission in developing countries? A survey of the empirical evidence. *Economic Systems, 37*(2), 187–216.

Mishra, P., Montiel, P., & Sengupta, R. (2016). Monetary transmission in developing countries: Evidence from India. *IGIDR; Working Paper, 2016-008.*

Mohanty, D. (2011, September). How does the Reserve Bank of India conduct its monetary policy? *Reserve Bank of India Bulletin.*

Mohanty, D. (2012, May). Evidence of interest rate channel of monetary policy transmission in India. *RBI Working Paper No. 6.*

Mohanty, M. S., & Kumar, R. (2016). Financial intermediation and monetary policy transmission in EMEs: What has changed post-2008 crisis? *Monetary and Economic Development, BIS Working Papers No. 546.*

Mohanty, M. S., & Turner, P. (2008). Monetary policy transmission in emerging market economies: What has changed? *BIS Papers, 35.*

Ray, P., Joshi, H., & Saggsar, M. (1998). New monetary transmission channels: Role of interest rates and exchange rate in conduct of Indian monetary policy. *Economic And Political Weakly, 33*(44).

Reserve Bank of India. (2004). Monetary transmission mechanism. *Report on Currency and Finance, 2003–04.* Mumbai: Reserve Bank of India.

Reserve Bank of India. (2011). *Report of the working group on operating procedure of monetary policy, chairman: Deepak Mohanty.* Mumbai: Reserve Bank of India.

Reserve Bank of India. (2014). *Report of the expert committee to revise and strengthen the monetary policy framework, Chairman: Urjit R. Patel.* Reserve Bank of India: Mumbai.

Reserve Bank of India. (2015–16). *Handbook of statistics on the Indian economy.* Mumbai: Reserve Bank of India.

Sengupta, N. (2014). Changes in transmission channels of monetary policy. *Economic and Political Weekly, XLIX*(49), 62–71.

Sims, C. A. (1972). Money, income and causality. *The American Economic Review, 62*(4), 540–552.

Sims, C. A. (1980). Macroeconomics and reality. *Econometrica, 48,* 1–48.

Chapter 4
Stock Indices and Inflation Through Industry Prisms

Abha Mohan, Tomy Mathew and K. Subramanian

Abstract The relationship between macroeconomic variables and stock price is a widely discussed and investigated topic both in developed and developing countries. But, so far industry specific studies are limited in Indian context. Among various macroeconomic variables, rate of inflation is considered to be a prominent economic indicator. The current study examined the long run association between Industry specific indices and inflation rate. Inflation rate measured in terms of CPI and four major sector indices of Bombay Stock Exchange such as S&P BSE Fast Moving Consumer Goods, S&P BSE Healthcare, S&P BSE Information Technology and S&P BSE Bankex were taken for industry specific analysis. In view of the fact that CPI numbers are measured monthly, the study used monthly data of inflation rate and BSE Sectoral Indices from January 2012 to October 2017. Econometric techniques such as Augmented Dickey Fuller test, Johansen Co-integration test, VECM and VAR models were applied to the time series data. The results established negative long run causality running from inflation rate towards FMCG and Banking indices, but no relationship was established with Pharmaceutical and IT indices.

Keywords Inflation · Stock price · Industry · Consumer price index
BSE sectoral indices

A. Mohan (✉) · K. Subramanian
School of Contemporary Knowledge Systems, ChinmayaVishwavidyapeeth,
Ernakulam, Kerala, India
e-mail: abha.mohan@cvv.ac.in

K. Subramanian
e-mail: subramanian.k@cvv.ac.in

T. Mathew
Department of Commerce, CMS College (Autonomous), Kottayam, Kerala, India
e-mail: tomycms@gmail.com

A. K. Mishra et al. (eds.), *Current Issues in the Economy and Finance of India*,
Springer Proceedings in Business and Economics,
https://doi.org/10.1007/978-3-319-99555-7_4

4.1 Introduction

Stock indices are considered as significant indicators of the well being of an economy. An Industry specific stock index is nowadays assessed to track the performance and growth of a sector, since it is considered to be a true reflector of the behaviour of a particular industry. Economists and financial researchers have always been very keen on the interaction of stock prices with the macroeconomic variables. Among various macroeconomic variables, inflation rate is considered to be a prominent one, as it plays vital role in the monetary policy decisions of a country.

Inflation is the continuing upward movement of general price level of various goods and services in a country over a period of time. Inflation rate in India was initially represented by Wholesale Price Index of selected basket of wholesale commodities. Later in April, 2014 Reserve Bank of India considered Consumer Price Index (combined) as the key measure of inflation (The Hindu 2014). CPI is the measure of change in the general level of retail prices of selected consumer goods and services. CPIs have been widely used as a macroeconomic indicator of inflation, and also as a tool by Government and Central Bank for targeting inflation and monitoring price stability. (Consumer Price Index: Changes in the Revised Series 2015).

The relationship between stock price and inflation rate is widely discussed and investigated topic both in developed and developing countries. There are many studies inland and abroad, examining the liaison between these two variables. But studies specifically investigating the relationship between inflation and stock indices of different industries are limited. Every industry need not behave in a common way to the change in inflation rate.

The current study aims to establish the long run relationship between inflation and industry specific stock indices. Since industry specific stock indices exhibit the behaviour of sectors, the effect of inflation on the chosen sector may be inferred. Investors and business decision makers may use the findings of the study to gauge the performance of a particular industry during the time of rise or fall in inflation rate and plan the strategies accordingly.

4.1.1 Stock Returns and Inflation

As per random walk theory, stock prices equip the information in the economy and promptly react to it. Therefore the stock market may become agog towards the fluctuation in macroeconomic variables. Being a major economic indicator, the variations in inflation rate may be an omen to stock market to either tank or surge prices.

Further, Arbitrage Pricing Theory developed by Stephen Ross, assumes return on any asset is linearly related to a set of systematic risk factors. The risk factors were again classified into macroeconomic and microeconomic risk factors. The macroeconomic variables; the spread between long and short interest rate, high and low grade bonds, Industrial Production and expected and unexpected inflation are significant risk factors that systematically affect the stock market (Chen et al. 1986). Hence the stock return can be linearly related to the major macroeconomic variable, inflation.

Fisher (1930) proposed that the expected nominal interest rate is the sum total of expected real interest rate and the expected inflation rate. From the Fisher's theory, it is inferred that there exists a positive relation between the stock returns and inflation. Fama and Schwert (1977) generalized Fisher's hypothesis on to various assets like real estate, government debt instruments, short term bills and stock returns, of which stock returns and inflation showed a negative relationship.

4.1.2 Selected Industries and Inflation

The study had chosen four major industries of India; Fast Moving Consumer Goods, Pharmaceutical, Information technology and Banking.

Fast moving consumer goods industry is one of the largest industries in India. It comprises of three main sectors; food and beverages, healthcare and household and personal care. The performance of this industry to a great extent depends on the purchasing power and demographic layout of the country. The purchasing power is explained by the CPI of a country. At the time of inflation the companies' costs goes up, sales get stagnated and companies may be in doldrums. The FMCG stocks are cyclical and are expected to react to macroeconomic variables.

Indian pharmaceutical industry is one of the fastest growing industries and plays a prominent role in the global pharmaceutical sector. Inflation may have an effect on cost of production and thereby profitability of the companies. But the Pharmaceutical stocks are defensive stocks that are expected to outperform even when the economy slows down, in view of the fact that the sector deals with drugs that are always essential for life.

The fast absorption of digital technology in India has contributed for the tremendous growth of IT industry. The cost competitiveness in providing IT services has given India a remarkable outlook in the global sourcing market. Since IT stocks are growth stocks, they are expected to withstand the changes in inflation rate.

Indian banking industry has always retained the confidence among the investors. The industry has remained stable in many of the global upheavals. The monetary policies largely depend upon the inflation rate prevailing in the country. At the time of rising inflation, RBI announces monetary tightening by raising the interest rate and/or reducing money supply. This may have an adverse effect on the banking activities which may in turn encumber companies' growth. Like FMCG stocks, Banking stocks are cyclical and are expected to change in accordance with inflation.

4.2 Literature Review

A large number of studies were carried out for investigating the relationship between stock prices and inflation rates. The survey on the literature exhibits varied results of relationship such as negative, positive and even no relationship between the variables. The studies of Fama (1981) and Schwert (1981) are the two major studies that confirmed negative relationship. According to Fama, there exists a positive relationship between stock returns and real activity and a negative relationship between inflation and real activity. As such he analysed the proxy hypothesis of negative relationship between stock returns and inflation and the study established the negative relationship between expected and unexpected components of inflation and stock returns. Schwert proved that the daily returns of S&P composite portfolio is negatively related to the announcement of unexpected inflation in the CPI.

Feldstein (1983) and Kaul (1987) intrigued the reason for inflation—stock relation. Feldstein found that the inverse relation between inflation and stock price is due to the basic features of US tax laws of that time. From the post war evidence, Kaul found that the negative inflation—stock relation in US, UK, Canada and Germany is due to the money demand and also due to some effect of counter cyclical money supply.

More recently, Bordo et al. (2009) found that the inflation shocks negatively impact the real stock price index (S&P 500) as well as stock market conditions. Geetha et al. (2011) established long run relationship between stock returns and both expected and unexpected inflation in Malaysia, US and China. Both expected and unexpected inflation had a negative impact on the stock market in Malaysia and a positive impact in US. Interestingly in China the expected inflation had a negative impact and unexpected inflation had a positive impact. However short run relationship was established only in China.

Ibrahim and Agbaje (2013) established positive and significant long run and short run relationship between inflation and Nigerian stock market. Later Uwubanmwen and Eghosa (2015) attempted to find the impact of inflation on the Nigerian Stock Market, but confirmed a negative but weak impact. They made a concluding remark that inflation is not strong predictor of Nigerian stock returns.

Amonhaemanon et al. (2014) found that Thai stock returns are negatively related to both unexpected and expected inflation and Vietnamese stock returns are negatively related to unexpected inflation only. But quite the reverse, the Vietnamese stock returns showed a positive relation with the expected inflation. However, the coefficients of these variables were not statistically significant. Afterwards, Hau (2017) found that 12 out 24 Vietnamese stocks have positive and significant relation with ex post inflation. But, he also found that all stocks are not related to the actual inflation.

A negative impact of inflation on stock prices was confirmed by Mahmood et al. (2014) in Pakistan stock market and Silva (2016) in Srilankan stock market. On the contrary, Floros (2004) could not find long run association between Greek

Consumer Price Index, which was considered as a proxy for inflation, and Athens Stock Exchange Price Index.

In the Indian context Patel (2012) found long run equilibrium between macroeconomic variables including inflation and stock market indices such as SENSEX and S&P CNX NIFTY. Also he stated that inflation is highly positively correlated with the indices. Ray (2012) tested the granger causality between stock prices and macroeconomic variables and found a unidirectional causality running from stock price to inflation, but not from inflation to stock price. Reddy (2012) opined that interest and inflation rate jointly have a negative influence on Indian stock price. Tripathi and Kumar (2014) conducted a study on BRICS stock markets and could not find any significant long term equilibrium relationship between inflation and Indian stock market. Similarly Gurloveleen and Bhatia (2015) found no significant relationship between inflation and Indian stock.

There are a few studies that concentrated on sectoral stock prices while examining the relationship. Lajeri and Dermine (1999) found that in France during the period of high volatility, the unexpected interest rate and inflation rate jointly showed a negative impact on the bank stock returns. Abadi (2006) confirmed negative and significant impact of expected inflation on the bank stock returns. Umashankar and Himabindu (2015) investigated the impact of inflation on the performance of FMCG stocks. They found a significant negative relation in four years and positive relation in three years. Nurhakim et al. (2016) investigated the influence of profitability and inflation on Pharmaceutical stock prices. The result shows that pharmaceutical stocks are not significantly influenced by the inflation rate.

4.3 Data and Methodology

The study is confined to four major industry specific stock indices of Bombay Stock Exchange such as S&P BSE Fast Moving Consumer Goods, S&P BSE Healthcare, S&P BSE Information Technology and S&P BSE Bankex. Inflation rate measured in terms of Consumer Price Index (CPI) is chosen for the study. The period of the study is from January 2012 to October 2017. The study has used EViews 9 for econometric analysis.

4.3.1 Objectives of the Study

The objective of the study is to examine the long run relationship between inflation rate and industry specific stock indices. More specifically the study investigates the long run causality running from Inflation to Industry specific sock indices.

4.3.2 Hypothesis

H0: There is no long run causality running from Inflation rate to Industry specific Indices.

4.3.3 Data Required and Source

The data required for the study are monthly inflation rates measured in terms of CPI and monthly index values of four selected indices from January 2012 to October 2017. Inflation rates are obtained from Database of Indian Economy website maintained by RBI and Index Values from BSE website.

4.3.4 Methodology

Various econometric tools are applied in this study. Initially the time series data are checked for stationarity using Augmented Dickey Fuller (ADF) Test. Since the whole set of data are stationary only at first difference; the study proceeds with the Johansen Cointegration Test to understand the existence and number of cointegrating vectors. Optimal number of lags for the cointegration test was arrived at using Akaike Information Criterion (AIC), Final Prediction Error (FPE) and Hannan-Quinn information criterion (HQ). Further when cointegration exists Vector Error Correction Model is used to examine and confirm the long run causality. If Johansen cointegration test reveals no cointegration between the variables, Vector Autoregressive Model is used to examine the significance of dynamic relationship. As the study is limited to examine the influence of inflation on stock return, the equations considering Stock indices as exogenous variable and inflation rate as endogenous variable are only taken.

4.4 Empirical Results and Analysis

4.4.1 Unit Root Test

The study deals with five set of time series data and hence to proceed further the stationarity needs to be checked. ADF test is used to examine the stationarity of all five variables: Inflation rate, S&P BSE FMCG, S&P BSE Healthcare, S&P BSE IT and S&P BSE Bankex. The stock index values are converted to natural log values, before testing for unit root.

H0: The time series has a unit root (Time series are non-stationary)

The study failed to reject null Hypothesis at level since, the critical values are less than the t-statistic at 1, 5 and 10% level of significance and the *p*-value is greater than 0.05. But it got rejected at the first difference for all the five variables. That means all the variables are stationary only at their first difference. The results of ADF test at first difference are shown in Table 4.1.

4.4.2 Lag Selection

Before proceeding with further econometric tools optimal lag length needs to be decided. There are many information criterions available for lag selection. In the current study, AIC, FPE and HQ are chosen. For each sector index and inflation rate set of data, two has been chosen as the optimum lag length.

4.4.3 Results of Johansen Cointegration Test

Since the data are stationery at first difference, Johansen cointegration test is applied to investigate whether the variables are cointegrated. Two variables are cointegrated if they have a long term equilibrium relationship (Gujarati et al. 2012). Johansen cointegration test uses λ_{trace} and λ_{max} statistics for finding the number of cointegrating vectors. The present study uses λ_{trace} statistic for testing the hypothesis.

Table 4.1 Results of ADF test

		D(INFLATION)	D(LNFMCG)	D(LNHEALTH)	D(LNIT)	D(LNBANK)
Exogenous		Constant	Constant, linear trend	Constant, linear trend	Constant, linear trend	Constant, linear trend
		t-statistic (Prob.*)	t-statistic (Prob.*)	t-statistic (Prob.*)	t-statistic (Prob.*)	t-statistic (Prob.*)
Augmented Dickey-Fuller test statistic		−6.25761	−9.111946	−9.643202	−9.56888	−7.549777
		(0.0000)	(0.0000)	(0.0000)	(0.0000)	(0.0000)
Test critical values:	1% level	−3.53003	−4.098741	−4.098741	−4.098741	−4.098741
	5% level	−2.904848	−3.477275	−3.477275	−3.477275	−3.477275
	10% level	−2.589907	−3.16619	−3.16619	−3.16619	−3.16619

*MacKinnon (1996) one-sided p-values
Source Test result, self computed

Table 4.2 Results of Johansen cointegration test between S&P BSE FMCG and inflation

Unrestricted cointegration rank test (Trace)				
Hypothesized No. of CE(s)	Eigenvalue	Trace statistic	0.05 Critical value	Prob.**
None*	0.185428	15.60286	15.49471	0.0482
At most 1	0.027403	1.861648	3.841466	0.1724

Trace test indicates 1 cointegrating eqn(s) at the 0.05 level
*denotes rejection of the hypothesis at the 0.05 level
**MacKinnon-Haug-Michelis (1999) *p*-values
Source Test result, self computed

Table 4.3 Results of Johansen cointegration test between S&P BSE healthcare and inflation

Unrestricted cointegration rank test (trace)				
Hypothesized No. of CE(s)	Eigenvalue	Trace statistic	0.05 Critical value	Prob.**
None	0.104664	11.79853	15.49471	0.1669
At most 1*	0.063440	4.391275	3.841466	0.0361

Trace test indicates no cointegration at the 0.05 level
*denotes rejection of the hypothesis at the 0.05 level
**MacKinnon-Haug-Michelis (1999) p-values
Source Test result, self computed

S&P BSE FMCG Index and Inflation: The Johansen Cointegration test rejects the null hypothesis of no cointegration between S&P BSE FMCG and Inflation, at 5% level of significance as the trace statistic is greater than the critical value. The test indicates the existence of at least one cointegrating equation, which means the variables are cointegrated. Therefore VECM can be applied. The results are shown in Table 4.2.

S&P BSE Healthcare index and Inflation: The test failed to reject the null hypothesis of no cointegration between S&P BSE Healthcare and Inflation as the trace statistic is less than the critical value. Since there is no long run equilibrium between the variables, VECM cannot be applied. As a result the study continues with VAR model. The results are shown in Table 4.3.

S&P BSE IT Index and Inflation: As per the results shown in Table 4.4, the test has failed to reject the null hypothesis of no cointegration at 5% level of significance. There exists no long run equilibrium between S&P BSE IT and Inflation and therefore VAR model will be used.

S&P BSE Bankex and Inflation: The results shown in Table 4.5 imply that the null hypothesis of no cointegration between S&P BSE Bankex and Inflation is rejected and there exists at least one cointegrating vector. VECM model will be used as there is long run equilibrium between the variables.

Table 4.4 Results of Johansen cointegration test between S&P BSE IT and inflation

Unrestricted cointegration rank test (trace)				
Hypothesized No. of CE(s)	Eigenvalue	Trace statistic	0.05 Critical value	Prob.**
None	0.101056	9.411613	15.49471	0.3287
At most 1	0.033368	2.273792	3.841466	0.1316

Trace test indicates no cointegration at the 0.05 level
**MacKinnon-Haug-Michelis (1999) p-values
Source Test result, self computed

Table 4.5 Results of Johansen cointegration test between S&P BSE bankex and inflation

Unrestricted cointegration rank test (trace)				
Hypothesized No. of CE(s)	Eigenvalue	Trace statistic	0.05 Critical value	Prob.**
None*	0.272168	21.89112	15.49471	0.0047
At most 1	0.009008	0.606252	3.841466	0.4362

Trace test indicates 1 cointegrating eqn(s) at the 0.05 level
*denotes rejection of the hypothesis at the 0.05 level
**MacKinnon-Haug-Michelis (1999) p-values
Source Test result, self computed

4.4.4 Results of Vector Error Correction Model

VECM is a restricted VAR designed for use when variables are cointegrated. With the existence of cointegrating vector that exhibits the long run relationship, long run causality must be analysed using VECM. VECM is applied for FMCG and Bankex indices, since they are found to be cointegrated with inflation.

Model 1: VECM equation for dependent variable S&P BSE FMCG Index

$$\begin{aligned} D(LNFMCG) = {} & C(1) * (LNFMCG(-1) + 0.0648759788411 * INF(-1) - 9.31444727087) \\ & + C(2) * D(LNFMCG(-1)) + C(3) * D(LNFMCG(-2)) \\ & + C(4) * D(INF(-1)) + C(5) * D(INF(-2)) + C(6) \end{aligned}$$

In the equation LNFMCG is the log value of FMCG index and INF is the Inflation rate. C(2) and C(3) are the coefficients of lagged values of dependent variable. C(4) and C(5) are the coefficients of lagged values of independent variable and C(6) is the constant. C(1) is the coefficient of cointegrating equation (LNFMCG (−1) + 0.0648759788411 * INF(−1) − 9.31444727087). It is the error correction term and is understood as the speed of adjustment towards long run equilibrium. The results of VECM estimates are shown in the Table 4.6. C(1) is negative and also significant at 5% level. This implies that there is long run causality running from Inflation rate to FMCG Index. Also the cointegrating equation: 'LnFMCG = 9.31 – 0.065 Inflation', shows that the variables are negatively associated in the long run.

Table 4.6 Results of VECM estimates—BSE FMCG index and inflation

	Coefficient	Std. error	t-statistic	Prob.
C(1)	−0.131082	0.049849	−2.629568	0.0108
C(2)	−0.112266	0.119179	−0.941994	0.3499
C(3)	0.057805	0.121295	0.476566	0.6354
C(4)	0.000697	0.007559	0.092203	0.9268
C(5)	−0.002966	0.007139	−0.415554	0.6792
C(6)	0.012886	0.005470	2.355815	0.0217

Source Test result, self computed

Table 4.7 Results of VECM estimates—BSE bankex and inflation

	Coefficient	Std. error	t-statistic	Prob.
C(1)	−0.233234	0.091388	−2.552125	0.0132
C(2)	0.157031	0.123439	1.272139	0.2082
C(3)	0.027958	0.127888	0.218614	0.8277
C(4)	0.010710	0.012474	0.858579	0.3939
C(5)	−0.012247	0.012576	−0.973829	0.3340
C(6)	0.011049	0.008212	1.345507	0.1834

Source Test result, self computed

Model 2: VECM equation for dependent variable S&P BSE Bankex

$$\begin{aligned} D(LNBANK) = {} & C(1) * (LNBANK(-1) + 0.103617920649 * INF(-1) - 10.4424952318) \\ & + C(2) * D(LNBANK(-1)) + C(3) * D(LNBANK(-2)) \\ & + C(4) * D(INF(-1)) + C(5) * D(INF(-2)) + C(6) \end{aligned}$$

From the Table 4.7, it is inferred that there is long run causality running from Inflation rate to BSE Bankex as C(1) is negative and significant at 5%. The cointegrating equation: 'LnBANK = 10.44 − 0.104 Inflation', shows that there is a long run negative association between the variables.

4.4.5 Results of Vector Auto Regression Estimate

VAR model is used to estimate the dynamic relationship when the variables are not cointegrated. VAR model is applied for BSE Healthcare index and BSE IT index as they are not cointegrated with Inflation rate.

Model 3: VAR Model with BSE Healthcare Index (LNHEALTH = log values) as dependent variable

Table 4.8 Results of VAR estimates—BSE healthcare index and inflation rate

	Coefficient	Std. error	t-statistic	Prob.
C(1)	−0.089236	0.126124	−0.707527	0.4819
C(2)	0.170505	0.127451	1.337812	0.1858
C(3)	−0.007252	0.008706	−0.833023	0.4080
C(4)	0.002551	0.008271	0.308447	0.7588
C(5)	0.010211	0.005994	1.703451	0.0935

Source Test result, self computed

Table 4.9 Results of VAR estimates—BSE IT index and inflation rate

	Coefficient	Std. error	t-statistic	Prob.
C(1)	0.813167	0.124785	6.516521	0.0000
C(2)	0.156963	0.126836	1.237531	0.2205
C(3)	0.002065	0.010993	0.187840	0.8516
C(4)	−0.000872	0.010323	−0.084487	0.9329
C(5)	0.272592	0.471900	0.577649	0.5656

Source Test result, self computed

$$D(LNHEALTH) = C(1) * D(LNHEALTH(-1)) + C(2) * D(LNHEALTH(-2)) + C(3) * D(INF(-1)) + C(4) * D(INF(-2)) + C(5)$$

The VAR estimates (Table 4.8) shows that none of the coefficients are significant at 5%, which means that BSE Healthcare Index is not influenced by Inflation rate.

Model 4: VAR Model with BSE IT Index (LNIT = log values) as dependent variable

$$D(LNIT) = C(1) * D(LNIT(-1)) + C(2) * D(LNIT(-2)) + C(3) * D(INF(-1)) + C(4) * D(INF(-2)) + C(5)$$

From Table 4.9, it can be seen that only C(1), which is the coefficient of LNIT (−1) is significant at 5%. It means that the present BSE IT index value associates with the previous month index value. All the other coefficients are insignificant at 5% level; therefore BSE IT Index is not influenced by Inflation rate.

4.5 Conclusion

The study explores the influence of inflation rate on the industry specific stock indices. FMCG index, Healthcare Index, IT Index and Banking Index of Bombay Stock Exchange were considered for the study. The study confirmed the long run causality running from inflation rate to FMCG index and Banking Index. Also the inflation rate is having a negative association with these indices. Healthcare and IT indices were found to have no association with the inflation rate. The results are an implication for the investment decisions in these sector stocks at the time of higher inflation.

FMCG and Banking Stocks are cyclical stocks and are expected to change in accordance with the inflation. Also the Pharmaceutical stocks being defensive stocks and IT stocks being growth stocks are expected not to have a causal relationship with the inflation especially in the long run. Therefore the finding of the present study is in confirmation with the existing knowledge base.

The study may be replicated with indices of various other sectors, to understand the impact of inflation on the performance of other sectors. Also Nifty sector indices may be included and compared to have a clear picture on the inflation impact. Studies investigating the influence of various macroeconomic variables on sector indices will be useful for the investors to make rational investment decisions.

References

Amonhaemanon, D., Annaert, J., De Ceuster, M. J., & Long, H. L. (2014). The Fisher hypothesis and investment assets: The Vietnamese and Thai case. *International Journal of Financial Research, 5*(4), 180–195. https://doi.org/10.5430/ijfr.v5n4p180.

Al-Abadi, M. I., & Al-Sabbagh, O. W. (2006). Interest rate sensitivity, market risk, inflation and bank stock returns. *Journal of Accounting, Business and Management, 13,* 25–38.

Bordo, M. D., Dueker, M. J., & Wheelock, D. C. (2009). Inflation, monetary policy and stock market conditions: Quantitative evidence from a hybrid latent-variable VAR. *Federal Reserve Bank of St. Louis.*

Chen, N.-F., Roll, R., & Ross, S. A. (1986). Economic forces and stock market. *Journal of Business, 59*(3), 383–403.

Consumer Price Index: Changes in the Revised Series. (2015). Retrieved November 26, 2017, from Ministry of Statistics and Programme Implementation. http://164.100.34.62:8080/PDFile/CPI-Changes_in_the_Revised_Series.pdf.

Fama, E. F. (1981). Stock returns, real activity, inflation, and money. *The American Economic Review, 71*(4), 545–565.

Fama, E. F., & Schwert, G. W. (1977). Asset returns and inflation. *Journal of Financial Economics,* 115–146.

Feldstein, M. (1983). Inflation and the stock market. In N. B. Research (Ed.), *Inflation, tax rules, and capital formation* (pp. 186–198). Chicago: University of Chicago Press.

Fisher, I. (1930). *Theory of interest.* New York: Macmillan Company.

Floros, C. (2004). Stock returns and inflation in Greece. *Applied Econometrics and International Development, 4*(2), 55–68.

Geetha, C., Mohidin, R., Chandran, V. V., & Chong, V. (2011). The relationship between stock market and inflation: Evidence from Malaysia, United States and China. *International Journal of Economics and Management Sciences, 1*(2), 01–16.

Gujarati, D. N., Porter, D. C., & Gunasekar, S. (2012). *Basic econometrics* (5th ed.). Chennai: McGraw-Hill Companies.

Gurloveleen, K., & Bhatia, B. S. (2015). An impact of macroeconomic variables on the functioning of Indian stock market: A study of manufacturing firms of BSE 500. *Journal of Stock & Forex Trading, 5*(1), 160–167. https://doi.org/10.4172/2168-9458.1000160.

Hau, L. L. (2017). Fisher theory and stock returns: An empirical investigation for industry stocks on Vietnamese stock market. *The International Journal of Engineering and Science, 6*(5), 39–45.

Ibrahim, T. M., & Agbaje, O. M. (2013). The relationship between stock return and inflation in Nigeria. *European Scientific Journal, 9*(4), 146–157.

Kaul, G. (1987). Stock returns and inflation. *Journal of Financial Economics, 18,* 253–275.

Lajeri, F., & Dermine, J. (1999). Unexpected inflation and bank stock returns: The case of France 1977–1991. *Journal of Banking & Finance, 23*(6), 939–953. https://doi.org/10.1016/S0378-4266(98)00121-6.

Mahmood, I., Nazir, F., Junid, M., & Javed, Z. H. (2014). Stock prices and inflation: A case study of Pakistan. *Journal of Asian Business Strategy, 4*(12), 217–223.

Silva, N. L. C. (2016). Effect of inflation on stock prices: Evidence from Sri Lanka. *International Journal of Scientific & Engineering Research, 7*(4).

Patel, S. (2012). The effect of macroeconomic determinants on the performance of the Indian stock market. *NMIMS Management Review, 22,* 117–127.

Ray, S. (2012). Testing granger causal relationship between macroeconomic variables and stock price behaviour: Evidence from India. *Advances in Applied Economics and Finance, 3*(1), 470–481.

Reddy, D. V. (2012). Impact of inflation and GDP on stock market returns in India. *International Journal of Advanced Research in Management and Social Sciences, 1*(6), 120–136.

Nurhakim, S. A., Yunita, I., & Iradianty, A. (2016). The effect of profitability and inflation on stock price at pharmaceutical industries. *Asia Pacific Journal of Advanced Business and Social Studies, 2*(2), 202–210.

Schwert, G. W. (1981). The adjustments of stock prices to information about inflation. *The Journal of Finance, 36*(1), 15–29.

The Hindu. (2014, April 02). Retrieved January 08, 2018, from *The Hindu* Web site. http://www.thehindu.com/business/Economy/rbi-adopts-new-cpi-as-key-measure-of-inflation/article5859713.ece.

Tripathi, V., & Kumar, A. (2014). Relationship between inflation and stock returns—Evidence from BRICS markets using panel cointegration test. *International Journal of Accounting and Financial Reporting, 4*(2), 647–658. https://doi.org/10.5296/ijafr.v4i2.6671.

Umashankar & Himabindu. (2015). Impact of inflation on FMCG stocks performance: An empirical study of HUL and ITC. *Indian Journal of Applied Research, 5*(7), 187–189.

Uwubanmwen, A., & Eghosa, I. L. (2015). Inflation rate and stock returns: Evidence from the Nigerian stock market. *International Journal of Business and Social Science, 6*(11), 155–167.

Chapter 5
Fundamental Drivers of Indian Stock Market

Rubina Barodawala and Diksha Ranawat

Abstract The paper sketches historically the emerging Indian stock market economy from the birth of the Bombay stock exchange and the National stock exchange to the present. It focuses on analyzing the return properties of securities on the stock market using higher moments of the return distribution viz., skewness and kurtosis. This is in recognition of the fact that return distributions are not normally distributed as assumed by Standard Mean-Variance portfolio models. Consequently, it would help the investors in their forecast of market risk and portfolio adjustments with the help of studying these higher moments to access the risk and return trade-off. This particular analysis, which tests for the significance of higher moments, is likely to yield a deeper insight into the dynamics of stock market crises and booms. Moreover, the attempt here is to describe the stylised facts at a fundamental level to comprehend the extent of diversion from the normal and the reason's causing the difference. Thus, when the fluctuating nature of Indian stock market is correlated with these rudimentary factors it would yield a model of the risk factors of the stock market in different phases of the market.

Keywords Booms and crises in the Indian stock markets · Skewness
Kurtosis · Macroeconomic variables

5.1 Introduction

The dynamics of financial markets is the consequence of a large number of individual decisions based on the heterogeneous information. Financial returns are assumed to be normally distributed for a long time and the strongest argument

R. Barodawala (✉) · D. Ranawat
Department of Economics, Faculty of Arts, The Maharaja Sayajirao University of Baroda, Vadodara 390002, Gujarat, India
e-mail: rubina.barodawala-be@msubaroda.ac.in

D. Ranawat
e-mail: diksharanawat10@gmail.com

A. K. Mishra et al. (eds.), *Current Issues in the Economy and Finance of India*, Springer Proceedings in Business and Economics,
https://doi.org/10.1007/978-3-319-99555-7_5

supporting this assumption is based on the Central Limit Theorem, which states that the sum of a large number of independent, identically distributed variables from a finite-variance distribution will tend to be normally distributed. However, financial returns depict another tale, they exhibit heavier tails, which is a possible source of infinite variance. Thus, the first part of our study concerns with the importance of inclusion of these characteristics of returns in investment decisions. There are numerous studies around the globe, which examines the impact of these idiosyncratic properties of the returns distributions, which initiate with the introduction of the mean-variance portfolio by Markowitz. While some found results in support of the Markowitz theory, there was evidence of the failure of the theory as well. Then after, there were studies which reported the significance of the inclusion of the third and fourth moment i.e. skewness and kurtosis.

This paper explores the relationship between these moments and returns distribution of the stock market since the two leading stock exchanges in India, the Bombay Stock Exchange, and the National Stock Exchange, began operating, using very basic methodologies. The shape of the return distribution remains controversial; therefore, one of the most important facets in the analysis of the stock returns is to determine an appropriate probability structure of the returns distribution as it helps to study and understand the characteristics of the market using the probability model. The second moment of returns, variance, has been the subject of a large literature in finance which has been widely used as a proxy for risk in financial returns. Thus, the properties of variance and its relationship with expected return have been important topics in financial return. Campbell (1987), Harvey (1989), Nelson (1991), Campbell Hentschel (1992), Hentschel (1995) and Glosten et al. (1993) have studied the intertemporal relation between return and risk (measured in the form of variance or covariance). The sign and magnitude of this trade-off have been an important concern. However, there are considerable affirmations that show the investor's preferences are delimited by the mean and variance to include higher moments: skewness and kurtosis. They are meticulously uptight about the significant losses i.e., downside risk which is a function of skewness and kurtosis.

Skewness and Kurtosis measures are generally used to elucidate shape characteristics of a distribution. Additionally, they are used in tests of normality and in studies of robustness to normal theory procedures, as, for example, in Wilcox (1990). Skewness, asymmetry in distribution, is found to be present in many important economic variables such as stock index returns and exchange rate. The returns of symmetrical distributions are scattered around the mean whereas for asymmetrical distributions they are scattered over the tails of the distribution depending upon the characteristics of the data.

In recent years many studies have empirically investigated the skewness and kurtosis of stocks' returns and prices. In addition, various financial decision models have been constructed to incorporate returns' skewness as well as kurtosis as a major factor. Therefore, the accurate estimation of stock-variables' skewness and kurtosis become an important issue. The presence of positive/negative skewness in stock return distributions has been well documented in the long history of financial literacy. Arditti and Levy (1967) and Scott and Horvath (1980) report that investors show a preference for positive skewness in return distributions under general assumptions. Later, Rubinstein (1973) and Kraus and Litzenberger (1976, 1983) developed models of expected returns that included skewness. Damodaran (1985) report that there is a positive relation between firm's propensity to release good news and stock returns. On similar grounds, McNichols (1988) finds that earning announcement periods carry positive skewness. Badrinath and Chatterjee (1991) demonstrate skewness properties across several stock groups, including industry groups, high and low-risk stocks, and small and large stocks. Aggarwal and Aggarwal (1993) show that skewness properties differ across the stock markets.

Barberis and Huang (2008), Brunnermeier et al. (2007), Mitton and Vorkink (2007) and Boyer et al. (2010) suggest that investor's portfolio decisions are often influenced by the skewness of individual securities.

On the other hand, the coefficient of kurtosis is informative about the tail behavior and spread of outliers in and around the tails of a series, an issue that has drawn substantial interest in the financial literature. In addition, it can be related to the variance of variance and, thus, can be used as a diagnostic for the correct specification of the return and variance dynamics. Mandelbrot (1963) and Fama (1965) proposed stable distributions as an alternative to the Gaussian distribution model. Balanda and MacGillivray (1988) suggested that, like location and scale, skewness and kurtosis can be described in many ways.

The risk of economic depression due to the stock market crash is more significant in emerging countries than developed which raises the concerns of drawdown and economic instability. Hence the second part of our study examines the behavior of the market and the linkages between the stock market and various aspects of the economy. To have a better understanding of the complexity of the market, it is important to understand its determinants. On these grounds, various studies have recognized essential macroeconomic and institutional factors that conceivably drive the stock market. These studies based on high technical methodologies have been carried out to understand the inter-relationship between the stock market, macroeconomic variables, and institutional variables. Our study delimits itself to few selected macroeconomic variables namely Inflation, Money Supply, Gross Fiscal Deficit, Call rates, Foreign Institutional Investment, Trade Balance, and Exchange rate (measured in terms of US Dollar) for the time period January 2011 to February 2018.

Although the theoretical literature on the determinants of the stock market is limited it can be broadly classified into macroeconomic factors and institutional factors. In this study, we discuss the association of few selected macroeconomic factors and the stock market in turn. The literature asserts that higher rates of inflation associated with less liquid and smaller equity markets (Ho and Iyke 2017). Boyd et al. (1998, 2001) point out that higher rate of inflation reduces the availability of credit and encourages lower-quality borrowers into the credit-seeking pool which leads to credit market frictions. Moreover, he also states that the relationship between inflation stock market development is highly non-linear.

Huybens and Smith (1999) and Choi et al. (1996) state that rationing of credit due to credit market frictions becomes severe when the rate of inflation rises.

The existing literature shows that stock prices may or may not be negatively affected by exchange rate (Ho and Iyke 2017). According to the modern portfolio theory, the exchange rate will not affect the stock market (Jorion 1991). While the arbitrage pricing theory states that exchange rate is negatively affected by the stock market by Ross (1976).

One of the reasons driving this research is the use of established statistical characteristics to better describe and understand the real-world financial data. Our purpose here is to comprehend these dynamics with the help of very basic tools and deduce the distribution pattern in the most lucid way and to estimate empirically the connection between stock market returns and selected macroeconomic variables.

5.2 Methodology

2.1. The paper aims to investigate two research issues. One, the presence of skewness and kurtosis on NSE and BSE from the time they began operating on a digital platform.
2.2. Second, to test the relationship between the stock market and rudimentary macroeconomic variables.

2.1. In order to study the presence of skewness and kurtosis, empirical data of about 27 (BSE) and 21 (NSE) years were collected. Daily closing prices were extracted from their respective websites resulting in 6529 data points for BSE and 5946 data points for NSE. Daily share returns or price at time t, R(t), is defined as the continuous rate of return or as first difference of log price.

To test the normality of the return distribution, we apply a non-parametric test of goodness of fit—The Kolmogorov-Smirnoff test. It tests for any differences in the distribution of the observed and the expected values with respect to a specified distribution. On the basis of cumulative frequency, if both observed and expected distribution is identical then the deviation among their cumulative frequencies would be approximately zero; otherwise, they would be large.

The Skewness and Kurtosis of the return distribution are calculated using the following formula:

$$\text{Skewness} : g1 = m3/m23/2 \tag{5.1}$$

where $m3 = \sum (x - \bar{x})3/n$ and $m2 = \sum (x - \bar{x})2/n$

$\bar{x}$ is the mean and n is the sample size. m3 is called the third moment of the data set. m2 is the variance, the square of the standard deviation.

$$\text{Kurtosis} : a4 = m4/m22 \tag{5.2}$$

where $m4 = \sum (x - \bar{x})4/n$ and $m2 = \sum (x - \bar{x})2/n$

$\bar{x}$ is the mean and n is the sample size.
M4 is called the fourth moment of the data set.
m2 is the variance, the square of the standard deviation.

If the bulk of the data is at the left and the right tail is longer, the distribution is skewed right or positively skewed. Alternatively, if the peak is toward the right and the left tail is longer, we say that the distribution is skewed left or negatively skewed. If skewness of a distribution is 0, the distribution is said to be perfectly symmetrical; however, the skewness of zero is unlikely in empirical data. If skewness is less than −1 or greater than +1, the distribution is highly skewed. If skewness is between −½ and +½, the distribution is approximately symmetric. While, kurtosis for a standard normal has a value of 3, whereas excess kurtosis is often presented as kurtosis −3. A distribution with kurtosis <3 is called platykurtic, compared to a normal distribution, its tails are shorter and thinner, and often its central peak is lower and broader. A distribution with kurtosis >3 is called leptokurtic, compared to a normal distribution its tails are longer and fatter and often its central peak is higher and sharper which is called a fat tail.

Lastly, we study skewness and kurtosis in case of positive/negative returns separately.

2.2. In order to assess the relationship between stock market returns and few selected macroeconomic variables such as Money Supply, Inflation, Call Rate, Gross Fiscal Deficit, Trade Balance, Foreign Institutional Investment, Exchange Rate the study employs Autoregressive Distributed Lag (ARDL).

Thus, to investigate the relationship following equation is modelled:

$$\text{NIFTY} = \alpha + \beta(\text{MS}) + \chi(\text{CPI}) + \rho(\text{GFD}) + \delta(\text{FII}) + \gamma(\text{CR}) + \phi(\text{USD}) + \eta(\text{TB}) + \mu_t \tag{5.3}$$

$$\text{SENSEX} = \alpha + \beta(\text{MS}) + \chi(\text{CPI}) + \rho(\text{GFD}) + \delta(\text{FII}) + \gamma(\text{CR}) + \phi(\text{USD}) + \eta(\text{TB}) + \mu_t \tag{5.4}$$

The Augmented Dickey-Fuller (ADF) test is applied to check the macroeconomic and stock market variables for unit root to avoid spurious regression.

The ARDL model is preferred for our analysis over conventional co integration testing as it can be used with a mixture of I(0) and I(1) integration and our data has a mixture of both the integration level. The integration levels of all the macroeconomic variables and stock market variable were integrated at level 1 except Foreign Institutional Investment and Trade Balance which were integrated at level 0. Additionally, it integrates the short-run impact of the given variables with a long-run equilibrium using an error correction term without dropping long-run information. Therefore, both short-run and long-run relationship between macroeconomic variables and stock market returns for India's stock exchanges can be assessed through this model.

The ARDL model regresses stock index (dependent) variable on their own lagged value; on stationary (short run) contemporary and lagged values of macroeconomic (independent) variables; and on non-stationary (long run) values of macroeconomic variables.

The equation used for testing the long run relationship is modeled as below:

$$\begin{aligned}\Delta(\mathrm{nft})_t = {} & \beta_0 + \beta_1(\mathrm{nft})_{t-1} + \beta_2(\mathrm{ms})_{t-1} + \beta_3(\mathrm{cpi})_{t-1} + \beta_4(\mathrm{gfd})_{t-1} + \beta_5(\mathrm{fii})_{t-1} \\ & + \beta_6(\mathrm{cr})_{t-1} + \beta_7(\mathrm{usd})_{t-1} + \beta_8(\mathrm{tb})_{t-1} + \sum_{i=1}^{p} \beta_9\Delta(\mathrm{nft})_{t-i} + \sum_{i=1}^{q} \beta_{10}\Delta(\mathrm{ms})_{t-i} \\ & + \sum_{i=1}^{r} \beta_{11}\Delta(\mathrm{cpi})_{t-i} + \sum_{i=1}^{s} \beta_{12}\Delta(\mathrm{gfd})_{t-i} + \sum_{i=1}^{t} \beta_{13}\Delta(\mathrm{fii})_{t-i} + \sum_{i=1}^{u} \beta_{14}\Delta(\mathrm{cr})_{t-i} \\ & + \sum_{i=1}^{v} \beta_{15}\Delta(\mathrm{usd})_{t-i} + \sum_{i=1}^{w} \beta_{16}\Delta(\mathrm{tb})_{t-i} + \cdots\end{aligned} \tag{5.4}$$

$$\begin{aligned}\Delta(\mathrm{ssx})_t = {} & \beta_0 + \beta_1(\mathrm{ssx})_{t-1} + \beta_2(\mathrm{ms})_{t-1} + \beta_3(\mathrm{cpi})_{t-1} + \beta_4(\mathrm{gfd})_{t-1} + \beta_5(\mathrm{fii})_{t-1} + \beta_6(\mathrm{cr})_{t-1} \\ & + \beta_7(\mathrm{usd})_{t-1} + \beta_8(\mathrm{tb})_{t-1} + \sum_{i=1}^{p} \beta_9\Delta(\mathrm{ssx})_{t-i} + \sum_{i=1}^{q} \beta_{10}\Delta(\mathrm{ms})_{t-i} \\ & + \sum_{i=1}^{r} \beta_{11}\Delta(\mathrm{cpi})_{t-i} + \sum_{i=1}^{s} \beta_{12}\Delta(\mathrm{gfd})_{t-i} + \sum_{i=1}^{t} \beta_{13}\Delta(\mathrm{fii})_{t-i} + \sum_{i=1}^{u} \beta_{14}\Delta(\mathrm{cr})_{t-i} \\ & + \sum_{i=1}^{v} \beta_{15}\Delta(\mathrm{usd})_{t-i} + \sum_{i=1}^{w} \beta_{16}\Delta(\mathrm{tb})_{t-i} + \cdots\end{aligned} \tag{5.5}$$

After regression of Eqs. (5.4) and (5.5), the Wald test (F-statistic) was computed to differentiate the long-run relationship between the concerned variables.

Further, the ECM version of modified ARDL is used to investigate the short-run dynamic relationships. The lagged value of the first difference of NIFTY/SENSEX, Money Supply, Inflation, Call Rate, Gross Fiscal Deficit, Trade Balance, Foreign Institutional Investment, Exchange Rate on lagged values is our explanatory variable of NIFTY /SENSEX with error correction variable at first difference as follow.

$$\Delta(\mathrm{nft})_t = \beta_0 + \sum_{i=1}^{p} \beta_9 \Delta(\mathrm{nft})_{t-i} + \sum_{i=1}^{q} \beta_{10} \Delta(\mathrm{ms})_{t-i} + \sum_{i=1}^{r} \beta_{11} \Delta(\mathrm{cpi})_{t-i} + \sum_{i=1}^{s} \beta_{12} \Delta(\mathrm{gfd})_{t-i} + \sum_{i=1}^{t} \beta_{13} \Delta(\mathrm{fii})_{t-i} + \sum_{i=1}^{u} \beta_{14} \Delta(\mathrm{cr})_{t-i} + \sum_{i=1}^{v} \beta_{15} \Delta(\mathrm{usd})_{t-i} + \sum_{i=1}^{w} \beta_{16} \Delta(\mathrm{tb})_{t-i} + \mathrm{ECT}_{t-1} \quad (6)$$

$$\Delta(\mathrm{ssx})_t = \beta_0 + \sum_{i=1}^{p} \beta_9 \Delta(\mathrm{ssx})_{t-i} + \sum_{i=1}^{q} \beta_{10} \Delta(\mathrm{ms})_{t-i} + \sum_{i=1}^{r} \beta_{11} \Delta(\mathrm{cpi})_{t-i} + \sum_{i=1}^{s} \beta_{12} \Delta(\mathrm{gfd})_{t-i} + \sum_{i=1}^{t} \beta_{13} \Delta(\mathrm{fii})_{t-i} + \sum_{i=1}^{u} \beta_{14} \Delta(\mathrm{cr})_{t-i} + \sum_{i=1}^{v} \beta_{15} \Delta(\mathrm{usd})_{t-i} + \sum_{i=1}^{w} \beta_{16} \Delta(\mathrm{tb})_{t-i} + \mathrm{ECT}_{t-1} \quad (7)$$

While the stationary contemporaneous and lagged values will determine the short-run relationship between macroeconomic variables and stock returns, the non-stationary ones will establish the long run relationship.

For diagnostic checking of the model the study uses:

- CUSUM and CUSUM—Q test for checking the stability of the model.
- Breusch-Godfrey Serial Correlation Lagrange Multiplier test to check for autocorrelation errors in the model.
- Breusch-Pagan-Godfrey test for testing heteroscedasticity in the model.

5.3 Data and Empirical Analysis

5.3.1 Data

To accomplish the first research objective daily data ranging from January 1991 to December 2017 of BSE and January 1994 to December 2017 of NSE are obtained which contains 6529 and 5894 data points respectively for the analysis. While for the second research objective the data ranging from January 2011 to February 2018 of both BSE and NSE were used for the analysis. The series of return is computed from daily closing data for the BSE and NSE index of the Indian Stock Exchange. The daily returns are computed using the natural logarithm of the closing price at time t divided by yesterday's adjusted closing price t − 1 (Table 5.1).

Table 5.1 Description of variables

Acronyms	Construction of variables	Data source
BSE	Returns of Bombay Stock Exchange from January 1991 to December 2017 (Daily data) and January 2011 to February 2018 (Monthly data)	BSE website
NSE	Returns of National Stock Exchange from January 1994 to December 2017 (Daily data) and January 2011 to February 2018 (Monthly data)	NSE website
Broad money (money supply)/MS	M2 from January 2011 to February 2018	RBI website
CPI (inflation)	General Index from January 2011 to February 2018	RBI website
Gross fiscal deficit/ GFD	January 2011 to February 2018	RBI website
Call rate/CR	January 2011 to February 2018	RBI website
Exchange rate/USD	US Dollar from January 2011 to February 2018	RBI website
Trade balance/TB	January 2011 to February 2018	RBI website
Foreign institution investment/FII	March 2011 to February 2018	RBI website

5.3.2 Analysis

The result of K-S test is presented in Table 5.2.

The values of skewness and kurtosis each are calculated annually using the daily returns of both the stock exchanges and presented in Table 5.2.

The skewness and kurtosis values from January 1991 to December 2017 in the case of BSE and January 1994 to December 2017 in the case of NSE reported in Table 5.2 has been classified into Moderately Skewed data (Yellow color), Highly Skewed data (highly positive-green color, highly negative-blue color) and approximately symmetric data (grey color) for Skewness; while Leptokurtic data (greater than 3, grey color), Mesokurtic/approximately symmetric (Blue color) and Platykurtic data (less than 3, pink color).

In 2009 we saw highly positively skewed data in NSE as well as BSE which signifies the existence of positively extreme values at the right tail of the distribution. Moreover, the kurtosis for the year has been greater than 3 for both the exchanges stating fat tails in the distribution. The Sensex topped from around 8000 to 17,000 points and NSE from 2000 to 8000 points after a fall down in 2008 due to the US sublime crises.

In contrast, 2004 and 2015 saw highly negative skewed in both the markets and a leptokurtic distribution stating higher negative values in the left tail of the distribution following the dramatic election results of May 2004 that swept away the

Table 5.2 Values of skewness and kurtosis over the period

Year	Skewness S	Kurtosis S	Normality	Sig.	Year	Skewness N	Kurtosis N	Normality	Sig.
1991	0.394	3.9358	0.043	0.02	1994	0.6079	2.0464	0.064	0.024
1992	-0.0349	2.6986	0.07	0.024	1995	-0.106	0.7515	0.044	0.011
1993	-0.4324	1.0881	0.042	0.032	1996	0.6955	1.1026	0.063	0.019
1994	0.5768	1.7834	0.07	0.008	1997	0.0584	7.5642	0.09	0
1995	0.1146	0.3853	0.035	0.042	1998	-0.0943	1.6166	0.062	0.021
1996	0.5044	0.9745	0.044	0.02	1999	0.0445	2.2468	0.077	0.001
1997	-0.3089	4.3148	0.06	0.033	2000	-0.1053	1.491	0.048	0.007
1998	-0.0456	1.3055	0.044	0.01	2001	-0.4615	2.2619	0.09	0
1999	0.0526	1.4921	0.063	0.018	2002	0.0777	1.4573	0.06	0.028
2000	-0.2428	0.9464	0.059	0.035	2003	-0.3365	0.4701	0.062	0.019
2001	-0.4625	1.6791	0.072	0.003	2004	-1.8018	14.397	0.092	0
2002	0.1421	1.4936	0.044	0	2005	-0.5167	0.5918	0.057	0.047
2003	-0.1898	0.133	0.041	0.05	2006	-0.6199	2.7313	0.114	0
2004	-1.554	13.7483	0.093	0	2007	-0.2582	1.5581	0.076	0.001
2005	-0.4421	0.4048	0.062	0.04	2008	-0.2834	1.6882	0.056	0.042
2006	-0.4845	3.0024	0.111	0	2009	1.5084	12.621	0.06	0.033
2007	-0.2099	1.4548	0.076	0.001	2010	-0.277	0.6703	0.044	0
2008	-0.0689	0.9038	0.048	0.002	2011	0.2704	0.0575	0.051	0
2009	1.3125	10.9219	0.07	0.006	2012	0.0756	0.6616	0.058	0.038
2010	-0.2544	0.6496	0.051	0.037	2013	-0.1156	1.5144	0.56	0.05
2011	0.2791	0.0583	0.052	0	2014	0.0146	0.5739	0.066	0.013
2012	0.0885	0.6232	0.058	0.041	2015	-1.0579	4.6216	0.066	0.011
2013	-0.1109	1.4288	0.056	0.05	2016	-0.0736	1.0319	0.069	0.006
2014	0.0946	0.6028	0.06	0.033	2017	-0.062	0.2972	0.056	0.05
2015	-1.0568	4.6817	0.066	0.011					
2016	-0.0431	1.0861	0.074	0.002					
2017	0.1514	1.4153	0.138	0					

Author's estimation

Bharatiya Janta Party (BJP)-led coalition government. Additionally, in 2015 RBI cut interest rates for four consecutive times followed by a rise in inflation driven highly by a surge in the prices of pulses including lentils, a staple of the Indian diet. A higher kurtosis was also reported in 1991 in BSE which saw an economic emergency declared in the country, in 1997 due to Asian currency crises and in 2006 due to the fluctuation in the prices of fuel and power.

The rest of the years saw either moderately higher/lower skewed or lower kurtosis following various financial and economic conditions globally along with that of the country.

The Table 5.3 presents the skewness and kurtosis separately in case of positive/negative returns. In case of positive returns, the skewness is found to be positive whereas in case of negative returns skewness is found to be negative. Excess kurtosis is found irrespective of the returns being positive or negative. This means

Table 5.3 Values of skewness and kurtosis with respect to positive and negative returns

Returns (NSE)	Positive	Negative	Returns (BSE)	Positive	Negative
Skewness	3.022	−2.834	Skewness	2.99	−2.75
Kurtosis	21.664	15.349	Kusrtosis	18.51	13.66

Author's estimation

during the periods of booms large positive values are present in the right tail of the distribution; while during crashes large negative values are found in the left tail of the distribution.

5.3.3 *Short Run and Long Run Relationship*

The following Table 5.4 presents the selected ARDL Model for NSE and BSE selected on the basis of lowest AIC criterion (Table 5.5).

The computed F-test for NSE and BSE modelis 9.379523 and 9.462815 respectively. While the relevant critical value bounds for this test at the 95% level is given by 2.17 (lower bound) and 3.21 (upper bound). Since the F statistic for both exceeds the upper bound of the critical value band the null hypothesis of no levels relationship between dependent and independent variables is rejected. Thus, the test results suggest the existence of long-run relationship between the stock market returns and the chosen macroeconomic variables.

The following table represents the short run as well as the long run coefficients for ARDL(1, 0, 1, 2, 0, 0, 0, 0) for NSE followed by ARDL(1, 0, 1, 0, 0, 2, 0, 0) for BSE.

The long run model corresponding to ARDL(1, 0, 1, 2, 0, 0, 0, 0) for NSE is

$$\begin{aligned} \mathrm{DNFT_t} = {} & 232.8111 - 62.75641(\mathrm{DCPI_t}) + 263.6318(\mathrm{DCR_t}) + 0.384008(\mathrm{DGFD_t}) \\ & + 0.023745(\mathrm{DMS_t}) - 0.002736(\mathrm{FII_t}) + 0.215809(\mathrm{TB_t}) - 0.618134(\mathrm{DUSD_t}) \end{aligned}$$

The long run model corresponding to ARDL(1, 0, 1, 0, 0, 2, 0, 0) for BSE is

$$\begin{aligned} \mathrm{DSSX_t} = {} & 669.009 - 175.8884(\mathrm{DCPI_t}) + 803.0238(\mathrm{DCR_t}) + 0.076402(\mathrm{DMS_t}) \\ & + 1.422237(\mathrm{DUSD_t}) + 1.338737(\mathrm{DGFD_t}) + -0.011046(\mathrm{FII_t}) + 0.606185(\mathrm{TB_t}) \end{aligned}$$

It is evident from Tables 5.6 and 5.7 that for both NSE and BSE the coefficient of Gross Fiscal Deficit (GFD) is significant at 5% level of significance indicating the existence of long-run relationship between stock market returns and Gross fiscal deficit while the Call Rate coefficients are found significant at 10% level of significance which states a long run relationship with the stock market. While the rest

Table 5.4 ARDL model, NSE

Dependent variable: DNFT				
Maximum dependent lags: 2 (Automatic selection)				
Model selection method: Akaike info criterion (AIC)				
Dynamic regressors (2 lags, automatic): DCPI DCR DGFD DMS FII TB DUSD				
Fixed regressors: C				
Selected model: ARDL(1, 0, 1, 2, 0, 0, 0, 0)				
Variable	Coefficient	Std. error	t-statistic	Prob.*
DNFT(−1)	−0.004339	0.141076	−0.030757	0.9756
DCPI	−63.02871	54.42946	−1.157989	0.2512
DCR	145.3094	110.3367	1.316964	0.1925
DCR(−1)	119.4664	102.5695	1.164736	0.2484
DGFD	0.134788	0.062937	2.141614	0.0360
DGFD(−1)	0.115271	0.072903	1.581167	0.1188
DGFD(−2)	0.135615	0.063304	2.142293	0.0360
DMS	0.023848	0.038048	0.626784	0.5330
FII	−0.002748	0.013982	−0.196545	0.8448
TB	0.216745	0.221417	0.978900	0.3313
DUSD	−0.620816	46.65235	−0.013307	0.9894
C	233.8213	163.6086	1.429151	0.1578
R-squared	0.159615	Mean dependent var		54.84737
Adjusted R-squared	0.015174	S.D. dependent var		294.4913
S.E. of regression	292.2484	Akaike info criterion		14.33702
Sum squared resid	5466186.	Schwarz criterion		14.70504
Log-likelihood	−532.8069	Hannan-Quinn criteria		14.48410
F-statistic	1.105055	Durbin-Watson stat		1.983390
Prob(F-statistic)	0.372111			

Author's estimation

*Note: *p*-values and any subsequent tests do not account for model selection

of the macroeconomic variable's coefficient was not found to be statistically significant.

On the other hand, the short run coefficient estimates show the dynamic adjustment of all variables. The short-run coefficient for DGFD(−1),D(GFD) And D(DGFD(−1)) are statistically significant at 5% level significance for both Indexes. Furthermore, D(CR(−1)) is found significant at 10% significance only in case of BSE.

The ECM coefficient λ i.e. CointEq(−1) is statistically significant and negative implying convergence to equilibrium in the model for both the indexes. Furthermore, the presence of significant coefficient of Error Correction Model confirms the existence of a stable long-run relationship and cointegration between the independent and dependent variables.

Table 5.5 ARDL model, BSE

Dependent variable: DSSX				
Maximum dependent lags: 2 (Automatic selection)				
Model selection method: Akaike info criterion (AIC)				
Dynamic regressors (2 lags, automatic): DCPI DCR DMS DUSD DGFD FII TB				
Fixed regressors: C				
Selected model: ARDL(1, 0, 1, 0, 0, 2, 0, 0)				
Variable	Coefficient	Std. error	t-statistic	Prob.*
DSSX(−1)	−0.007771	0.140959	−0.055130	0.9562
DCPI	−177.2552	173.4655	−1.021847	0.3107
DCR	418.2221	348.9396	1.198552	0.2351
DCR(−1)	391.0420	324.6182	1.204621	0.2328
DMS	0.076996	0.120464	0.639164	0.5250
DUSD	1.433289	147.8671	0.009693	0.9923
DGFD	0.482134	0.199302	2.419119	0.0184
DGFD(−1)	0.414704	0.232426	1.784242	0.0791
DGFD(−2)	0.452302	0.201057	2.249619	0.0279
FII	−0.011132	0.044280	−0.251393	0.8023
TB	0.610896	0.700239	0.872411	0.3862
C	674.2084	517.4402	1.302969	0.1973
R-squared	0.162754	Mean dependent var		165.7175
Adjusted R-squared	0.018852	S.D. dependent var		934.6660
S.E. of regression	925.8139	Akaike info criterion		16.64316
Sum squared resid	54856409	Schwarz criterion		17.01117
Log-likelihood	−620.4402	Hannan-Quinn criteria.		16.79024
F-statistic	1.131006	Durbin-Watson stat		1.970091
Prob(F-statistic)	0.352943			

Author's estimation

*Note: *p*-values and any subsequent tests do not account for model selection

The value of λ is equal to $\lambda = -1.00$ and -1.01 for NSE and BSE respectively. It implies that that dependent variable i.e. stock market returns will return aftershock in independent (macroeconomic) variable in log run at a speed of 100 and 101% per year for NSE and BSE respectively.

5.3.4 Diagnostic Checking

1. CUSUM and CUSUM-Q TEST

The stability of the model and the coefficients are checked through the CUSUM and CUSUM-Q while the graphical presentation of the recursive coefficients is used

Table 5.6 ARDL model—short run and long run relationship, NSE

Variable	Coefficient	Std. error	t-statistic	Probability
C	233.8213	0.023848	1.429151	0.1578
DNFT(−)*	−1.004339	−0.002748	−7.119144	0.0000
DCPI**	−63.02871	0.216745	−1.157989	0.2512
DGFD(−1)	264.7757	−0.620816	1.897294	0.0623
DGFD(−1)	0.385674	145.3094	2.306787	0.0243
DMS**	0.023848	0.134788	0.626784	0.5330
FII**	−0.002748	−0.135615	−0.196545	0.8448
TB**	0.216745	0.023848	0.978900	0.3313
DUSD**	−0.620816	−0.002748	−0.013307	0.9894
D(DCR)	145.3094	0.216745	1.316964	0.1925
D(DGFD)	0.134788	−0.620816	2.141614	0.0360
D(DGFD(−1))	−0.135615	145.3094	−2.142293	0.0360
Levels equation:				
DCPI	**−62.75641**	**57.34510**	**−1.094364**	**0.2779**
DCR	**263.6318**	**143.9725**	**1.831126**	**0.0717**
DGFD	**0.384008**	**0.170971**	**2.246044**	**0.0282**
DMS	**0.023745**	**0.038300**	**0.619975**	**0.5375**
FII	**−0.002736**	**0.013993**	**−0.195544**	**0.8456**
TB	**0.215809**	**0.219310**	**0.984034**	**0.3288**
DUSD	**−0.618134**	**46.42273**	**−0.013315**	**0.9894**
C	**232.8111**	**163.3964**	**1.424824**	**0.1591**
CointEq(−1)*	−1.004339	0.103061	−9.745136	0.0000

Author's estimation
* *p*-value incompatible with t-Bounds distribution
** Variable interpreted as Z = Z(−1) + D(Z)

to judge the stability of the coefficients. Graphical representations of CUSUM and CUSUM square are shown in Fig. 5.1 for our model.

As it is clear from Figs. 5.1 and 5.2, the plots of both the CUSUM and CUSUM square within the boundaries and hence these statistics confirm the stability of the long run coefficients of regressors.

2. Breusch-Godfrey Serial Correlation Lagrange Multiplier test to check for autocorrelation errors in the model (Table 5.8).

In case of both the markets, Breusch-Godfrey with the null hypothesis of no serial Autocorrelation is accepted. Therefore, there is no serial correlation in the model.

3. Breusch-Pagan-Godfrey test for testing heteroscedasticity in the model (Table 5.9).

Table 5.7 ARDL model—short run and long run relationship, BSE

Variable	Coefficient	Std. error	t-statistic	Prob.
C	674.2084	517.4402	1.302969	0.1973
DSSX(−1)*	−1.007771	0.140959	−7.149388	0.0000
DCPI**	−177.2552	173.4655	−1.021847	0.3107
DCR(−1)	809.2641	442.0926	1.830531	0.0718
DMS**	0.076996	0.120464	0.639164	0.5250
DUSD**	1.433289	147.8671	0.009693	0.9923
DGFD(−1)	1.349140	0.531626	2.537761	0.0136
FII**	−0.011132	0.044280	−0.251393	0.8023
TB**	0.610896	0.700239	0.872411	0.3862
D(DCR)	418.2221	348.9396	1.198552	0.2351
D(DGFD)	0.482134	0.199302	2.419119	0.0184
D(DGFD(−1))	−0.452302	0.201057	−2.249619	0.0279
Level's equation:				
DCPI	**−175.8884**	**181.1534**	**−0.970936**	**0.3352**
DCR	**803.0238**	**452.4096**	**1.774993**	**0.0807**
DMS	**0.076402**	**0.120797**	**0.632483**	**0.5293**
DUSD	**1.422237**	**146.7917**	**0.009689**	**0.9923**
DGFD	**1.338737**	**0.538967**	**2.483894**	**0.0156**
FII	**−0.011046**	**0.044228**	**−0.249747**	**0.8036**
TB	**0.606185**	**0.692423**	**0.875455**	**0.3846**
C	**669.0095**	**516.0686**	**1.296358**	**0.1995**
CointEq(−1)*	−1.007771	0.102957	−9.788309	0.0000

Author's estimation
*p-value incompatible with t-Bounds distribution
**Variable interpreted as Z = Z(−1) + D(Z)

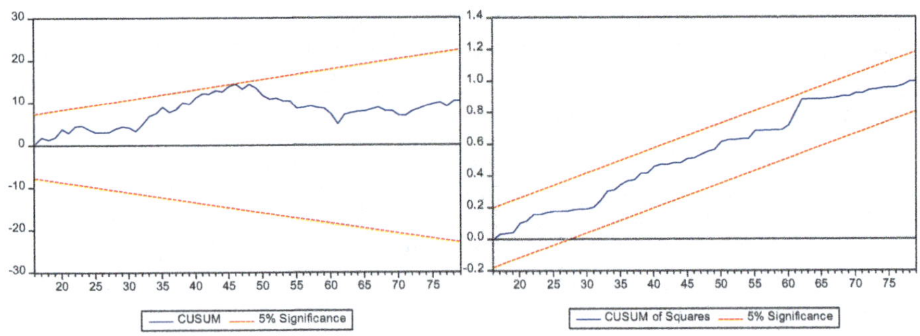

Fig. 5.1 NSE CUSUM and CUSUM-Q

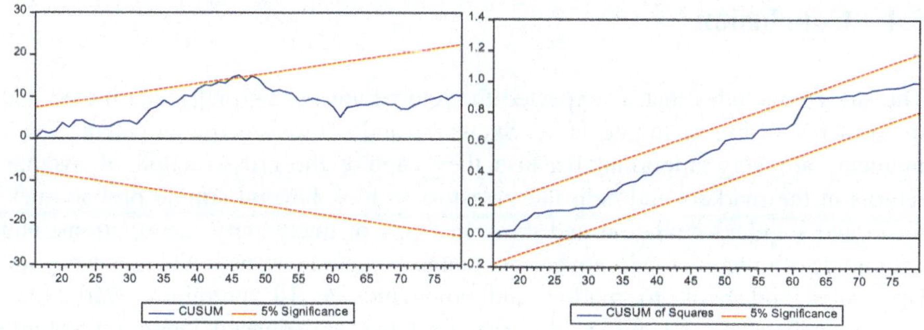

Fig. 5.2 BSE CUSUM and CUSUM-Q

Table 5.8 Serial correlation test

Stock markets	F-statistic	Prob. F(2,62)	Obs* R-squared	Prob. Chi square(2)
NSE	0.091212	0.9129	0.222962	0.8945
BSE	0.045293	0.9557	0.110879	0.9461

Author's estimation

Table 5.9 Heteroscedasticity test

Stock markets	F-statistic	Prob. F (11,64)	Obs* R-squared	Prob. Chi square (11)	Scaled explained SS	Prob. Chi-square (11)
NSE	0.875172	0.5684	9.937185	0.5360	6.313152	0.8517
BSE	0.913431	0.5330	10.31265	0.5025	6.740228	0.8197

Author's estimation

The *p*-value of the diagnostic test run on the residuals of the long-run equation presented above indicates no evidence of Heteroscedasticity in the model.

A similar study carried out in the developed economies such as the US show that the US stock market exhibits a positive and significant relationship with its Gross Domestic Product (GDP) and Industrial Production Index (IIP), while a negative and significant relationship with the unemployment and interest rates variables. In case of China, the stock returns fluctuations over long term are strongly related to their economic factors. The results indicate that exchange rate and inflation have a positive impact on stock market while interest rate have a negative impact on Shanghai stock exchange. Stock prices are influenced by investors' expectations and these expectations responds quickly to any changes in the economy therefore the effect of real economy on markets matters to a great extent.

5.4 Conclusion

The study concludes that as expected the returns are not normally distributed and the presence of higher moments i.e. Skewness and Kurtosis is quite evident. These moments are very important because they capture the cross-section of average returns in the markets and help the investors to look beyond simple probabilities, mean and standard deviation and think in terms of uncertainty, expectations, and magnitude of outcomes. Moreover, it explains expected returns in the assets beyond beta, size, and book to market and commands a risk premium every year. A negatively skewed signifies that the asset has experienced increased volume relative to the trend over a period, had positive returns in the past and are larger in terms of market capitalization. Behavioral finance suggests that investors prefer multiple small gains and a large loss than multiple losses and a large gain.

As Taleb (2007) points out "agents underestimate the extreme values of a distribution in a surprising manner; violations are far more excessive than one would expect: events that are estimated to occur less than 2% of the time will take place up to 49%." According to him, investors believe that extremities don't exist until a bubble burst exactly like how literature didn't believe black swans exist until they spot some in Australia. Thus, the booms and crises are a result of inefficiency on the part of investors to predict the outcomes of extremely high or extremely low returns.

The second part of the paper investigates the relationship between Stock market returns and selected macroeconomic variables using ARDL model to enhance investors portfolio understanding and evaluation in terms of sensitivity of respective stock market prices to the systematic effect of the selected macroeconomic variables. The study found the existence of long-run relationship significantly between the stock market and selected macroeconomic variables especially Gross Fiscal deficit and Call Rate at various levels of significance. This would help the policymakers and regulators to formulate appropriate policies in order to improve the conditions of fiscal deficit and for the banks to design relevant measures. Moreover, the efficient market hypothesis points out that the market responds to the arrival of new information which comes randomly.

The findings would help the investors and portfolio managers to make effective investment decisions because the knowledge of the inter-relationship among the stock market and macroeconomic variables provides a better understanding of portfolio selection and diversification of risk, risk-return relationship and macroeconomic risk according to the economic conditions of the country as well as global markets.

In addition to the above-mentioned results presented by the study, it also reflects on the depth of the stock market activities through the speed of adjustments towards the long-run equilibrium by estimating the error term. This term is found to be negative and significant in the study, as a result, we can say that the system is adjusting at the speed of 100% towards long-run equilibrium for both the markets. This may help decision-makers at all the levels form investors to portfolio managers to the policymakers by focusing on the varying significance of the economic risk factors.

References

Aggarwal, R., & Aggarwal, R. (1993). Security return distributions and market structure: Evidence from the NYSE/AMEX and the NASDAQ Markets. *Journal of Financial Research,* 209–222.

Arditti, F. D., & Levy, H. (1967). Portfolio efficiency analysis in three moments: The multiperiod case. *Journal of Finance, 30,* 797–809.

Badrinath, S. G., & Chatterjee, S. (April 1991). A data-analytic look at skewness and elongation in common stock return distributions. *Journal of Business and Economic Statistics,* pp. 223–233.

Balanda, K. P., & MacGillivray, H. L. (1988). Kurtosis: A critical review. *The American Statistician, 42*(2), 111–119. https://doi.org/10.1080/00031305.1988.10475539.

Barberis, N., & Huang, M. (2008). Stocks as lotteries: The implications of probability weighting for security prices. *American Economic Review, 98,* 2066–2100.

Brunnermeier, M., Gollier, C., & Parker, J. (2007). optimal beliefs, asset prices and the preference for skewed returns. *American Economic Review Papers and Proceedings, 97,* 159–165.

Boyd, J. H., & Smith, B. D. (1998). Capital market imperfections in a monetary growth model. *Economic Theory, 11,* 241–273.

Boyd, J. H., Levine, R., & Smith, B. D. (2001). The impact of inflation on financial market performance. *Journal of Monetary Economics, 47,* 221–248.

Campbell, J. Y. (1987). Stock returns and the term structure. *Journal of Financial Economics, 18,* 373–399.

Campbell, J. Y., & Hentschel, L. (1992). No news is good news: An asymmetric model of changing volatility in stock returns. *Journal of Financial Economics, 31,* 281–318.

Choi, S., Smith, B., & Boyd, J. (1996). Inflation, financial markets, and capital formation. *Federal Reserve Bank of St. Louis Review, 78,* 9–35.

Damodaran, A. (December 1985). Economic events, information structure, and the return-generating process. *Journal of Financial and Quantitative Analysis,* pp. 423–434.

Dubauskas, G. (2005). Autoregressive conditional skewness, kurtosis and Jarque-Bera in Lithuanian stock market measurement. Engineering Economics No 5, 45.

Fama, E. (1965). The behavior of stock prices. *Journal of Business, 38,* 34–105.

Glosten, L. R., Jagannathan, R., & Runkle, D. E. (December 1993). On the relation between expected value and the volatility of the nominal excess return on stocks. *Journal of Finance, 48,* 1779–1801.

Harvey, C. R. (1989). Time-varying conditional covariance in tests of asset pricing models. *Journal of Financial Economics, 24,* 289–317.

Harvey, C. R., & Siddique, A. (2000). Conditional skewness in asset pricing tests. *Journal of Finance, 55,* 1263–1295.

Hentschel, L. (1995). All in the family: Nesting symmetric and asymmetric GARCH models. *Journal of Financial Economics, 39,* 71–104.

Ho, S-. Y., & Iyke, B. N. (2017). Determinants of stock market development: A review of the literature. *Studies in Economics and Finance, 34*(1), 143–164. https://doi.org/SEF-05-2016-0111.

Huybens, E., & Smith, B. (1999). Inflation, financial markets, and long-run real activity. *Journal of Monetary Economics, 43,* 283–315.

Jareno, F., & Negrut, L. (2016). US stock market and macroeconomic factors. *Journal of Applied Business Research,* https://doi.org/10.19030/jabr.v32i1.9541.

Jorion, P. (1991). The pricing of exchange rate risk in the stock market. *Journal of Financial and Quantitative Analysis, 26,* 361–376.

Ross, S. (1976). The arbitrage theory of capital asset pricing. *Journal of Economic Theory, 13,* 341–360.

Joshi, P. (2015). Relationship between macroeconomic variables and stock market development: Evidence from the Indian Economy. (Doctoral dissertation). Retrieved from http://shodhganga.inflibnet.ac.in/bitstream/10603/84912/1/thesis_pooja.pdf.

Khan, M. K., Teng, J-Z., Parvaiz, J., & Chaudhary, S. (2017). Nexuses between economic factors and stock returns in China. *International Journal of Economics and Finance, 9*(9); ISSN-1916-971X. E-ISSN 1916-9728.

Kraus, A., & Litzenberger, R. H. (1983). Skewness preference and the valuation of risk assets. *Journal of Finance, 31,* 1085–1100.

Mandelbrot, B. (1963). The variation of certain speculative prices. *Journal of Business,* 394–419.

McNichols, M. (October 1988) A comparison of the skewness of non-earnings announcement dates. *Journal of Accounting and Economics,* 239–273.

Mitton, T., & Vorkink, K. (2007). Equilibrium under-diversification and the preference for skewness. *Review of Financial Studies, 20,* 1255–1288.

Nelson, D. B. (1991). Conditional heteroscedasticity in asset return: A new approach. *Econometrica, 59,* 347–370.

Rubinstein, M. (1973). The fundamental theorem of parameter-preference security valuation. *Journal of Financial and Quantitative Analysis, 8,* 61–69.

Scott, R. C., & Horvath, P. A. (1980). On the direction of preference for moments of higher order than the variance. *Journal of Finance, 35,* 915–919.

Sirucek, M. (2012). Macroeconomic variables and stock market: US review. *International Journal of Computer Science and Management Studies,* ISSN (online): 2231–5268.

Shah, A. A., Aamir, M., & Saba, I. (2012). Empirical analysis of long and short run relationship among macroeconomic variables and Karachi stock market: An auto regressive distributive lag (ARDL) approach. *Pakistan Journal of Social Sciences, 32*(2), 323–338.

Taleb, N. N. (2007). Fooled by randomness: The hidden role of chance in life and in the markets. (2nd ed.). Penguin Books.

Tripathi, V., & Kumar, A. (1989). Do macroeconomic variables affect stock returns in BRICS markets? An ARDL approach. *Journal of Commerce & Accounting Research, 4.* https://doi.org/10.21863/jcar/2015.4.2.008.

Wilcox, R. R. (1990). Comparing the means of two independent groups. *Biometrical Journal, 32,* 771–780.

Part II
Financial Institutions, Instruments and Markets

Chapter 6
Information Transmission in Post-recession Era: Evidence from India, China, Hong Kong and Japan

Ashish Kumar and Swati Khanna

Abstract The study proposes to investigate lead lag relationship in price discovery, volatility spillover and leverage effect in stock exchanges of four Asian economies namely India, China, Hong Kong and Japan. Data comprises of daily closing values of the indices Hang Seng Composite for Hong Kong, Nikkei for Japan, Shanghai Composite Index for China and Sensex for India. Johansson Co-integration Test, VEC model, Granger Causality Test, ARCH LM test and EGARCH model have been employed to examine and explore price discovery, volatility behavior and leverage effect from one country to another. In post crisis period India is co-integrated with China but is not integrated with Hong Kong and Japan. China is co-integrated with Hong Kong but not with Japan. Hong Kong and Japan are co integrated with each other. India leads China in price discovery process. Hong Kong leads China and Japan in price discovery process. Volatility spillovers have been found among these Asian countries in post-recession era. Leverage effect is observed among all market pairs except for Hong Kong and China. The study further shows that good news information transmission generates less volatility for stock markets of India, Hong Kong and Japan but on the contrary it generates more volatility for stock markets of China. The research contributes to existing literature on lead lag relationship in price discovery, volatility spillovers, leverage effect in stock markets, and is one of the very few studies conducted for select Asian countries.

Keywords Volatility · Volatility spillover · Co-integration · VEC model
Granger causality · EGARCH model

A. Kumar (✉) · S. Khanna
University School of Management Studies, GGSIP University,
Dwarka, New Delhi, India
e-mail: ashish_prl@yahoo.com

A. K. Mishra et al. (eds.), *Current Issues in the Economy and Finance of India*,
Springer Proceedings in Business and Economics,
https://doi.org/10.1007/978-3-319-99555-7_6

6.1 Introduction

Degree of stock market assimilation tends en route for amendments over time, particularly around phase manifested by crisis. Yang et al. (2003) International financial crisis originated in USA transmitted its end product to developed and developing countries of the world due to numerous diverse factors from one country to another (Abdelbaki 2010; Saeid and Saeid 2012; Singhania and Anchalia 2013). Pessimistic consequences of financial crisis are, decrease in value of US$, decline in value of assets, economic stagnation, increased inflation rate and decreased interest rates go together with decreased incentives for savings, investments and economic development (Malik et al. 2009; Abdelbaki 2010). Global Financial crisis of 2007–2009 is a by-product of several economic crises occurring from time to time over centuries. Few of the prominent economic crises in the history are 1772 crisis of London when 20 important banks went bankrupt, 1893—Banking crisis of Australia when commercial banking system of Australia collapsed, 1994–1995 was sourced by speculative attack and default on Mexican debt, 1997–1998 Asian Financial crisis caused by currency devaluations and banking crisis in Asian economies, 1998 economic crisis of Russia also known as Ruble crisis sourced by declining productivity and a high fixed exchange rate between ruble and foreign currencies and chronic fiscal deficit, 2000–2001 Turkish economic crisis was backed by heavy reliability on foreign investments. All major crises originate from flawed financial applications and incompetent regulatory administration. Finally, in 2008; subprime crisis erupted in United States but gradually embraced the entire world. Worldwide economies experienced a severe depression in 2008 and 2009 and its impact on GDP and macroeconomic policies could be sensed over a longer period of time. Crises become global due to the transmission mechanismof risk aversion and financial market volatility along global supply chains (Gros and Alcidi 2010; Biggs and Mayer 2010). Current policies of financial adjustment would have been sufficient if the crises were only financial, but the crises are due to serious factor namely distribution inequalities specifically income distribution etc. (Pressacco and Seravalli 2009).

Stock markets of the world are interlinked and are interdependent. Macroeconomic announcements in different financial markets lead to information transmission (Wongswan 2006). Information signals transmit, link and spill from one market to another, known as information transmission. To measure and determine the flow of information transmission, return spillover and volatility spillover analysis are conducted. Volatility spillovers and return spillovers have been observed in emerging and mature stock markets by many studies namely; Errunza and Losq (1985), Jorion and Schwartz (1986), King and Wadhwani (1990), Dungey and Martin (2007), Khuong Nguyen and Bellalah (2008), Mitton (2002), Fidrmuc and Korhonen (2010) and Sheng (2009) in Asian context.

Assessment of stock indices in post financial crisis era on the basis of return, volatility spillovers and information transmission in stock markets of major Asian economies is of utmost importance to outline potential policy measures and to improve the market efficiency so as to prevent long and severe effects of crisis and to prevent such crisis in years to come. The study aims to examine return spillover, volatility spillover and information transmission in stock markets of India, China, Hong Kong and Japan for last 6 years. Static and dynamic cointegration tests and multivariate generalized autoregressive conditional heteroscedasticity (MGARCH) models are employed to conduct the research study.

Present study is distinctive in numerous facets as it aims to explore volatility spillovers and information transmission effects in major stock markets of Asia. The study has practical inferences for investors, academicians, researchers and policy makers as the results of our study will help them not only in understanding the behaviour of information transmission in the post recession era for select stock markets but will also be useful in framing an investment strategy to prevent and curb crisis in near future.

6.2 Review of Literature

Financial literature has a plethora of studies that investigate and examine information transmission among the stock markets of the world. Reviewed literature is divided into three sections as follows.

(i) Literature related to inter-linkageamong various stock markets of the world.
(ii) Literature related to return and volatility spillovers.
(iii) Literature related to impact of global financial crisis.

Most of the preliminary studies analyzed short term correlations of returns across mutually supporting developed markets and concluded the existence of international diversification prospects (Levy and Sarnat 1970; Solnik 1974; Eun and Shim 1989). Globalization and liberalization policies across the world strengthened financial relations among the emerging and mature market economies. This led to information linkage between the stock markets of the world. Many researchers have examined linkages between most influential US stock market and other stock markets of the world (Taylor and Tonks 1989; Chen, et al. 2002; Manning 2002). These studies suggest that because of these linkages amongst the economies there occur limited gains from portfolio diversification for the investors (Serrano and Revero 2003). In contrast to the above studies a study by Phylaktis and Ravazzolo (2005) which analyzed the linkages between US, Japan and Pacific Basin stock markets did not find significant influence of US and Japan on pacific basin markets. So, we may say that degree of integration between the stock markets changes over time and is influenced by multiple economic factors.

In this study keeping in mind the objective of information transmission, literature related to return spillover and volatility spillover has been reviewed. Return and volatility spillovers have been observed across North America, Europe and Asian stock markets and it is found that regional influence between Asian and European stock markets is greater (Singh et al. 2010). Return and volatility transmission have been analyzed among European and Asian stock markets and significant co-movement of returns have been observed (Dedi and Yavas 2016).

Inter and intra regional information transmission is foundacross emerging and developed stock markets of Asia, America and Europe (Yarovaya et al. 2016). Long term information linkages measured by volatility spillovers have been observed in stock markets of US, Europe and Asia (Ng 2000; Miyakoshi 2003; Wang and Firth 2004; Maderitsch 2015).

Studies related to volatility and return spillovers have emerged from different parts of the world but research gap still persists. Studies related to the existence of bidirectional volatility and return spillovers among emerging and developed markets are in abundance (Bhar and Nikolova 2009; Maderitsch 2015; Dedi and Yavas 2016; Liu 2016) but studies related to price discovery, information transmission and volatility spillovers among Asian stock markets are few (Mukherjee and Mishra 2010). In addition to analysis of inter linkages among various stock markets, volatility transmission and dynamic correlations researchers have also explored the impact of US Financial crisis, 2008 on various stock markets across the world (e.g. Adamu 2010; Ravichandran and Maloain 2010; Ali and Afzal 2012; Singhania and Anchalia 2013). Few mentionable studies which have studied the effect of US financial crisis, 2008 on India, China and other emerging Asian stock markets are Lim et al. (2008), Fidrmuc and Korhonen (2010) and Zhang and Chen (2011).

The impact of US financial Crisis of 2008 has not been same on all the economies. Ravichandran and Maloain (2010) in their study on Gulf economies find that during the US crisis period there was an adverse impact on these economies which eased out once the crisis was over.

Singhania and Anchalia (2013) in their study find that there was a positive impact of US financial crisis on volatility of returns of stock markets China, Japan and India; however no such effect has been observed in case Hong Kong.

From the review of literature made for the present study it may be concluded that in recent years of globalization there have been many instances of stock market integration and commercial inter-relationships through information transmission and the degree of integration and volatility of stock returns has been affected by the 2008 US financial crisis. Our study is contribution to volatility in returns and spillovers in Asian countries in post crisis period.

6.3 Objectives, Data and Research Methodology

6.3.1 Objectives of the Study

a. To understand the lead-lag relationship and price discovery among the sample stock markets in post crisis era using Vector Error Correction Model.
b. To measure leverage effect and impact of information transmission on volatility among the sample stock markets using EGARCH model.

6.3.2 Data

The present study explores the behavior of volatility of select Asian countries. The sample consists of developing and emerging economies of Asia, which are India, China, Japan and Hong Kong. Data considered in the study is collected for a period from 1/April/2010 to 28/October/2016. The data consist of daily market indices of Hang Seng Composite for Hong Kong, Nikkei for Japan, Shanghai Composite Index for China and Sensex for India (Table 6.1).

6.3.3 Research Methodology

This section describes the methodologies used to measure information linkages among India, Hong Kong, Japan and China. To determine lead lag relationship and to gain insight into price discovery process Cointegration technique has been used. To examine the leverage effect EGARCH model methodology is explained below.

6.3.3.1 Johansson's Cointegration Test

Johansson cointegration test determines co integrating relationships by means of bivariate co integration test, based on vector autoregressive framework. If individual time series are co integrated then VAR model can be expressed by an Error correction model as follows:

$$\Delta X_t = \tau_0 + \tau_1 \Delta X_{t-1} + \tau_2 \Delta X_{t-2} + \cdots + \tau_{k-1} \Delta X_{t-k+1} + \pi X_{t-1} + \varepsilon_t$$

or

$$\Delta X_t = \tau_0 + \sum_{i=1}^{k-1} \tau_i \Delta X_{t-i} + \pi \Delta X_{t-1} + \varepsilon_t \tag{6.1}$$

where $\pi \Delta X_{t-1}$ is the error correction term (ECT), $\pi = \alpha\beta'$ is the coefficient matrix and $\varepsilon_t \sim \text{iid}\ (0,\sum)$.

Table 6.1 Sample stock markets and their indices: 1/4/2010 to 28/10/2016

Country	Stock market index
India	Sensex
China	Shanghai Composite Index
Japan	Nikkei
Hong Kong	Hang Seng

Unrestricted VAR model is used to estimate coefficient matrix π under the hypothesis testing of r co integrating vectors. Error Correction model depicts the feedback process, short run adjustment parameters are elements of matrix α to long run relationship in matrix β. Therefore long run and short run dynamics are identified by hypothesis testing on α and τ. Causal relationships among co integrated series are calculated by Granger's Causality test pair wise.

6.3.3.2 Stationarity, Homoscedasticity and EGARCH Model

To make the data time consistent and less skewed we have taken the return of each market index in the following form and return variables have been named as Return_China, Return_Hong Kong, Return_India and Return_Japan. The continuously compounded return has been computed as follows:

$$R_t = \ln p_t - \ln p_{t-1} \tag{6.2}$$

The stationarity of all the return series have been tested by applying ADF (Augmented Dickey Fuller Test) unit root test.

Further, to analyze the leverage effect, information transmission and volatility spillover between chosen economies EGARCH model has been used. In order to develop EGARCH Model, data should meet the two important prerequisite i.e. there should be (a) volatility clustering and (b) Arch Effect. The Lagrange Multiplier (LM) test developed by Engle (1982) examines the existence of heteroscedasticity and the necessity of using EGARCH model to identify leverage effect. The null hypothesis assumes that the regression model is homoscedastic as the following form:

$$y_t = ax_t + u_t \tag{6.3}$$

Here u_t is the Gaussian white noise. By rejecting the null hypothesis we conclude that u_t ARCH effect. If ARCH effect is detected future value of u_t^2 can be predicted by past values of u_t^2 (i < t).

To validate the existence of leverage effect EGARCH model analysis is carried out. EGARCH equation is given by:

$$\log \sigma_t^2 = \omega + \beta \log \sigma_{t-1}^2 + \alpha \left| \frac{\varepsilon_{t-1}}{\sigma_{t-1}} \right| + \gamma \left| \frac{\varepsilon_{t-1}}{\sigma_{t-1}} \right| \tag{6.4}$$

The logarithmic of conditional variance implies the leverage effect is exponential. The leverage effect is considered if value of is $\gamma < 0$ and p-value is significant.

6.4 Data Analysis

6.4.1 *Descriptive Statistics*

Table 6.2 shows the descriptive statistics for the return series of 4 select Asian countries. According to the results Chinese stock markets have the lowest average return of (−0.0000298) and Japanese stock market generates the highest daily return (0.000334) in post recession era.

Volatility is highest in Chinese stock markets and lowest in Indian stock markets. So, we can say that Indian stock market is the most stable market among sample stock markets. The coefficient of skewness is negative for sample stock markets which show market returns negatively skewed. The Jarque-Bera values are larger than the critical value for all the nations, which helps to reject the null of a normal distribution. From the kurtosis statistic it can be concluded that all stock markets are leptokurtic (measure of kurtosis being more than 3).

6.4.2 *Unit Root Tests*

Table 6.3 shows the result of unit root test. According to Augmented Dickey-Fuller Test all the return variables are found to be stationary at level and hence normally distributed.

Table 6.2 Descriptive statistics sample: 1/4/2010 to 28/10/2016

	Return China	Return Hong Kong	Return India	Return Japan
Mean	−0.0000298	0.0000342	0.000315	0.000334
Median	0.000176	3.96E−0.5	0.000553	0.000665
Maximum	0.066423	0.073665	0.41456	0.074262
Minimum	−0.089058	−0.064225	−0.061197	−0.111534
Std. Deviation	0.016179	0.012753	0.010908	0.014968
Skewness	−0.790049	−0.237451	−0.193058	−0.556043
Kurtosis	8.233657	6.111369	4.468608	7.429941
Jarque-Bera	1838.105	609.2282	141.8126	1285.718
Probability	0.00000	0.000000	0.000000	0.000000
Sum	−0.043955	0.050550	0.464562	0.493124
Observations	1476	1476	1476	1476

Source Authors' calculations

Table 6.3 Results of unit root test post-crisis era sample: 1/4/2010 to 28/10/2016

Variables	ADF p-value	Stationarity
Return_India	0.0000	Stationary
Return_Hong Kong	0.0001	Stationary
Return_China	0.0000	Stationary
Return_Japan	0.0001	Stationary

Source Authors' calculations

6.4.3 *Johansson co-integration Test*

Table 6.4 shows the cointegration results of four select Asian countries. In post crisis period India is co-integrated with China but is not integrated with Hong Kong and Japan, China is co-integrated with Hong Kong but not with Japan and Hong Kong and Japan are co integrated with each other.

6.4.4 *Vector Error Correction Model*

Table 6.5 provides the estimated coefficients and t-statistics [] of the VEC model of the bivariate co integrated series as identified. The speed adjustment co-efficient is also known as error correction term. India's, speed of adjustment coefficient is

Table 6.4 Results of pair wise Johansson co-integration test: 1/4/2010 to 28/10/2016

Market pair	Co-integration	P-value
India–China	Co-integrated	0.0663
India–Hong Kong	Not co-integrated	0.3068
India–Japan	Not co-integrated	0.3964
China–Hong Kong	Co-integrated	0.0190
China–Japan	Not co-integrated	0.5294
Hong Kong–Japan	Co-integrated	0.0400

Source Authors' calculations

Table 6.5 Results of VEC model: 1/4/2010 to 28/10/2016

Market pair	Co-efficient	Market	Co-efficient
India China	−0.212705 [−1.76978]	China India	0.008306 [1.39877]
China Hong Kong	0.004121 [0.73878]	Hong Kong China	−0.102699 [−0.63583]
Hong Kong Japan	−0.001870 [0.016850]	Japan Hong Kong	0.067007 [2.97774]

Source Authors' calculations *the values in [] parenthesis are t-statistics

greater for China. So, India leads China in price discovery process. Hong Kong, speed of adjustment coefficient is greater for China. So, Hong Kong leads China in price discovery process. Therefore, China lags India and Hong Kong in price discovery process. Hong Kong, speed of adjustment coefficient for is greater for Japan.So, Hong Kong leads Japan in price discovery process.

6.4.5 Granger Causality Test

Table 6.6 exhibits the causal relationships among co-integrated market pairs, obtained by conducting Granger Causality test. The results of the bivariate test state that there is no cause and effect relationship between Hong Kong–China, India–China and Japan–China. However unidirectional causality has been reported from India to Hongkong, India to Japan and Japan to Hongkong.

6.4.6 ARCH LM Test

Table 6.7 represents the pair wise results of ARCH LM test for the sample nations. Presence of ARCH effect in the residuals is observed as *p*-value of Observed

Table 6.6 Results of Granger Causality Test: 1/4/2010 to 28/10/2016

Pair	Null Hypothesis	F-Statistic	Probability	Causality direction
1	Hong Kong does not Granger cause China China does not Granger cause Hong Kong	0.15525 1.08384	0.8562 0.3386	No effect
2	India does not Granger cause China China does not Granger Cause India	1.61577 1.17565	0.1991 0.3089	No effect
3	Japan does not Granger cause China China does not Granger Cause Japan	0.09303 0.60863	0.9112 0.5442	No effect
4	India does not Granger cause Hong Kong Hong Kong does not Granger Cause India	9.51540 0.50743	0.00008* 0.6021	Unidirectional
5	Japan does not Granger cause Hong Kong Hong Kong does not Granger Cause Japan	0.13740 2.77182	0.8716 0.0629**	Unidirectional
6	Japan does not Granger cause India India does not Granger Cause Japan	0.17612 16.1169	0.8385 0.0000*	Unidirectional

Source Authors' calculations

Table 6.7 Results of Arch test pair wise: 1/4/2010 to 28/10/2016

Market pair	Observed R-squared	*P*-value
India and China	5.022249	0.0250
India and Hong Kong	4.570397	0.0325
India and Japan	5.123203	0.0236
Hong Kong and India	8.354489	0.0038
Hong Kong and China	1.438176	0.2307
Hong Kong and Japan	8.552322	0.0034
China and India	66.84478	0.0000
China and Hong Kong	64.92641	0.0000
China and Japan	88.55850	0.0000
Japan and India	105.9863	0.0000
Japan and Hong Kong	114.1662	0.0000
Japan and China	66.19562	0.0000

Source Authors' calculations

R-squared is significant for all the market pairs i.e. it is less than 0.05 accept for Hong Kong and China. This shows that there is an ARCH effect present in the residuals and we may apply ARCH/GARCH family models to all the market pairs except for Hong Kong and China.

6.4.7 Results of EGARCH Model

Table 6.8 shows the pair wise results of leverage effect. In this model the leverage effect can be identified by variable C(6). The value of variable C(6) for pairs India and China, India and Hong Kong and India and Japan are negative and significant, which means bad news generates more volatility than good news for Indian stock markets in the post crisis era.

Similar results are seen for market pairs Hong Kong and Japan, Hong Kong and India, Japan and India, Japan and China and Japan and Hong Kong. So, it may be concluded that good news generates less volatility than bad news for stock markets of Japan and Hong Kong as well in post recession era. On the contrary leverage effect given by variable C(6) for China with stock markets of Hong Kong, Japan and China are positive and insignificant. This proves that good news generates more volatility than bad news for stock markets of China. Leverage effect for Hong Kong and China could not be determined as ARCH LM test was not satisfied for this market pair.

Table 6.8 Results of EGARCH test pair wise: 1/4/2010 to 28/10/2016

Market returns	Mean equation			Variance equation			
	C	Return_India (−1)	Return_China (−1)	C(4)	C(5)	C(6)	C(7)
Return_India	0.00184 [0.4950]	0.063122 [0.0286]	0.028514 [0.1094]	−0.668248 [0.0000]	0.087348 [0.0006]	−0.141976 [0.0000]	0.933995 [0.0000]
	C	Return_India (−1)	Return_Japan (−1)	C(4)	C(5)	C(6)	C(7)
Return_India	0.000179 [0.5083]	0.052817 [0.0724]	0.002517 [0.8989]	−0.646476 [0.0000]	0.087425 [0.0000]	−0.139654 [0.0000]	0.936370 [0.0000]
	C	Return_India (−1)	Return_HK(−1)	C(4)	C(5)	C(6)	C(7)
Return_India	0.000183 [0.4966]	0.037441 [0.2353]	0.026392 [0.3189]	−0.645987 [0.0000]	0.086668 [0.0005]	−0.140301 [0.000]	0.936367 [0.0000]
	C	Return_China (−1)	Return_India (−1)	C(4)	C(5)	C(6)	C(7)
Return_China	0.000612 [0.6213]	−0.007516 [0.8026]	0.066235 [0.0502]	−0.16445 [0.0000]	0.123546 [0.0000]	0.00519 [0.9395]	0.991270 [0.0000]
	C	Return_China (−1)	Return_Japan (−1)	C(4)	C(5)	C(6)	C(7)
Return_China	0.000094 [0.7743]	0.018780 [0.5430]	−0.049777 [0.0249]	−0.15961 [0.0000]	0.121916 [0.0000]	0.001500 [0.8224]	0.991680 [0.0000]
	C	Return_China (−1)	Return_Hong Kong (−1)	C(4)	C(5)	C(6)	C(7)
Return_China	0.000151 [0.6513]	0.020425 [0.5330]	−0.022722 [0.4509]	−0.16226 [0.0000]	0.122778 [0.0000]	0.001161 [0.8630]	0.991434 [0.0000]
	C	Return_HK (−1)	Return_India (−1)	C(4)	C(5)	C(6)	C(7)
Return_HK	0.000039 [0.8979]	−0.033523 [0.2868]	0.136234 [0.0000]	−0.32482 [0.0000]	0.080437 [0.0000]	−0.06783 [0.0000]	0.970084 [0.0000]
	C	Return_HK(−1)	Return_Japan (−1)	C(4)	C(5)	C(6)	C(7)
Return_HK	0.00006 [0.8285]	0.037440 [0.2110]	0.016337 [0.4916]	−0.26473 [0.0000]	0.065406 [0.0000]	−0.06702 [0.0000]	0.975564 [0.0000]
	C	Return_HK (−1)	Return_China (−1)	C(4)	C(5)	C(6)	C(7)

(continued)

Table 6.8 (continued)

Market returns	Mean equation			Variance equation			
	C	Return_India (−1)	Return_China (−1)	C(4)	C(5)	C(6)	C(7)
Return_HK	**ARCH Test Not Satisfied**						
	C	Return_Japan (−1)	Return_India (−1)	C(4)	C(5)	C(6)	C(7)
Return_Japan	0.000348 [0.2972]	−0.061790 [0.0436]	0.159901 [0.0000]	−0.81324 [0.0000]	0.210165 [0.0000]	−0.10998 [0.0000]	0.923523 [0.0000]
	C	Return_Japan (−1)	Return_China (−1)	C(4)	C(5)	C(6)	C(7)
Return_Japan	0.000359 [0.2910]	−0.012027 [0.6916]	0.011810 [0.5664]	−0.76013 [0.0000]	0.208165 [0.0000]	−0.11037 [0.0000]	0.929391 [0.0000]
	C	Return_Japan (−1)	Return_HK(−1)	C(4)	C(5)	C(6)	C(7)
Return_Japan	0.000371 [0.2743]	−0.024502 [0.4505]	0.036325 [0.3052]	−0.77373 [0.0000]	0.207521 [0.0000]	−0.11057 [0.0000]	0.927770 [0.0000]

Source Authors' calculations, values in parentheses represents p-values

6.5 Conclusion

This study examines lead-lag relationship and impact of information transmission on volatility using leverage effect in four major Asian countries namely China, Hong Kong, India and Japan based on daily market indices of Hang Seng Composite for Hong Kong, Nikkei for Japan, Shanghai Composite Index for China and Sensex for India. Data considered in the study is collected for a period from 1/April/2010 to 28/October/2016. Johansson Co-integration test, vector error correction model, Granger causality test and EGARCH modelshave been appliedfor this purpose. The main conclusions of this study are as follows:

The daily return of the stock market is positive for India and Japan whereas the same is negative for Hong Kong and China for the study period. The Indian stock market is least volatile whereas the Chinese markets are most volatile for the study period among the four stock markets included into the study. The results of Johanson's Co-integration test reveal that India is co-integrated with China but not with Hong Kong and Japan. Similarly, China is co-integrated with Hong Kong but not with Japan. Also, Hong Kong and Japan are also co-integrated with each other. The results further reveal that India leads China; Hong Kong leads China and Japan in price discovery process. There are spillovers of volatility amongst all the countries in the study. The leverage effect has been observed for all the market pairs except for Hong Kong and China. The results of EGARCH model state that good news information transmission generates less volatility for stock markets of India, Hong Kong and Japan. On the other hand, good news information transmission generates more volatility for stock market of China.

The results obtained from this study can be useful for investors in formulating better strategies and exploiting the inefficiency in Asian stock markets.

References

Abdelbaki, H. H. (2010). Assessing the impact of the global financial crisis on GCC countries.

Adamu, A. (2010). Global financial crisis and Nigerian stock market volatility.

Ali, R., & Afzal, M. (2012). Impact of global financial crisis on stock markets: Evidence from Pakistan and India. *Journal of Business Management and Economics, 3*(7), 275–282.

Bhar, R., & Nikolova, B. (2009). Return, volatility spillovers and dynamic correlation in the BRIC equity markets: An analysis using a bivariate EGARCH framework. *Global Finance Journal, 19*(3), 203–218.

Biggs, M., & Mayer, T. (2010). The output gap conundrum. *Intereconomics/Review of European Economic Policy, 45*(1), 11–16.

Chen, G. M., Firth, M., & Rui, O. M. (2002). Stock market linkages: Evidence from Latin America. *Journal of Banking & Finance, 26*(6), 1113–1141.

Dedi, L., & Yavas, B. F. (2016). Return and volatility spillovers in equity markets: An investigation using various GARCH methodologies. *Cogent Economics & Finance, 4*(1), 1266788.

Dungey, M., & Martin, V. L. (2007). Unravelling financial market linkages during crises. *Journal of Applied Econometrics, 22*(1), 89–119.

Eun, C. S., & Shim, S. (1989). International transmission of stock market movements. *Journal of Financial and Quantitative Analysis, 24*(2), 241–256.

Errunza, V., & Losq, E. (1985). International asset pricing under mild segmentation: Theory and test. *The Journal of Finance, 40*(1), 105–124.

Fidrmuc, J., & Korhonen, I. (2010). The impact of the global financial crisis on business cycles in Asian emerging economies. *Journal of Asian Economics, 21*(3), 293–303.

Gros, D., & Alcidi, C. (2010). The impact of the financial crisis on the real economy. *Intereconomics, 45*(1), 4–20.

Jorion, P., & Schwartz, E. (1986). Integration vs. segmentation in the Canadian stock market. *The Journal of Finance, 41*(3), 603–614.

Khuong Nguyen, D., & Bellalah, M. (2008). Stock market liberalization, structural breaks and dynamic changes in emerging market volatility. *Review of Accounting and Finance, 7*(4), 396–411.

King, M. A., & Wadhwani, S. (1990). Transmission of volatility between stock markets. *The Review of Financial Studies, 3*(1), 5–33.

Lim, K. P., Brooks, R. D., & Kim, J. H. (2008). Financial crisis and stock market efficiency: Empirical evidence from Asian countries. *International Review of Financial Analysis, 17*(3), 571–591.

Liu, C. (2016). Spillover effects in major equity markets: A GARCH BEKK approach. *Open Access Library Journal, 3*(02), 1.

Levy, H., & Sarnat, M. (1970). International diversification of investment portfolios. *The American Economic Review, 60*(4), 668–675.

Manning, N. (2002). Common trends and convergence? South East Asian equity markets, 1988–1999. *Journal of international Money and Finance, 21*(2), 183–202.

Maderitsch, R. (2015). Information transmission between stock markets in Hong Kong, Europe and the US: New evidence on time-and state-dependence. *Pacific-Basin Finance Journal, 35*, 13–36.

Malik, N. I., Ullah, S., Azam, K., & Khan, A. (2009). The impact of recent global financial crisis on the financial institutions in the developing countries: Global perspectives. *International Review of Business Research Papers, 5*(5), 85–95.

Mitton, T. (2002). A cross-firm analysis of the impact of corporate governance on the East Asian financial crisis. *Journal of Financial Economics, 64*(2), 215–241.

Miyakoshi, T. (2003). Spillovers of stock return volatility to Asian equity markets from Japan and the US. *Journal of International Financial Markets, Institutions and Money, 13*(4), 383–399.

Nath Mukherjee, K., & Mishra, R. K. (2010). Stock market integration and volatility spillover: India and its major Asian counterparts. *Research in International Business and Finance, 24*(2), 235–251.

Ng, A. (2000). Volatility spillover effects from Japan and the US to the Pacific-Basin. *Journal of international money and finance, 19*(2), 207–233.

Pressacco, F., & Seravalli, G. (2009). The real origins of the global crisis. *Transition Studies Review, 16*(3), 791.

Phylaktis, K., & Ravazzolo, F. (2005). Stock market linkages in emerging markets: Implications for international portfolio diversification. *Journal of International Financial Markets, Institutions and Money, 15*(2), 91–106.

Saeid, M., & Saeid, M. (2012). The effect of financial crisis of 2007 on business integration (G15) countries. *World Applied Sciences Journal, 18*(11), 1593–1601.

Sheng, A. (2009). *From Asian to global financial crisis: An Asian regulator's view of unfettered finance in the 1990s and 2000s*. New York: Cambridge University Press.

Fernández-Serrano, J. L., & Sosvilla-Rivero, S. (2003). Modelling the linkages between US and Latin American stock markets. *Applied Economics, 35*(12), 1423–1434.

Ravichandran, K., & Maloain, A. M. (2010). Global financial crisis and stock market linkages: Further evidence on GCC market. *Journal of Money, Investment and Banking, 16*, 46–56.

Singh, P., Kumar, B., & Pandey, A. (2010). Price and volatility spillovers across North American, European and Asian stock markets. *International Review of Financial Analysis, 19*(1), 55–64.

Solnik, B. H. (1974). An equilibrium model of the international capital market. *Journal of economic theory, 8*(4), 500–524.
Singhania, M., & Anchalia, J. (2013). Volatility in Asian stock markets and global financial crisis. *Journal of Advances in Management Research, 10*(3), 333–351.
Taylor, M. P., & Tonks, I. (1989). The internationalisation of stock markets and the abolition of UK exchange control. *The Review of Economics and Statistics,* 332–336.
Wongswan, J. (2006). Transmission of information across international equity markets. *The Review of Financial Studies, 19*(4), 1157–1189.
Wang, S. S., & Firth, M. (2004). Do bears and bulls swim across oceans? Market information transmission between greater China and the rest of the world. *Journal of International Financial Markets, Institutions and Money, 14*(3), 235–254.
Yang, J., Kolari, J. W., & Min, I. (2003). Stock market integration and financial crises: The case of Asia. *Applied Financial Economics, 13*(7), 477–486.
Yarovaya, L., Brzeszczyński, J., & Lau, C. K. M. (2016). Intra-and inter-regional return and volatility spillovers across emerging and developed markets: Evidence from stock indices and stock index futures. *International Review of Financial Analysis, 43,* 96–114.
Zhang, C., & Chen, X. (2011). The impact of global oil price shocks on China's stock returns: Evidence from the ARJI (-ht)-EGARCH model. *Energy, 36*(11), 6627–6633.

Chapter 7
A Statistical Re-assessment of Capital Adequacy and Insolvency Risk in Commercial Banks of India

Nupur Moni Das and Joyeeta Deb

Abstract This paper is an attempt to empirically explore the association of capital adequacy and insolvency risk of the Indian Commercial Banks, while controlling for various other bank specific and macro-economic factors which also affects the risk level of the banks. To find the inter-relationship of Capital Adequacy Ratio (CAR) and insolvency risk, data of 21 years and 43 banks have been taken into consideration. Simultaneous Equations Model (SEM) is used to examine the association between Risk and Capital Adequacy Ratio and Two Stage Least Squares (2SLS) method is being used to estimate the parameters of the Simultaneous Equations Model. The findings reflect that both variables have inverse impact on each other. The other micro and macro-economic variables also have significant impact on risk and capital of the banks.

Keywords Capital adequacy · Simultaneous equations · Basel norms
Two stage least squares (2SLS) · Insolvency risk

7.1 Introduction

Risk is inherent part of any business organization in general and the banking organizations in particular due to its highly leveraged business structure. As stated by Singh (2011) Financial Risk is often defined as the unexpected variability or volatility of returns and thus includes both potential worse-than-expected as well as better-than-expected return. The banks chiefly depend on deposits of the customers for the purpose of lending and investment. At most times, the short term deposits act as a shoulder for the banks to lend out money and make investment for long term which gives rise to liquidity and maturity mismatches followed by higher risk. Banks also become a victim of credit risk due to non-repayment of the dues by the borrowers. There are various other types of risk which banks faces during their

N. M. Das (✉) · J. Deb
Department of Commerce, Assam University, Silchar, India
e-mail: nupurmonid430@gmail.com

A. K. Mishra et al. (eds.), *Current Issues in the Economy and Finance of India*,
Springer Proceedings in Business and Economics,
https://doi.org/10.1007/978-3-319-99555-7_7

operations. The extent of risk taking by banks effects the possibility of bank failure on the micro level, and it influences the sustainability of the banking system at the macro level. The risky behaviour can be noticed either through the rise of the credit risk in the loan portfolio or through the fall of capital level "buffer" or both simultaneously (Louati et al. 2015). Bank shareholders like other shareholders may have incentives for greater risk taking to maximize the value of their call option on the residual value of the firm (Cebenoyan et al. 1995). A certain level of risk taking is essential for growth of an organization and it is not dangerous until banks are competent enough to manage and absorb the risk. As per (Kunt and Huizinga 2004) to restrain bank risk taking, financial safety net relies on two mechanisms: Market Discipline and Bank Regulation. Capital is considered by the bank regulatory authorities as the most important element to regulate the banking business and advises the banks to maintain sufficient capital proportionate to the risk assumed by the banks. Capital serves as a method of co-insurance whereby higher capital levels require the banks to absorb greater losses in the event of failure and encourages additional prudence in management (Kim and Santomero 1988). Dearth of sufficient quantum of its own capital leads bank to make default in servicing its debt which also leads to total failure. As, the banking sector is highly leveraged and deals with customer's money, returning the money with due interest in due time is highly important for survival and maintaining confidence in the banking system. Therefore, maintenance of sufficient amount of capital is very important for stability as well as profitability of the system.

Historically, capital, inter alia, was only a factor considered for assessing the performance and health of the banks. However, currently it is the main factor for judging the efficiency and stability of the units (Das and Deb 2017). Maintenance of capital is not a new practice. It has been in practice ever since when there was no formal banking system. The practices varied from country to country. The original form of capital controls is that the regulatory authorities define the highest limit of bank debt ratio (Zheng et al. 2012). However, lone focus on the leverage and no emphasis on the asset quality of the banks failed to serve the purpose and called for more stringent supervision. History of Capital adequacy regulation in India can be dated back to 1985, when Reserve Bank of India (RBI) introduced measures for dealing with liquidity, credit and foreign exchange risk through health coding system. The health coding system indicates the health of the assets by dividing it to eight categories namely-Satisfactory, Irregular, Sick but viable, Sick: not viable/ sticky, Advances recalled, Suit filed accounts, Decreed debts, Bad and doubtful debts (Roy et al. 2013).

During financial liberalisation, banks encounter greater competition and expose themselves to greater risks (Dhumale 2000) and thus raised difficulties for banks to absorb it. A large number of bank failures, degrading quality of assets, deteriorating level of capital, deregulation of interest rates, increase in cross border activities of banks all over the world posed various challenges and questioned the stability of the sector. Moreover, the process of liberalisation, globalisation and privatisation also brought its own pros and cons. All these factors led the think-tank of the banking industry to intervene and take necessary actions against the odds. The regulatory authorities also felt a need to set uniform standards internationally for effective and efficient cross-border operations. In 1988, the G10 countries came together and constituted the Basel Committee on Banking Supervision (BCBS) under the patronage of Bank for International Settlements (BIS). After rounds of deliberations, the first set of norms (Basel I) were introduced which is formally known as '*International Convergence of capital measurement & Capital Standards*'. The regulatory authorities mainly focussed on maintenance of a minimum capital in relation to the Risk Weighted Assets (RWAs) in order to act as a cushion against losses to prevent bank failures and to ensure stability of the banking industry and the economies at national as well as international level. India too started adopting the Basel I norms in 1992 in a phased and systematic manner.

However, as the banking crisis had not affected Indian banks and keeping into consideration other country specific characteristics, there is a debate regarding the adoption of Uniform Capital Adequacy guidelines based on regulations of developed country.

On this backdrop, this paper intends to have an insight into the mechanism of capital and risk of the banks after bestowing regulatory eye in the form of capital standards i.e. to find how the Indian banking sector is reacting to this set of regulation. In simple words, the paper endeavours to examine how the uniform capital ratio impacts the risk of the Indian commercial banks and whether the risk level of the banks also impacts capital simultaneously. Moreover, the paper particularly emphasizes on insolvency risk of the banks.

The rest of the paper is organized as follows. Section 7.2 provides a brief review of the existing literature related to capital and risk relationship. The Data description and methodology is accommodated in Sect. 7.3 of the paper. The Sect. 7.4 is devoted to the empirical analysis part and the last section i.e. Sect. 7.5 provides the summary and conclusion of the paper.

7.2 Related Literature

Capital Adequacy of the banking sector has been a highly discussed area in the banking literature since a long time by the bankers, regulators and the academicians. However its significance has increased after the introduction of the standard capital adequacy guidelines prescribed by the Basel Committee on Banking Supervision (BCBS) in 1988. The views regarding the effectiveness and fit of the uniform guideline have been different from parties to parties. It has been studied from different angles viz. its impact on profitability, risk, small scale industries, smaller banks, its effectiveness and so on.

Literature on the relationship between capital and risk provides two different views. One view is that Capital and risk are negatively related. The parties supporting this view argue that higher the amount of capital better is the cushion for absorbing the risk and thus reduces the risk and increases stability. Moreover, one more argument in this favour is that as cost of raising equity is higher than other sources, they prefer to take lesser risk in order to maintain sufficient level of capital. Another outlook is that capital and risk are positively related which indicates that as the capital increases, the risk also increases. Arguments in favour of this thought are (1) In order to comply with higher capital requirements and maintaining profitability simultaneously, banks tend to take more risk. Secondly, as the banks requires to keep only a proportion of RWA's as capital, they are able to take more risk compared to the amount invested as capital. Some of the existing studies associated with capital and risk relationship are summarised below:

Kim and Santomero (1988) assessed the role played by banking capital regulation in controlling risk by a risk-variance framework and stated that traditional uniform capital ratio regulation is not an effective way to control the possibility of bank insolvency. They too states that if risk weights are chosen optimally, risk of banks will be lesser than before which is very pertinent for effective implementation of the recent step towards capital adequacy. Blum (1999) theoretically analysed the capital—risk relationship and stated that when the restrictions are tightened, the expected profits of the banks are reduced and the banks has less to lose in the event of insolvency. Therefore, banks tend s to take more risks. Similarly, Nachane (1999) in his paper stressed that abrupt rush along the Basle norms which mandates inflexible CRAR's which the Narsimham II Committee recommended is not advisable. Besides, a positive correlation between capital and risk is established which is explained by substitution of leverage by assets risk. Hovakimian and Kane (2000) pointed out that weak capital regulation and deposit pricing policy leads to risk shifting by the banks to safety net. Regulators should undertake market based capital adequacy measures in an attempt to prevent risk shifting incentives by the banks. Nachane et al. (2001) theoretically evaluated how banks respond to different types of capital regulation and expressed that regulations leading to cosmetic changes are not likely to accomplish the goals of effective increases in the capital to ensure stability of the banking sector as a whole. Chen et al. (2006) also specified that recent guidelines such as granularity adjustment proposed in Basel II do not consider the correlated nature of individual loan default risks and hence continue to potentially miscalculate the level of economic capital that banks should hold to ensure the regulatory system is fairly priced. Ma et al. (2011) assessed the impact of capital constraints on risk taking behaviour of commercial banks and established that when the stringency in capital standards increases, there is more structural adjustment in credit towards efficiency and thus lead to more stability and lesser risk. Bougatef and Mgadmi (2016) elucidated the association between regulatory capital and the risk level. They established insignificant relationship of capital and risk and thus stated that the regulation are not effective to make any change in the risk level of the banks which is believed to be due to particularity of the country itself and maintenance of more than minimum capital by the banks due to which banks are not pressurized to make any type of change.

On the other hand, some researchers have studied the simultaneous relationship between capital and risk. Nguyen and Nghiem (2015) studied the inter-linkage among default risk, capital ratio and efficiency using simultaneous equations model on a balanced panel data. The study revealed that better capitalized banks assume lower risk of insolvency and higher efficiency. Maji and De (2015) surveyed the association between regulatory capital and risk in Indian context using simultaneous equation model and an inverse relationship between risk and capital is observed. They explained this association by arguing that overcapitalized banks may decrease the capital base keeping the risk level constant or increase the level of risk in order to maintain minimum risk based capital ratio whereas undercapitalized bank can increase capital base for the same purpose. But Zheng et al. (2012) found significant positive correlation between capital and risk while scrutinising internal mechanism between capital buffers and risk adjustments. They noticed that banks with adequate capital adjust their capital buffer and risk positively. However for low capital banks the relationship is the reverse. This is attributed to avoid the cost of violence of regulatory requirements. The results of Miah and Shameen (2015) investigating the linkage between risk, efficiency and capital and comparing the conventional and Islamic banks revealed positive bidirectional relationship of capital and risk for Islamic banks whereas they found no significant relation on the part of conventional banks. The further concluded that the banks having higher capital are believed to have sufficient cushion for losses and thus assume higher level of risk which again calls for higher capital requirement.

It is clearly visualized from the review that although capital adequacy is studied from different angles, the results are inconclusive and inconsistent which varied from researcher to researcher. It may be due to different study area, study period and different samples.

Although research has been carried on this particular area i.e. Capital and Risk taking behaviour of the banks, there are a few studies which focussed on Indian banks. On the other hand, among the Indian studies, different researchers employed different methodology, time period and found inconsistency in the results. Thus, this study is proposed to study the relationship between capital and insolvency risk covering all the three Basel guidelines i.e. from 1996 to 2016.

7.3 Data and Methodology

7.3.1 Description About the Data

The study is based on panel data set of 43 Indian commercial banks which comprises of 25 Public Sector Banks and 18 Private Sector Banks with 21 years of relevant time series data commencing from the financial year 1996 to 2016. The required data have been extracted from various secondary sources viz. statistical tables relating to commercial banks of India of Reserve Bank of India, website of planning commission, indiastats.com, world bank and so on. The study considered all the Indian Commercial banks which has been operating since 1992 and continuing its service as of now.

7.3.2 Tools and Techniques

Simultaneous Equations Model:

Survey of literature related to this area brings us to a conclusion that the two variables Capital Adequacy Ratio and Risk are found to be influencing each other. Therefore, the paper employed Simultaneous Equation Model to find out the Impact of Capital Adequacy Ratio on insolvency risk of the banks and vice versa as single equation model will not provide efficient results. Simultaneous Equations Models are used when there is a two way influence among the economic variables or when some of the regressors are endogenous (Gujarati et al. 2012) Insolvency Risk is the probability of not being able to service its debt by an entity. Two Stage Least Squares (2SLS) method is used to estimate the coefficients of the models.

Variance-Inflation Factor (VIF) Test:

When large number of variables are used in a regression model, it is always important to assure non-existence of multicollinearity between the explanatory variables. Otherwise, regression model may produce misleading results. Variance Inflation Factors test is used to detect the extent of collinearity among the variables. As a rule of Thumb, if the VIF exceeds 10, that variable is said to be highly collinear (Gujarati et al. 2012).

Hausman-Specification test

Additionally, Hausman Specification test is also done in order to check for existence of endogeneity or simultaneity among the variables. If there is no simultaneity between CAR and Z_Score, 2SLS will not produce efficient results.

7.3.3 Variables and Their Measurements

The study intends to assess the impact of capital adequacy ratio on the overall risk of the banks. Risk is the dependent variable and CAR is considered to be endogenous in nature. Although the emphasis is mainly to gauge the impact of CAR on risk, there are also other variables which influence the risk taking behaviour of the banks. Therefore, the paper includes some other exogenous bank-specific and macroeconomic variables for a controlled experiment. All the explanatory variables used in the study are suggested by various earlier researchers. The variables and their measurements are described below:

Risk: Risk is the dependent variable employed in the study. Z-Score is widely used to measure the overall risk of the banks (Nguyen and Nghiem 2015; Khan et al. 2016; Odonkor et al. 2016). The Z-Score index is given by

$$Z - Score = \frac{\text{ROA} + \text{Capital to Assets Ratio}}{Standard\ Deviation\ of\ ROA}$$

Regulatory Capital: Equity to assets ratio and Capital to Risk weighted Asset ratio are two broadly used measures for regulatory capital. However, the latter is considered as more efficient. Thus, the study used Capital Adequacy Ratio (CAR) calculated by the commercial banks as per the guidelines of the BCBS and RBI to represent the regulatory capital. It is expected to be negatively associated with the risk of the banks as the main objective of the imposition of CAR is to reduce risk of the banks and maintain consistency. The CAR is given by

$$CAR = \frac{\text{Total Capital}}{\text{Risk} - \text{Weighted Assets}}$$

Size of the banks: The banks' size is measured by the log of total assets of the banks. It is hypothesized to have negative association with risk as the large sized banks are able to diversify and lower their risk taking activities due to availability of better risk management expertise. Moreover, it is expected to have positive relationship with capital because usually, the larger sized banks have better access to capital markets and enjoy economies of scale in their operations.

Income Diversification: Diversification of Income is proxied by the ratio of Non-Interest Income to Total Assets (NNITA). As, diversification is done to "not to put all the eggs in one basket", it is hypothesized to bear an inverse relationship with risk. On the other hand, it is also expected to bear a positive association with CAR because when the banks start earning from different sources rise, it automatically push the overall profits of the banks and thereby helps the banks to raise more capital.

Profitability: The variable profitability is proxied by Net Interest Income (NII) which is one of the standard measures used by banks to gauge the profitability of the banks. Relationship with capital is expected to be positive as higher the earnings, banks will be able to raise more capital in the form of retained earnings.

Economic Growth: Economic growth is a macroeconomic variable which is quantified by the Gross Domestic Product (GDP). It is projected to have negative impact on risk and capital as the financial health of borrowers and market remains stable and during favourable economic conditions thus keeping risk at acceptable level followed by lesser capital proportionately with risk.

Inflation: It is measured by Consumers Price Index (CPI). The financial health of the borrowers is weak and the market behaviour is instable during inflationary pressure, thus increases the risk level and thereby the capital of the banks. Thus, it is projected to bear positive relationship with capital and risk.

Operating inefficiency: If the operations in an organization are managed efficiently, it generally raises the profits and capital and reduces the risk of the banks and vice versa. It is taken as an instrumental variable and measured by the ratio of Operating Expenses to Total Assets (OETA). Hence, lower the ratio, higher is the efficiency level and is projected to have negative impact on capital followed by probability of increasing the risk level.

Liquidity: The ratio of total loans to total assets is included as an instrumental variable in order to capture the liquidity aspect. It is expected to influence the capital level negatively as highly liquid banks are considered to be less leveraged and thus allowed to operate with lower capital level.

Lagged Risk: The lagged risk is expected to have an inverse function with the present risk level as if the risk is high in the previous period, the banks will try to reduce it to an acceptable level and if the risk level is less and there is a scope to take some more risk without hampering the stability, the banks will assume some risk in order to increase the profits.

a. ***Empirical Models***:

The following two systems of equation have been developed to examine the association of capital and risk keeping in view the simultaneous association between these two variables. Thus Z-Score (measure of risk) and CAR (measure of capital) are considered to be endogenous variables and all the other right hand side variables are exogenous.

$$Z - Score = a_{0t} + \beta_{1t}CAR + \beta_{2t}TA + \beta_{3t}NNITA + \beta_{4t}GDP + \beta_{5t}INFL + \beta_{6t}Z\_Score_{t-1} + \mu_{7t}$$

$$CAR = a_{0t} + \beta_{1t}Z - Score + \beta_{2t}TA + \beta_{3t}NNITA + \beta_{4t}NII + \beta_{5t}GDP + \beta_{6t}INFL + \mu_{7t}$$

7.4 Empirical Results

Tables 7.1 and 7.2 give a glimpse of the major performance indicators of the Public Sector and Private Sector Banks in India after and during the introduction of capital adequacy norms. Return of Assets (ROA) indicates about the profitability of the banks. On the other hand, NPA/Net Advances and CAR reflects the riskiness of the banks and banks' capital positions respectively. Comparing the two tables, it is clearly visible that the overall Average ROA and CAR of the private sector banks is better than the public sector banks and the differences between the two groups are significant as evident from the results of t-test which is displayed in Table 7.3 as the p value is less than 0.05. Whereas, the average of the NPA to Net Advances of the Private sector banks is lower as compared to the public sector banks. However, the differences are not significant as per the t test results as the probability value is higher than 0.05. It can be pictures from the overall result that the private sector banks are in a better position in comparison to the public sector banks in terms of non-performing assets and resilience to threats from any risk.

The collinearity statistics as depicted in Table 7.4 shows that the VIF is much less than the rule of thumb i.e. 10 in case of all the variables. Moreover, the

Table 7.1 Descriptive statistics of major performance indicators of public sector banks in India

	ROA		NPA/net advances		CAR	
	AVG	SD	AVG	SD	AVG	SD
Basel I	0.64	0.83	7.48	4.48	10.82	3.64
Basel II	0.95	0.34	1.50	5.36	12.71	1.17
Basel III	0.35	0.51	3.48	2.01	11.57	0.90
Overall	0.70	0.66	4.44	5.20	11.68	2.66

Source Computed by author based on data extracted from Reserve Bank of India

Table 7.2 Descriptive statistics of major performance indicators of private sector banks in India

	ROA		NPA/net advances		CAR	
	AVG	SD	AVG	SD	AVG	SD
Basel I	1.09	0.57	5.53	3.18	12.85	3.90
Basel II	0.95	0.78	1.22	1.17	14.56	6.22
Basel III	1.02	0.83	1.25	1.13	13.86	2.21
Overall	1.02	0.71	3.04	3.09	13.69	4.77

Source Computed by author based on data extracted from Reserve Bank of India

Table 7.3 Results of t-test

	ROA	NPA/net advances	CAR
t-critical value	2.039513	2.028094	2.0210754
P value	0.001613	0.132807	0.00001801
t stat	−3.45572	1.537943	−4.8681424

Source Computed by author based on data extracted from Reserve Bank of India

tolerance is very high. All the variable's tolerance value is more than 0.5. Thus none of the variables have the nature of multicollinearity.

The result of Hausman specification test shows that the variable CAR and Z-Score are endogenous as their predicted value is found to be significantly associated with the dependent variable, i.e. Risk (Z-Score) and CAR which is reflected in Table 7.5. In this case, the OLS estimators will provide biased results and thus 2SLS is used to estimate the parameters of the equation.

The results of 2SLS presented in Table 7.6 regarding the impact of Capital Adequacy on Banks' risk exhibits that the variable CAR has a positive significant impact on the dependent variable Z_Score. Higher, Z_Score Implies lower probability of insolvency. Thus, positive association between CAR and Z_Score

Table 7.4 Collinearity statistics

(Dependent variable: Z_Score)			(Dependent variable: CAR)		
Variables	Tolerance	VIF	Variables	Tolerance	VIF
CAR	0.99	1.01	Z_SCORE	0.89	1.13
TA	0.96	1.04	TA	0.62	1.61
NNITA	0.87	1.15	NNITA	0.79	1.26
GDP	0.96	1.04	GDP	0.96	1.04
INFL	0.92	1.09	INFL	0.91	1.09
–	–	–	NII	0.63	1.59

Source Computed by the author using SPSS

Table 7.5 Results of Hausman error specification test (panel estimated generalized least squares)

	Coefficient	Std. Error	t-statistic	Prob.
Dependent variable (Z-score)				
PR_CAR	1.891328	0.177187	10.67418	0.0000
Dependent variable (CAR)				
PR_Z-SCORE	1.109858	0.109434	10.14176	0.0000

Source Computed using E-views by the author

Table 7.6 Results of 2SLS (risk equation)

Variables (Dependent = Z_Score)	Coefficient	Std. Error	t-statistic	Prob.
C	−4.95868	2.42E−08	−2.05E + 08	0.0000**
CAR	1.88395	1.13E−09	1.67E+09	0.0000**
TA	−1.12013	2.30E−09	−4.88E+08	0.0000**
NNITA	−2.15424	5.70E−09	−3.78E+08	0.0000**
GDP	0.53343	4.58E−10	1.16E+09	0.0000**
INFL	−0.020500	5.44E−10	4.75E+08	0.0000**
Z_SCORE-1	2.03129	3.66E−09	5.55E+08	0.0000**
F-statistic	310.695**			
j-statistic	0.20961			
R-Squared	−6.81			
Adjusted R-squared	−6.887			
Instruments	Constant TA NNITA GDP INFL NII OETA TLTA			

Source Computed using E-views
**indicates significance at 5% level

suggests that as the CAR increases, the risk of the banks reduce. The results show that one unit change in the CAR moderates 1.88 unit changes in risk. This, accepts our hypothesis that CAR and Risk has a negative association. The result is similar to the earlier researchers (Ma et al. 2011; Nguyen and Nghiem 2015; Bougatef and Mgadni 2016) and against the results found by Nachane (1999), Zheng et al. (2012) and Miah and Shameen (2015). The exogenous variable TA turned out to bear a negative significant impact on Z_Score of the banks which rejects our hypothesized relationship between these two variables. This entails that larger the size of the banks, greater the risk they assume. This might be due to the fact that larger sized banks are given greater autonomy by the regulators and possession of "too big to fail attitude" by the bank authority. The variable GDP is negatively associated with risk level of banks as GDP Shows positive association with Z_Score. Table 7.6 reflects that one unit change in GDP brings 0.53 unit change in the risk level which indicates that changes in risk is lesser in proportion to change in GDP. The reason for negative association between two variables is as expected as increase in GDP improves financial health of individuals and every unit in the economy which in turn reduces the risk of non-payment and bearish market. Inflation is found to be positively influencing the risk level of banks. This relationship is also obvious with respect to the fact that inflation curtails purchasing power in the economy and influences the financial health negatively which consequently reduces the risk of the banks. Similarly, the variable Revenue Diversification (NNITA) also positively impacts the risk taking behaviour of the banks. This is against the expected relationship. The reason behind might be because of excessive introduction of Non-conventional sources of income without taking proper precautions. The impact of lagged risk on current risk is negative which also tally the expected result. If the risk level is higher in the current period, an attempt is always made to bring it to an acceptable level in order to avoid regulatory costs as well as to trade-off between profitability and stability.

On the other hand, the results displayed in Table 7.7 gives the glimpse of impact of Risk on Capital of the bank. It shows that Risk influences CAR inversely which is evident from the positive coefficient of Z_Score and is significant at 5% confidence level. The reason behind it might be that when the risk of the bank increases, automatically the CAR reduces if additional capital is not raised immediately as CAR is a ratio of Capital to Risk Weighted Assets. The result is in line with (Maji and De 2015). However, the results contradicts the result of Blum (1999), Nachane (1999) Zheng et al. (2012) and Miah and Shameen (2015). Besides, Miah and Shameen (2015) found positive association only in case of Islamic Banks but for Conventional banks the association was insignificant. The exogenous variable TA showed significant positive beta coefficient which implies larger the size of the banks, higher the amount of capital held and vice versa. This can be explained by the hypothesis that larger banks have easy access to capital markets, thus are able to maintain capital at higher level and at lower cost. Both NNITA and NII impacts the level of capital positively which signifies the contribution of profits through traditional and non-traditional banking activities to the capital, where Retained earnings from increasing profits might be the way out. On the other hand, the beta coefficient for GDP is negative. Additionally, the relationship between inflation and Capital is also turned out to be negative.

Table 7.7 Capital equation

Variable (Dependent variable = CAR)	Coefficient	Std. Error	t-stats	Prob
C	7.946417	2.17E−08	3.67E+08	0.000**
Z_Score	0.728154	3.73E−10	1.95E+09	0.000**
TA	0.210893	1.55E−09	1.36E+08	0.000**
NNITA	0.453094	6.32E−10	7.17E+08	0.000**
NII	5.92E−07	7.16E−15	82685251	0.000**
GDP	−0.227667	9.56E−11	−2.38E+09	0.000**
INFL	−0.098118	6.03E−11	−1.63E+09	0.000**
F-statistic	180.8930**			
j-statistic	0.337047			
R-squared	0.159741			
Adjusted R-squared	0.154114			
Instruments	Constant TA NNITA GDP Z-SCORE $_{t-1}$ TLTA OETA			

Source Computed using E-views
**indicates significance at 5% level

The Risk Model (Table 7.6) reflects that the R-Squared and Adjusted R-Squared value is negative. However, this does not signify bad fit of the models. These two values happen to be negative when the sum of squared residuals for instrumental variables is larger than the total sum of squares (Al-Kayed et al. 2014). The value of Hansen j statistic is more than 0.05 in both the models which implies that the restrictions implied by the existence of more instruments than endogenous regressors are valid. In addition, as the F value is considerably high and significant as evidenced by the F-value and P (F-statistic) which is displayed in the Tables 7.6 and 7.7, it ensures the significance of the whole regression model.

7.5 Summary and Conclusion

The paper attempted to gauge the inter-linked association of regulatory capital and insolvency risk of the Indian commercial banks using a sample of 43 banks (25 public sector and 18 private sector banks) over 21 financial years (1996–2016). The study applied Two-Stage-Least-Squares method to find the estimates of the simultaneous equation model. The findings reflects that bi-directional negative association subsists amid capital and insolvency risk i.e. capital has a negative impact on the risk of banks and risk also impacts capital negatively in turn. Besides, the other explanatory variables too have significant influence on the endogenous variable. The overall picture that can be viewed from the results of both the models (given the negative association of capital and risk, positive association of TA with risk and capital, positive relationship of NNITA with risk and Capital, positive association of NII with capital, positive association of GDP with risk and negative with capital, and positive association of inflation with risk and negative with capital) is that higher is the profitability, better is the capital position of the banks as large banks with better profitability have easier access to capital market in addition to the retained earnings through profits and vice versa followed by squeeze in risk taking which follows the hypothesis that higher the capital, greater the security and lesser the risk. However, larger sized banks although with higher capital, take more risk. In addition, the association of NNITA with risk and capital indicates that increase in non-conventional sources of income raises the riskiness of the banks due to the inherent risk within the activities. However, the capital adequacy improves in response to the diversification. Increase in overall profitability might be the reason behind this. Again, relationship of GDP with both the variables can be explained by the fact that, during favourable times, apparently there is less risk. The capital adequacy position shrinks with increase in GDP which might be due to optimistic views of the bankers.

The overall study concludes that with higher capital adequacy standard, the banks control the riskier activities. This study can be a helping hand to the policy makers and the public as a whole. However, it is just an exploration of the existing affairs. It is very important to peep deeper into this area through more scientific research as inspite of strict regulatory measures; the non-performing assets of the banks are alarming in the recent years. Moreover, only a single measure is used for risk of insolvency. Thus, there is a further scope to counter check the results using different risk measure and different methodology.

References

Alkadamani, K. (2015). Capital adequacy, bank behaviour and crises: Evidence from emergent economies. *European Journal of Sustainable Development, 4*(2), 329–338.

Al-Kayed, L. T., Raihan Syed Mohd Zain, S., & Duasa, J. (2014). The Relationship between capital structure and performance of Islamic Banks. *Journal of Islamic Accounting and Business Research, 5*(2), 158–181.

Blum, J. (1999). Do capital adequacy requirements reduce risks in banking. *Journal of Banking & Finance 23,* 755–771.

Bougatef, K., & Mgadmi, N. (2016). The impact of prudential regulation on bank capital and risk taking: The case of MENA countries. *The Spanish Review of Financial Economics, 14,* 51–56.

Cebenoyan, A. S., Cooperman, E., & Register, C. A. (1995). Deregulation, reregulation, equity ownership and S&L risk taking. *Financial Management, 24*(3), 63–76.

Chen, C. R., Steiner, T. L., & Whyte, A. M. (2006). Does stock option based executive compensation induce risk-taking? An analysis of the banking industry. *Journal of Banking and Finance, 30*(3), 915–945.

Das, N., & Deb, J. (2017). Regulatory capital and its impact on credit risk: The case of Indian Commercial Banks. *IUP Journal of Bank Management, XVI*(4), 7–22.

Demigruc-Kunt, A., & Huizinga, H. (2004). Market discipline and deposit insurance. *Journal of Monetary Economics, 1,* 375–399.

Dhumale, R. (2000). *Capital adequacy standards: Are they sufficient?* Working Paper No. 165 related to CBR Research Programme on Industrial Organisation, Competitive Strategy and Business Performance. ESRC Centre for Business Research, University of Cambridge.

Gujarati, D. N., Porter D. C., & Gunasekar S. (2012). Basic econometrics; McGraw Hill Education (India) Edition.

Hovakimian, A., & Kane, E. J. (2000). Effectiveness of capital regulation at U.S Commercial Banks, 1985–1994. *The Journal of Finance, 55*(1), 451–468.

Khan, M. S., Scheule, H., & Wu, E. (2016). Funding liquidity and bank risk taking. *Journal of banking and Finance* 000, 1–14.

Kim, D., & Santomero, A. M. (1988). Risk in banking and capital regulation. *The Journal of Finance, 43*(5), 1219–1233.

Louati, S., Gargouri Abida, I., & Boujelbene, Y. (2015). Capital adequacy implications on Islamic and non-Islamic Bank's behaviour: Does market power matter? *Borsa Istanbul Review, 15*(3), 192–204.

Ma, L., Dai, J., & Huang, X. (2011). Effect of capital constraints on risk preference behaviour of commercial banks. *China Finance Review International, 1*(2), 168–186.

Maji, S. G., & De, U. K. (2015). Regulatory capital and risk of Indian Banks: A simultaneous equation approach. *Journal of Financial Economic policy, 7*(2), 140–156.

Miah, M. D., & Shameen, K. (2015). Relationship between capital, risk and efficiency. *International Journal of Islamic and Middle Eastern Finance and Management, 8*(2), 203–221.

Nachane, D. M (1999). Capital adequacy ratios: An agnostic viewpoint. *Economic and Political Weekly, 34*(314), *Money, Banking and Finance*; 155–160.

Nachane, D. M., Narain, A., Ghosh, S., & Sahoo S. (2001). Bank response to capital requirements: Theory and Indian evidence. Economic and Political Weekly, 36(4); *Money, Banking & Finance,* 329–331 + 333–335.

Nguyen, T. P. T., & Nghiem, S. H. (2015). The interrelationship among default risk, capital ratio and efficiency-evidence from Indian Banks. *Managerial Finance, 41*(5) 507–525.

Odonkor, T. A., Osei, B. A., & Sjö, B. (2016). Risk-taking, ownership and excess reserves in the Ghanaian Banking system. *Journal of Emerging Market Finance, 15*(2), 147–168.

Roy, D. G., Kohli, B., & Khatkale, S. (2013). Basel I to Basel II to Basel III: A risk management journey of Indian Banks. *AIMA Journal of Management & Research, 7*(2/4).

Singh, N. (2011). *Tejamani*. Risk Management: Maxford Books.

Zheng, C., Xu, T., & Liang, W. (2012). The empirical research of banks' capital buffer and risk adjustment decision making. *China Finance Review International, 2*(2), 163–179.

Chapter 8
Examining the Linkages Between Financial Development and Energy Consumption in India

Seema Saini and Yadawananda Neog

Abstract This paper examines the long-run equilibrium and the existence of the causal relationship between financial development, energy consumption, economic growth and FDI in India for the period 1978–2014. The Johansen-Juselius maximum likelihood procedure in the multivariate framework and Granger causality in the vector error correction framework (VECM) is employed to examine the co-integration and causal association between the considered variables. The results of Johansen-Juselius co-integration test shows that there is long-run equilibrium relationship among variables. We also find that there is no long-run causality between the variables, but there exists bi-directional short-run causality between financial development and energy consumption in India. Based on these results, suitable growth policies are also discussed for India.

Keywords Energy-finance · Co-integration · Causality

8.1 Introduction

According to the *Global Energy Statistical Yearbook 2015*, India is the most significant energy consumer agent, just behind China and US. As per world Development indicators, energy consumption in India has almost doubled since 2000 which is contributing to 10% of the global energy demand while the potential for further rapid growth GDP is higher. Energy consumption plays a vital role in economic development, so the link between energy consumption and economic growth is now well researched in literature.

S. Saini
Department of Economics Sciences, IIT Kanpur, Kanpur, India
e-mail: saini@iitk.ac.in

Y. Neog (✉)
Department of Economics, Banaras Hindu University, Varanasi, India
e-mail: yadavneog@gmail.com

A. K. Mishra et al. (eds.), *Current Issues in the Economy and Finance of India*, Springer Proceedings in Business and Economics,
https://doi.org/10.1007/978-3-319-99555-7_8

Huo (2009) examines the link between economic growth and energy consumption and he finds that economic growth Granger causes energy consumption and energy consumption Granger causes economic growth respectively in context of China.

Energy consumption and financial development also have the very complicated relationship. On the one hand, financial development has a positive correlation in the sense that if there is financial development in an economy, it leads to economic growth, which in turn has a positive relationship with energy consumption. The financial development also causes an increase in investment in new technology which in lieu lowers the energy consumption. The increased investments in new technology will lead to increase in investment in that machinery which will use less energy. I.e., they will invest more in inventing energy efficient technology.

If we see the accumulated result, it will lead to the positive impact of financial development on energy consumption. This means the effect of a reduction in energy consumption due investment surpasses by the direct positive impact of financial development on energy consumption. Even our result also shows this accumulated result by showing a positive effect of financial development on energy consumption.

Domestic credit judges the financial development in our case to the private sector as a % of GDP which is the proxy for financial development. If there is an increase in the domestic credit to private sector, it means that people have excess money to invest and that is also at less rate of interest. They have many investments project become profitable after this decrease in interest rate. This leads to more projects to be incorporated by the investors for a higher profit. Higher investment through this leads to more growth and development. This makes our way clearer to use domestic credit to private sector.

A large group of studies has examined the nexuses between growth-energy, FDI-growth, CO_2-finance, and growth-finance in advanced and emerging economies but nexus between energy-finance is insufficient in the Indian context. Karanfil and Li (2015) is the first who introduces the financial element in the energy-growth framework.

The rest of the paper is organized as follows. In the second section, we will discuss the literature review in the context of India and other countries. In the third section, we have presented the methodology used in this study. In the next section, we have shown the empirical findings and conclusion.

8.2 Literature Review

Importance of energy consumption for economic growth is best shown in 1973–1974 when oil-producing countries of the Middle-East restricted the output. As a result, prices have increased fourfold in few months. This has given a great backdrop to developing nations by decreasing the supplies of raw material to industrialized countries. This is the significant evidence of the relationship between energy consumption and economic growth.

There many studies like Chebbi and Boujelbene (2008), Jumbe (2004) and Siddiqui (2004), etc. which suggest that energy consumption and economic growth have a high correlation. Whereas, other studies like Gbadebo and Chinedu (2009), Noor and Siddiqi (2010) support a negative relationship. Sarkar et al. (2010) and Yusma reported the non-causality relationship between them. Other studies which have reported bi-directional causality are Pradhan (2010), Loganathan, et al. (2010). Riaz and Stern (1984) showed that changing energy consumption with economic growth is defined by the historical, social and economic progress of the country, so it is a multidimensional phenomenon. Ghosh (2010) finds that in the short-run if we try to correct the problem of carbon emissions, it could lead to a reduction in the national income of the country because economic growth is directly related with the utilization of resources which produces carbon emission at larger quantities. But the long run causality is not defined by economic growth on carbon emissions as it is also defined by various other factors which are responsible for growth and development process of an economy. In India, various methods have been used to check energy preservation and energy proficiency to minimize wastage of energies across the value chain. Some methods are narrowing down energies of demand and supply gap, and long run witness of eco-friendly technologies which one side increases growth with less production of emissions and economy is not affected at all. Jayanthakumaran et al. (2012) examine that China and India are two different countries whose growth and carbon emissions are affecting them differently and they are having differences in utilization of energy resources for growth. India is a country of the informal economy while China is different depends on formal sectors, so the contribution to growth and carbon emissions are different, China's emissions are defined by per capita income of the people while India's not. Alam et al. (2011) suggest that in the long run both dynamic modelling and accounting methods has shown null results of energy consumption and CO_2 emissions on real incomes. So, it shows India could use energy prevention and its efficiency development without harshing economic growth of the country and will combat the problem of global warming. Hou (2009) narrated that energy is the key indicator of economic development, in China it has been shown economic growth and energy consumption is having casual effects with each other. Sadorsky (2010) investigates the role of financial development as a driver of economic growth in 22 emerging countries from period 1990 to 2006. To examine the linkages, they use the generalised method of moment and different measures of financial development. They find that there is positive and statistically significant relationship between the energy consumption and financial development. Mallick and Mahalik (2014) explored the relationship between financial development, energy consumption and economic growth using ARDL approach to co-integration in India from 1971 to 2009. Results show that proportion of the urban population in the total population positively and significantly affect the energy consumption whereas it affects negatively to the financial development. Khan et al. (2007) study that energy plays a significant role on the demand and the supply sides of economy. This implies that there is a causal association running from energy consumption to economic growth. Jumbe (2004) observes that if causation runs from energy consumption to GDP then it infers that an economy is energy reliant on and hence energy is an incentive to economic growth deficiency of energy may affect economic growth and may cause unfortunate economic performance leading to a decrease of income and employment. On the other hand, if causality runs from GDP to energy consumption, reverse will happen Abul and Masih (1997). Therefore, energy conservation policies may be pursued without affecting the economy Jumbe (2004). Fröling (2011) study that development of energy in the transition from sluggishness to growth. Sehrawat et al. (2015) examine that in India, environmental degradation is positively associated with increasing pace of economic growth, energy consumption and support of financial development for running different projects, like conversion of smart cities lead to expansion in urbanization. Shahbaz et al. (2017) find that adverse shocks to energy consumption have influences on economic growth. Mallick (2009) assesses that energy consumption and capital formation is neither having any casual relationship and nor energy consumption affects economic growth process. Siddiqui (2004) examines that current rise in energy prices, shrinking prevailing resources, and the examination for other sources of energy and energy preservation technologies have transported into attention the question of interconnection between energy use and economic growth. Energy development is likely to lead to higher growth and its deficiency may retard the growth process. The influence of all fonts of energy on economic growth is not the same. The influence of electricity and petroleum products as well as that of electricity only is highly and statistically significant. Boutabba (2014) find the evidence of long run and causal relationship between carbon emission, energy, income, financial development and trade openness for India. They recommend that while making environmental policies for reducing CO_2 emission financial development should be taking into account. Komal and Abbas (2015) investigate the nexus of finance-growth-energy by employing the GMM technique for period 1972–2012 for Pakistan. Their Results shows that financial development positively affects the energy consumption. For D8 countries, Razzaqi et al. (2011) have found both long run as well as short run relationship in between energy consumption and economic prosperity. Shahbaz (2016) apply the co-integration test proposed by Bayer and Hanck (2012) the and find the long-run and short-run relationship among globalization and energy consumption for India using panel data from period 1971 to 2013. They suggest that both globalization and financial development help in increase in economic growth in India.

From the above literature, we found that energy consumption is not having any long-run effects on the growth of the economy, but at times of emergencies, energy plays a significant role in overwhelming the problems of growth. Technology and innovations have shown tremendous alternatives for the well being of the economies, energy is just meant to the growth process, but if we talk about sustainability then both energy and growth are having causality in them.

8.3 Data and Methodology

8.3.1 Data

This study covers the period for India from 1978 to 2015. The annual time series data for the variables are extracted from the World Development Indicator of World Bank. All the variables are transformed into their logarithmic form. Thus, the first difference variable can be interpreted as the growth rate. Variables with their measurement, definition, and sources are mentioned in Table 8.1.

Financial development mainly has two aspects of domestic development. One is stock market development and another is intermediary development. Our study is limited only to the intermediary development because the availability of the data for stock market development proxied by the different indicator in the literature is not available for the initial years. Thus, in our study financial development is measured by domestic credit to the private sector which is intermediary development. According to King and Levine (1993) financial system that transfers funds to the private sector firms than government sector will offer more services. Chorfoon tang and Bee wan tan (2014) finds that it not only measures the efficiency of credit provision by financial intermediaries but also shows the level of private activities within the economy. In literature number of proxy has been used but it has its pros and cons.

8.3.2 Methodology

In the present study, firstly we will check for the stationarity in the variables using Augmented Dickey-Fuller (ADF) unit root test (Dickey and Fuller 1979; Ames and Watson 1989). To study the long run equilibrium relationship and long-term causality among variables we have employed Johansen-Juselius maximum likelihood procedure in the multivariate framework. After that, Granger causality test has been applied to check for the direction of the causality.

Model:

In this study we will use the following model:

$$\ln EC_t = \alpha_0 + \alpha_1 \ln GDP_t + \alpha_2 FD_t + \alpha_3 FDI_t + \varepsilon_t \tag{8.1}$$

Here, ln represents the natural logarithm, EC_t is the per capita energy consumption (measured in kg of oil equivalent), GDP_t is the per capita gross domestic product, FDI_t is the foreign direct investment as a % of GDP, FDt is the Financial development indicator proxied by domestic credit to private sector as a % of GDP and ε_t is the error term which follows the white noise process.

Table 8.1 Variables used in the empirical analysis

Variable	Measurement	Definition	Source
GDP	GDP per capita is measured by gross domestic product divided by midyear population (constant 2010 US$)	GDP is the sum of gross value added by all sectors of an economy during a period	World development indicators
Energy consumption	Kg of oil equivalent per capita	Energy use means the use of primary energy before any transformation to end-use fuels	World development indicators
FDI	Foreign direct investment, net inflows (% of GDP)	Net inflows (new investment inflows less disinvestment) in the economy from foreign investors and is divided by country's GDP	World development indicators
Financial development (FD)	Domestic credit to private sector (% of GDP)	Financial resources that provided to the private sector by financial corporations	World development indicators

Unit Root test:

ADF test is for the unit root of time series. This test is applied by assuming that our error term may be correlated with each other. A slight modification is made to DF test, and it can be seen in the ADF model.

$$\Delta y_t = (\delta - 1)y_{t-1} + \sum_{i=1}^{m} \alpha \Delta y_{t-i} + u_t \tag{8.2}$$

The difference is that in this equation the lagged value of the dependent variable is added to the explanatory variable to overcome the problem of autocorrelation. The null hypothesis (H0: δ = 1) for the ADF test is that the series has a unit root or non-stationary. And the alternative hypothesis is that the series is stationary. The null hypothesis tested with the use of t (tau) statistics. The null hypothesis will be rejected if the calculated t value is greater than the tabulated t value. If the series becomes stationary at levels, then we called it integrated of order 0, i.e., I (0). And if the series becomes stationary after taking the first difference, then we will call it integrated of order 1, i.e., I(1). Therefore, in general form, a series can be said integrated of order d, i.e. I (d), if we take d time differentiation for making series stationary.

Co-integration:

Johansen Maximum Likelihood Procedure will be performed to examine the level of co-integration among energy consumption, GDP, Financial development and FDI for India. This procedure follows two steps. Firstly, we will check for the order of integration of the logarithm variables. In the second step, VAR[1] approaches are used to check for the number of co-integrating equations in the model. Trace statistics and maximum eigenvalue statistics have been employed to test the co-integrating rank. The Trace test is a joint test, the null hypothesis (ro $\leq$ r) is that the number of co-integrating vectors is less than or equal to r, against a general alternative hypothesis that there is more than r. The Maximal Eigenvalue test conducts separate tests on each eigenvalue. The null hypothesis, i.e. (ro = r) is that there are r co-integrating vectors present against the alternative that there are (r + 1) present. The optimal value of lag is determined by Akaike (AIC) and Schwarz–Bayesian (SBC) model selection criteria.

Granger Causality:

Granger causality is performed to examine the direction of causality between the variables energy consumption, GDP, Financial development and FDI. If variables are I (1) individually and co-integrated causality test within the first difference VAR model will be misleading (Engle and Granger 1987). Therefore, Granger causality is detected by Vector error correction term (VECM) framework as follows:

$$\Delta \ln EC_t = \alpha_0 + \gamma ECT_{t-1} + \alpha_1 \sum_{i=1}^{k} \ln EC_{t-i} + \alpha_2 \sum_{i=0}^{k} \ln GDP_{t-i} + \alpha_3 \sum_{i=0}^{k} \ln FD_{t-i} + \alpha_4 \sum_{i=0}^{k} \ln FDI_{t-i} + \varepsilon_t \tag{8.3}$$

$$\Delta \ln FD_t = \alpha_0 + \gamma ECT_{t-1} + \alpha_1 \sum_{i=1}^{k} \ln FD_{t-i} + \alpha_2 \sum_{i=0}^{k} \ln GDP_{t-i} + \alpha_3 \sum_{i=0}^{k} \ln EC_{t-i} + \alpha_4 \sum_{i=0}^{k} \ln FDI_{t-i} + \varepsilon_t \tag{8.4}$$

$$\Delta \ln FDI_t = \alpha_0 + \gamma ECT_{t-1} + \alpha_1 \sum_{i=1}^{k} \ln FDI_{t-i} + \alpha_2 \sum_{i=0}^{k} \ln GDP_{t-i} + \alpha_3 \sum_{i=0}^{k} \ln EC_{t-i} + \alpha_4 \sum_{i=0}^{k} \ln FD_{t-i} + \varepsilon_t \tag{8.5}$$

$$\Delta \ln GDP_t = \alpha_0 + \gamma ECT_{t-1} + \alpha_1 \sum_{i=1}^{k} \ln GDP_{t-i} + \alpha_2 \sum_{i=0}^{k} \ln FDI_{t-i} + \alpha_3 \sum_{i=0}^{k} \ln EC_{t-i} + \alpha_4 \sum_{i=0}^{k} \ln FD_{t-i} + \varepsilon_t \tag{8.6}$$

[1]Vector Auto-Regression. See Sims (1972, 1980).

These are the four equations for Granger representation of VECM model. Here Δ symbol represents the first difference. ECT is the Error Correction Term, which denotes the speed of adjustment in the long run. The error term (ϵ) is assumed to be normally distributed and white noise. For the analysis of short-run causal relationship, we have applied homogeneity Wald test first difference lagged explanatory variables.

8.4 Empirical Results

8.4.1 Results of Unit Root Analysis

Table 8.2 shows the results of unit root test. We have applied the ADF test to check for the stationarity of variables. The optimal lag length of the ADF is determined by the Akaike's Information Criterion (AIC). All the variables i.e. energy consumption, GDP, Financial development and FDI are non-stationary at level. But becomes stationary at 5% level of significance with the order of integration is one as we can see from the table. Therefore, uniformity of order of integration insists on employing cointegration test for to check for the long run relationship.

8.4.2 Results of co-integration Analysis

As all the variables are integrated of order one I(1) so, we can now examine the existence of long-run equilibrium relationship between energy consumption, GDP, Financial development and FDI in India. We have performed the Johansen-Juselius

Table 8.2 Summary of unit root test

Variable		1% level	5% level	10% level	T-Statistics	Prob.	Results
Energy	level	−4.234972	3.540328	−3.202445	0.002248	0.9947	Non-stationary
	1st Diff.	−4.243644	−3.544284	−3.204699	−5.489048	0.0004	*Stationary
GDP	level	−4.234972	−3.540328	−3.202445	−2.150632	0.5014	Non-stationary
	1St Diff.	−4.243644	−3.544284	−3.204699	−8.109511	0.0000	*Stationary
Credit	level	−4.273277	−3.557759	−3.212361	−3.009564	0.1453	Non-stationary
	1st Diff.	−2.634731	−1.951000	−1.610907	−1.939691	0.0512**	Stationary
FDI	level	−4.234972	−3.540328	−3.202445	−3.045382	0.1346	Non-stationary
	1st Diff.	−4.296729	−3.568379	−3.218382	−4.883328	0.0025*	Stationary

*, ** and ***denote significance at the 1, 5 and 10% levels respectively

Table 8.3 Johansen-Juselius Multivariate likelihood co-integration tests summary

Trace-statistics				
Dependent variable = energy consumption				
Null hypothesis	Alternative hypothesis	Trace statistics	0.05 critical value	Prob. **
r = 0	r ≥ 1	68.13531	47.85613	0.0002
r ≤ 1	r ≥ 2	35.52143	29.79707	0.0098
r ≤ 2	r ≥ 3	12.38056	15.49471	0.1396
Max-Eigen statistics				
Null hypothesis	Alternative hypothesis	Trace statistics	0.05 critical value	Prob. **
r = 0	r = 1	32.61388	27.58434	0.0103
r = 1	r = 2	23.14086	21.13162	0.0257
r = 2	r = 3	9.052976	14.26460	0.2818

**Mackinnon et al. (1999) *p* value

co-integration test. Results of the Johansen–Juselius co-integration test are shown in Table 8.3.

Probability values for trace statistics and Max-Eigen statistics reveal that we can reject the null hypothesis. The null hypothesis of trace statistics (r ≤ 1), i.e., of at most one co-integrating rank for co-integration is rejected at 5% level of significance. The null hypothesis of Max-Eigen statistics (r = 1), i.e. of one co-integrating equation is also rejected at 5% level of significance. From Table 8.3, it is clear that there is at least two co-integrating equation in our model. Therefore, our variables show that there is long-run equilibrium relationship between energy consumption, GDP, Financial development and FDI in India.

8.4.3 Results of Granger Causality

From Table 8.3, we have witnessed that variables are co-integrated in the long run. But co-integration does not provide us the direction of the causal relationship between variables. Therefore, VECM Granger Causality test is employed to test the direction of causality in variables (Table 8.4).

As the following Table 8.4 depicts, our Error Correction Term is negative but insignificant at 5% level. That means there is no long-run causality in between variables. The speed of adjustment is nil for our model. For the case of short-run Granger causality, we have found one bidirectional relationship between energy consumption and financial development. These causal relationships are (a) financial development does cause energy consumption in India and (b) Energy consumption also cause financial development for India. All other short run causal relationships become insignificant in our case. The recent development of the financial sector in

Table 8.4 Long run and short run Granger causality test summary

Dependent variable	ΔlnEC	ΔlnFD	ΔlnFDIt	ΔlnGDPt	ECTt − 1
ΔlnECt	–	4.325374 (0.0375)*	0.178422 (0.6727)	0.306393 (0.5799)	
ΔlnFDt	4.605078 (0.0319)*	–	0.166730 (0.6830)	0.090487 (0.7636)	
ΔlnFDIt	1.008558 (0.3152)	0.287205 (0.5920)	–	0.501008 (0.4791)	
ΔlnGDPt	0.244227 (0.6212)	0.005895 (0.9388)	0.170755 (0.6794)	–	−0.219864 (0.1541)

Parentheses represent probability values
*Significant at 5% level

India leads better financial resources to the people. The rapid growth of industries, infrastructure, and small-scale entrepreneurship assist more energy consumption in the Indian case. From the sustainable development prospective, it is not a positive aspect, because high consumption of energy will always lead to environmental pollution. Though the rise in the use of energy consumption also causes financial development, a country's overall development also depends upon its environmental quality also.

8.5 Conclusion

In the present study, we examine the relationship between financial sector, energy consumption, economic growth and FDI in India for the period 1978 to 2014. The main findings of this study are as follows. There is evidence from Johansen-Juselius cointegration test that all the variables are cointegrated. This indicates that there is long-run equilibrium relationship between the variables, though there might be some divergence in the short run. Results of Granger causality shows that bidirectional causality is running between energy consumption and financial development. Therefore, both long run and short run results suggest that in India energy is an important input for the blooming of financial sector development. The policy-makers should adopt the dual approach that, on the one hand, they can encourage the research and development in the green technology to reduce the consumption of fossil fuel and on the other hand, they can increase the investment in the energy infrastructure for the development of the financial sector. The government should also emphasize on the effective banking system which will lead to an efficient financial system which will provide the funds for fulfilling their demand for energy in India.

References

Abul, M. M., & Masih, R. (1997). On the temporal causal relationship between energy consumption, real income, and prices: Some new evidence from asian-energy dependent NICs based on a multivariate cointegration/vector error-correction approach. *Journal of Policy Modeling*, *19*(4), 417–440.

Alam, M. J., Begum, I. A., Buysse, J., Rahman, S., & Van Huylenbroeck, G. (2011). Dynamic modeling of causal relationship between energy consumption, CO_2 emissions and economic growth in India. *Renewable and Sustainable Energy Reviews, 15*(6), 3243–3251.

Ames, S. H. & Watson, M. W., (1989). New indexes of coincident and leading economic indicators. *NBER Macroeconomics Annual*, *4*, 351–409.

Bayer, C. & Hanck, C. (2012). Combining non-cointegration tests. *Journal of Time Series Analysis*, *34*(1), 83–95.

Boutabba, A. M. (2014) The impact of financial development, income, energy and trade on carbon emissions: Evidence from the Indian economy. *Economic Modelling*, *40*, 33–41.

Chebbi, H. E., & Boujelbene, Y. (2008). CO_2 emissions, energy consumption and economic growth in Tunisia. European Association of Agricultural Economists, 2008 International Congress, August 26–29.

Dickey, A. D., & Fuller, A.W. (1979). Distribution of the estimators for autoregressive time series with a unit root. *Journal of the American Statistical Association*, *74*(366), 427–431.

Engle, R. F., & Granger C. W. J. (1987). Co-integration and error correction: Representation, estimation, and testing. *Econometrica*, *55*(2), 251–276.

Fröling, M. (2011). Energy use, population and growth, 1800–1970. *Journal of Population Economics, 24*(3), 1133–1163.

Gbadebo, O. O., & Chinedu, O. (2009). Does energy consumption contribute to economic performance? Empirical evidence from Nigeria. *Journal of Economics and International Finance*, *1*(2), 44–58.

Ghosh, S. (2010). Examining carbon emissions economic growth nexus for India: A multivariate cointegration approach. *Energy Policy, 38*(6), 3008–3014.

Hou, Q. (2009). The relationship between energy consumption growths and economic growth in China. *International journal of economics and finance, 1*(2), 232.

Jayanthakumaran, K., Verma, R., & Liu, Y. (2012). CO_2 emissions, energy consumption, trade and income: A comparative analysis of China and India. *Energy Policy, 42,* 450–460.

Johansen, S. (1988). Statistical analysis of cointegration vectors. *Journal of Economic Dynamics and Control*, *12*(2–3), 231–254.

Jumbe, C. B. L. (2004). Cointegration and causality between electricity consumption and GDP: Empirical evidence from Malawi. *Energy Economics*, *26*(1), 61–68.

Karanfil, K., & Li, Y. (2015). Electricity consumption and economic growth: Exploring panel-specific differences. *Energy Policy*, *82*, 264–277.

Khan, M. A., Qayyum, A., & Ahmad, E. (2007). Dynamic modelling of energy and growth in South Asia [with Comments]. *The Pakistan Development Review*, 481–498.

King, G. R., & Levine, R. (1993). Finance and growth: Schumpeter might be right. *The Quarterly Journal of Economics*, *108*, 717–737.

Komal, R., & Abbas, F. (2015). Linking financial development, economic growth and energy consumption in Pakistan. *Renewable and Sustainable Energy Reviews*, *44*, 211–220.

Mallick, H. (2009). Examining the linkage between energy consumption and economic growth in India. *The Journal of Developing Areas, 43*(1), 249–280.

Mallick, H., & Mahalik, M. (2014). Energy consumption, economic growth and financial development: A comparative perspective on India and China. *Bulletin of Energy Economics*, *2*(3), 72–84.

MacKinnon, J., Haug, A., & Michelis, L. (1999). Numerical distribution functions of likelihood ratio tests for cointegration. *Journal of Applied Econometrics*, *14*(5), 563–577.

Noor, S., & Siddiqi, M. W. (2010). Energy consumption and economic growth in South Asian Countries: A co-integrated panel analysis. *International Journal of Energy and Power Engineering*, *4*(7), 1731–1736.
Pradhan, P. R. (2010). Financial deepening, foreign direct investment and economic growth: Are they cointegrated. *International Journal of Financial Research*, *1*(1), 37–43.
Razzaqi, S., Bilquees, F., & Sherbaz, S. (2011). Dynamic relationship between energy and economic growth: Evidence from D8 countries. *The Pakistan Development Review*, 437–458.
Riaz, T., & Stern, N. H. (1984). Pakistan: Energy consumption and economic growth [with comments]. *The Pakistan Development Review*, *23*(2/3), 431–456.
Sadorsky, P. (2010). The impact of financial development on energy consumption in emerging economies. *Energy Policy*, *38*(5), 2528–2535.
Sarker, A. R., & Alam, K. (2010). Nexus between electricity generation and economic growth in Bangladesh. *Asian Social Science*, *6*(12), 16–22.
Sims, C. A., (1972). The role of approximate prior restrictions in distributed lag estimation. *Journal of the American Statistical Association*, *67*(337), 169–175.
Sims, C. A. (1980). Macroeconomics and reality. *Econometrica*, *48*(1), 1–48.
Sehrawat, M., Giri, A. K., & Mohapatra, G. (2015). The impact of financial development, economic growth and energy consumption on environmental degradation: Evidence from India. *Management of Environmental Quality: An International Journal*, *26*(5), 666–682.
Shahbaz, M., Van Hoang, T. H., Mahalik, M. K., & Roubaud, D. (2017). Energy consumption, financial development and economic growth in India: New evidence from a nonlinear and asymmetric analysis. *Energy Economics*, *63*, 199–212.
Siddiqui, R. (2004). Energy and economic growth in Pakistan. *The Pakistan Development Review*, 175–200.

Chapter 9
Leverage Effect and Volatility Asymmetry

Parthajit Kayal and S. Maheswaran

Abstract The leverage effect, the relationship between asset volatility and returns is generally examined at contemporaneous or inter-temporal level. Instead, this paper examines the leverage effect over a period by classifying days into positive-return and negative-return days. We also examine the volatility asymmetry in leverage effect by decomposing the volatility into *up* and *down volatilities*. This paper makes use of extreme value estimators to examine 14 indices from different Emerging economies and 10 indices from developed economies. We document that the evidence of a negative relationship between volatility and returns is more prevalent in developed markets. This study also observes a dominance of *down volatility* over *up volatility* during negative-return days.

Keywords Leverage effect · Volatility asymmetry · Extreme value estimators

9.1 Introduction

A negative correlation between asset's volatility increments and price returns is referred as leverage effect. In this paper, we look at this leverage effect and its asymmetry from a unique perspective to establish a general behaviour of investors and traders. We do not deal with the contemporaneous or inter-temporal relationship between asset volatility and returns. Instead, we try to examine the leverage effect over a period using daily data and by classifying them into positive-return days and negative-return days. We believe that estimation of contemporaneous and intertemporal can have misleading results. Usage of high-frequency data in

P. Kayal (✉)
Madras School of Economics, Gandhi Mandapam Road,
Behind Government Data Center, Kottur, Chennai 600025, Tamil Nadu, India
e-mail: parthajit@mse.ac.in

S. Maheswaran
Institute for Financial Management and Research, 24, Kothari Road, Nungambakkam, Chennai 600034, Tamil Nadu, India

A. K. Mishra et al. (eds.), *Current Issues in the Economy and Finance of India*,
Springer Proceedings in Business and Economics,
https://doi.org/10.1007/978-3-319-99555-7_9

estimating contemporaneous leverage effect draws the problem of noise and inter-temporal estimation requires well-defined periods. The advantage of our approach is that the estimation will be noise free and also not have the selection bias of periods. We also examine the volatility asymmetry in much detail by decomposing it into *up* and *down volatility*. We first examine this on emerging economies (EM) and then on developed economies. This allows us to draw a comparison among them.

This paper documents evidence of a negative relationship between volatility and returns using daily index data. Moreover, this is more prevalent in developed markets. We also observe convincing evidence of the dominance of *down volatility* over *up volatility* during negative-return days. The results are similar for both EM and developed markets. To examine asymmetric property in volatilities we use daily open, high, low, and close (OHLC) data. The basic idea is based on the changes of daily extreme prices of an asset. First, we use the daily opening and closing prices to identify the upward and downward market. We define days as *Good Days* when closing price is higher than opening price i.e., days when markets have moved up over the trading hours. *Bad Days* are the days when closing price is lower than opening price i.e., days when markets have moved down over the trading hours.[1] Then we use daily high and low prices to estimate volatility. Daily high prices are almost always buyer-initiated trades and daily low prices are almost always seller-initiated trades (Corwin and Schultz 2012). Therefore, the estimated values using daily high and low prices reflect the fundamental volatility of an asset (Corwin and Schultz 2012). To estimate volatility, we use the extreme value estimators by Rogers and Satchell (1991) and Yang and Zhang (2000). Rogers and Satchell (RS) estimator is a popular volatility estimator which makes use of daily high and low prices. The estimator derived by Yang and Zhang (YZ) includes opening jumps which were ignored in RS estimation. In this paper, we define the *Good Days* and *Bad Days* on basis of daily data and opening jumps need to consider previous days' closing price. Therefore, in the context of this paper, opening jumps are not very important and hence, the RS estimator is better suited. However, for comparison purposes, we also estimate YZ from daily data and finds that YZ estimation does not alter our conclusion. The advantage of using RS and YZ estimator to calculate volatility is that both the estimators are derived under very general conditions. Therefore, it is easy to calculate and can be applied to a variety of markets with different market structures.

Our general conclusion is that volatility in *Bad Days* is significantly higher than that of *Good Days*. This result is consistent with the theory of leverage effect and can also be explained by simple observation that says traders and investors hurry to close their positions to minimise their losses and consider putting money elsewhere during *Bad Days* and react slower in *Good Days* as there is no rush to rebalance their portfolios. We also observe a dominance of *down volatility* over *up volatility*

[1]Our definition of *Good Days* and *Bad Days* are based on daily opening and closing data hence does not consider intra-day changes in the price movements.

during *Bad Days*. We show that these facts are pervasive using index data from different emerging and developed countries.

This paper is organised as follows. We discuss related literature in Sect. 9.2. In Sect. 9.3, we present the data and discuss the methodologies in detail. We document the results in Sect. 9.4. We investigate the robustness of our result in Sect. 9.5. Section 9.6 briefly summarises and concludes.

9.2 Literature Survey

Leverage effect is a well-known and well-documented stylized fact in finance. The prevalent explanation in the literature is that if the asset price declines, the value of the debt rises relative to its equity for the associated company. Naturally, the asset becomes riskier; hence volatility increases (Black 1976; and Christie 1982). However, this explanation has been adopted only to describe the statistical regularity. The correlation does not necessarily imply causality. Alternative explanations referred as volatility feedback effect suggest an inter-temporal relationship; rise in anticipated volatility requires an expected higher return. This interpretation supports the basic idea of investment: 'High-risk, High-reward' concept. Increases in anticipated volatility lead to negative returns in future (French et al. 1987; Campbell and Hentschel 1992). The idea of leverage effect can be a contemporaneous or inter-temporal relationship between asset volatility and returns. This relationship has been tested in almost in all financial markets and assets using different frequencies in the data.

This leverage effect in assets is asymmetric in general. The magnitude of volatility increment during fall in asset prices is much higher than that of during rising in asset prices (Black 1976; Schwert 1989, 1990; Nelson 1991; Engle and Ng 1993). The literature on volatility asymmetry in leverage effect is not vast. El Babsiri and Zakoian (2001) showed that asymmetry in conditional heteroskedasticity models by treating the volatility of positive and negative returns as two distinct processes. The fact that, investors' positions (long or short) risk is associated with movements of the asset's price (up or down) established the motivation for this research field. Therefore, for an unbiased measure, it is wise to separate the volatility of *Good* and *Bad* days.

Using a high-frequency data, Barndorff-Nielsen et al. (2008) estimated the realised semi variances of negative and positive intra-daily returns. They separately measured the volatility of negative and positive returns to identify that downside realised semi-variance has more information than the normally realised variance statistic. Chen and Ghysels (2011) decomposed the intra-daily volatility in *down* and *up*. In a very recent study, Palandri (2015) analysed the dynamics of estimated *down* and *up* volatilities using daily returns. He used a bivariate generalisation of the standard EGARCH model. He showed that good and bad news affect differently in the volatilities of positive and negative daily returns. In this paper, we do not deal with realised semi-variance but tries to separately measure the variance of negative and positive returns days using extreme value estimators. We also decompose the volatilities of *Good* and *Bad Days* into *down* and *up volatility* for possible differences in structural information about volatility that characterises the *Good* and *Bad Days*.

This study looks at the volatility from the same perspective as seen by El Babsiri and Zakoian (2001) and Palandri (2015) with a different objective. This paper aims to establish the fact that the relationship between volatility and returns calculated over a period is consistent with leverage effect. We show that volatility in *Good Days* is significantly different than that of *Bad Days*. We also examine whether these facts are pervasive using data from emerging and developed countries. To achieve superiority in our estimation process, we measure unconditional volatility. We make use of daily extreme prices (OHLC) to get an efficient estimation (Chou et al. 2010).

Although this paper is also related to the literature of asymmetric volatility[2] which was documented as an empirical phenomenon (see, Engle and Ng 1993), we do not look at the impact of asymmetric volatility. This study highlights the need for separating the volatilities of *Good* and *Bad* times in any research which make use of volatility by establishing the evidence of significant differences in volatility using daily data. In a very recent study, Bekaertet al. (2015) use a model that distinguishes between good (low) and bad (high) volatility. Our paper shows that volatility can also be distinguished between *Good* and *Bad Days*.

9.3 Data and Methodology

To incorporate the dynamic characteristic of price process of an asset and estimate volatility, the generalised autoregressive conditional heteroskedasticity (GARCH)[3] and the stochastic volatility (SV[4]) models are well-known measures. However, both the GARCH and SV models are based on the closing prices; hence these estimations are not very accurate and efficient as they fail to use the information content in the reference period (Alizadeh et al. 2002; Brandt and Diebold 2006; Chou 2005). In other words, these estimation models ignore the path of the price movements or daily price range. If the market drops and then recovers by the end of the trading hours, the traditional volatility estimators will under-estimate the actual volatility (Kayal and Maheswaran 2018). This study uses daily Open, High, Low and Close (OHLC) data for all the assets. Although the above models are good for estimating the time-varying conditional volatility of assets, this paper focuses on unconditional volatility. The aim of our research is to find the difference between volatilities of

---

[2]See Bekaert and Wu (2000) for an overview of the literature on asymmetric volatility.

[3]GARCH family of models was initially proposed by Engle (1982) and Bollerslev (1986) and from then it has been extensively used in literature with major improvements.

[4]SV models were first advocated by Taylor (1986).

Good Days and *Bad Days*, not the time-varying estimation of volatilities. We use Rogers and Satchell (1991) i.e., RS estimator to check the difference of volatilities between *Good* and *Bad Days*. We also use Yang and Zhang (2000) method to cross-check our results and to see if opening jumps have any effect on our results. As already said, these RS and YZ estimators are derived under very general conditions, hence comparatively easy to calculate and can be applied to a variety of markets with different market structures. Another advantage is that both the estimator use OHLC prices and thereby able to capture the significant amount information inside the reference, unlike GARCH and SV models (Kayal and Maheswaran 2017). Usage of all the daily extreme prices (OHLC) in the estimation process achieve superiority and gives a more efficient estimation as it reflects more information about the price changes (Chou et al. 2010).

9.3.1 Data

The data used in this study are daily prices of 14 indices from 14 different Emerging economies[5]and 10 indices from developed economies (See Table 9.1 and Table 9.2). The reason behind using index level data is that we wanted to establish the results irrespective of market size and value factors of firms. Index level data act as a well-diversified and liquid equity portfolio and hence removes much of idiosyncratic risk and industry specific systemic risk which would have affected our results. We collect daily time series OHLC data for all the indices from Bloomberg database. OHLC data reveals more information about the variation of asset prices and exhibits the direction of the price changes over a whole day.

We employ daily time series of OHLC data (five working days per week excluding days of respective public and other holidays) for all the assets used in the study. This study uses 8 years of data starting from January 2009 to December 2016. OHLC data was not available for earlier dates for most of the stock indices. To maintain uniformity in our data we have considered only 2009–2016 period. The Specification of the methodology is described below.

9.3.2 Methodology

The RS and YZ are extreme value (EV) volatility estimators which are based on the high and the low prices. In finance literature, EV volatility estimators have been accepted as highly efficient estimators. These EV estimators are classified in two

[5]We started with 23 emerging economies (listed in the Morgan Stanley Capital International (MSCI) emerging markets Index) but many of these countries do not have open, high and low data prior to 2010. Our estimation process requires OHLC data at the daily level. Therefore, we have excluded those countries from our sample.

Table 9.1 List of emerging countries and respective stock indices

Indices from emerging countries	
Country name	Index name
Brazil	Ibovespa Brasil Sao Paulo stock exchange index
China	Shanghai composite index
Czech Republic	SE PX index
Egypt	Egyptian EGX 30 index
India	S&P CNX Nifty index
Indonesia	Jakarta stock exchange composite index
Mexico	Mexican Bolsa IPC index
Nigeria	Nigerian stock exchange all-share index
Pakistan	Karachi stock exchange KSE100 index
Philippines	Philippines stock exchange PSEi Index
Russia	Russia MICEX index
South Africa	FTSE/JSE Africa all share index
South Korea	Korea composite stock price index
Turkey	Borsa Istanbul 100 index

This table reports selected stock market indices from 14 countries featured in the MSCI Emerging Markets Index. As discussed earlier we had to exclude 9 emerging economies as OHLC data was not available for their stock indices. Brazil and Mexico are from the South American continent. Czech Republic, Turkey, and Russia are from Europe. Egypt, Nigeria, and South Africa represent the African continent here. Among the Asian countries we have China, India, Indonesia, Pakistan, Philippines, and South Korea

sets, first is *Method of Moments* (MM) (Garman and Klass 1980; Parkinson 1980; Rogers and Satchell 1991; Kunitomo 1992; Yang and Zhang 2000 etc.) and the second set is *Maximum Likelihood* (ML) estimators (Ball and Torous 1984; Magdon-Ismail and Atiya 2003; Horst et al. 2012 etc.). The ML estimators are considered to have complexity due to the intricacy of the joint density functions, being non-expressive in the closed-form (Maheswaran and Kumar (2013)) and difficulty in assessing the sensitivity to outlier observations. Hence, the MM-estimators have an advantage over ML estimators. The RS and YZ estimators are of the best among the all the MM-estimators which provide a closed-form solution for the volatility estimation that can be easily programmed and not computer-time intensive, unlike 'Maximum Likelihood' (ML) estimation measures which require an iterative process.

We assume that the intra-day price series follow a geometric Brownian motion which evolves as a diffusion process with instantaneous drift (mean) μ and volatility (variance) σ^2. Hence, the natural logarithm of stock price follows Brownian motion, a most common used underlying model in finance literature (Alizadeh et al. 2002). The data, we use are put through the logarithm transformation to get the Brownian motion in the price series.

Suppose $p_{t,n}$ is the price of an asset at time t, on day n. Now $P_{t,n}$ represents logarithm of the price $p_{t,n}$. Here, $t = 0$ when markets open and $t = 1$ when markets

Table 9.2 List of developed countries and respective stock indices

Indices from developed countries	
Country name	Index name
USA	Dow Jones industrial average
USA	The NASDAQ composite index
USA	S&P 500 index
United Kingdom	FTSE 100 index
Germany	DAX index
France	CAC 40 index
Europe	EURO STOXX 50 index
Japan	Nikkei 225 index
Hong Kong	Hang Seng index
Japan	Tokyo Price index

This table reports ten popular and mature stock market indices. The first three indices are from the USA. The Financial Times Stock Exchange Index (FTSE 100) belongs to the London Stock Exchange. The DAX index is an index of 30 largest German companies. The CAC 40 index contains the top-40 stocks listed on Euronext Paris. The Euro Stoxx 50 is a weighted index of 50 Eurozone stocks. The Nikkei 225 belongs to the Tokyo Stock Exchange (TSE). The Hang Seng index represents almost 67% of the capitalization of the Hong Kong Stock Exchange. The Tokyo Price Index, commonly known as TOPIX, is also an important stock market index for the TSE in Japan

close. When n = 1, it denotes the starting day of the sample and n = N the last day of the sample.

$$P_{t,n} = \log_e(p_{t,n}) \qquad 0 \le t \le T \tag{9.1}$$

Following Kayal and Maheswaran (2016), we have normalised the High (maximum), Low (Minimum) and Closing (Terminal) prices by the opening price (see Eqs. 9.2–9.5).

$$b_n = \sup_{0 \le t \le T} P_{t,n} - P_{t=0,n} \tag{9.2}$$

$$c_n = \inf_{0 \le t \le T} P_{t,n} - P_{t=0,n} \tag{9.3}$$

$$x_n = P_{t=1,n} - P_{t=0,n} \tag{9.4}$$

$$o_n = P_{t=0,n} - P_{t=1,n-1} \tag{9.5}$$

RS estimation for *Good Days* and *Bad Days*

The RS is an attractive EV estimator because it is an estimator for the unconditional variance and is also unbiased for any value of the drift in the context of Brownian motion. Using the prices (b_n, c_n, x_n) as shown in Eqs. 9.2–9.4, we can calculate $uxvx_n$ prices directly using the formula below in Eq. 9.6.

$$uxvx_n = b_n^2 + c_n^2 - x_n(b_n + c_n) \tag{9.6}$$

These estimated $uxvx_n$ prices from daily OHLC data can be used to get RS estimator. Here, we calculate the RS estimator separately for the *Good Days* and *Bad Days*.

$$RS^+ = \frac{1}{N1}\sum_{n=1}^{N1} uxvxI_{x>0} \tag{9.7}$$

$$RS^- = \frac{1}{N2}\sum_{n=1}^{N2} uxvxI_{x<0} \tag{9.8}$$

Here I_x is the indicator function taking the value 'One' if the argument x is true, otherwise 'Zero'. N1 and N2 are a total number of *Good* and *Bad Days* respectively. Equations 9.7 and 9.8 estimate volatilities of *Good Days* and *Bad Days* respectively. To check for the difference in volatilities between *Good* and *Bad Days*, we calculate the difference of RS (DRS) i.e., *Bad Days'* RS—*Good Days* RS, in Eq. 9.9. We can also get RS estimate for the full sample by just adding Eqs. 9.7 and 9.8.[6]

$$DRS = RS^- - RS^+ \tag{9.9}$$

Here, as we focus on price volatility over the trading periods, overnight returns are excluded (which we include in YZ volatility estimation). We avoid the need to adjust prices for splits or dividends as that will have impacted not only closing prices but opening, high and low prices also. Our prices are normalized and hence, adjustment for splits or dividends are not necessary. The announcement for splits and dividends would impact the volatility which would be in anyway embedded in our estimation.

[6]The definition of *Good Days* and *Bad Days* consider only those days when opening prices and closing prices are not same. The RS and YZ estimate for the full sample will thus ignore those days when opening and closing prices are same (in the case of no trade or all trades occur at the same price). This kind of issue is there when a stock or asset is not liquid enough and generally seen to happen for small stocks. Our study doesn't deal with individual stocks. Despite that, we still find instances where limited number of days in our data with either all the OHLC prices is same or opening and closing prices are same due to errors done by data sources. During the cleaning of data, we have deleted those days from our samples.

Decomposing the volatility estimated by RS

Equation 9.6 gives us the easy way to calculate daily volatility $uxvx_n$ using b_n, c_n, and x_n prices. This study also tries to decompose the daily volatility estimated from RS into *up volatility* and *down volatility* to explore more information about volatility that characterizes the effect of *Good* and *Bad Days*. For that we can estimate daily *up volatility* and *down volatility* using Eqs. 9.10 and 9.11 respectively.

$$ux_n = \frac{1}{2}\left(u_n^2 - x_n^2\right) \tag{9.10}$$

$$vx_n = \frac{1}{2}\left(v_n^2 - x_n^2\right) \tag{9.11}$$

Here, $u_n = 2b_n - x_n$ and $v_n = 2c_n - x_n$. We can also estimate the daily volatility $uxvx_n$ as in Eq. 9.6 by just taking a simple arithmetic average of Eqs. 9.10 and 9.11.

Yang Zhang volatility estimation for *Good Days* and *Bad Days*

Although asset prices (stocks, indices etc.) are generally more volatile during the trading hours than at other times, non-trading periods often also experience significant moves in prices (French and Roll 1986; Harris 1986). The YZ estimator, which is also an estimator for the unconditional variance and unbiased for any value of the drift, incorporates opening jumps[7] in the estimation of volatility. We should not expect the similar results from YZ estimation as the YZ estimation process is meaningfully different from that of RS. The YZ estimation is a weighted sum of the RS (estimates high-to-low volatility), open-to-close volatility and overnight volatility. We use the YZ estimation just as an alternative measure to check for the leverage effect but not to compare with the results from RS estimation.

$$YZ^+ = Var(o_n)I_{x>0} + k * Var(x_n)I_{x>0} + (1-k) * RS^+ \tag{9.12}$$

$$YZ^- = Var(o_n)I_{x<0} + k * Var(x_n)I_{x<0} + (1-k) * RS^- \tag{9.13}$$

Here $k = \frac{0.34}{1.34 + \frac{N+1}{N-1}}$ and I_x is the sane indicator function used earlier in Eqs. 9.7 and 9.8, taking the value one if the argument x is true, else zero. N = N1 when *Good Days* as N1 represents the total number of *Good Days* and N = N2 when it is for *Bad Days*. Similarly, like DRS in Eq. 9.9, we estimate difference of YZ (DYZ) i.e., *Bad Days'* YZ—*Good Days* YZ, to find the difference in volatilities estimated using YZ method between *Good* and *Bad Days* (see Eq. 9.14).

$$DYZ = YZ^- - YZ^+ \tag{9.14}$$

[7]We also calculate overnight volatilities and close-to-close volatilities separately for *Good* and *Bad Days* for all the assets. We do not find any significant differences.

Asymmetry Ratios

To check for the level of asymmetry in *Good* and *Bad Days* volatilities, we estimate asymmetry ratios using RS and YZ volatilities estimation. These ratios (see Eqs. 9.15 and 9.16) will give the relative differences in volatilities of both types of days. To compare the asymmetry between both types of days, one would ideally maintain the same volatility mid-point. Therefore, we divide the difference of volatilities in numerators by taking an average of them in denominators.

Asymmetry ratios are defined as the volatility spread between *Good* and *Bad Days* relative to the average volatility,

$$\emptyset_{RS} = \frac{RS^{-} - RS^{+}}{RS^{*}} \tag{9.15}$$

$$\emptyset_{YZ} = \frac{YZ^{-} - YZ^{+}}{YZ^{*}} \tag{9.16}$$

These ratios measure the level of asymmetry in volatilities in two different situations by comparing the difference of volatilities with the average level of volatility ($RS^*$and YZ^*) from both situations.

9.4 Empirical Results

During a bear market, investors often sell their assets and choose safer investment options. This effect is commonly known as 'Flight to quality'. We argue that this effect exists even in daily level also due to the presence of day traders in the markets. In the stock markets, if a security or indices take a downturn (During *Bad days*), then investors or daily traders hurry to close their positions to minimise their losses and consider putting money elsewhere. This causes high uncertainty and panic in the markets, finally leading to high volatility at the daily level when markets fall. In the case of an upturn or *Good Days*, investors or traders generally react slower as they will not be in hurry to change their portfolios. Therefore, we expect estimated volatility will be much lower in *Good Days*.

We first calculate the DRS and DYZ (see Eqs. 9.9 and 9.14) for 14 emerging stock indices in our data. We use the 10,000 bootstrap simulations for data of each country to generate standard errors. Table 9.3 reports the DRS and DYZ along with and standard error[8] and t-statistics for all the countries. We find that t-statistics for DRS are significant at 5% level for indices from eight emerging countries (Brazil, Czech Republic, Indonesia, Mexico, Pakistan, Philippines, South Africa, and

[8]Mean of DRS and DYZ generated through 10,000 bootstrap simulation is the almost same as actual estimate. Therefore, we have presented only the actual numbers in Tables 9.3 and 9.4 for brevity.

Table 9.3 Volatility differences between Good and Bad days (Bad days–Good days)—emerging countries

	Difference of RS			Difference of YZ		
Country	Actual	Std. Err.	t-stat	Actual	Std. Err.	t-stat
Brazil	0.00003	0.00001	3.03804	0.00003	0.00001	2.71298
China	0.00003	0.00002	1.61945	0.00004	0.00002	1.74050
Czech Rep	0.00004	0.00001	3.34787	0.00003	0.00001	3.06317
Egypt	0.00001	0.00001	0.52780	0.00001	0.00001	1.24490
India	0.00004	0.00003	1.38804	0.00002	0.00003	0.88740
Indonesia	0.00005	0.00001	6.45695	0.00005	0.00001	6.35047
Mexico	0.00002	0.00001	3.18628	0.00002	0.00001	3.21010
Nigeria	0.00001	0.00001	1.58563	0.00001	0.00001	1.01643
Pakistan	0.00002	0.00001	2.92841	0.00002	0.00001	2.74508
Philippines	0.00002	0.00000	4.91972	0.00002	0.00001	3.24948
Russia	0.00004	0.00002	1.85047	0.00003	0.00002	1.70140
S Africa	0.00003	0.00001	5.30212	0.00003	0.00000	5.18820
S Korea	0.00001	0.00001	1.26640	-0.00001	0.00001	-0.78735
Turkey	0.00004	0.00001	3.47226	0.00001	0.00001	0.98216

This table reports the actual volatility difference between *Good* and *Baddays* (*Baddays–Gooddays*) for 14 emerging countries listed in MSCI. The volatility differences were estimated from two different extreme values estimators, RS and YZ. We also report the standard errors and t-statistics obtained using bootstrap sampling of the actual data. The difference of mean VRatios from bootstrap sampling are almost same as the difference of actual VRatios therefore; we do not report it here

Turkey) out of fifteen. The t-statistic for DRS is significant for a stock index of Russia at 10% level. Although, for the other countries t-statistics are not significant but the value of DRS is positive. Hence, our results support the leverage effect to be common in emerging markets (EM). The comparison of DRS and DYZ in EM is presented in Fig. 9.1.

We also check whether we see a similar pattern exists in stock indices from developed countries (see Table 9.4; Fig. 9.2). In our study, all the 10 indices of developed countries show positive DRS with 7 (Dow Jones, NASDAQ Composite, S & P 500, FTSE 100, CAC 40, Nikkei 225, and Tokyo Price Index) of them significant at 5% level and 2 (DAX and EURO STOXX 50) of them at 10% level. The DRS value for Hong Kong Hang Seng index is positive (almost near to zero) but statistically insignificant. In our findings, the volatility differences in *Good* and *Bad Days* are more prominent in the case of developed indices.

We explore the issue further by examining the DYZ and found a similar result (see Table 9.3; Fig. 9.1). In the case of DYZ also, t-statistics are again significant at 5% level for seven countries (Brazil, Czech Republic, Indonesia, Mexico, Pakistan, Philippines, and South Africa) out of fourteen. The t-statistics for DYZ are significant for a stock index of China and Russia at 10% level. Our results show that

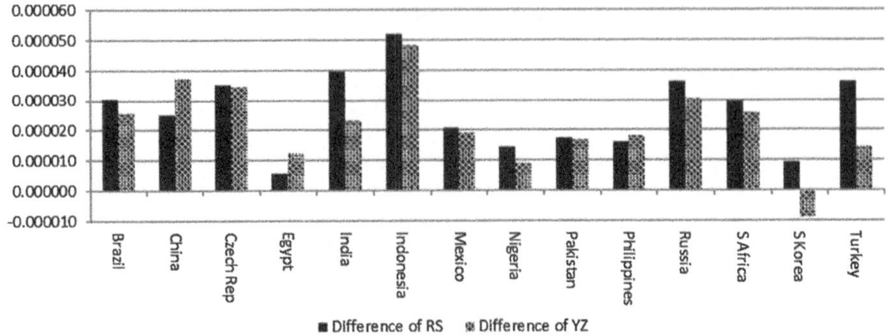

Fig. 9.1 Volatility difference between Good days and Bad days for stock indices—emerging countries.
Note This figure reports the volatility differences (RS and YZ) between *Good days* and *Bad days* for stock indices of all the emerging countries considered in this study. The differences were calculated by subtracting measured volatility of *Good days* from that of *Bad days*

Table 9.4 Volatility differences between Good and Bad days (Bad days–Good days)—developed countries

	Difference of RS			Difference of YZ		
Index name	DRS	Std. Err.	t-stat	DYZ	Std. Err.	t-stat
Dow Jones	0.00002	0.00001	2.96140	0.00002	0.00001	3.08892
NASDAQ composite	0.00002	0.00001	2.63521	0.00002	0.00001	1.30848
S & P 500	0.00002	0.00001	2.95975	0.00002	0.00001	3.21131
FTSE 100	0.00003	0.00001	3.00244	0.00002	0.00001	3.05391
DAX	0.00002	0.00001	1.86447	0.00000	0.00002	0.10616
CAC 40	0.00002	0.00001	2.10757	0.00001	0.00001	0.79481
EURO STOXX 50	0.00002	0.00001	1.85091	0.00002	0.00001	1.72501
Nikkei 225	0.00002	0.00001	2.44214	0.00002	0.00001	1.99248
Hang Seng	0.00000	0.00001	0.33655	0.00000	0.00001	0.22640
Tokyo price index	0.00002	0.00001	2.07657	0.00002	0.00001	1.81642

This table reports the actual volatility difference between *Good* and *Bad days* (*Bad days–Good days*) for 10 indices from developed countries. The volatility differences are estimated from two different extreme values estimators, RS and YZ. We also report the standard errors and t-statistics obtained using bootstrap sampling of the actual data. The difference of mean VRatios from bootstrap sampling are almost same as the difference of actual VRatios therefore; we do not report it here

almost all the countries with significant differences in RS and YZ are common (except China).

In the case of indices of developed countries (see Table 9.4; Fig. 9.2), all the stock indices show positive DYZ with 3 (Dow Jones, S & P 500, FTSE 100, and Nikkei 225) of them significant at 5% level and 2 (EURO STOXX 50 and Tokyo

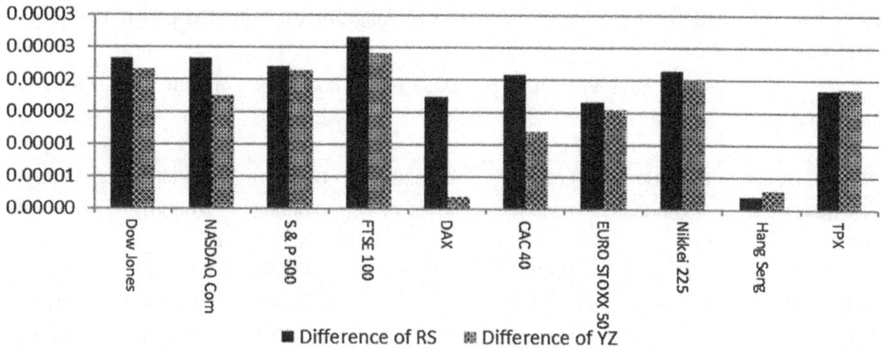

Fig. 9.2 Volatility difference between Good days and Bad days for stock indices—developed countries.
Note This figure reports the volatility differences (RS and YZ) between *Good days* and *Bad days* for all the developed stock indices considered in this study. The differences were calculated by subtracting measured volatility of *Good days* from that of *Bad days*

Table 9.5 Difference of Up volatility and Down volatility for both Good and Bad days—emerging countries

	Good Days Vol. Diff. (*Up–Down*)			*Bad Days* Vol. Diff. (*Up–Down*)		
Country	Actual	Std. Err.	t-stat	Actual	Std. Err.	t-stat
Brazil	0.00003	0.00001	2.04115	−0.00007	0.00002	−4.62460
China	−0.00010	0.00002	−6.00679	−0.00002	0.00002	−0.75385
Czech Rep	0.00000	0.00001	−0.25639	−0.00005	0.00002	−2.68957
Egypt	0.00005	0.00002	2.93774	−0.00002	0.00001	−1.55364
India	0.00000	0.00001	−0.41383	−0.00009	0.00005	−1.58013
Indonesia	0.00000	0.00001	−0.62345	−0.00009	0.00001	−6.82779
Mexico	0.00001	0.00001	1.60812	−0.00004	0.00001	−3.40668
Nigeria	−0.00002	0.00001	−2.83676	−0.00003	0.00002	−1.68226
Pakistan	0.00001	0.00001	2.17514	0.00001	0.00001	1.62890
Philippines	0.00000	0.00000	−0.61498	−0.00003	0.00000	−6.32561
Russia	−0.00001	0.00002	−0.46433	−0.00007	0.00003	−2.68494
S Africa	0.00001	0.00001	1.66080	−0.00004	0.00001	−4.57246
S Korea	−0.00003	0.00001	−3.93480	−0.00004	0.00001	−3.69573
Turkey	−0.00007	0.00001	−4.58434	−0.00004	0.00001	−3.40210

This table reports the actual difference between *Up* volatility and *Down* volatility for 14 emerging countries listed in MSCI. We report the differences for both *Good* and *Bad days*. The level of volatility is estimated through the RS. We also report the standard errors and t-statistics obtained using bootstrap sampling of the actual data. The mean differences from bootstrap sampling are almost same as the difference of actual estimation therefore; we do not report it here

Table 9.6 Difference of Up volatility and Down volatility for both Good and Bad days—developed countries

	Good days Vol. Diff. (*Up–Down*)			*Bad days* Vol. Diff. (*Up–Down*)		
Index name	Actual	Std. Err.	t-stat	Actual	Std. Err.	t-stat
Dow Jones	0.00000	0.00001	−0.66280	−0.00006	0.00001	−3.78659
NASDAQ composite	−0.00003	0.00001	−4.76279	−0.00002	0.00001	−1.71400
S & P 500	−0.00002	0.00001	−2.92493	−0.00004	0.00001	−3.31182
FTSE 100	0.00000	0.00001	0.14315	−0.00006	0.00001	−4.04467
DAX	−0.00003	0.00001	−2.32164	−0.00004	0.00001	−4.03343
CAC 40	−0.00003	0.00001	−2.82183	−0.00004	0.00002	−2.77970
EURO STOXX 50	−0.00004	0.00001	−3.20659	−0.00003	0.00001	−2.37342
Nikkei 225	0.00000	0.00001	−0.80174	−0.00001	0.00002	−0.71666
Hang Seng	−0.00001	0.00001	−0.83276	−0.00004	0.00001	−5.93402
Tokyo Price index	−0.00001	0.00001	−1.17526	−0.00002	0.00002	−1.18222

This table reports the actual difference between *Up* volatility and *Down* volatility for 10 indices from developed countries. We report the differences for both *Good* and *Bad days*. The level of volatility is estimated through the RS. We also report the standard errors and t-statistics obtained using bootstrap sampling of the actual data. The mean differences from bootstrap sampling are almost same as the difference of actual estimation therefore; we do not report it here

Price Index DAX) at 10% level. The DYZ values for other 3 indices (NASDAQ Composite, DAX CAC 40, and Hang Seng) indices are positive but not significant. The differences in DRS and DYZ values are due to consideration of opening jumps in YZ estimation. Overall results reveal a similar pattern in DRS and DYZ which supports the presence of leverage effect tin emerging markets. Moreover, it is more prevalent in developed markets. The probable reason behind that is the presence large number of traders and investors in stock markets of developed countries than that of EM markets.

We explore the results further to see whether any structural information about volatility that characterises the effect of *Good* and *Bad Days* can be identified. For the same purpose, we decompose the RS volatility estimation into *up volatility* and *down volatility* as shown earlier in Eqs. 9.10 and 9.11. We calculate the *up* and *down volatility* separately for both *Good* and *Bad Days* and then subtract *down volatility* from *up volatility* to make a comparison for both types of days. We also perform 10,000 bootstrap simulations to generate standard error and t-statistics (see Tables 9.5 and 9.6; Figs. 9.3 and 9.4).

The results (see Tables 9.5 and 9.6; Figs. 9.3 and 9.4) show that the differences of *up* and *down volatility* are not very obvious in the case of *Good Days*. The differences are positive for some countries and negative for the rest, hence not conclusive for *Good Days*. It is possible that there is no specific pattern of price movements during *Good Days*. Convincing evidence is present in the case of *Bad*

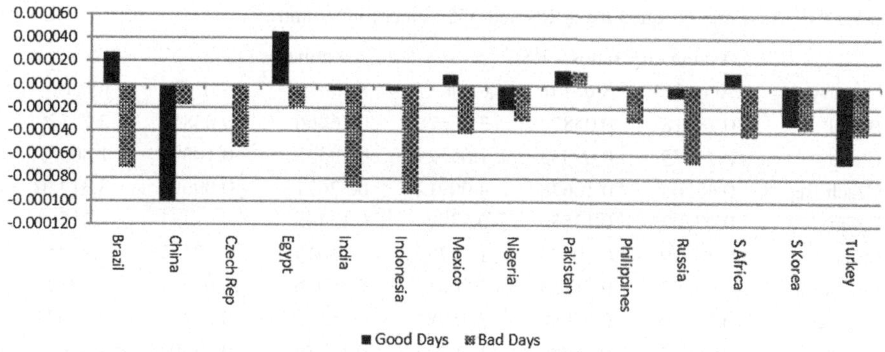

Fig. 9.3 Difference of Up volatility and Down volatility for both Good and Bad days—emerging countries.
Note This figure reports the actual difference between *Up volatility* and *Down volatility* for stock indices of all the emerging countries considered in this study. We report the differences for both *Good* and *Bad days*. The level of volatility is estimated through the RS

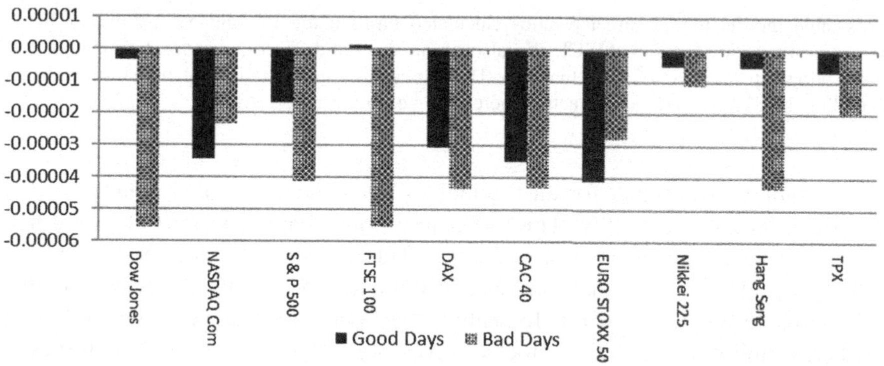

Fig. 9.4 Difference of Up volatility and Down volatility for both Good and Bad days—developed countries.
Note This figure reports the actual difference between *Up volatility* and *Down volatility* for all the developed stock indices considered in this study. We report the differences for both *Good* and *Bad days*. The level of volatility is estimated through the RS

Days. The volatility difference is negative for all the indices (indices from EM and developed countries) with most of them significant in *Bad Days*. This finding reveals that *Bad Days* are associated with panic sell which contributes towards high *down volatility* through momentum trading. This suggests a significant relationship between negative returns over the trading hours and *down volatility*. This evidence is consistent with the notion that in *down* market investors panic and initiate more sells than buys, this lead to larger price movements.

Tables 9.7; 9.8 and Figs. 9.5; 9.6 show the volatility asymmetry level (defined earlier in Eqs. 9.15 and 9.16). The level of asymmetry compares the difference of volatilities with the average level of volatility ($RS^{*}$and YZ^{*}) from both situations.

Table 9.7 Asymmetry ratios using RS and YZ—emerging countries

	Asymmetry ratios—RS			Asymmetry ratios—YZ		
Country	Actual	Std. Err.	t-stat	Actual	Std. Err.	t-stat
Brazil	0.18218	0.05870	3.06678	0.16266	0.05859	2.75129
China	0.15975	0.09333	1.65129	0.19335	0.10377	1.80357
Czech Rep	0.43506	0.10678	4.00912	0.32631	0.09690	3.31436
Egypt	0.07402	0.13536	0.53994	0.14446	0.11321	1.25584
India	0.36730	0.20589	1.64789	0.18019	0.17755	0.92857
Indonesia	0.65357	0.08288	7.90417	0.55066	0.07451	7.39692
Mexico	0.26740	0.07659	3.45282	0.25510	0.07315	3.44674
Nigeria	0.26875	0.15395	1.70323	0.14233	0.13407	1.02434
Pakistan	0.21109	0.07012	2.97674	0.20240	0.07115	2.80625
Philippines	0.35101	0.06970	5.01407	0.27643	0.08353	3.32963
Russia	0.17243	0.09243	1.85906	0.15093	0.08722	1.71511
S Africa	0.32541	0.05779	5.60803	0.29917	0.05444	5.46933
S Korea	0.13523	0.10438	1.29431	−0.07150	0.09058	−0.79133
Turkey	0.25502	0.07259	3.50782	0.08179	0.08388	0.99279

This table reports the asymmetry ratios calculated through the RS and YZ estimators for 14 emerging countries listed in MSCI. We also report the standard errors and t-statistics obtained using bootstrap sampling of the actual data. The average asymmetry ratios obtained from bootstrap sampling are almost same as the actual therefore; we do not report it here

These findings show that for all the indices (Developed and EM countries), *Bad Days* exhibit more volatility. This is because price changes in *Bad Days* are negatively skewed than those of *Good Days*. This is relevant since in *Bad Days*, a rational agent should purchase more stocks thinking price will rise eventually than he would during *Good Days*. In reality, they perceive that price will fall even further, enabling quick sell of stocks, drives price further away and contribute to market volatility. During *Good Days*, agents tend to relax and react slower unless they observe extreme jumps in positive returns. It creates a trading imbalance between Good and Bad Days which leads to asymmetry in volatilities. Overall our results are pervasive and not EM specific indices.

9.5 Robustness Check

The estimated volatility of *Good* and *Bad Days* are subject to the empirical model used and its' underlying assumptions. To match our estimated RS volatility, we also use YZ methodology which considers opening jumps over RS estimation. Overall our findings are similar and support our conjecture.

Table 9.8 Asymmetry ratios using RS and YZ—developed countries

	Asymmetry ratios—RS			Asymmetry ratios—YZ		
Index name	Actual	Std. Err.	t-stat	Actual	Std. Err.	t-stat
Dow Jones	0.36304	0.10584	3.38578	0.34365	0.09735	3.49068
NASDAQ composite	0.29491	0.10308	2.83606	0.14426	0.10878	1.32624
S & P 500	0.32395	0.09653	3.28647	0.31297	0.08734	3.52374
FTSE 100	0.30327	0.09607	3.16393	0.28914	0.09011	3.21607
DAX	0.13710	0.07353	1.85783	0.01151	0.08973	0.13382
CAC 40	0.16863	0.07809	2.15846	0.07028	0.08428	0.80207
EURO STOXX 50	0.12667	0.07068	1.85348	0.11041	0.06599	1.73181
Nikkei 225	0.28311	0.10523	2.67795	0.13870	0.06799	2.06269
Hang Seng	0.02593	0.07849	0.33897	0.01833	0.08466	0.23421
Tokyo price index	0.26782	0.11169	2.30506	0.14545	0.07461	1.88829

This table reports the asymmetry ratios calculated through the RS and YZ estimators for 10 indices from developed countries. We also report the standard errors and t-statistics obtained using bootstrap sampling of the actual data. The average asymmetry ratios obtained from bootstrap sampling are almost same as the actual therefore; we do not report it here

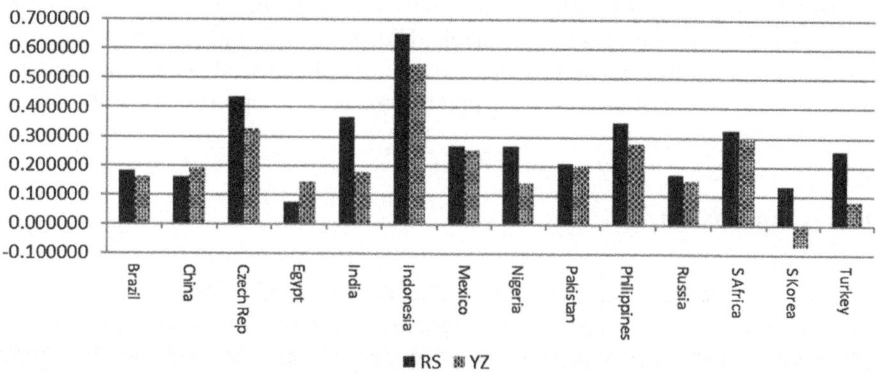

Fig. 9.5 Asymmetry ratios—emerging countries.
Note This figure reports the actual asymmetry ratios calculated through the RS and YZ estimators for stock indices of all the emerging countries considered in this study

The models used in this study are based on extreme values hence; it is possible that our results are impacted by outliers. To overcome that, we have checked our data range and removed all outlier values which fall in the range of top and bottom 5%.

There may be some overlapping of data in *Good* and *Bad Days* if the prices have not changed over a day. In this situation, OHLC prices will be same for a given day. This could be also due to misreporting of data which is very common in the case of EM indices. We have looked at our data carefully and estimated the volatility with overlapping and non-overlapping data separately for each index. The output doesn't

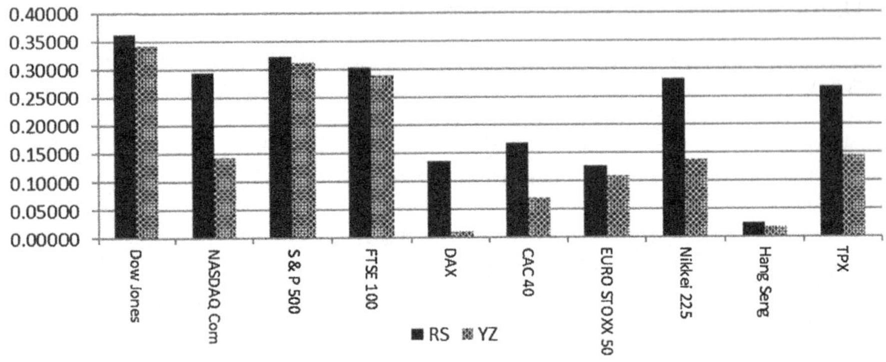

Fig. 9.6 Asymmetry ratios—developed countries.
Note This figure reports the actual asymmetry ratios calculated through the RS and YZ estimators for all the developed stock indices considered in this study

vary much and hence, continue to support our argument. However, we had to trim the data for some countries when daily OHLC prices were reported to be constant over the days for a very long period. This happens due to unavailability and misreporting of actual data.

We have repeated the analysis on 2007–08 (sub-prime crisis period) data for some indices for which data was available. However, the number of *Bad Days* was much higher than the number of *Good Days* during this period, we did not find any evidence against out conjecture. For brevity, we do not report the output.

9.6 Conclusion

We present evidence of an asymmetry in the unconditional volatility as we find that volatility in *Bad Days* is significantly higher than that of *Good Days*. This result is consistent with the theory of leverage effect and can also be explained by simple observation that says traders and investors hurry to close their positions to minimise their losses and consider putting money elsewhere during *Bad Days* and react slower in *Good Days* as there is no rush to rebalance their portfolios. In our findings, the volatility asymmetry is more prominent in the case of developed indices. The probable reason behind that is the presence large number of traders and investors in stock markets of developed countries compared to that of EM markets.

We also observe a dominance of *down volatility* over *up volatility* during *Bad Days*. However, the differences of *up* and *down volatility* are not very obvious in the case of *Good Days*. The differences are positive for some countries and negative for the rest, hence not conclusive for *Good Days*. Convincing evidence is present only in the case of *Bad Days*. This finding reveals that *Bad Days* are associated with panic selling which contributes towards high *down volatility* through momentum trading. *Good Days* are less likely to have any price pressure. We show that these facts are pervasive using index data from different emerging and developed countries.

Although these findings may not be used to form a proper long-term investment strategy due to high trading cost and relatively lesser time to trade, these results are important in explaining the pattern of market volatility and can influence investors' or traders' decisions to enter markets or close positions.

Our results have important implications for research in asset pricing. First, these results suggest that investors will be able to take better decision looking at price direction. If the market looks highly volatile, it is more likely that price will go down. Second, our empirical findings raise an interesting question for future research. Our investigation focuses on daily data (OHLC), but it also suggests that using high-frequency OHLC data may provide new insights. While we know remarkably little about this topic, the current approach offers an initial framework for further explorations. Although we do not aim to find complete explanations for this anomaly in this study, these methods exhibit novel evidence of directional asymmetry in volatility. There is a certain need for more work to develop a better understanding of how directions of prices affect volatility in financial assets.

References

Alizadeh, S., Brandt, M. W., & Diebold, F. X. (2002). Rangebased estimation of stochastic volatility models. *The Journal of Finance, 57*(3), 1047–1091.

Bekaert, G., & Wu, G. (2000). Asymmetric volatility and risk in equity markets. *Review of Financial Studies, 13*(1), 1–42.

Bekaert, G., Engstrom, E., & Ermolov, A. (2015). Bad environments, good environments: A non-gaussian asymmetric volatility model. *Journal of Econometrics, 186*(1), 258–275.

Ball, C. A., & Torous, W. N. (1984). The maximum likelihood estimation of security price volatility: Theory, evidence, and application to option pricing. *Journal of Business, 57*(1), 97–112.

Barndorff-Nielsen, O. E., Hansen, P. R., Lunde, A., & Shephard, N. (2008). Designing realized kernels to measure the ex post variation of equity prices in the presence of noise. *Econometrica, 76*(6), 1481–1536.

Black, F. (1976). Studies of stock price volatility changes. In *Proceedings of the 1976 Meetings of the American Statistical Association*, pp. 171–181.

Bollerslev, T. (1986). Generalized autoregressive conditional heteroskedasticity. *Journal of econometrics, 31*(3), 307–327.

Brandt, M., & Diebold, F. X. (2006). A no-arbitrage approach to range-based estimation of return covariances and correlations. *Journal of Business, 79,* 61–74.

Campbell, J. Y., & Hentschel, L. (1992). No news is good news: An asymmetric model of changing volatility in stock returns. *Journal of Financial Economics, 31,* 281–318.

Chen, X., & Ghysels, E. (2011). News—Good or bad—And its impact on volatility predictions over multiple horizons. *Review of Financial Studies, 24*(1), 46–81.

Chou, R. Y. T. (2005). Forecasting financial volatilities with extreme values: the conditional autoregressive range (CARR) model. *Journal of Money, Credit, and Banking, 37*(3), 561–582.

Chou, R. Y., Chou, H., & Liu, N. (2010). Range volatility models and their applications in finance. In *Handbook of quantitative finance and risk management* (pp. 1273–1281). Springer US.

Christie, A. A. (1982). The stochastic behavior of common stock variances: Value, leverage and interest rate effects. *Journal of Financial Economics, 10*(4), 407–432.

Corwin, S. A., & Schultz, P. (2012). A simple way to estimate bid-ask spreads from daily high and low prices. *The Journal of Finance, 67*(2), 719–760.

El Babsiri, M., & Zakoian, J. M. (2001). Contemporaneous asymmetry in GARCH processes. *Journal of Econometrics, 101*(2), 257–294.

Engle, R. F. (1982). Autoregressive conditional heteroscedasticity with estimates of the variance of United Kingdom inflation. *Econometrica, 50,* 987–1007.

Engle, R. F., & Ng, V. K. (1993). Measuring and testing the impact of news on volatility. *The Journal of Finance, 48*(5), 1749–1778.

French, K. R., & Roll, R. (1986). Stock return variances: The arrival of information and the reaction of traders. *Journal of Financial Economics, 17*(1), 5–26.

French, K. R., Schwert, G. W., & Stambaugh, R. F. (1987). Expected stock returns and volatility. *Journal of Financial Economics, 19,* 3–29.

Garman, M. B., & Klass, M. J. (1980). On the estimation of security price volatilities from historical data. *Journal of Business, 53,* 67–78.

Harris, L. (1986). A transaction data study of weekly and intradaily patterns in stock returns. *Journal of Financial Economics, 16*(1), 99–117.

Horst, E. T., Rodriguez, A., Gzyl, H., & Molina, G. (2012). Stochastic volatility models including open, close, high and low prices. *Quantitative Finance, 12*(2), 199–212.

Kayal, P., & Maheswaran, S. (2016). *A study of excess volatility of gold and silver.* Paper presented at Commodity Markets Conference, Leibniz University Hannover, Germany, 3–4 June.

Kayal, P., & Maheswaran, S. (2017). Is USD-INR really an excessively volatile currency pair? *Journal of Quantitative Economics, 15*(2), 329–342.

Kayal, P., & Maheswaran, S. (2018). Speed of price adjustment towards market efficiency: Evidence from emerging countries. *Journal of Emerging Market Finance, 17*(1_suppl), S112–S135.

Kunitomo, N. (1992). Improving the Parkinson method of estimating security price volatilities. *Journal of Business, 65*(2), 295–302.

Maheswaran, S., & Kumar, D. (2013). An automatic bias correction procedure for volatility estimation using extreme values of asset prices. *Economic Modelling, 33,* 701–712.

Magdon-Ismail, M., & Atiya, A. F. (2003). A maximum likelihood approach to volatility estimation for a Brownian motion using high, low and close price data. *Quantitative Finance, 3* (5), 376–384.

Nelson, D. B. (1991). Conditional heteroskedasticity in asset returns: A new approach. *Econometrica, 59,* 347–370.

Palandri, A. (2015). Do negative and positive equity returns share the same volatility dynamics? *Journal of Banking & Finance, 58,* 486–505.

Parkinson, M. (1980). The extreme value method for estimating the variance of the rate of return. *Journal of Business, 53*(1), 61–65.

Rogers, L. C. G., & Satchell, S. E. (1991). Estimating variance from high, low and closing prices. *The Annals of Applied Probability, 1*(4), 504–512.

Schwert, G. W. (1989). Why does stockmarket volatility change over time? *Journal of Finance, 44,* 1115–1153.

Schwert, G. W. (1990). Stockmarket volatility. *Financial Analysts Journal, 46,* 23–34.

Taylor, S. J. (1986). *Modelling financial time series.* Chichester: Wiley.

Yang, D., & Zhang, Q. (2000). Drift-independent volatility estimation based on high, low, open, and close prices. *The Journal of Business, 73*(3), 477–492.

Part III
Regional Economic Development Issues

Chapter 10
Structural Change and Economic Growth in India—A State-Wise Analysis

Kshamanidhi Adabar and Trupti Mayee Sahoo

Abstract This paper reviews the recent literature on structural change, human capital and economic growth and examines the relationship between structural change and economic growth across 14 major Indian states from 1993–94 to 2011–12. Calculating income share for various economic activities and following in the line with Dietrich for NAV and MLI, McMillan and Rodrik for within and static effects, Timmer et al. for within effect, static and dynamic effects, it estimates structural change in income for 14 major states from 1993–94 to 2011–12. There has been an increasing trend in patterns of structural change as evident by NAV and MLI across sectors to contribute to the growth process of per capita real income. Using catch up regression for absolute convergence, it finds the evidence of absolute beta divergence meaning by relatively richer states have grown faster than poorer counterparts. Including structural change in income and employment in industrial sector (high intensity) along with other control variables such as per capita investment, human capital, initial level of per capita real income in cross-sectional regressions, it finds significant contribution of structural change for economic growth across Indian states during this period. However, some of the fundamental variables are although in expected line, they are not significant which calls for re-examination of these issues within suitable framework such as dynamic panel data analysis that will sort out some of the problems encountered in cross-sectional growth regression.

Keywords Structural change · Economic growth · Human capital
Convergence

K. Adabar (✉) · T. M. Sahoo
Centre for Studies in Economics and Planning (CSEP),
Central University of Gujarat, Sector-29, Gandhinagar, India
e-mail: kshama@cug.ac.in

T. M. Sahoo
e-mail: trupticug@gmail.com

A. K. Mishra et al. (eds.), *Current Issues in the Economy and Finance of India*,
Springer Proceedings in Business and Economics,
https://doi.org/10.1007/978-3-319-99555-7_10

10.1 Introduction

There has been vast literature on economic growth. Many studies have analyzed various determinants of economic growth within neoclassical and endogenous growth theory framework to explain differences in levels and growth rates of income across countries and regions (Barro 1991; Mankiw et al. 1992; Levine and Renelt 1992; Acemoglu et al. 2001 among others). They have identified saving or investment rate, population growth rate, urbanization rate, human capital, levels of technology, size of government, rule of law, quality of social and political institutions etc. that affect economic growth. Recently there are a few studies that attempted to analyze structural change and economic growth and productivity (Cortuk and Singh 2013; Sen 2016; Teixeira and Queiros 2016; Timmer and De Vries 2009 among others). Structural change and economic growth may be correlated and impacting with each other over time. Since economic growth is originating out of various sectors, the nature and patterns of these structural changes will affect the quality of growth processes.

Structural transformation generally referred to as long term changes in the composition of an aggregate that is attributable to changes in the relative significance of the sectors in the economy to changes in the location of economic activity (urbanization) and to other concomitant aspect of industrialization which take place together (see, Singariya 2014). Structural change in modern development include a relocation of workforce from agriculture towards non-agricultural production. Most often it has recognized that, structural changes do not only characterized economic development, they are also indispensable for economic growth. Structural change as a source of economic growth has been excessively studied in literature on endogenous growth (Kaldor 1996; Lewis 1954; Romer 1987; Fisher 1939; Clark 1940/51; Kuznets 1971). Because structural change come out with a change in final demand, new method of production, which allows for a more efficient allocation of resources or innovation of a new product line which itself augment the value of the produce, that form the essence of the growth process (Zagler 2009). In addition to that, development of an economy is also regarded as a process that entails sustained increase in output per-capita accompanied by structural change in productive capital and employment (Roy 1980). However structural change does not come without a cost. The most evident social cost of structural change is unemployment and underemployment. The reason is that, firm producing a product in a declining market will lay off workers. Workers specializing in a particular mode of production make their qualification redundant until these workers re-qualify and are matched to a new job in an expanding product segment or in a new technology, these workers will suffer from the spell of unemployment (Zagler 2009). India is pragmatic example of such growth. Because unlike other developed and developing countries, India is not following same kind of structural change in terms of income and employment (see, Papola 2012). As a result of which economic growth has been accompanied by a much lower rate of growth in employment and by zero or negative growth of what the ILO has termed as "Decent Work" (Bagchi 2005).

The higher economic growth in the post reform period has been accompanied by a slower growth in employment. Employment growth has infact, declined with the acceleration of growth rate of GDP. Thus, structural change has not delivered on employment front as they have on GDP front (Papola 2012). This type of growth is widely recognized as "jobless growth".

Therefore, for a developing country like India where socio economic problem such as poverty, unemployment and inequality influences policy decisions it becomes important to study structural change and its relationship with economic growth and employment, so that growth and employment impulses emerging sectors could be identified and foster to sustain economic growth momentum. An in depth understanding of structural change from time to time become all more important for policy makers to design effective policies to achieve broader objective of inclusive growth. In this backdrop, the present study attempts to examine structural change across 14 Indian states in term of income. It also tries to relate it with economic along with other factors of growth from 1993–94 to 2011–12 within growth regression framework. The following section gives the review of literature. Section third deals with data and methodology. Empirical results are discussed in section four. A concluding remark is given at the end.

10.2 Literature Review

History has witnessed that economic growth is completely associated with structural change. Structural economists like Kuznets empirically validated that growth is conveyed by change in sectorial composition. Structural change is a long process that reallocates labor and capital from one sector to another resulting in differences in labor and capital productivity across different sectors. Demand side factor such as income elasticity of demand is considered as the driving force behind changes in product structure of an economy. The supply side factors such as change in technology, geographical condition, intuitional responses and trade inter-industry division of labor also led to relocation of activities from one sector to another sector. Whatever may the reason of structural change, it leads to economic growth in all aspect.

By using Generalized Method of Movements of dynamic panel data model for highly developed 21 OECD countries for the period 1960–2011 and for transition and Mediterranean countries over a shorter time period from 1990 to 2011, Teixeira and Queiros (2016) analyzed the impact of two core variables such as (1) human capital measured by the average educational attainment of adults (2) structural change measured by share of employment in knowledge/technology intensive industries on economic growth. Some control variables like investment, public consumption, population growth, institutional environment have used in the study which considered as relevant factors for economic growth. The study has observed that, countries with a higher stock of human capital tend to grow faster than others. A higher stock of human capital improves the workers skill which has a positive impact on productivity. Countries that experiencing changes in productive structure towards a greater share of technology/knowledge intensive industries will tend to observe high economic growth. Therefore, growth rate of countries that observe an increase in the specialization in high level industries tend to be higher. The estimated result replicates that, the estimated, isolated impact of human capital and structural change on economic growth is higher for OECD countries for long period of time (1960–2011) than European and Mediterranean countries over shorter time span (1990–2011). It seems evident that, the effects of the interaction between structural change and human capital only appear in long term yielding opposite results in shorter period. Regarding the control variable it has observed that, investment/physical capital variable plays an important role in economic growth both for more developed, western countries and eastern European, emergent economies. High public consumption can create market distortions than negatively affect economic growth. The study confirms that, a negative relationship between population growth and economic growth for developed OECD countries but it failed to find any evidence that population growth matters for economic growth for less developed countries. It has observed that, more democratic, freer countries have on average higher economic growth.

Sen (2016) analyzed various factors responsible for structural change in different countries like Malaysia, Republic Korea, Taipei, China and India etc. it has observed that, countries that have been able to successfully transfer workers from low productivity to high productivity sectors are seen to have sustained inclusive growth. It has argued that, the pace of structural transformation is determined by two independent set of factors such as the demand for labor from high productivity sectors and the supply of labor from low productivity sectors. Further, both government failures and market failures can negatively affect the demand for labor from high productivity sectors as well as constrain mobility of labor from low productivity sectors. Government failures such as labor regulations and product market regulations can have negative impact on the demand for labor in high productivity sector such as manufacturing, while land policies can create impediments in the smooth out movement of labor from low productivity sectors such as agriculture. Market failure such as lack of coordination in investment and credit market imperfections can have negative impact on the demand for labor in the modern sector of the economy unless addressed by effective industrial and financial policies while human capital-related market failures can limit the supply of skilled workers from low productivity sectors to high productivity sectors. With respect to India, the review has suggested that, stringent labor regulations, burdensome land acquisition policies, market failure related to human capital formation and skill development of labor force act as hindrances in the path of structural transformation. Given the very large share of workers employed in Indian agriculture and need to increase the rate of structural transformation in the economy requires easing government policies relating to functioning of land and labor market.

McGreor and Verspagen (2016) have analyzed the structural change process of Asian countries, observed that, structural change and productivity growth are interrelated because broad sectors of the economy offer different possible ways for productivity growth. In particular, sectors in which more developed countries tend to relocate more labor than developing countries, tend to offer better opportunities for reaching high productivity levels. The agriculture sector dominates in low income countries, the manufacturing sector as well as service sector rise in middle income countries and the manufacturing share falls in high income countries with service sector. The findings revealed that, productivity growth within the sector is in most of the cases, the largest component of productivity growth in Asia. This is called static structural effect which is especially strong in countries with intermediate level of productivity growth. Whereas the dynamic structural effect had a negative impact on the Asian productivity growth. The dynamic effect measures the interaction between the change of sectorial employment share and change in the productivity of in a sector. The negative effect in many cases results from a process of deindustrialization where manufacturing declines in terms of employment share but at the same time it shows strong productivity increases. It has observed that structural changes are most important variable in determining potential productivity growth.

Dietrich (2011) has observed that, aggregate growth causes structural change and in terms of employment or in terms of real value added for most of the countries especially those with largest economics. Here, structural change decelerated in every short period of time and accelerated in every long period of time. Economic growth has a decelerating impact on structural change if the structural change measured in terms of change in employment. If the structural change measured in terms of real value added, the aggregate impact is positive which means that, change in sectorial structure of output is driven by changes in demand due to rising income or productivity growth differences. Second for the opposite case, that structural changes cause economic growth, the result for the employment and real value-added show less significant result, but the conclusion remains the same as structural change promotes economic growth or at least does not decelerate it. For France, Japan, Netherlands and US for the case of employment and for Germany, Italy and US for the case of real value added, a significant positive influence of structural change on economic growth has observed. Only for UK the result is inconclusive in this matter. It appears to be the case that, rigidities impede growth and therefore structural change is needed for economic growth.

There are many studies focusing on nature and patterns of structural change of different sectors of states as well as Indian economy. Setthy (2003) has analyzed the structural change across states over the period from 1980–81 to 1999–2000 by using the gross and net SDP and per capita SDP data. To observe the nature of structural change, sectorial composition GSDP and NSDP have examined based on different base period like 1960–61, 1970–71, 1980–81 and 1993–94. Until 1980s the share of agriculture has remained at one half or above for many states like Bihar, Uttar Pradesh, Madhya Pradesh, Rajasthan, Orissa, Punjab and Haryana and Himachal Pradesh. The share of service sector has risen in almost all states but the most rapid expansion has taken place in states like Kerala and Maharashtra. The manufacturing sector has also experienced relatively adverse terms of trade in 1990s.

Rao (1979) has analyzed various fact about structural change in Indian economy for the period 1950–51 to 1976–77 and observed that, there is a fall in the share of primary sector in each of three sub periods covered the period 1950–1977. The share of secondary sector fell marginally in the first period and rises in the second and third period while the share tertiary sector recorded a rise in all these three periods. Bhattacharya and Mitra (1990, 1993) have analyzed about growth of service sector and its implications in India for the time period 1950–51 to 1986–87. They have observed that service sector is growing much faster than the commodity sector. It appears that income from service sector is growing much faster than the demand generated for service by commodity sector. These changes are in the direction of modernization and increasing share of secondary and tertiary sector. Nevertheless, Indian economy continue to be dominated by unorganized and private sector. However, starling feature of structural change is the failure of occupational structure to coincide with sectorial NDP structure. Papola (2012) has analyzed the process of structural change in India for the time period 1950 to 2004. He has divided the whole period into four parts from independence to mid-1960s, mid 1960 to 1980s, 1980 to early 1990s and from 1990s to 2004–05. It has observed that, the first three decades rate of economic growth followed by industrial sector.

Cortuk and Singh (2013) examined the changes in growth rate and how the rate of growth is different for 16 major Indian states for the period 2000–2006. It also analyzes the relationship between growth rate and structural change between states for the same period. The regression between SDP per capita and growth rate of the states shows a slight positive relationship which indicates the phenomenon of divergence among Indian states. Again, the regression between the structural change index (NAV) and growth rate of states shows somewhat flatter regression line through with a positive slope indicating a weak positive relationship between structural change and growth over this period. There is a clear negative relationship observed between per capita SDP and structural change. This indicates that India's richer states have seen less structural change over this period. The basic regression result shows that structural change In Indian economy is significant in explaining growth of economy for the period 2000–2006 but not vice versa. Growth does not seem to lead to structural change. However, the result emerges only if specification of disturbance term is carefully done. In particular, the study has allowed hetero-scedastic, auto-correlated type of AR (1) and cross-sectional correlated error terms. Otherwise both the lagged growth and lagged structural change have insignificant effects in explaining its impact on growth and structural change of current period. The study also analyzed that, the growth is more persistent and cumulative in richer states.

Bagchi et al. (2005) have analyzed the how Gujarat model of growth has benefited most of the population for the period from 1970–71 to 2000–01. It has observed that economic growth is sustained by growth of tertiary and secondary sector which has a little impact on the growth rate of primary sector. Growth rate of service sector has increased from 5% during 1970s to 7% during 1980s further to 8% during in 1990s. Within the tertiary sector, trade, hotels, Insurance, storage, transport, communication and real estate play a leading role in generating income growth during these periods. Therefore, it seems that the economy of Gujarat grew in a volatile and unbalanced fashion over the period under consideration. Agriculture accounted for 52% of workforce and 13% of NSDP during 2000–01. Such a discrepancy seriously damaging the implications for income and security of people engaged in the sector. The share of number of factory employees to the all India total has increased only marginally, but the corresponding shares of productive capital, value of output and net value added increased at a much faster rate especially in 1990s. The factory sector has undergone a high degree of concentration than in the rest of India. Similarly, in case of manufacturing sector the share of the sector in GDP is much higher than the share of employment. The productivity of labor in manufacturing sector was also more than its wage rate.

10.3 Data and Methodology

This study is based on secondary data for 14 major states. To analyze structural change in term of income, data on disaggregated NSDP are collected from online EPW research foundation for the period 1993–94 to 2011–12. Disaggregated NSDP for this period corresponds to three different series such as 1993–94, 1999–00 and 2004–05. Series 1993–94, 1999–00 are converted to 2004–05 series to arrive at a comparable data for the total period. To understand sectorial contribution to NSDP of each state, percentage is used. NAV and MLI are calculated using these sectoral shares in income and are considered as structural change in income. Trend growth rate of per capita real income at 2004–05 constant prices is estimated from semi-log model which takes into account all years during a period. This is treated as dependent variable in case of regression analysis. Similarly, enrolment and gross enrolment ratio for higher education, and population data are also collected from online EPW research foundation database. Enrolment per ten thousand population is used as proxy human capital for 1993–2011 and GER for 2004–2011. Credits extended by all scheduled commercial banks are taken as proxy for investment data from www.rbi.org.in. Share of employment in industry sector is used from different quinquennial round for 1993–2011. This could be considered as another proxy for structural change in employment.

10.3.1 Estimation of Structural Change in Income

Structural change is calculated using the following methodology as available in the recent literature. This estimated structural change is alternately considered as one of control variables in Eq. (10.5) to explain differences in growth rate of per capita real income across states in India.

Norm of Absolute Value Index

The norm of absolute value (NAV) is a simplest index to measure structural change given by Dietrich (2009). Let ϕi, T be the share of sector i in the final period T and $\phi_{i,S}$ be the share of sector i in the initial period S. The NAV index can be written as

$$\mathrm{NAV} = \frac{1}{2}\sum_{i}^{S} \left| \Phi_{i,T} - \Phi_{i,S} \right| \tag{10.1}$$

NAV index can take a value from zero, if the sectorial shares remain constant, to unity, if the change in all sectors is at its highest implying that the whole economy undergoes a total change. According to this index, structural change is equal to the overall change in the distribution of economic activity across the sector.

Modified Lilien Index

Lilien index was originally used to measure the sectorial growth rate for the demand for labor from period S to period T and employed to measure the degree of liquidity of factor allocation. However, Deitrich (2012) modified the Lilien index by augmenting it with weights of the share of the sector in both periods. The MLI can be written as follows.

$$MLI = \sqrt{\sum_{i}^{S} \Phi_{i,S}\Phi_{i,T}\left(\log\frac{\Phi_{i,S}}{\Phi_{i,T}}\right)^2} \tag{10.2}$$

A low MLI implies that the structural change in the economy is taking place at a slow rate, while a high MLI means that structural change is occurring at a rapid rate. A major drawback of the MLI and NAV indices is that while they provide a useful summary of the change in the structure of the economy, they do not provide any information on how the change in the economy impacts productivity.

McMillan and Rodrik Index

McMillan and Rodrik (2011) consider the base period employment shares and final period productivity levels. More specifically, the change in labor productivity is decomposed as where Δy is the change in aggregate labor productivity between final and initial period, and y_{it} and y_{is} are the sectorial labor productivity levels in the final and initial period, respectively. Similarly, ϕ_{it} and ϕ_{is} are the final and initial employment shares of the various sectors. The first term is positive when the weighted change in labor productivity levels in sectors is positive, and reflects the contribution to overall productivity change from an increase in sectorial labor productivity. This is referred to as the within effect. The second term in Eq. 10.3 is the reallocation effect, which reflects the change in labor productivity due to reallocation of employment across sectors, and is positive when labor moves from less to more productive sectors. This is also referred to as structural change in McMillan and Rodrik (2011) and Hansen et al. (2001).

$$\Delta Y = \sum_i \left(y_{i,T} - y_{i,S}\right)\Phi_{i,S} + \sum_i \left(\Phi_{i,T} - \Phi_{i,S}\right)y_{i,T} \tag{10.3}$$

Timmer and De Vries Index

Timmer and De Vries (2009) argue that the structural change term in the McMillan and Rodrik index is only a static measure of the reallocation effect as it depends on the differences in productivity level and not their growth rates. They use the base periods for the productivity levels as well as employment share, and introduces a third interaction term.

$$\Delta Y = \sum_i^s \left(y_{i,T} - y_{i,S}\right)\Phi_{i,S} + \sum_i^s \left(\Phi_{i,T} - \Phi_{i,S}\right)y_{i,S} + \sum_i^s \left(y_{i,T} - y_{i,S}\right)\left(\Phi_{i,T} - \Phi_{i,S}\right) \tag{10.4}$$

Here, the first term as before reflects the contribution to overall productivity change from an increase in sectorial labor productivity (the 'within effect'). In the second term, the term within parenthesis would be positive for sectors that have witnessed an increase in employment share and negative for sectors that have experienced a decline in employment share. So, a positive second term would imply that sectors, which witnessed an increase in employment share, were the ones that had a higher level of initial productivity. The third term, which is the interaction term, represents the joint effect of changes in sectorial productivity levels and employment shares. A positive term implies that workers are moving into sectors where productivity levels are increasing.

Thus, the reallocation effect term in Eq. (10.3) is broken into two different terms in Eq. (10.4) where the first term represents if labor has moved into sectors that have above average productivity levels and the second term indicates if sectors that have witnessed an increase in employment shares have also experienced productivity growth. De Vries et al. (2015) refer to the first term as 'static reallocation effect' and the second term as 'dynamic reallocation effect'.

Growth Regression Framework

In the line with Teixeira and Queiros (2016), econometric specification is based on catch up equation (Barro and Sala-i-Martin 2003) that can be given as

$$Y_i = \beta_0 + \beta_1 IPCIi + \beta_2 SCI_i + \beta_3 INV_i + \beta_4 SCI_i + \beta_5 HC_i + \beta_6 (SC_i \times HC_i) + u_i \tag{10.5}$$

where

Y_i	is the trend growth rate of per capita real income of state *i*
IPC	Initial level of per capita income
SCI	Structural change in income
INV	Average per capita investment
SCE	Structural change in employment in industrial sector
HC	Enrollment in higher education per thousand population
$HCI \times HC$	Interaction between structural change in employment in industrial sector and enrollment in higher education per thousand population
u	random error term
i	1, 2, … 14 Indian states.

10.4 Empirical Results on Structural Change in Income

Using Eqs. (10.1) and (10.2), NAV and MLI are calculated and presented in Table 10.1. These indices are based on the change in income shares from 1993–94 to 2011–12. This period is divided into three sub-periods: 1993–1999, 2004–2011 and 1993–2011. NAV index lies "between" 0 and 1. Except Andhra Pradesh and West Bengal, NAV index for all other states is greater than one for all the sub-periods. According to this index structural change is equal to the overall change in the

Table 10.1 NAV and MLI in income across 14 states from 1993–94 to 2011–12

Index		NAV			MLI	
Time Period	1993–1999	2004–2011	1993–2011	1993–99	2004–2011	1993–2011
AP	0.85	0.75	1.07	0.25	0.48	0.34
BI	1.32	2.24	1.12	0.78	0.38	0.45
GJ	1.20	2.33	1.18	0.66	0.36	0.34
HY	1.52	2.18	1.17	0.58	0.40	0.42
KN	1.30	1.64	1.31	0.45	0.39	0.35
KR	1.58	3.25	1.13	1.40	0.39	0.66
MP	1.17	1.11	1.40	0.33	0.48	0.34
MH	1.30	2.07	0.97	0.63	0.30	0.37
OR	1.50	1.71	1.43	0.49	0.48	0.42
PN	1.26	1.75	1.33	0.62	0.42	0.44
RJ	0.97	1.57	1.18	0.53	0.36	0.32
TN	1.11	2.08	1.12	0.68	0.36	0.33
UP	1.07	1.39	1.21	0.41	0.38	0.33
WB	0.57	6.94	6.48	2.85	2.90	0.16

Source Author's calculation from Eqs. (10.1) and (10.2)

distribution of economic activity across the sector. One of the possible explanations for this high index is due to the conversion of series 1993–94 into 2004–05 which might have resulted in over estimation of the value of income or output before the year 2004–05.

Lilien index is originally used to measure the degree of liquidity of factor reallocation. Dietrich (2012) modified the Lilien index (MLI) by augmenting with weights of the share of sectors in both periods. A low MLI implies that the structural change in the economy is taking place at a slow rate, while a high MLI indicates that structural change in occurring at a rapid rate. The calculated values for this index for different periods are given in Table 10.1. During 1993–2011, MLI ranges from 0.16 (West Bengal) to 0.66 (Kerala). This means that structural change in West Bengal is slow and it is high in Kerala. Since this estimation is different from Sen Gupta et al. (2016) in terms of sample size and time period. NAV and MLI index values may not be comparable.

McMillan and Rodrik (2011) decompose change in labour productivity based on period employment share and final period productivity levels to evaluate the contribution to growth arising from reallocation of workers/labour force across the sectors (within and between effects). Using this concept from Eq. (10.3), decomposition is evaluated in per capita income/output and the estimated average productivity is given in Table 10.2.

During 1993–2011, within effect is more than between effect to contribute to growth of per capita income for all the states. Positive within effect reflects the increase in sectoral productivity to overall change in growth whereas, positive between effects reflects the change in labour productivity due to reallocation of employment across sectors from less to more productive sectors. The calculated values for this decomposition are in lower side for all these states as population is used instead of employment.

De Vries et al. (2015) argue that structural change estimation in McMillan and Rodrik index is only a static measure of the reallocation effect as it depends on the differences in productivity level and not their growth rates. They suggest alternative decomposition method to account for differences in growth and levels across the sectors, which may be negatively correlated. It uses the base periods for productivity levels and employment share as well as joint effect of changes in sectoral productivity levels and employment shares to evaluate within effect, static effect and dynamic effect. In fact, the reallocation effect is divided into static and dynamic effect. Static effect relates to movement in labour from less average productive to above average productivity levels. Dynamic effect indicates if sectors that have witnessed an increase in employment share have also experienced productivity growth. Table 10.3 reveals the calculation of this index. The values of static effects are negative for industry that has not moved less productive sector to more productive sectors. Since it is based on population figure instead of employment, values of within, static and dynamic effect for decomposition may need further examination.

Table 10.2 McMillan and Rodrik index for 14 states from 1993 to 2011

Time period	1993–1999			2004–2011			1993–2011		
Decomposition	Within effect	Between effect	Total growth	Within effect	Between effect	Total growth	Within effect	Between effect	Total growth
AP	0.51	−0.14	0.38	0.57	−0.10	0.47	0.63	−0.12	0.51
BI	3.18	−0.74	2.45	−0.10	0.00	−0.10	1.04	−0.27	0.77
GJ	0.57	0.14	0.71	−0.14	0.03	−0.11	0.15	0.08	0.23
HY	2.05	−0.38	1.67	−0.10	−0.02	−0.11	0.66	−0.09	0.57
KN	0.96	−0.05	0.92	−0.19	0.01	−0.18	0.20	0.05	0.24
KR	−0.47	0.15	−0.32	0.01	−0.03	−0.02	−0.02	0.02	0.00
MP	2.27	−0.26	2.00	−0.18	−0.02	−0.20	0.69	−0.07	0.62
MH	−0.47	0.04	−0.43	−0.01	0.06	0.05	−0.22	0.05	−0.17
OR	3.37	−0.22	3.15	−0.12	0.02	−0.11	1.08	0.11	1.19
PN	1.73	−0.57	1.16	−0.03	0.00	−0.03	0.61	−0.18	0.43
RJ	1.16	−0.30	0.86	−0.08	0.02	−0.06	0.36	−0.09	0.27
TN	0.19	0.18	0.38	−0.07	0.00	−0.07	0.09	0.07	0.16
UP	−0.31	−0.12	−0.43	−0.14	−0.02	−0.16	−0.26	−0.04	−0.30
WB				−6.90	−0.10	−7.00	0.37	0.03	0.39

Source Author's calculation from Eq. (10.3)

Table 10.3 de Vries, Timmer and de Vries index for 14 states from 1993 to 2011

	1993–1999				2004–2011				1993–2011			
	Within	Static	Dynamic	Total growth	Within	Static	Dynamic	Total growth	Within	Static	Dynamic	Total growth
AP	4.61	−1.30	−0.08	3.22	6.25	−1.85	0.80	5.20	13.21	−3.61	1.24	10.83
BI	27.58	−5.45	−1.93	20.19	−1.10	−0.82	0.80	−1.12	21.92	−7.27	1.21	15.85
GJ	5.45	−1.65	3.07	6.87	−1.50	−0.35	0.69	−1.16	3.17	−2.10	3.10	4.18
HY	19.29	−3.25	−0.57	15.47	−1.08	−1.05	0.87	−1.26	13.87	−5.21	3.40	12.06
KN	9.64	−1.33	0.85	9.16	−2.13	−0.65	0.80	−1.99	4.12	−2.43	3.35	5.05
KR	−1.00	−11.31	12.81	0.49	0.14	−1.14	0.78	−0.22	−0.32	−18.78	18.38	−0.72
MP	21.83	−1.54	−1.10	19.20	−2.00	−1.46	1.29	−2.17	14.50	−3.91	2.17	12.75
MH	−4.26	−1.63	2.03	−3.87	−0.16	0.21	0.46	0.52	−4.59	−1.82	2.70	−3.71
OR	31.84	−1.87	−0.30	29.67	−1.37	−1.06	1.24	−1.19	22.77	−3.69	6.01	25.09
PN	15.62	−4.43	−1.32	9.87	−0.35	−0.97	0.98	−0.34	12.71	−6.15	2.46	9.02
RJ	10.14	−2.96	−0.05	7.13	−0.91	−0.43	0.69	−0.64	7.55	−3.96	1.83	5.43
TN	2.66	−1.23	3.08	4.51	−0.74	−0.71	0.70	−0.75	1.97	−1.72	3.10	3.35
UP	−3.50	−2.21	1.04	−4.67	−1.53	−0.99	0.81	−1.72	−5.37	−3.78	2.94	−6.22
WB	180.49	7.96	634.09	822.54	−75.95	−62.39	61.29	−77.05	7.69	−0.31	0.83	8.21

Source Author's calculation from Eq. (10.4)

10.4.1 Empirical Analysis of Structural Change and Economic Growth

Given that our estimation for McMillan and Rodrik index and de Vries, Timmer and de Vries index for within and between effects (static and dynamic) are fragile, NAV and MLI index are used to represent structural change. This structural change may be occurring due to some other factors such as investment, demography and urbanization, human capital, level of technology, quality of social and political institutions etc. Therefore, structural change interaction with these control variables over long period of time can affect the growth process.

An attempt is made here to estimate Eq. (10.5) to examine the effects of structural change, investment per capita, gross enrolment ratio (GER) for higher education, share of employment in industry, and interaction of human capital and structural change on economic growth across 14 Indian states during 1993–2011. Treating trend growth rate of per capita real income as dependent variable and using different specifications for independent variables, five different models have been tried within cross-sectional growth regression framework and estimated results are given in Table 10.4.

Table 10.4 Cross-sectional regression of economic growth, investment, human capital and structural change for 14 major Indian states during 1993–2011

Dependent variable: trend growth rate of per capita real income (1993–2011)					
Variables	Model 1	Model 2	Model 3	Model 4	Model 5
Constant	−9.834 (−1.38)	−9.823 (−1.32)	1.454 (1.02)	0.639 (0.39)	2.766 (1.15)
Initial level of per capita real income	1.486* (2.22)	1.480 (1.96)*	−2.026 (−1.31)		
Structural change in income		0.002 (0.04)	0.037 (0.82)	0.031 (0.69)	−0.081 (−1.16)
Per capita investment			5.89E−05 (1.93)*	0.000 (0.91)	0.000 (0.75)
Structural change in employment in Industrial sector (SCE)			0.140 (2.43)**	0.162 (2.61)**	0.156 (2.89)**
Human capital (HC)				0.154 (0.97)	0.151 (1.09)
Structural change (emp)*HC					0.009 (1.98)*
R-sq	0.253	0.253	0.525	0.570	0.710
Adj R-sq	0.191	0.117	0.383	0.379	0.529
F-stat	4.067	1.865	3.685	2.982	3.917
Prob (F-statistic)	0.067	0.201	0.051	0.080	0.043

Note t-values are given in parentheses. ** & * significant at 5 and 10% level, respectively
Source Equation (10.5)

Given the other control variables constant, growth rate of per capita real income is regressed on the initial level of per capita real income for Model 1 to observe absolute convergence or divergence across 14 Indian states. The positive and significant coefficient implies the evidence of absolute divergence during the period 1993–2011. This means that relatively rich states with higher initial level of per capita real income have grown faster than the relatively poor states in India during this period.

Model 2 is estimated by taking initial per capita real income and structural change in income as independent variables. It shows that growth rate of per capita real income is positively and significantly related with initial level of per capita real income. This shows the divergence pattern of growth across Indian states during 1993–2011. But, structural change coefficient is negative and not significant. Similar kind of insignificant impact is found if MLI is also used. However, the regression model in this case is not significant as indicated by F-statistics of the model.

Once more number of variables such as initial level of per capita real income, structural change in income, per capita investment and structural change in employment are included in the Model 3, the explanatory power of the model has improved to 53% as reflected in R-squared value. The estimated coefficients of per capita investment and structural change in employment are positive and significant. States with higher investment in different economic activities and higher employment share in industrial sector have grown more than that of others across 14 Indian states during 1993–2011. Shift in labor/workers from agricultural to especially construction of industrial sector has significantly impacted the growth process of the states. The coefficient of initial level of per capita real income is negative implying the tendency of divergence across the states. The coefficient of structural change indicator for income is positive. However, they are not statistically significant from zero.

Model 4 is estimated including human capital along with the variables used in Model 3. The explanatory power of the model has marginally increased from 0.53 to 0.57. Except structural change in employment in industrial sector, none of the estimated coefficients are statistically significant from zero. Shift in workers from less productive rural areas to productive construction activities in rural and urban areas has contributed to the growth of per capita real income across the states during the period 1993–2011. However, the positive signs of the coefficients of structural in income, investment and human capital show the positive direction to affect the growth processes.

Since structural change in employment in industrial sector and human capital are interacting and positively associated each other, interacting variable is created to see its impact on growth of income. It is positive and significant in Model 5 implying that productive industrial sectors have attracted the skill work force and the combination of the two has resulted into positive economic growth. Human capital as measured by enrolment in higher education alone cannot affect the growth. However, positive coefficient for human capital indicates that there is positive tendency of human capital to impact economic growth.

10.5 Conclusion

This paper reviews the recent growing body of literature on structural change, human capital and economic growth, and examines impact of structural change on economic growth. After calculating the share of different sectors in NSDP and following in the line with Dietrich for NAV and MLI, McMillan and Rodrik for within and static effects, de Vries et al. for within effect, static and dynamic effect, it estimates structural change in income for 14 major states from 1993–94 to 2011–12. There is an increasing trend in patterns of structural change as evident by NAV and MLI across sectors to contribute to the growth process of per capita real income. However, since it is based on population instead of employment data for labor productivity, these estimates are fragile. Using employment data, labor productivity can be found as per McMillan and Rodrik and de Vries et al. for fine tuning the estimates of structural change.

Regression analysis shows that it finds the evidence of absolute beta divergence indicating the relatively richer states have grown faster than the relative poorer states in India. Including structural change in income and employment in industrial sector (high intensity) along with other control variables such as per capita investment, human capital, and initial level of per capita real income in cross-sectional regressions, significant contribution of structural change for economic growth across the states during this period.

Most of the important fundamental variables as identified and verified by neoclassical and endogenous growth theories are not statistically significant due to typical problems in cross-sectional regression framework that usually suffer from many econometric problems. The estimated coefficients of these variables can be improved in direction and magnitudes with better measurements of variables and suitable econometric techniques. Due to conversion of series from 1993–94 to 2004–05, disaggregated NSDP data might be overestimated because of changes in output and price levels over time. Since the sample is small (14), there is degree of problem. If we include more number of variables into the model, this problem can be dealt with. Average of variables between the periods will not consider all values of all years. Since human capital, investment and growth are correlated to each other, is problem of simultaneity. Independent variables are also highly correlated to each other giving rise to problem of multicollinearity. Many of these problems can be sorted out once we increase the sample size, longer period. There may also be omitted variable bias. Further, fixed effect and dynamic panel data models can take care of most of these problems since lagged dependent variables is appearing as one of the independent variables.

References

Acemoglu, D., & Robinson, J. A. (2001). The colonial origins of comparative development: An empirical investigation. *American Economic Review*, 1369–1401.

Bagchi, A. K., Das, P., Chattopadhyay, S. K. (2005). Growth and structural change in the economy of Gujarat, 1970–2000. *Economic and Political Weekly*, 3039–3047.

Barro, R. (1991). Economic growth in a cross section of countries. *The quarterly journal of economics*, *106*(2), 407–443.

Barro, R. J., & Sala-i-Martin, X. (2003). *Economic growth* (2nd ed.). New York: Mcgraw-hill.

Bhattacharya, B. B., & Mitra, A. (1993). Employment and structural adjustment: A look at 1991 census data. *Economic and Political Weekly*, 1989–1995.

Bhattacharya, B. B., & Mitra, A. (1990). Excess growth of tertiary sector in Indian economy. *Economic and Political Weekly*, 2445–2450.

Clark, C. (1940). The conditions of economic progress, revised and reprinted in 1951. Macmillan London.

Cortuk, O., & Singh N. (2013). Analyzing the structural change and growth relationship in India: State-level evidence. *Economic and Political Weekly*.

Dietrich, A. (2011). *Does growth cause structural change, or is it the other way around? A dynamic panel data analysis for seven OECD countries* (pp. 915–943). Springer.

Fisher, A. G. (1939). Production, primary, secondary and tertiary. *Economic record*, *15*(1), 24–38.

Hansen, B. E. (2001). The new econometrics of structural change: dating breaks in US labor productivity. *Journal of Economic perspectives*, *15*(4), 117–128.

Kaldor, N. (1996). *Causes of slow rate of growth in the United Kingdom*. Cambridge University Press.

Kuznets, S. (1966). *Modern economic growth: Rate, structure, and speed*. New Delhi: Oxford Publication.

Kuznets, S. (1971). *Economic growth of nations: Total output and production structure*. Cambridge: Harvard University Press.

Levine, R., & Renelt, D. (1992). A sensitivity analysis of cross-country growth regressions. *The American economic review*, 942–963.

Lewis, W. A. (1954). *Economic development with unlimited supplies of labor*. The Manchester School, 139–191.

Mankiw, N. G., Romer, D., & Weil, D. N. (1992). A contribution to the empirics of economic growth. *The quarterly journal of economics*, *107*(2), 407–437.

McGregor, F. N., & Verspagen, B. (2016). *The role of structural transformation in potential of Asian economic growth*. ADB economics working paper series. Asian Development Bank, NO-407.

McMillan, M. S., & Rodrik, D. (2011). Globalization, structural change and productivity growth. *National Bureau of Economic Research, w17143*.

Papola, T. S. (2012). *Structural changes in Indian Economy: Emerging patterns and implications*. Working Paper, Institute for Studies in Industrial Development, 1–30.

Rao, V. K. R. V. (1979). Changing structure of Indian economy. *Economic and Political Weekly*, 2049–2057.

Romer, P. M. (1987). Growth based on increasing returns due to specialization. *The American Economic Review*, *77*(2), 56–62.

Roy, S. (2008). Structural change in employment in India since 1980s: How Lewisian is it? *Economic and Political Weekly*, 47–68.

Sen, K. (2016). *The determinants of structural transformation in Asia: A review of literature*. ADB economics working paper, Asian Development Bank, No-478.

Setthy, S. L. (2003). Growth of SDP and structural changes in states. *Economic and Political Weekly*, 5189–5199.

Singariya, M. R. (2014). Links between structural changes and economic growth in India. *Asian Online Journal, 1*, 1–7.

Teixeira, A. C. A., & Queiros, S. S. A. (2016). *Economic growth, human capital and structural change: A dynamic panel data analysis* (pp. 1636–1647). Elsevier.

Timmer, M. P., & De Vries, G. J. (2009). Structural change and growth accelerations in Asia and Latin America: a new sectoral data set. *Cliometrica, 3*(2), 165–190.

Zagler, M. (2009). *Economic growth, structural change, and search unemployment* (pp. 63–78). Springer.

Chapter 11
Financing MSMEs Rife with Problems—A Demand Side Analysis

Chinmayee Sahoo and Alok Ranjan Behera

Abstract MSME sector faces a number of marketing, infrastructural, financial and other constraints and challenges which put hindrance on the way to achieve a faster growth of this sector. Among the other constraints, lack of access to sufficient financing especially in developing countries, has been identified as a major bottleneck in realising the potential of this sector. Odisha is one of the top ten States in creation of job (20,839 person in 2006–07 and 107,011 in 2014–15) by MSME sector although it is positioned at 11 in respect of number of MSME units set up as compared to other States. Credit flow to the MSME sector declined during recent period in the state (41%) as against an increasing trend in the country (48%) (RBI Report 2015). This brought to the forefront to study about the demand side issues for accessing institutional finance by MSME because of banks are reluctant to provide credit to this sector. The study is conducted in Bhubaneswar city (No 1 smart city in India) of Odisha and chosen two clusters through cluster sampling technique. The total of 60 enterprises has been drawn randomly for the demand side analysis. To collect the data Personal interview method is used by taking semi structured questionnaire schedule for sample entrepreneurs. Factor analysis with rotate varimax normalization method is used to find out the major constraints faced by the MSMEs and to rank their problem, is presented through an index. It identified six major factors among its interest rate is the number one constraint in the demand side which impedes the growth of MSMEs not only is the financial problem but also in addition to that competition from well-running firm and lack of Labour are the major problem faced by the sample entrepreneurs. The results plot that manufacturing sector rife with more financial issues.

C. Sahoo
School of Humanities and Social Sciences, National Institute of Science Education and Research, Khorda 752050, Odisha, India
e-mail: Chinmayeesahoo44@gmail.com

A. R. Behera (✉)
Department of Analytical & Applied Economics, Utkal University, Bhubaneswar 751004, Odisha, India
e-mail: alokranjan78@gmail.com

A. K. Mishra et al. (eds.), *Current Issues in the Economy and Finance of India*, Springer Proceedings in Business and Economics,
https://doi.org/10.1007/978-3-319-99555-7_11

Keywords MSME · Demand · Manufacturing sector · Financial constraints

11.1 Introduction

The potential of Micro Small and Medium Enterprises (MSMEs) in achieving various economic objectives such as generation of productive investment and employment, promoting economic growth and export is widely accepted in both developed & developing countries. It also documented by policy makers and previous research activities. Besides these in developing countries like India, it helps in the development of the rural and backward areas thus reducing regional imbalance by providing equitable distribution of national income and wealth. The 44.77 million MSME units present in the country with 101.26 million of employment of people in 2011–12. This sector contribute around 45% of total industrial production and 8% of GDP in 2011–12 which was about 39.74% of industrial production a decade ago (1999–2000) and was contributing up to 5.86% of GDP initially. Highest growth of credit was achieved in the year 2008 (67.71%) with least growth seen in the year 2012 (7.19%) (Munda 2014).

According to the Ministry of Micro, Small & Medium Enterprises, the sector consisting of 36 million units, as on January 2016, has significant contribution in employment generation which has provided employment to over 80 million persons in 2006–07 to 117 million in 14–15. Moreover, the labour capital ratio in the MSME is high compared to large industries and they are widely disbursed in their presence making them important for achieving the national objective of growth with equity and inclusion. Fostering new entrepreneurship and providing volume to the industrial base of the economy which speaks of better utilisation of capacity (Salwan 2012).

In spite of this, MSMEs are considered to be less privileged than the large industries. Weaker should be protected against the stronger one (Lalhunthara 2014). The industrial sector is not performing well and its growth remaining constant since independence. MSME sector faces a number of marketing, infrastructural, financial and other constraints and challenges which put hindrance on the way to achieve a faster growth of this sector. Among the other constraints, lack of access to sufficient financing especially in developing countries, has been identified as a major bottleneck because until the gap between demand and supply side does not end that financial problems among the MSMEs will remain as the serious problem. There is a need of greater attention on the financing requirement of MSME sector. Irjayanti (2012) completely did demand side analysis to identify reasons for inability in competing in global market by considering several barrier factors faced by MSMEs. Through a supply side analysis (Ramlee 2013), reckons that MSMEs contend, finance for MSMEs is abundant however the supply of bank financing is largely unavailable to them.

11.1.1 Overview: Odisha Context

Odisha is one of the top ten states in creation of job (20,839 persons in 2006–07 and 107,011 in 2014–15) by MSME sector although it is positioned at 11 in respect of number of MSME units set up as compared to other states. Credit flow to the MSME sector declined during recent period in the state (41%) as against an increasing trend in the country (48%) (RBI Report 2015). Before 1991 in Odisha Industrial atmosphere was not there almost. Very few enterprises came into existence. People even didn't know what industry was. After 1991, because of the new industrial policy Odisha government took initiatives to set up more and more industries. They came to the point that not only the Farm sector but also the non-farm sector should come forward for the employment generation. People realised younger generation should proceed for the entrepreneurship and that was the track when the 1st generation of new entrepreneurs of Odisha lead the entrepreneurial activities. It is not like that the small scale industries were not previously set up. But there was no consciousness and awareness about setting up an industry, which is a professional thing and people were not aware of.

Initially only two government institutions were there to finance MSME sector. One was Odisha state financial corporation (OSFC) & another one was Industrial Promotion & Investment Corporation of Odisha limited (IPICOL). OSFC was most probably financing to the micro and small unit and IPICOL was financing to the medium scale industries. Up to 2005 things were going on work. After 2005 slowly things were changed as these two institutions stop financing to the MSME sector because most of the industries didn't succeed. Side by side there was a huge competition arises among the banking sector and also good number of public and private banking penetration which lead to the cash flow to this sector. 2005 onwards as the availability of money to this sector increased and banks came forward to finance the MSMEs, then the hindrance occur to MSMEs when the Non-Performing Assets (NPA) was more in this sector because most of the industries were hit up. And it was not possible for the bank to extend more finance to those people who were not capable of. Most of the projects got sick and the financing institutions themselves became bankrupted. This study tries to find out the financial constraints which MSMEs are still facing.

11.2 Literature Review

General thing inferred that the MSME development organisation earlier known as small industries development organisation (SIDO) was set up in 1954 as an apex body for sustained and organised growth of MSME. The president of India amended the Government of India rules 1961. Pursuant to this amendment, the ministry of agro and rural industries and ministry of small-scale industries were merged into a single ministry, the ministry of MSME. To act as the principal financial institution for the promotion, financing and development of the MSME sector the small industries development bank of India (SIDBI) was set up in 1990. Then the huge step was that, the Govt. of India enacted the MSMED act 2006 on June 16, 2006 which was notified on October 2, 2006. Munda (2014) reckon that the growth rate of MSME unit set up during a year and employment has been increasing over the years. Public sector banks are playing the dominant role in providing credit to MSME. The high growth of credit witnessed during 2008 is on account of re-classification of MSMEs as per MSMED Act, 2006. Growth of MSMEs is reflected when the firms with higher initial levels of productivity are more likely to survive and grow in size.

Stiglitz and Weiss (1981) in his theory, equilibrium credit rationing argues that the selection of borrowers in the loan market are more difficult, as rationing credit will enhance the adverse selection and moral hazard problems among borrowers. Asymmetric information arises in credit markets between the borrower and lender when one of the counterparties (usually the lender) does not have sufficient information or knowledge of the other counterparty involved in the loan transaction, which makes it difficult to make accurate lending decisions. Because of that there is arises gap between the demand and supply side.

The foreigners (Dermot Carey 2005) has employed that there is evidence of increases in bank rates over the past two years with limited switching between banks to avail of better rates. Banks operating in the SME sectors are on target for Basel II adaptation, Irish SMEs remain unaware and unprepared for the possible implications of this change. The improvement of managerial competence in entrepreneurs will lead to formation of good enterprises in the society. Kanitkar (1994) recognised that for the successful entrepreneurship, trained and educated entrepreneur should venture into business and there is need of redesigning the working of the financial institution.

Most of the study concern that entrepreneur are very much dependent on banks for credit and defines many of the issues from demand side which they are facing like high rate of interest, late sanction of credit, uneducated facing greatest difficulties in raising finance and problems like not having good partnership with the banks etc. The scarcity of credit can be resolved by borrowing from diverse source of credit (Akoten 2006) and many of the study distinguished the formal and informal source of access to credit by MSME. Most of the studies represent the supply side factors like lending technology, lending infrastructure, business environment, risk factor, high transaction cost factor, collateral & loan application challenges, number of sick units etc. these are those factors which may affect the performance of bank reluctant to provide credit to MSMEs. Quader (2009) from Bangladesh, by using factor analysis found that the high lending rate surfaced as the biggest constraint in the growth of SMEs. Regulatory constraints related to utility and labour comes in second position. Large established enterprises possess the necessary economic and human resource potential to cope with regulatory constraints and overcome difficulties but this is not happening in case of SMEs. Most of the study ascertains there is a need for better coordination between the government and commercial banks in the interest of the survival and growth of MSMEs.

11.3 Structure and Methodology

The main aim of this study is to provide further insight to make the demand factor available. The study sought to identify the problems which MSME borrowers have experienced about their credit, the supply and demand decision. So the focus is to identify demand side problems of accessing institutional finance by MSMEs in Odisha.

The data and methods, which has been utilised to analyses the objective which are taken in this study is quantitative analysis of survey data. The data obtained in this study is based on primary sources. Primary Data used in the study, has been collected through personal interview of the enterprises from the demand side. The study represents the MSMEs status of entire Odisha and finds out the issues generated to them through a sample survey. Odisha is one of the 29 states of India, located in the eastern coast. It is surrounded by the states of West Bengal to the northeast, Jharkhand to the north, Chhattisgarh to the west and south west, and Andhra Pradesh to the south. It is the 9th largest state by area and 11th largest by population. There are 30 districts in Odisha and this study is conducted in Bhubaneswar of Khorda district. To collect the data accurately first one pilot survey has been conducted. Through that pilot survey the information about number of MSME cluster and working enterprises in Bhubaneswar city has been collected form District Industrial Centre (DIC). The feature found from this pilot survey gave a route to this study. For the study Khorda district of Odisha has been taken purposively because the district down to its line and came to the 5th position in set up of MSME units in 2015–16. According to DIC, the number of MSME units is found to be abundant in Bhubaneswar city than other places of Khorda district. So, the study is conducted in Bhubaneswar city using convenience sampling technique. Therefore, it is thought that Bhubaneswar represents the whole of Khorda district. Cluster sampling is used to choose two clusters randomly (Mancheswar & Santrapur) out of five clusters of MSME in BBSR. From the list of registered MSMEs collected from the DIC, 50 sample units from the 1st cluster and 10 sample units from the 2nd cluster has been taken through simple random technique. To collect the primary data Personal interview method is used by taking semi structured questionnaire schedule.

This Study finds the major constraints faced by the MSMEs in Odisha selected from nine sub-sectors and miscellaneous such as; Handy crafts (stone carving), Fabrication work, Fishing net, Animal feed, Wood products, Aluminium & stainless steel utensils, Electricity & Stabilizer, Tools & Machines and Tiles &marbles. The study used Factor analysis with rotate varimax normalization method based on primary questionnaire survey in the demand side and interpreted the factor constraints according to their level of severity. Data has analysed through Statistical Package for Social Science (SPSS) and Microsoft Excel software. Descriptive statistical tools like frequency, percentage and mean is used to analyse the data and their interpretation is presented in the form of tables with suitable implications.

11.4 Demand Issues in MSME Financing (Demand Side Assay)

Demand side represents the borrower side, which means those who are accessing credit from the bank. To better understand the demand side, the study undertook every individual sampled enterprise; personal interviews were held with a semi-structured questionnaire and an effective discussion has been made with them also. The demand side questionnaire were designed to determine sector type, nature of the organisation, total turnover, types of problems in selling the output, sources of borrowing credit, perception about Rate of Interest, problems in repaying loan and other financial related issues.

The study has been conducted to analyse different MSME units as per their activities. The study has been taken the nine sub sector of MSME manufacturing unit. The final sample units have been selected among these nine sub sector of MSMEs named, handicrafts, fabrication work and tools and machinery having 8 MSME sample units from each. Five MSME sample units has been chosen from each of the following activity as fishing net, animal feed, wood products, aluminium and stainless steel utensils, electricity & stabilizer and tiles and marbles. Six MSME has been chosen from miscellaneous activities such as manufacturing of Plastic Scrap, Steel Almirah, Pharmaceutical products, Paper plates& Cardboard box, Powder Coating, Anodizing (Table 11.1).

There are 27 micro enterprises in the study out of which 22 are proprietor, 2 are having enterprise in partnership and 3 entrepreneurs are private limited. Out of 4 medium enterprises major are private limited. Small enterprises constitute 29 from which 12 are each proprietor and private limited and 5 entrepreneurs nature of

Table 11.1 Activities involved by the entrepreneurs in the study area

Sl. No	Activities Manufacturing unit	No. of entrepreneur	Percentage
1	Handy crafts (stone carving)	8	13.3
2	Fabrication work	8	13.3
3	Fishing net	5	8.3
4	Animal feed	5	8.3
5	Wood products	5	8.3
6	Aluminium & stainless steel utensils	5	8.3
7	Electricity & stabilizer	5	8.3
8	Tools & machines	8	13.3
9	Tiles & marbles	5	8.3
10	Miscellaneous	6	10
	Total	60	100

Note Miscellaneous part such as; Manufacturing of Plastic Scrap, Steel Almirah, Pharmaceutical products, Paper plates & Cardboard box, Powder Coating
Source Primary survey

Table 11.2 Nature of organisation with tire wise distribution (%)

Nature of organisation	Micro	Small	Medium	Total
Partnership	2	5	0	7
Proprietor	22	12	1	35
Private limited	3	12	3	18
Total	27	29	4	60

Source Primary survey (April–May 2017)

Table 11.3 Initial source of finance

Source	Number of entrepreneur	Percentage
Personal savings	30	50
Friends& relatives	5	13.3
Bank credit	8	8.3
Both 1 & 2	14	23.3
Other	3	5
Total	60	100

Note Other such as; Jami bandha, LIC loan, Share holder
Source Primary survey

enterprise is partnership. We can generalise from this table that medium term enterprises are very less in number in Odisha. Micro and Small enterprises are quite more in number and most of them are proprietors. They need a proper guidance to maintain their growth stability (Table 11.2).

Fifty percent of the enterprises had used personal saving as their initial source of finance to build up entrepreneurial activities. 13% of enterprises used initial finance from friends and relative. In the study more number of entrepreneurs (23.3%) was preferred both personal savings and hand loans from friends and relatives to get start their enterprise. Very few of them are said they were not used any kind of personal savings, hand loans and bank credit rather they used other kind of sources such as Jami bandha, LIC loan and loan from shareholder as initial source of finance (Table 11.3).

There are 70% of enterprises take loan from formal sources. Informal source of finance constitutes 18.3% of enterprises. There are 11.7% of enterprises who have not applied for any kind of loan. The reason for hand loan/informal loan is mainly;

Table 11.4 Formal and informal loan by the entrepreneurs

Loan structure	Number of entrepreneur	Percentage
Formal loan	42	70
Informal loan	11	18.3
Not apply for any loan	7	11.7
Total	60	100

Source Primary survey

lengthy bank documents, high processing charge in bank, rate of interest is less than the bank rate of interest. The 11.7% of the entrepreneurs those who are not applied for any loan, speaking with strongly that they need not any kind of bank loan rather they used their retained profit for further development of their enterprise due to the rules and regulation enacted in the bank (Table 11.4).

At the initial stage most of the entrepreneurs used personal saving and hand loans to start their business. But presently most of the entrepreneurs access credit from the bank. As the time passed the things were changed because banking sector and government make started conscious towards this sector. The table shows that 61.7% of entrepreneurs access credit form the bank followed by credit from hand loan 16.7, 11.7% from retained profit, 8.3% from the NBFIs (Table 11.5).

Public bank constitute the half of the financial assistance to enterprises. Seven enterprises depend on private bank for financial assistance. Only 8.3% access credit form other institutions such as NBFIs. 30% of the entrepreneurs are not accessing any kind of formal loans because they do not want to fall into the banking mess (Table 11.6).

The table represents how many entrepreneur change the bank because of the constraints they were facing in the previous bank. Mainly the changes occur from public sector banks to private banks or others institutions. The above table represent 28.57% entrepreneurs claimed that they have changed their bank to different banks. 20% are said that previously they accessed credit from public sector bank but now they changed to another public sector bank, 57.14% of the total private bank

Table 11.5 Present source of finance

Source	Number of entrepreneur	Percentage
Bank loan	37[a]	61.7
Retained profits	7	11.7
NBFI	5	8.3
Hand loan	10	16.7
Other	1	1.7
Total	60	100

Notes Other such as; Loan from shareholder
[a]Out of 37 one Entrepreneur applied for Gold Loan
Source Primary survey

Table 11.6 Types of formal loan wise distribution

Type of formal loan	Number of entrepreneur	Percentage
Public bank	30	50.0
Private bank	7	11.7
Other	5	8.3
No formal loan	18	30
Total	60	100

Note Other represents; Bajaj Finance & Tata Capital
Source Primary survey

Table 11.7 Bank changed by the entrepreneurs

Type of Bank	Change the bank	Bank changed by entrepreneurs	Bank not changed by entrepreneurs	Currently not using any bank	Total
Public sector	Public to public bank	6(20%)	22(73.33%)	2(6.7%)	30
Private sector	Public to private bank	4(57.14%)	3(42.86%)	0(0.0%)	7
Other institution	Public to other	2(40%)	3(60%)	0(0.0%)	5
Total		12 (28.57%)	28(66.67%)	2(4.76%)	42

Note Other represents; Bajaj Finance & Tata Capital-Study taken in 2017
Note The percentage in the parenthesis is the row percentage
Source Primary survey

account holder are said they changed public to private bank, 40% of other account holder are said that they changed public sector bank to other institutions like Bajaj Finance & Tata Capital. Some are currently closed the bank account. The reasons for these are the public sector bank (SBI) take more time to sanction credit than the private bank and other institutions. Also the rate of interest from public banks is more for the entrepreneurs than the private and other institutions. MSMEs always think about economies of scale so that the lower rate of interest would be beneficial for them. The sample entrepreneurs are repaying loan proportionately more than they save capital for their further investment (Table 11.7).

The above table represents that 15% of the entrepreneur said that they are irregular in repayment of the loan (Table 11.8).

Out of 9 entrepreneurs 55.56% are said due to low turnovers they are not able to repay loan regularly followed by high monthly amount and others. The problems like; competition, transportation problem, financial problem, price fluctuation, market size affecting more to the MSME units in the study area. Odisha market size is not so large and most of the raw materials are imported from the other state of the country. There is mostly delay of raw materials due to the problem in transportation. Competitions affecting the most to the entrepreneurs like customer made an order to the enterprise, if that order is not completed in time, due to competition

Table 11.8 Repayment of loan by the entrepreneurs

Repaying loan regularly	Number of entrepreneur	Percentage
Yes	33	55
No	9	15
Not applied for formal loan	18	30
Total	60	100

Source Primary survey

Table 11.9 Reasons for not repaying loan regularly

Reasons	Number of entrepreneur	Percentage
High monthly amount	2	22.2
High rate of interest	1	11.1
Low turnovers	5	55.56
Lack of seriousness	0	0.0
Other	1	11.1
Total	9	100

Source Primary survey

Table 11.10 Growth constraints of entrepreneurs

Growth constraint	Number of entrepreneur	Percentage
Lack of finance	15	25
Competition & low demand	10	16.7
Labour	15	25
Rate of interest	14	23.3
Red tapism by Govt & taxes	6	10
Total	60	100

Source Primary survey

prevailing the market, the order is gets cancelled and become transfer to another enterprise. This is hampering a lot and having impact on enterprise turnovers (Table 11.9).

The above table shows the type of constraints which borrowers are facing for the growth of their enterprise in Odisha. Majority are saying labour is a big problem followed by lack of finance, Rate of interest, competition & low Demand etc. 25% are said lack of finance is the major growth constrains to their enterprises followed by the labour. Labour are not interested to get involved in this sector because of government 1 Rs. rice subsidy no one get ready to do hard work. Government gives subsidies like capital, interest rate etc. to the small and medium unit more on the basis of their turnover. But micro units fail to achieve those subsidies (Table 11.10).

Factor Analysis

Factor analysis is a useful tool for investigating variables relationship. The key concept of factor analysis is that multiple observed variables have similar patterns of responses because they are all associated with a latent variable when is not directly measure. Each factor causes a certain amount of overall variables and the factors are always listed in order of how much variation they explain. Eigen value in the factor analysis is a major to explain how much of variance the observed variables or the factors have. A factor explains more variance than the single observed variable. The basic purpose of factor analysis is to explore the underlying variance structure of a set of correlation coefficient (Quader 2009). Steps Taken in Factor Analysis:

1st Step: Setting Up a Binding Constraint of Mean Value:

In the factor analysis first step is to find the major component factors and for that those factors mean are above score 2 are taken as a major component factor. As the study used three point Lickert scale so for this score 2 is set to find the major binding Constraints (Table 11.11).

The above mean value ranked the binding constraints those values are equal to mean score value 2 or more than 2. Statistically these 6 binding constraints are having more variance which means theses are affecting hugely in financing MSME sector in the study area. As per the rank high rate of interest is the major constraint in financing MSME. It is observed from the survey that there are many factors which affect the chance of Obtaining Credit from the Bank. Due to these financial constraints factor, the MSMEs found it difficult to promote their products and services. Not only is the financial problem but also in addition to that competition from well-running firm and lack of Labour due to having no interest to get involved in this sector are another major problem faced by the sample entrepreneurs.

Table 11.11 Mean value of the factors

Constraints	Mean value
High rate of interest	**2.65**
Red tapism in banks	1.90
Sanction time for loan	**2.37**
Competition	**2.13**
Credit score	0.48
Collateral	1.13
Red tapism in govt. agencies	1.57
Bank commission	1.83
Education	0.95
Business size	0.87
Credit sale	**2.50**
Bad debt	0.73
Lengthy loan application	**2.25**
Other* Problems	**2.00**

Source Compiled by Author

Note RANK 1—High Rate of Interest (ROI); RANK 2—Credit sale (CS); RANK 3—Sanction time for loan (STL); RANK 4—Lengthy loan application (LD); RANK 5—Competition (COM); RANK-6—(Labour)* (L)

Bold values are equal to mean score value 2 or more than 2

Table 11.12 KMO and Bartlett's test

Kaiser-Meyer-O measure	0.62
Approx. chi-square	140.849
Bartlett's test of sphericity (df)	78
Sig.	0.000

Source Compiled by Author

2nd Step: Kaiser-Meyer-Olkin (KMO) Measure of Sampling Adequacy (Table 11.12):

KMO test is used to test the sampling adequacy. The above table shows that KMO value is more than the minimum value of 0.5 which shows the sample which are taken are very good in nature. This is having significant result at 1% level of significance.

3rd Step: Factor Extraction (Factor Extraction is Done Through PCA):

The third step of factor analysis is to extract the factor through which we can get the Eigen value. Generally those values are greater than 1 that represent as the Eigen value. Factor Extraction is done using PCA or Maximum likelihood or GLS in order to determine the prominent factors. In PCA the linear combinations of observed variables are formed. The 1st PCA is the combination accounting to the highest variance in the sample. The 2nd PCA gives the next highest variance in the remaining sample and is uncorrelated with the 1st PCA and so on. In the below table the high rate of interest (Factor 1) was rated as the most serious problem followed by Credit sale (Factor 2), sanction time for loan (Factor 3), Lengthy loan application (Factor 4), competition (Factor 5) and Labour problem (Factor 6) are the major problem facing by the borrowers (Table 11.13).

From the above table it is found that 6 factors are having Eigen value more than one which means that these factors are having more variance and volatility in nature. The cumulative percentage of their variance is 73.03% which is very high.

Table 11.13 Representation of eigen value

	Eigen value	Cumulative% of variance
FACTOR 1	**2.75**	21.155
FACTOR 2	**1.74**	34.538
FACTOR 3	**1.414**	45.417
FACTOR 4	**1.331**	55.659
FACTOR 5	**1.196**	64.855
FACTOR 6	**1.063**	73.034
FACTOR 7	0.723	78.594
FACTOR 8	0.6	83.212
FACTOR 9	0.513	87.157
FACTOR 10	0.493	90.951
FACTOR 11	0.463	94.516
FACTOR 12	0.397	97.57
FACTOR 13	0.316	100

Source Compiled by Author

Generally bold values are greater than 1 that represent as the Eigen value

Table 11.14 Factors loading

	Factor 1	Factor 2	Factor 3	Factor 4	Factor 5	Factor 6
Credit score	−0.753					
RT bank	−0.726					
ST for loan	0.722					
competition	0.664					
others		−0.79				
RT govt		0.784				
Lengthy documents			0.853			
Bad debt						
ROI				0.841		
Credit sale					0.812	
collateral					0.668	
education						0.896
Bank cmtn			−0.509			

Source Compiled by Author

4th Step: Factor Rotation with Varimax Normalisation (Table 11.14):

The above table shows that these major 6 underlying factors loads the other observed variable factors which are highly correlated with them. The factor 1 loads the 4 observed variable such as lending technology, red tapism from bank, sanction time for loan and competition. Factor 2 loads 2 variables which are highly correlated with them. Likewise all the factor include one or more variables with them but except Bad debt. Bad debt is not included to any factors. That means it is not a major problem to the entrepreneurs.

Index Calculation

It is observed from the survey that there are many factors, which affect the chance of Obtaining Credit from the Bank. Due to these financial constraints factor, the MSMEs found it difficult to promote their products and services. Not only is the financial problem but also in addition to that competition from well-running firm and lack of Labour due to having no interest to get involved in this sector are another major problem faced by the sample entrepreneurs. The characteristics of financial problems faced by the entrepreneurs, is presented through an index in the Table 11.15.

Formula for rating percentage

$$P = X/N \times 100 \quad (11.1)$$

(P = Rating Percentage; X = weighted Score obtained; N = Total Score)

The above index presents the rank to different problems, which are facing by the borrowers. The high rate of interest was rated as the most serious problem

Table 11.15 Index calculation

Borrower problems	Entrepreneurs' ranking of financial problems			Not response	Weighted score	Rating (%)	Rank
	1	2	3				
High rate of interest	43	14	2	1	159	11.34	1
Red tapism in banks	19	19	19	3	114	8.13	8
Sanction time for loan	30	23	6	1	142	10.13	3
Competition	35	20	3	2	128	9.13	5
Credit Score	1	6	14	39	29	2.07	14
Collateral	7	12	23	18	68	4.85	10
Red Tapism in Govt. agencies	16	15	16	13	94	6.70	9
Bank Commission	21	18	11	50	110	7.85	7
Education	3	9	30	18	57	4.07	11
Business size	2	10	26	22	52	3.71	12
Credit sale	35	22	1	2	150	10.70	2
Bad debt	6	8	10	36	44	3.14	13
Lengthy loan application	24	29	5	2	135	9.63	4
Other problems (Specify)[a]	32	7	10	11	120	8.56	6
Total	274	212	178	218	1402	100	

Note [a]Other problem includes labours
Source Compiled by Author

(11.34%), followed by Credit sale (10.70%), sanction time for loan (10.13%), Lengthy loan application (9.63%), competition (9.13%) and Labour problem (8.56%) etc. are the major problem facing by the borrowers. In other words, 71.6% of the entrepreneurs indicated high rate of interest as the number one problem. Over 23.3% of the entrepreneurs felt high interest rate as the second most important problem, while 3.3% of them considered it as the third most important problem. The scarcity of finance poses a serious challenge to the development of entrepreneurship in Odisha.

11.5 Conclusion

In the study some enterprises view that because of the low finance, demand exceeds the supply. Customers are demanding the products but due to not approval and availability of the finance at the correct time, the entrepreneurs facing the problem of cancellation of orders. The common problem they are facing is that bank commission is more at the time of loan sanction. Public sectors banks are not suitable for the enterprise because banks are not heartily supporting and total loan process depends up on managers own interest. Rate of interest for the enterprises as compare to other countries is very high. In China ROI is 4% and in Bangladesh it is 6%. The entrepreneurs those who are not applied for any loan, speaking with strongly that they need not any kind of bank loan rather they used their retained profit for further development of their enterprise due to the rules and regulation enacted in the bank. The six major factors are the six different problems or constraints, which are facing by the borrowers. The high rate of interest is rated as the most serious problem followed by the Credit sale, loan availability in time, lengthy documents, competition and Labour problem etc. are the major problem facing by the borrowers. The scarcity of finance poses a serious challenge to the development of entrepreneurship in Odisha.

The study concludes that not only is the financial problem but also in addition to that competition from well-running firm and lack of Labour due to having no interest to get involved in this sector are another major problem faced by the sample entrepreneurs. As what I identified while going through the survey is that usually, entrepreneur starts well in the initial stage but somewhere lacks and miss the route to success. The study identify, due to competition prevail in the market the order is always get cancelled and become transfer to another enterprise. This is hampering their growth and also reduces enterprise turnovers. As the study found Labour are not interested to get involved in this sector because government provide subsidy (rice etc.) for that reasons no one get ready to do hard work. Government gives subsidies like capital, interest rate etc. to the small and medium unit more on the basis of their turnover but micro units fail to achieve those subsidies. Credit sale also create financial problem for the entrepreneurs.

The study reveals that the high rate of interest is the most serious financial problem faced by the MSMEs in Bhubaneswar city, of Odisha. Also in Odisha, the loan recovery from manufacturing units of MSME sector is very poor. There is an immediate need for intervention by the state government and commercial banks, especially the public sector banks to expand access to credit and banking facilities of the MSMEs and this sector always think about economies of scale so that the lower rate of interest would be beneficial for them. The government and banks need to work hand-in-hand for better coordination on a continuous basis. This study also having limitations like the sampling unit of the study is less due to time and money constraints. Only manufacturing sector of MSME is covered in the study. Considering both manufacturing and service sector would have provided for more significant results. The awareness potential and actual must be increasing so that more entrepreneurs are getting registered. Last but not the least, government should take action for which bank would be willing to provide loan to this sector.

References

Akoten, J. (2006). The determinants of credit access and its impacts on micro and small enterprises: The case of garment producers in Kenya. *Economic Development and Cultural Change, 54*(4), 927–944.

Dermot Carey, A. F. (2005). Is bank finance the Achilles' heel of Irish SMEs? *Journal of European Industrial Training, 29*(9), 712–729.

Irjayanti, M. (2012). Barrier factors and potential solutions for Indonesian SMEs. *Procedia Economics and Finance, 4,* 3–12.

Kanitkar, A. (1994). Entrepreneurs and micro-enterprises in rural India. *Economic and Political Weekly*, M25–M30.

Lalhunthara, N. J. (2014). Financial problems of microenterprises in Mizoram: Issues and dimensions. *IUP*.

Munda, S. K. (2014). Micro, small and medium enterprises (MSME) in India; financing by banks. *International Journal of Business and Management Invention, 3*(1), 07–16.

Quader, S. M. (2009). Constraints to SMEs: A rotated factor analysis approach. *A Research Journal of South Asian Studies, 24*(2), 334–350.

Ramlee, S. (2013). Barrier Factors and Potential Solutions for Indonesian SMEs. *Financing gap in Malaysian small-medium enterprises: A supply-side perspective, 16,* 115–126.

Salwan, P. (2012). Co-creation: An exploratory study of MSMEs & large banks in India. *Indian Journal of Industrial Relations, 48*(1), 1–18.

Stiglitz, J. E., & Weiss, A. (1981). Credit rationing in markets with imperfect information. *American Economic Review, American Economic Association, 71*(3), 393–410.

Chapter 12
Impact of MGNREGS on Rural Labour Markets and Agriculture: A Study of Madhya Pradesh

T. Prabhakara Reddy and V. Suresh Babu

Abstract MGNREGS is an opportunity for revitalising agriculture, restoration of ecosystems besides providing livelihood security to the poor and unemployed. It was to assess the impact of MGNREGS on rural labour markets, ascertain the changes in land use, cropping pattern and micro irrigation development in agriculture. The study concluded that for both male and female workers in rural areas, the scheme made a difference in terms of increasing real and money wage rates, especially more rapidly for female workers. During 2004–05 and 2007–08, person days of employment of rural women in public works increased around 4.4 times. There was no gender gap in the wages paid while average wages received in MGNREGS were significantly higher compared to other kinds of work. The impact is direct in terms of higher wages paid to women; indirect in terms of effects on women workers' reservation wages and bargaining power. The scheme had already positive effects on women workers in rural labour markets and resulted in real wages to rise, gender gaps to come down and open unemployment rates of women to decrease. Irrigation potential improved and the land brought under cultivation has been increased. Besides, the *kapildhara* wells and field bunding have resulted in improvement in micro irrigation, enabled changes in cropping pattern towards cash crops. Stop dams and check dams across *nalas* and small rivers enabled recharging of ground water and restoration of ecosystem benefiting all types of farmers while providing immediate irrigation. Public investment accompanied by private investment created assured irrigation.

T. P. Reddy (✉)
Satavahana Development Society, Hyderabad, India
e-mail: tprabha9@gmail.com

T. P. Reddy
SDS and Consultant (former) P P E, UNICEF, Patna, India

V. S. Babu
Centre for Climate Change and Disaster Mitigation, National Institute of Rural Development and Panchayati Raj, Hyderabad, India

A. K. Mishra et al. (eds.), *Current Issues in the Economy and Finance of India*, Springer Proceedings in Business and Economics,
https://doi.org/10.1007/978-3-319-99555-7_12

Keywords Rural labour markets · Realwages · Micro-irrigation and cropping pattern

12.1 Introduction

The Mahatma Gandhi National Rural Employment Guarantee Scheme (MGNREGS) can be construed as an opportunity for revitalising agriculture, restoration of ecosystems besides providing livelihood security to the poor and unemployed. The eight categories of works under MGNREGA largely address the key concerns of agriculture. MGNREGS aimed at enhancement of livelihood security in rural areas by providing at least 100 days of guaranteed wage employment in a financial year to every household whose adult members volunteer to do unskilled manual work and to create durable assets and thereby strengthen the natural resource base (NREGA, Operational Guidelines 2008). MGNREGS, India's main public works programme is unique, being large in size and intended to cover long periods, disburse huge funds and be dynamically responsive to climatic and rainfall conditions.

The Act has two major implications for the Indian economy. Firstly, it will address the rural crisis and the consequent demand deficiency (effective market demand) that has emerged in the post economic reforms period, and secondly, it will use the surplus manpower, especially women, for generating assets that expand the labour absorbing capacity of the mainstream economy to raise the rate of growth of sustainable employment in the countryside. Both these implications are interrelated and together, they are capable of promoting pro-poor growth and rural livelihoods in the economy (Hanumantha Rao 2010).

Brief Review of Literature

It has been established that MGNREGS has generated positive impact on agriculture and livelihoods of small, marginal and landless households in the rural areas. While real wage rates and the female labour participation have improved, the bargaining capacity of labourers registered an improvement resulting in additional incomes to the rural labour families (Chandrasekhar and Ghosh 2011). Besides, the scheme contributed to crop diversification in agriculture, micro irrigation development and reduced gender wage gaps in rural areas. The studies have shown that the real wage rates have increased after MGNREGS implementation when compared to pre-MGNREGS period for both male and female agricultural labourers in all the major farming operations (Narayanamoorthy and Bhattarai 2013; Gulati et al. 2013). The rate of increase in wage rates has been found to be higher across the female agricultural labourers as compared to their male counterparts. Further, it was argued, based on the regression analysis, that the average days of employment per household by MGNREGS, productivity of food grains and road density have positively fuelled the growth rate of wages for both male and female farm labourers. However, it was argued that while farm wage and non-farm wage of male labour has increased at a higher rate, the latter has experienced higher rate of increase than the former one (Nagaraj et al. 2014).

Although there have been many studies that have attempted to capture the impact of MGNREGS on a range of outcomes including employment and wages, income, consumption and welfare, women's empowerment (Khera and Nayak 2009) there has been little attention paid to the impact of the scheme on agriculture. Therefore, the present study assumes significance in understanding the impact of the scheme on agriculture and rural labour markets.

About Madhya Pradesh

As per Census 2011, the State had a population of 725.98 lakhs (6% of total population) as compared to 603.48 lakhs (Census 2001) thereby registering a decadal growth of 20.3%. The State population has grown 1.87% per annum during 2001–11 as against 1.64% p.a. at national level (NABARD 2014–15). As per Census 2011, the combined population of scheduled castes and scheduled tribes is about 36.72% of the total population as against all India average of 25.2%. In fact, they are all dependent on agriculture and seeking additional employment and income from MGNREGS in the state. The performance of agriculture is critical for economic growth and maximisation of welfare and well-being in Madhya Pradesh (MP) as agriculture accounts for 27% of the state's income in 2011–12, and employs over 73% of the workforce (NABARD 2014–15). At national level, it contributes 14% of national income and employs 61% of the workforce.

The importance of irrigation is too obvious to augment the productivity of agriculture and also for productive labour absorption. In 2000–01, the net irrigated area in MP was only 24% of geographical area compared to national average of 54.7%, but this has gradually increased to 30% by 2004–05. The cropping intensity was 124 for MP compared to134 for All India, and irrigation intensity was 131-compared to 167 at all India level (MPHDR 2007). Thus, resource use efficiency in MP agriculture is lower so concerted efforts are needed to strengthen the natural resource base and also to enhance the resource use efficiency. However, the cropping intensity has improved to 145 by 2010–11(NABARD 2014–15).

Other infrastructure conditions also matter greatly. Transport conditions determine the access of the farmers to both input and product markets; they allow for the promotion of non-agricultural activities that positively affect agriculture in turn. Energy has become increasingly important as more and more farmers become dependent on electricity for pumping water, and both the availability and the price of electricity affect the economics of cultivation. Rural connectivity and improvement of economic infrastructure (irrigation, electricity) would have positive impact on agriculture. At present, the availability of electricity is a problem in the countryside due to lack of adequate supply and as a result farmers are increasingly using diesel pump sets. However, irrigation facilities are improved under MGNREGS works in the state.

The paper is divided into four sections; section one dealt with introduction, brief review of literature, and the background of Madhya Pradesh; section two discussed the methodology adopted in the study and study area viz., Betul and Mandla; section three described the results and discussion and finally section four summed up conclusions and recommendations for further action.

12.2 Methodology

(i) **Objectives**

- To assess the impact of MGNREGS on rural labour employment;
- To ascertain the changes in land use, cropping pattern and micro irrigation development in agriculture.

(ii) **Hypotheses**

- H1: Improved irrigation facilities and land development through MGNREGS has led to productivity enhancement
- H2: there has been a positive change in labour markets in terms of increased wages etc.

Before and After Evaluation design has been followed to assess the impact of MGNREGS on agricultural wages, labour use, cost of cultivation. The control group data were used to isolate the effects of other factors (Experimental-Control design) and establish the net effect of MGNREGS on these key parameters.

- Agricultural wages for the base year 2005–06 and 2009–2010 (study period) were collected from the field and State Agriculture Department/Labour Bureau and NSSO, to analyse the changes in agricultural wages.
- By administering the structured schedule, primary data were collected from the respondents to assess the availability of labour during critical agricultural operations viz., land preparation, sowing, weeding, fertilizer and pesticide applications, harvesting and post harvest technologies. The baseline data pertaining to 2005–06 were compared with the 2009–2010 information with a view to ascertain the direct and indirect contribution of MGNREGS to changes in key parameters. Average wage was calculated from primary data and compared with MGNREGS wages in order to understand the changes in real income of labourers.
- Shifts in land use pattern and cropping pattern and extent of mechanization, were studied based on the primary data collected from the field. First hand information was collected from the respondents on the changes in cropping pattern and cropping system due to improved irrigation facilities through MGNREGS. The data were analysed to examine the changes in resource use caused by MGNREGS.
- Focus Group Discussions (FGDs) at Gram Panchayat level were organised to elicit information on rise in agricultural wages due to MGNREGS, rise in land value due to MGNREGS activities, soil quality improvement due to silt

application, rise in water table in the individual open wells due to water harvesting structures in Common Property Resources and land development activities, maintenance and durability of the assets created under MGNREGS.

(iii) **Methodology for Hypotheses Testing**

- In order to test the first hypothesis we have considered the variables such as number and type of works under MGNREGS, area developed through IBS and CPRs and productivity enhancement. Further, we have calculated the productivity per acre.
- Changes in Labour market have been examined by looking at the wages received by men and women and their participation in terms of days finally, it was presented with the help of percentages, number of days and number of persons.

(iv) **Sampling Design**

Two districts from different agro-climatic regions were selected and these are Mandla and Betul (representing irrigated and rainfed areas) from first phase of MGNREGS implementation were randomly selected. As a matter of fact, both the years happen to be normal years with normal rainfall and agricultural years.

Within each district, two blocks characterised by irrigated and rain-fed conditions were chosen randomly wherein MGNREGS works were taken up substantially. Thus, the total number of blocks selected for the purpose of the study was 2 from each district. From each block, two Gram Panchayats were selected on random basis on the number of activities taken upunder MGNREGS. Again from each Gram Panchayat 20 small and marginal farmers were selected for a detailed investigation who participated in MGNREGS. Further, in each GP two to three Focus Group Discussions were conducted with small and marginal farmers as one group, medium and large farmers as another group and a group of wage seekers.

(v) **Data Collection Methods**

The data and information were collected in four ways; firstly, culling out the necessary data from secondary sources; secondly, adopting survey method with a structured questionnaire; thirdly, using focus group discussion; and finally cross checking the information with key informants and other sources.

- The first objective was examined in terms of rise in agricultural wages, work participation rates with a focus on women, bargaining power of labourers, prevalence of migration and the gender gaps etc.
- The second objective was studied in terms of land use pattern, cropping pattern, cost of cultivation, net income and yield per acre among others.
- The third objective was studied in terms of availability of labour for agriculture, extent of mechanisation, land lease-in/out (tenancy), and fallow lands among others.

- The fourth objective was looked into in terms of investments in individual lands (especially SCs and STs) vis-à-vis common property resources, improved availability of irrigated area, net sown area and productivity enhancement etc.

(vi) **Study Period**

A comparative static framework was used and the data on two time periods (2005–06 and 2009–10) were compared to analyse the changes taking place in agriculture and rural labour markets. In fact, both are normal years as the study districts have experienced normal rainfall during these years.

About Betul

Betul is highly dominated by rural population (81.43%) who are mostly engaged in agriculture. As per 2001 census, the average land holding size was 2.6 ha. The average annual rainfall is 1000 mm. The district is known for high seasonal migration in the absence of gainful employment and income to the rural households. The type of soil is mostly alluvial which is amenable for easy percolation. Therefore, recharging takes place immediately resulting in improved irrigation in the district. Given the type of lands, agriculture is mostly dependent upon well irrigation. Under MGNREGS 20,900 dug wells were sanctioned whereas 16,002 were completed as on January 2011 resulting in an increase of 9% in irrigated area. According to NABARD estimates, while 60.6% of cultivated area is irrigated through dug wells, 24% through medium tanks and dams, 2.1% through other tanks, 8.2% through tube wells and the rest is through other sources. The farmers were adopting subsistence farming and cultivating crops like kodu kutki, jowar and maize (NABARD 2006).

About Mandla

Mandla is predominantly a tribal district (58%) with undulating landscape and a rainfall of 1400 mm per annum. As the district is having undulating landscape the irrigation potential is limited except for some nalas or streams. Mandla with a population of 8,94,236 with almost equal number of males and females reflected a balanced sex ratio in the district. Net sown area has increased to approximately 30% whereas the fallow lands have been reduced to 2%. About 62% of area is covered by forests and designated as Scheduled Area.

12.3 Results and Discussion

State Level Performance of MGNREGS

Madhya Pradesh is characterised by a high incidence of poverty based on 66th Round NSS which is 36.7% in 2009–10, sex ratio was low which registered 930 compared to national level of 940, the lowest literacy rate 70.6 as against 74% at the national level and the highest rate of child mortality. It is at the bottom of the ranking based on composite index of socio-economic and demographic indicators.

None of the districts figure among the first 100 districts. Lack of diversification is the chief characteristic of its economy-86% of its rural workers (72% of the total workers) depend on agriculture for their livelihood. Unirrigated agriculture which account for two-thirds of the cultivated land is highly degraded and characterised by low agricultural productivity, low wages, high distressed seasonal migration and high incidence of child and bonded labour (Parikh and Radhakrishna 2004–05). However, Madhya Pradesh is one of the better performing states, stood second after Rajasthan, both in terms of having a better coverage and creating a relatively larger number of days of employment per household, thus providing better wage income to the rural households. The state level progress is examined by looking at four parameters viz., the percentage of households covered under MGNREGS, the number of MGNREGS employment days per household, the total state level MGNREGS expenditure and the average wage accruals per household. According to official data of 2007–08 the performance of MGNREGS in Madhya Pradesh is summarised in Table 12.1.

Performance of MGNREGS in Study Area The study was undertaken in two districts viz., Betul and Mandla of Madhya Pradesh for the purpose of analysing the impact of MGNREGS on agriculture and rural labour markets. Here, we would like to present the performance of MGNREGS in terms of coverage and number of days of employment created, changes in land use and cropping pattern taking place in study area.

The performance of the scheme in study districts for the year 2009–10 can be gauged from Table 12.2.

Person days of employment per household received by labourers in Betul are ranging from 60 to 70 whereas in Mandla it is 55–70 and some households have completed 100 days in both the districts. On an average, a family has earned Rs. 5000–10,000 per annum from MGNREGS. Those who completed 100 days of employment earned Rs. 10,000 and above. Only in one or two villages of Mandla we found that the number of days of employment is less than 50 which is due to failure to take up adequate number of MGNREGS works and it is also due to little role played by Panchayats whereas Panchayats are active in Betul district. The participation of female workers, on an average, is in the range of 40–50 days in both the districts (the study area).

The achievement of 100 days of employment in some cases (or up to 70 days) is due to awareness and active participation of a family in MGNREGS. On the other

Table 12.1 Performance of MGNREGS in Madhya Pradesh, 2007–08

Name of the state	Amount distributed on NREGS (millions Rs.)	% rural households participating in NREGS	Average days of NREGS work/HH	Wage accrual in Rs./HH
Madhya Pradesh	16,520	54.4	63	5383

Source Abusaleh Shariff, IJLE, vol. 52, No. 2 (2009), p. 248

Table 12.2 Coverage and number of days of employment under MGNREGS, 2009–10

Particulars	Betul	Mandla	MP
Households provided wages (in lakhs)	1.48	1.73	33.96
Total person days generated (in lakhs)	83.22	154.29	1280.9
Women person days (in lakhs)	37.84	81.29	519.02
Person days generated for SCs/STs (%)	73.41	65.29	50.79
Person days generated for women (%)	45.46	–	40.51
Amount spent (Rs. Cr)	126.04	179.23	–
utilisation of funds per cent	70.69%	66%	–
Average no. of days of employment per household	60–70	70	–

Source District Administration Report (2009–10)

hand, less number of days of employment to the labourers is due to several reasons; one is inadequate number of works planned under MGNREGS, engagement of family in its own cultivation, delay in wage payment, migration for a better wage and employment and finally local politics that may exclude some people in getting wage employment. It was observed in our study that the first three reasons are prominent in not being able to get more number of days of employment by the labourers. However, it was found in couple of villages that the local politics have influenced to exclude some families in accessing wage employment under MGNREGS. The kind of works taken up and its distribution in community property resources as well as individual lands are discussed in the following table. The net result is also presented in the last two columns of the Table 12.3.

It is clear from the above table that though Individual Beneficiary Scheme (IBS) is given priority under MGNREGS it varied from district to district. While more number of kapildhara wells (42%) has been taken up in Betul depending on the landscape of the district, field bunding (39%) is accorded priority in Mandla district. Further, the cost of each kapildhara well is in the range of Rs. 100,000–115,000 while field bunding in IBS costs around Rs. 15,000–25,000. Both the initiatives are successful in improving the water levels for agriculture. However; the former one is a productive and durable asset. While the latter one is not a permanent structure and thus it cannot be treated as a durable asset.

The permanent structures like stop dams, kapildhara wells, and cement roads in few places have been taken up under MGNREGS while not so permanent structures are gravel roads, check dams, field bunding, tank excavation and horticultural plantations.

Stop dams and check dams across *nalas* and small rivers provided very good recharging of ground water to all types of farmers while providing immediate irrigation to the nearby fields. The difference between stop and check dam is that one is earthen one whereas other one is a concrete structure. By seeing the water conservation measures under MGNREGS some farmers have invested money in

Table 12.3 Type and distribution of works taken up in study area

Districts	Type of works taken up	Individual beneficiary scheme	Community property resources
Betul	Kapildhara well (42%)	Improved irrigation and Productivity enhancement	NA
	Field bunding (5%)	Improved irrigation and Productivity enhancement	NA
	Road connectivity (22%)	NA	Improved connectivity
	Tank/pond excavation (6%)	NA	Recharging of ground water tables
	Nandanphalodyan (7.5%)	Horticultural plantation and additional income	Horticultural plantation and additional income
	Stop dams (11%)	NA	Improved irrigation facility
	Check dams (6.5%)	NA	Improved irrigation facility
Mandla	Kapildhara well (18%)	Improved irrigation and Productivity enhancement	NA
	Field bunding (39%)	Improved irrigation and Productivity enhancement	NA
	Road connectivity (12%)	NA	Improved connectivity
	Tank/pond excavation (10%)	NA	Recharging of ground water tables
	Nandanphalodyan (10%)	Horticultural plantation and additional income	Horticultural plantation and additional income
	Stop dams (5%)	NA	Improved irrigation facility
	Check dams (6%)	NA	Improved irrigation facility

Source Field data
Note The figures in () represent the percentage of works taken up in study area whereas the net result is given in the next two columns

digging bore wells whereas others have spent on land levelling etc. Strictly speaking, the private investment was forthcoming though in a small way but went hand in hand and thus it is a clear cut shift in the overall agriculture. Public investment accompanied by private investment created assured irrigation and resulted in changes in cropping pattern which is in favour of cash crops.

Laying roads and tank excavation in common property resources is a successful activity that has benefited all the farming community irrespective of the land ownership. Improved road connectivity, it is reported, has yielded enhanced price for the agricultural produce in many places while desilting of tanks and ponds has

Table 12.4 Distribution of operational holdings in MP, 2007–08

Sl. No.	Particulars						
	Farmer category/DOH	Marginal	Small	Semi-medium	Medium	Large	Total
1.	Distribution of Operational holdings (As per 2000–01) (%)	38.55	26.5	20.21	12.45	2.25	100

Source Agriculture, Centre for Monitoring Indian Economy (CMIE) June (2010)

resulted in improved productivity through enhanced irrigation facility. As a result, per acre land prices have increased in study area. For instance, the price of land per acre was Rs. 100,000 previously went up to Rs. 4–5 lakhs now in Betul district (Table 12.4).

About 85% of operational holdings are small and marginal which are without proper irrigation and economically unviable. As per 2000–01 operational holdings, large farmers accounted for 2.25% whereas medium farmers are 12.5% in the state and together operate 15% of the operated area (Table 12.4). It is clear from the Table 12.5 that the gross irrigated area is just 32% and therefore most of the areas are designated as rain fed.

However, according to official records of 2007–08 net irrigated area as a percentage of net sown area is 43.7% increased to 52.47% by 2011–12. However, Madhya Pradesh agriculture is backward and characterised by subsistence farming. Whatever is produced it is meant for self-consumption but not for market sale. However, the situation is changing as the farmers began cultivating commercial crops like soyabean and paddy which are fetching good incomes.

As far as land utilisation pattern in MP is concerned, net sown area is just 48% and the land under forests is 28%. Uncultivated land is 24% including fallows and related categories. Area under food grains and non-food grains is 56 and 44% of total cultivated area respectively (Table 12.5. Gross irrigated area is 32% while net irrigated area as a per cent of net sown area is 44%. The sources of irrigation revealed that the agriculture in the state is predominantly well irrigated (66%)

Table 12.5 Land utilisation particulars (official records) of MP, 2007–08

a.	Land under forests (%)	28.3
b.	Gross cropped area (Ha)	20,416,000
c.	Net sown area (%)	47.75
d.	Land not available for cultivation (%)	11.03
e.	Fallow land (%)	4.66
f.	Other uncultivated land excluding fallows (%)	8.26
g.	Area under food grains (% of GCA)	55.29
h.	Area under non-food grains (% of GCA)	44.71
i.	Gross irrigated area	32.17
j.	Net irrigated area (% of NSA)	43.70

Source Agriculture, Centre for Monitoring Indian Economy (CMIE) June (2010)

Table 12.6 Irrigation and yield per hectare in MP

Particulars	Total canals	Tanks	Total wells	Other sources	Total	
Sources of Irrigation (% of NIA)	16.38	2.15	66.31	15.16	100	
	Rice	Wheat	Jowar	Rapeseed & Mustard	Cotton	
Gross Irrigated Area (% of GCA)	16.17	91.74	0.19	52.83	42.35	
Fertilizer Consumption per Hectare (kgs.)	63.76					
	Rice	Jowar	Bajra	Maize	Ragi	Small Millets
Yield per Hectare (kgs.)	938	1117	1402	1288	250	272
Wheat	Barley	Gram	Arahar	R Mustard	Soyabean	Cotton
1612	1163	711	670	927	1091	233

Source Agriculture, Centre for Monitoring Indian Economy (CMIE) June (2010)

followed by canals (16%) (Table 12.6. The fact is that the undulating character of the landscape has given rise to more number of open wells in the state. As a matter of fact, the cropping and irrigation intensities are less than all India levels which require concerted efforts in strengthening the natural resource base of the state economy.

Crop wise gross irrigated area as a percentage of gross cropped area revealed that the wheat (92%), mustard (53%) and cotton (42%) are predominantly cultivated under irrigated areas when compared to paddy (16%). As regards the cropping pattern wheat, mustard and cotton are cultivated in the order of preference during 2009–10 whereas kodukutki, jowar and other millets were sown prior to 2005–06. Fertiliser consumption per hectare is mere 64 kgs in paddy cultivation (Table 12.6). Yield per hectare is also less when compared to other states. As per agriculture Census 2010–11, total land holdings in the State were 88.72 lakhs in 2010–11 while the average size of land holding declined from 2.22 ha (2000–01) to 1.78 ha (2010–11). The marginal and small farmers account for 71% and operate 34% of the total area. The gross cropped area during 2011–12 was 217.55 lakh ha with a cropping intensity of 144.87% and the net sown area was 150.17 lakh ha constituting 49% of the total geographical area.

Betul District: Land Use and Cropping Pattern

Betul consisting of 10 blocks is predominantly a tribal district (46%) in Madhya Pradesh having around 40% forest area. It is also characterised by high poverty rates (51%) and a low per capita income of Rs. 14,346 in 2006–07 (GoMP 2007). The landscape is undulating with ridges and valleys with lot of catchment area but

Table 12.7 Land use pattern in Betul, 2004–05

Sl. No.	Particulars	%
1	Forests	39
2	Net sown area	40
3	Fallow land	7
4	Cultivable waste land	4
5	Land not available for cultivation	7
6	Other uncultivated land excluding fallow and cultivable waste land	3
7	Total geographical area	100

Source MP Human Development Report, 2007 p.154

not command area. Although five rivers originate in Bhandwa area of the district they are either flowing into Maharashtra or other parts of the Madhya Pradesh.

Agro-climatic Situation

Betul is highly dominated by rural population (81.43%) who are mostly engaged in agriculture. As per 2001 census, the average land holding size was 2.6 ha. The average annual rainfall is 1000 mm. The district is known for high seasonal migration in the absence of gainful employment and income to the rural households. While net sown area is 40 and 21% of land was not able to use due to various reasons (Table 12.7).

The type of soil is mostly alluvial which is amenable for easy percolation. Therefore, recharging takes place immediately resulting in improved irrigation in the district. Given the type of lands, agriculture is mostly dependent upon well irrigation. Under MGNREGS 20,900 dug wells were sanctioned whereas 16,002 were completed as on January 2011 resulting in an increase of 9% in irrigated area. According to NABARD estimates, while 60.6% of cultivated area is irrigated through dug wells, 24% through medium tanks and dams, 2.1% through other tanks, 8.2% through tube wells and the rest is through other sources.

The farmers are adopting subsistence farming and cultivating crops like kodukutki, jowar and maize. They take agricultural loans from local 'shahukaars' (the money lenders) who take away their output immediately after harvesting. It also indicates that the land, labour and credit markets are interlocked to such an extent wherein the farmer is not able to take the advantage of support price announced by the Government of India. As a result, we could observe that there is a practice of 'distress sales' adopted by the farmers not only small and marginal but also medium farmers. Further, some labourers are attached to large farmers from whom they get financial support during emergencies and who provide them wage labour continuously for a reasonable number of days. When MGNREGS works were taken up the labourers could not participate as they were engaged in agriculture work belonging to large farmers. Only when those agricultural operations are over the attached labourers are free to work in MGNREGS.

Changing Scenario

The pattern of land utilisation showed that there exists 43% agricultural land, 39% forest land, 14% barren land and followed by 4% grazing land. About 3% fallow land has been brought under cultivation in the last five years. As regards the irrigation sources and its potential it is clear that 61% is through dug wells followed by minor tank irrigation (16%) tube wells (8%) medium tanks and dams (8%) and other sources (5%). While irrigation is improving due to MGNREGS works the land brought under cultivation is also rising (Table 3.5). It is a fact that the kapildhara wells have become a successful initiative in the district given the suitability and the need for irrigation in an undulating land.

Socio Economic Situation

About one and a half lakh households have been provided wages through MGNREGS so far. Total person days of employment generated is 83.22 lakhs whereas average person days generated per household is 56.38 (MGNREGA Administration, 2009–10, Betul). Under MGNREGS the percentage of man days generated for SCs, and STs is 73.41 per annum in the district against the state average of 50.79 indicated that the effective targeting of marginalised sections took place in the district. Similarly, the percentage of employment days generated for women is 45.46 as against the state average of 40.51 in 2009–10.

The financial parameters showed that the district has been able to utilise the funds to the tune of 71% during 2009–10. The category of works undertaken depicted (prioritisation) that first priority is given to dug wells (42.2%) with a view to enhance the irrigation facility to the small and marginal farmers; 22% of works pertain to rural road connectivity followed by 18% relating to water conservation. Another 12% of works are concerned with drought relief and afforestation (MGNREGA Administration, 2009–10, Betul).

Substantial awareness has been generated through various methods like conducting camps, street plays, distribution of pamphlets, posters, flexi boards, sign boards and wall writings etc. According to district administration data the district is leading in terms of MIS data; wage payments are made early (within 2–3 weeks time) by deputing a special employee in each Janpad Panchayat to coordinate between Bank and GP. Publication of 'fund flow' information in local newspapers as part of transparency, toll free number for resolving complaints, Lok Adalat and Lok Kalyan Shibirs and Rojgar Divas are measures to benefit the labourers are worth appreciating. Several measures are taken up to monitor the progress and keep vigilance on the work of MGNREGS in the district. A cyber roll as a pilot attempt in order to mark the attendance of workers by taking finger prints using biometric machine and e-muster website connected through GPS and finally to the MIS software is an important initiative taken up by the district administration. As a result, the records are being maintained up to date and payments are being made immediately.

Mandla District

Mandla district has 90% of rural population in which majority are dependent upon agriculture for their livelihood. The landless families in the district are 26,000 out of 1, 96,766 total rural families which account for 12%.

Socio Economic Eituation

The literacy rate was 60% in 2004–05. The total inhabited villages in the district are 1214 while it has 40 forest villages. It has 57.2% ST population whereas SC population is about 4.6%. The work participation rate of females was 48.3 during 2004–05 has increased to more than 55% by 2009–10 (Table 12.8).

Agro-climatic Situation

Mandla is predominantly a tribal district (58%) and is receiving an average rainfall of 1400 mm per annum. As the district is having undulating landscape the irrigation potential is limited except for some nalas or streams. Mandla with a population of 8, 94,236 with almost equal number of males and females reflected a balanced sex ratio.

The land use pattern has undergone changes in the last five years reflecting more land brought under cultivation. Net sown area has increased to approximately 28% whereas the fallow lands have been reduced to 2%. About 62% of area is covered by forests and designated as Scheduled Area. The average land holding size was 1.8 ha. Tractors per 10 villages were 4.6 in the year 2004 while it has increased to 12 by 2009–10. Apart from tractors, the number of sprayers has increased tremendously in the district. Mechanisation has picked up at a rapid rate in the past four to five years in Mandla which may be due to shortage of labour during peak agricultural operations.

There is a striking difference between both the districts though they are designated tribal areas. Mandla which is predominantly tribal district has more area under forests (62%) less Net Sown Area (NSA) (28%) while Betul which is also a tribal district but undergoing transformation has relatively more NSA (40%) less forest coverage (39%). One of the plausible reasons is that Betul is directly connected to New Delhi and other places through Indian Railways thus amenable for change whereas Mandla is not.

Table 12.8 Land use pattern in mandla, 2004–05

Sl. No.	Particulars	%
1	Forests	61
2	Net sown area	23
3	Fallow land	6
4	Cultivable waste land	2
5	Land not available for cultivation	6
6	Other uncultivated land excluding fallow and cultivable waste land	2
7	Total land	100

Source MP Human Development Report, 2007 p.230

Mandla consists of nine Janpad Panchayats, 486 Gram Panchayats, 1247 villages and 74 forest villages. Although Narmada River flows in the district, the irrigated area is just 6.5% of cultivable area. The main crops of the district are paddy, maize, soyabean, kodukutki, during Kharif season and wheat, pulses, rai and mustard in Rabi season. Although it depicts a typical subsistence farming economy practising rain-fed cultivation, gradually the farming community is learning new methods of cultivation through 'demonstration effect'. The application of fertilisers and pesticides per acre is still relatively less. As a result, the productivity of crops was also low especially before launching of MGNREGS. At present, the MGNREGS has provided 'field bunding' to many small and marginal farmers popularly known as "*med bandhaan*" which is a successful initiative in the district. Added to it, *kapildhara* wells have improved the irrigation facilities thus, enhancing the productivity of crops significantly.

Further, the district experienced interlocked markets wherein the land, labour and credit markets are controlled by rural gentry who are economically well off and take the advantage of support price announced by the Government of India. We observed that there is a practise of 'distress sales' adopted by the farmers not only small and marginal but also medium farmers. Therefore, the provision of institutional credit and subsidised inputs would make a real difference in farmers' life. Added to it, fallow lands have been converted into cultivated area and there have been changes in cropping pattern too. On the whole, with the introduction of MGNREGS the district has experienced additional guaranteed income to the labourers and productivity enhancement to the farmers. However, it was revealed that the farmers in Mandla need works such as land levelling, renovation of old wells, contour bunding and bund across nala/stream under MGNREGS.

Changing Scenario

As per Census 2001 the literacy rate is 61%. Though schools exist in many villages there is a shortage of teachers and quality of education is a casualty. Potable drinking water facility is 38% whereas the use of sanitary toilets is 5% only. As per Human Development Index Madhya Pradesh state secured 38th rank while Gender Development Index showed much ahead to others with 8th rank. While rural electrification is 94% the household electricity connectivity is only 30%. The district is lagging behind in infrastructure, human development, Infant Mortality Rate and Child Mortality Rate.

More number of field bunding activities has resulted in recharging of water in small farm holdings benefiting majority of small and marginal farmers in the district. The initiative is eco-friendly and cost-effective which is also providing enormous wage employment. Further, the farmers are able to cultivate two crops who were cultivating single crop hither to. As a result, land value has risen considerably in the district. There is not much socio-economic difference between labourers and small farmers as majority of farmers are also labourers. Therefore, the relationships between these two occupational groups are cordial.

Migration is observed in the district with excess labourers in a family moving out of subsistence farming and going to places like Bhopal, Jabalpur and Nagpur especially for earning higher wages. It is a *sine qua non* of development wherein the labour move out of agriculture and are being absorbed in non-farm activities. Further, the distress migration has been controlled to a great extent due to the introduction of MGNREGS activities. Culturally speaking, the tribal population is the happiest people when their basic necessaries are fulfilled. In fact, they do not work for 3–4 months in a year during rainy season and Rabi season as they keep adequate stocks of food grains.

Changes in Cropping Pattern

There is a 'paradigm shift' in the rural economy as the tribal population is moving from minor forest produce to agriculture in so far as their livelihood is concerned. Again, the tribal population is moving from subsistence agriculture to commercialised agriculture due to assured irrigation created under schemes like MGNREGS. There is a marked change in cropping pattern in the districts. Five to 6 years back they were cultivating traditional crops like kodukutki, jowar, maize and paddy in a limited area. It was mostly rain fed agriculture in the absence of assured irrigation facilities. But now they are cultivating wheat, soyabean and vegetables like tomatoes, beans, brinjal, mutter etc., as a result of improved irrigation through stop dams, check dams and dug wells taken up under MGNREGS. As a result, there is a change in their food consumption and habits too.

Further, considerable land has been brought under cultivation in the districts. As a matter of fact, the fallow lands are reduced and the tenancy is on the rise due to irrigation facilities created under the programme. Fallows have been reduced due to small and marginal farmers who are not only taking up MGNREGS work but also taking the lands of others on lease and cultivating them with wheat, chana and vegetables among others. Large farmers who are in towns either due to service or children's education have a tendency of leasing out lands to others for cultivation. The ground water table is improved as a result of water conservation activities and the *kapildhara* dug well initiative has been reported as a successful one since it has provided assured irrigation to majority of small and marginal farmers in Betul district. Having received open wells many tribal families began cultivating commercial crops within a short span of 2 years.

Given the situation of improved irrigation facilities through public investment reflected in terms of stop/check dams across streams and tributaries in some villages of study area the big farmers began investing in agriculture in the form of digging bore wells, land levelling, purchase of pump set and other activities. Private investment is flowing into agriculture in a small way but there is a clear cut shift in their investment. One of the big farmers from Mandla district was saying that let the government provide us irrigation we will cultivate commercial crops in two seasons and improve the productivity. It is, in fact, a complementary effort by the big farmers towards public investment especially made in MGNREGS programme.

Though they are tribals with limited education they have adjusted to changes very easily and introduced new methods of agriculture. They are adopting mechanisation, applying fertilisers and pesticides and it appeared that the farmers have been experiencing improved productivity. Having seen the profits in agriculture from crops like soyabean and wheat, the farmers are taking the lands of others on lease and cultivating them. The tenancy is oral and output of the crop and the expenses incurred are shared equally by the owner of the land and the tenant (share cropping) (Table 12.9).

Table 12.9 A comparative picture of impact on both the districts in Madhya Pradesh

Item of examination	Betul	Mandla
Objectives		
(a) Impact on rural labour markets	Wages have risen by double the amount	Wages have risen not as much as in Betul
• Gender wage gap	Gender disparities are reduced	Gender disparities are reduced to a great extent
	Women workers participation increased (45–50 days) changing their status from marginal worker to main worker	Women workers participation also improved (40–45 days p. a.)
• Bargaining capacity	Qualitative changes like bargaining capacity of labourers has improved tremendously	Bargaining capacity of labourers improved to some extent
• Migration	Migration continued unabated but there is no distress migration in the district	Migration got reduced but there is no distress migration
• Decentralised Governance	Implementative framework is decentralised to a great extent therefore, more number of works, immediate wage payment and high coverage of the scheme	Not so decentralised; administration oriented; less number of works in remote areas like Sagar Panchayat;
(a) Changes in land use	Marked changes in land use pattern	Fallow lands have been brought under cultivation
Improved irrigation	Fallow lands have been brought under cultivation Improved assured irrigation	Improved availability of irrigated area
Cropping pattern	Changes in cropping pattern from dry land crops to irrigated crops; traditional to cash crops	Changes in cropping pattern from dry land crops to irrigated crops; traditional to cash crops
Cost of cultivation (COC)	CoC increased due to irrigation charges, diesel, electricity bills, fertilisers and pesticides; 50% in human labour	CoC increased due to irrigation charges, diesel, electricity bills, fertilisers and pesticides; 38% in human labour

(continued)

Table 12.9 (continued)

Item of examination	Betul	Mandla
Other aspects		
Guaranteed wage employment and enhanced incomes to the labourers	Increased number of employment days and enhanced incomes	enhanced incomes
Supplementary income	To small and marginal farmers	To small and marginal farmers
Gender disparities	Reduced; wages have risen and	Reduced, wages have risen and participation improved from marginal workers to main workers
Rise in cost of cultivation to small and marginal farmers	Affected adversely but adopted a system of exchange of labour to cope with the situation	Affected adversely but adopted a system of exchange of labour (in a limited way) to cope with the situation

12.4 Conclusions and Recommendations

The study has concluded that for both male and female workers in rural areas, the MGNREGS has made a difference in terms of increasing the wage rates for casual work. The real wages increased for both male and female workers and indeed more rapidly for female workers. They also argued that during 2004–05 and 2007–08 person days of employment of rural women in public works increased around 4.4 times, a remarkable shift in terms of involvement in paid work. This was possible because there is hardly any gender gap in the wages paid and secondly, average wages received in MGNREGS were significantly higher than those received by casual labour in other kinds of work.

It was found that there is a reduction in the gender wage gap due to the MGNREGS. The impact is direct in terms of the higher wages paid to women in this scheme; indirect in terms of the effects on women workers' reservation wages and bargaining power. Finally, it can be concluded that despite limitations, the scheme has positive effects on women workers in rural labour markets. It has caused real wages to rise, gender gaps to come down and open unemployment rates of women to decrease. Another important change that has been observed is that there is a tremendous improvement in micro irrigation through *Kapildara* wells and *Medbandhan* (field bunding) which has become a success in the state and resulted in changes in cropping pattern and established that the resources can be used in a sustainable manner.

It was suggested to enhance public investment in irrigation, rejuvenation of dry land areas through soil and water conservation, revamping agricultural research and extension, developing market infrastructure including transport and cold storage etc. Further, to ensure the quality and permanent assets convergence of various programmes with concomitant funds, techniques, human resources and institutions is needed.

Acknowledgements The authors would like to thank Prof. K. Hanumantha Rao, Head, CWEPA, NIRD & PR, Hyderabad for his guidance and research support in completing the project successfully. It is part of a larger study conducted by National Institute of Rural Development & Panchayati Raj, Hyderabad for Ministry of Rural Development, Government of India, New Delhi, 2011.

References

Agriculture: Centre for Monitoring Indian Economy (CMIE) (2010). June pp. 123–143.

Adhikari, A. & Bhatia K. (2010). NREGA wage payments; can we bank on the banks? *Economic and Political Weekly, January 2, XLV* (1) 30–37 (2010).

Chandrasekhar, C. P. & Ghosh, J. (2011). Public works and wages in rural India. *Business Line date* 11.01.2011 p-9 Col. No. 1–8.

District Administration Reports of Betul and Mandla (2010). Mahatma Gandhi National Rural Employment Guarantee Scheme, 2009–10 pp. 45–49.

Government of Madhya Pradesh (2007). Bhopal; Madhya Pradesh Human Development Report, pp. 230–232.

Gulati, A., Jain, S., & Satija, N. (2013). *Rising farm Wages in India: The Pull and Push Factors, Discussion Paper, CACP*. Ministry of Agriculture, and Government of India.

Hanumanatha Rao, C. H. (2010) Inclusive Growth: An Overview of Performance and the Challenges Ahead. *The Indian Economic Journal, 58*(1) April-June pp. 23–27 (2010).

Khera, R., & Nayak, N. (2009). Women Workers and perceptions of the National rural employment Guarantee act. *Economic and Political Weekly, 44*(43), 49–57.

Madhya Pradesh Human Development Report. (2007). Government of M.P., Bhopal, pp. 4–6.

Murgai, R., & Martin, R. (2005). Employment Guarantee in Rural India; What would cost and how much would it reduce poverty? *Economic and Political Weekly, 30,* 3450–3455.

NABARD (2006). Mumbai; The Status of Madhya Pradesh Agriculture, pp. 32–45.

NABARD. (2015). State Focus Paper 2014–15. Madhya Pradesh, Bhopal.

Nagaraj, N., Bantilan, C., Pandey, L., & Roy, N. S. (2014). Impact of MGNREGA on rural agricultural wages in SAT, India. In *Paper presented at National Symposium on "Dynamics of Rural Labor Markets; Implications for Agricultural Growth and Rural Transformation* (pp. 15–16) September 2014, New Delhi. pp. 25.

Narayanamoorthy, A., Bhattarai, M. (2013). Rural employment scheme and agricultural wage rate nexus: an analysis across states. *Agricultural Economics Research Review, 26*(Conference Number), 149–163.

National Rural Employment Guarantee Act (2008). Operational Guidelines, pp. 1–5.

Parikh, K. S., Radhakrishna, R. (2005). India Development Report 2004–05, Oxford University Press and Indira Gandhi Institute of Development Research, New Delhi, pp. 12–49.

Shariff, A. (2009). Assessment of outreach and benefits of national rural employment guarantee scheme of India. *Indian J. Labour Econom, 52*(2), 248–259.

Part IV
Public Policy Economics and Analysis

Chapter 13
Reforming Tax Systems: Key Policy Considerations from South and South-West Asia

Matthew Hammill and Jose Antonio Pedrosa-Garcia

Abstract In South and South-West Asia, tax systems face several challenges which are reflected in poor efficiency in trying to mobilize and manage public financial resources. The complexity of tax structures and the granting of exceptions undermine effectiveness, introduce regressiveness in tax systems and hinder the social contract, all of which take a toll on tax morale and promote informality. Tax reforms are necessary to avoid this vicious circle, while streamlining the tax systems to make them simpler, faster and more effective. Special attention should be paid to coordination of tax administration at different administrative levels, increasing the tax base and strengthening transparency to deter corruption—which may thrive due to the many possibilities for interpreting tax systems. Reforms may not be easy to undertake because the costs of implementing them are borne in the short term, but their benefits are realized in the medium to long run. However, reforms will be the only way to go if South and South-West Asia is to implement the 2030 Agenda.

Keywords Tax reforms · South Asia · South West Asia

M. Hammill
United Nations ESCAP, New Delhi, India

J. A. Pedrosa-Garcia (✉)
United Nations ESCAP, Bangkok, Thailand
e-mail: pedrosagarcia@un.org

A. K. Mishra et al. (eds.), *Current Issues in the Economy and Finance of India*, Springer Proceedings in Business and Economics,
https://doi.org/10.1007/978-3-319-99555-7_13

13.1 Introduction: Challenges in Financing Sustainable Development Through Tax Systems

Countries should have significant resources to invest in sustainable and inclusive development. To do so, the most common yardstick is the tax-to-GDP ratio, which is a measure of the economic importance of the public sector in a country's economy. On average, South and South-West Asia's tax-to-GDP ratio is 12.6%, one of the lowest in the world, below that of other developing countries in the Asia-Pacific region, at 15.2%, and much lower than that of OECD countries, at 25.1%.[1] Several countries in the sub-region have tax-to-GDP ratios under 10%: Afghanistan, Bangladesh, the Islamic Republic of Iran and Pakistan, with Afghanistan's being the lowest in the Asia-Pacific region at just 7.6% (IMF 2018).

The Addis Ababa Action Agenda is a vital part of the 2030 Agenda and relates to financing for development (ESCAP 2018a), setting a target tax-to-GDP ratio at 20%.[2] Given the considerable financing requirements, the current tax-to-GDP ratios will not suffice (Schmidt-Traub 2015). Consequently, the 10 countries comprising the South and South-West Asian sub-region are unlikely to achieve the Sustainable Development Goals without first implementing comprehensive and difficult reforms to improve this situation. Hence, investing in domestic resources through smarter tax policies and more inclusive public expenditure is the largest untapped finance opportunity for those countries to effectively pursue implementation of the 2030 Agenda (Long and Miller 2017). Domestic resource financing must be infrastructure- and public service-intensive to support the various generational transformations under way in South and South-West Asia, such as urbanization, women's empowerment, youth bulge or population ageing; such financing is also needed for the economic transformation from labour-intensive agriculture to capital-intensive industry and services (ESCAP 2017a).

It is possible and advisable to increase the tax-to-GDP ratio in this sub-region because the ratio is considerably below its potential. Various international standards have suggested that tax-to-GDP ratios should be between 15 and 20%; this range remains a realistic goal for South and South-West Asian countries to achieve before reaching in 2022 the halfway point for achieving the Sustainable Development Goals. Recent studies would suggest that developing countries in the Asia-Pacific region are realizing only one half to two thirds of their tax potential (ESCAP 2014). For the South and South-West Asian sub-region, these estimates of tax potential would suggest tax-to-GDP ratios of 12–13% for the Islamic Republic of Iran and

---

[1]The countries considered in South and South-West Asia are: Afghanistan, Bangladesh, Bhutan, India, the Islamic Republic of Iran, Maldives, Nepal, Pakistan, Sri Lanka and Turkey.

[2]The IMF standard recommendation for low income countries, which for South and South-West Asia includes only Afghanistan, is an arbitrary 15% to fuel development growth sprints. Recent reports by the World Bank and GIZ reinforce recommended ratios in this range (Long and Miller 2017).

Pakistan.[3] Countries in the sub-region are working to improve their tax-to-GDP ratio. For example, in Bangladesh a flat 15% value-added tax has been introduced —although, owing to pressure from the business sector, its implementation (initially planned for 1 July 2017) has been pushed forward to 2019 (EIU 2018a).

13.2 Challenges Facing Tax Systems in South and South-West Asia

It should be acknowledged that South and South-West Asian countries have different tax structures and therefore face different challenges. Such diversity is reflected in the average tax rates—and especially in the tax types that are zero, as can be appreciated in Table 13.1. While some countries such as Bangladesh have gaps in social security, others such as Afghanistan could reinforce their revenue from indirect taxes.

Tax rates by themselves do not explain the fundamental sources of the diversity of tax systems; specific country circumstances should also be considered. For instance, the fragile security situation and weak government control over parts of Afghanistan pose great challenges for the collection of taxes. It is estimated that 47.5% of the country's total revenue comes from domestic resources, with the remainder being derived from external grants (EIU 2018a). In India, while it has been acknowledged that its goods and services tax (GST) has reduced the complexity of its taxation system, its tax laws are still perceived to be second most complex in the Asia-Pacific region—after those of China: well over half of private sector companies in India believe that complexity in the tax regime has increased in the last three years—"complexity" referring to the perceived level of difficulty in interpreting the tax law and rules in the relevant jurisdictions (Deloitte 2017). In Sri Lanka, the 2018 budget is aimed at streamlining the corporate income tax system and reducing exemptions to improve compliance and increase revenues (EIU 2018c). In Pakistan, most tax revenue is derived from indirect taxes, making the tax system relatively regressive (ESCAP 2018b), which does not favour inclusion.

To the extent that generalizations can be made about the tax systems in South and South-West Asia, it may be said that they are complex, inefficient and not very conducive to the collection of large tax volumes. For example, India has a tax administration index of 58.4%, which is below the average index for the entire Asia-Pacific region at 60.3% (ESCAP 2018b).

Inefficiency in the tax system does not favour inclusion, which in turn lowers tax morale. Financial contributions by people and businesses to their Government depend on the perception of the public goods and services received, such as

[3]The ratio could increase potential/gap: Afghanistan 15.0/6.2; Bangladesh 18.0/7.5; Bhutan 16.0/6.7; Islamic Republic of Iran 13.1/7.2; Maldives 16.5/5.8; Nepal 16.1/0.9; and Pakistan 12.1/1.8. Estimates do not include India (ESCAP 2014).

Table 13.1 Average tax rates, by type, in selected countries

	Indirect	Corporate	Individual	Social security (Employee)	Social security (Employer)
Afghanistan	0	20	20	20	50
Bangladesh	15	25	30	0	0
India	15	34.61	35.43	12	12.5
Pakistan	17	31	20	0	0
Sri Lanka	11	28	16	8	12

Source KPMG Tax Rates Online Tool (2018)

education, health care, basic utilities or responsive government administration. In most countries and sectors in the sub-region, this social contract is broken. The result can be a vicious cycle of tax avoidance which hampers financing decent public goods and government services, and subsequent low-quality, exclusionary service delivery.

13.3 Factors Limiting Tax System Effectiveness

The complexity of the structure and composition of tax systems in South and South-West Asia can be gauged by considering the multiplicity of taxes, cumbersome assessment procedures, inefficiency of tax administrations, delays in resolving disputes, unequal exemptions granted to certain groups and corruption. Because of such complexity, the sub-region's tax systems tend to be dependent on indirect taxes for most tax revenue. Value-added taxes (VAT) are increasingly popular and expanding in coverage as a strategy to capture tax revenue without the complex assessment of household incomes and wealth, and they lower the disincentives to business compared with direct corporate taxation.

An element that can aggravate complexity in the tax system is the highly decentralized structures of countries in the sub-region. Subnational public expenditures are one third greater than subnational public revenues in Bangladesh. They are twice as large in India and more than six times as large in Pakistan (ESCAP 2017a). Central tax collection results in greater uniformity and simplicity across provinces, states and districts, but requires a transparent and equitable process for distribution of revenues. In addition, various provincial/state and local-level taxes typically remain in place, which increases coordination costs. For example, Indian states apply a separate state goods and services tax along with the federal equivalent on relevant transactions. In Pakistan, property taxes are collected at the state and provincial levels, but are more difficult to administer and apply due to valuation requirements and their greater complexity. Some cases in other regions show local taxation as more effective than central grants in delivering good-quality social infrastructure when coordination is poor.[4]

Goods and services taxes and VAT have often been introduced without differentiation and adopt various rates and exemptions during passage of legislation, in order to appease key interest groups, or attempt targeting to lighten the burden on those left behind.[5] Each modification imposes additional complexities, making tax administration more difficult. India's recent introduction of national and state GST occurred after some delay; its final form currently affords goods and services exemptions for food and agricultural products. Sri Lanka increased VAT rates from 11 to 15% in 2015 and expanded VAT to include telecommunications and private health care (IMF 2016), but left food and medicine VAT exempt. In Bangladesh, a new VAT law increasing the rate from 11 to 15% was supposed to be implemented in 2017; however, implementation has been delayed until 2019 after resistance from various special interest groups (EIU 2018a).

Indirect taxes instead of direct taxes tend to be heavily applied in the sub-region. This means that those who are wealthier pay relatively less tax, because indirect taxes have regressive scale effects. Consequently, well-designed and well administered tax systems are necessary to offset regressive indirect taxation. Fragmented indirect taxes and regressive tax revenue streams can be addressed and offset by direct taxation policies, pro-poor public spending and more effective tax administration. However, South and South-West Asian countries face additional challenges in all three areas, leaving regressiveness as a key characteristic of sub-regional tax systems.

Across South and South-West Asia, the collection of personal income tax and property tax tends to be below potential, as a result of high thresholds and various exemptions, thus making tax administration burdensome and inefficient. In 2013, the sub-region's share of personal income tax in total tax revenue was only 14% on average, the lowest in Asia and the Pacific.[6] Tax reforms in various countries in the sub-region have increased personal income tax thresholds over time, decreasing the scope of their tax net (Bhutan, Ministry of Finance 2017). By taking such measures, countries "untax" or remove the tax burden for the vast majority of the poorer population, in particular those who work informally,[7] but they also leave much of the population permanently outside the tax administration system (ESCAP 2017b).

---

[4]For example, in Brazil, increases in municipal taxation were used to improve both the quality and quantity of education infrastructure, while increases in federal grants had no impact on infrastructure spending at all (Gadenne 2016).

[5]For example, in India the first goods and services tax proposal contained one universal rate and no exemptions. The final legislation contains five rates (Economic Times 2018) and various exempted categories that must be defined, categorized and reported in tax returns.

[6]As an unweighted average. Latest data available are from the IMF Government Finance Statistics. Available from www.imf.org/en/Data.

[7]Rising income levels translate into higher tax intake when there is deliberate government action to modernize the tax system and incentivize formalization of the economy (Besley and Persson 2014).

Property taxes also contain numerous exemptions in the sub-region's tax systems, often being undervalued and poorly implemented. In Pakistan, property tax intake is low due to generous exemptions and undervaluation, such as in Pakistan's Punjab Province; the level of undervaluation has been estimated at 45–80% (Bahl et al. 2015).

Corporate tax rates in many South and South-West Asian countries are not considerably lower than those in other regions of the world, mirroring the relatively high rates for many businesses in developing countries (World Bank 2017). However, corporate taxes across countries also contain numerous exemptions in an attempt to increase investment and encourage productivity. These exemptions can be arbitrary and create vested interests in maintaining special conditions when economies and structures have substantially changed. In Bangladesh, corporate income tax rates are not especially lower, but revenue is diminished by numerous exemptions, tax holidays and depreciation allowances, as well as challenges in enforcing compliance (Mansur et al. 2011). In Pakistan, broad discretion in exemptions to the payment of corporate taxes meant for industries involved in the China-Pakistan Economic Corridor and in special economic zones, has led to exemptions being applied to unrelated projects (Abbasi 2017).

Poor capacity and ineffective tax administration is also hampering resource mobilization in South and South-West Asia. The problem of adding complexity to each tax is that it burdens the tax administration and its capacity for accurate, timely and transparent tax collection. Across the sub-region there are large gaps in capacity to administer the complex tax web. As a result, on one hand the frequent thresholds and exemptions leave large shares of the population outside the tax system. On the other, the complexity of the tax system delays tax administration and gives extensive discretion to working-level officials to make tax assessment decisions, thus making those decisions less transparent and reducing overall accountability. A simpler progressive tax system with fewer loopholes and greater manageability would outperform designs that are only better on paper (ESCAP and Oxfam 2017c).

Small tax bases are a key constraint in the sub-region's tax systems, driven by informal economies, loopholes, exemptions and poor administration for obtaining compliance. Afghanistan's small tax base includes a miniscule group of large taxpayers contrasted with the wider potential taxpayer population that is largely non-compliant and unidentified (Grut 2017). In Bangladesh, the top 10 large taxpayers paid more than 78% of VAT collected by the large taxpayers' unit, and 50% of all tax revenue collected by the unit came from just one company (World Bank 2017). For business and corporate taxation in Nepal, about 1000 companies contribute half the tax revenue (GIZ 2018). Pakistan had only 750,000 payers of income tax registered in 2014 in a country of 190 million people; remarkably, almost half (46%) of the 1167 members of the 6 houses of parliament (national assembly, senate and four provincial assemblies) paid no tax at all, thus demonstrating the weak tax morale even among legislators (ESCAP 2017a).

Tax competition and base erosion is also hampering domestic resource mobilization. The capacity to capture tax revenues on a sustained basis from corporations and enterprises is also challenged by the increasing globalization of production and value chains. Countries in the sub-region have responded with tax competition, among other investment incentives, for attracting corporate presence into the country with benefits of tax flows, productivity and employment, although the evidence for these gains is weak (ESCAP and Oxfam 2017c). At the same time, multinational enterprises are more strategic in their use of profit shifting and transfer pricing to erode traditional tax bases and take advantage of arbitrage gains in tax loopholes between countries. Increasing the corporate tax based and avoiding its erosion for countries in the sub-region requires unanimous cooperation for reversing eroding tax incentives and for coordinating treatment of multinational enterprises to close tax loopholes between countries (KPMG 2017).

13.4 Policy Recommendations

The countries in the sub-region need to design tax systems and taxes that incentivize and accelerate transitions to sustainable economies and environmentally friendlier technologies. In South and South-West Asia, inclusive tax design requires addressing disincentives and perverse effects in two areas: gender equality and environmental sustainability. Tax design is gender blind in the sub-region. Personal income tax structures are often based on traditional household models of a single male head of household and breadwinner, with women being dependents. Rates reflect this model and penalize secondary income earners, mostly women, with higher marginal tax rates and fewer options for tax deductions (ESCAP and Oxfam 2017c). Greater gender mainstreaming in tax design should be matched by improved pro-poor gender-responsive budgeting to link tax revenues to spending priorities that better empower women and promote equal voice and control in society and the economy (ESCAP and Oxfam 2017c).

In leveraging technology, both filing tax returns and making payments are vital as they address the complexity of taxation systems. Both operations should be done electronically, and countries in the sub-region have been active in opening up their tax systems so that taxpayers can file their tax returns electronically and make payments electronically as well. Afghanistan has introduced electronic filing for large taxpayers and plans to roll out a system for medium-sized taxpayers in the coming year (Byrd and Payenda 2017). The country also has an electronic revenue collection system for making payments (Afghanistan, Ministry of Finance 2017). Bangladesh and Nepal have also recently introduced electronic filing and a payments system which simplifies individual and VAT processes. In Nepal, 98% of income and VAT returns were filed electronically in 2016 (GIZ 2018).

Tax and spending coordination and negotiation between different levels of government is critical for revenues collected centrally to be spent effectively at the provincial/state and municipal levels. This requires very country-specific policies to be tailored to specific challenges (ESCAP 2018b), but countries should consider reforming the bottlenecks that they experience in overall fiscal management. Specific tools that they can use to identify those bottlenecks may be, for example public expenditure benefit-incidence analysis, which can capture the distributional impacts of public spending across categories of gender, geography and social groups. That tool showed that access to and utilization of public spending is regressive in India, with gender-differentiated patterns.

Increasing the tax base may require a carrot-and-stick approach, which also can be highly country-specific. In Bangladesh, the stick approach in 2017 increased the number of individual tax filers from 1 million to 1.55 million by requiring tax submission from all government officials with monthly salaries exceeding 16,000 taka (about $190) and by requiring private sector managers and executives to file returns so that their employers would not be fined (World Bank 2017). In contrast, Bhutan increased its number of personal income tax filers by more than 10% in the 2016 fiscal year, despite reduced exemptions, because individuals were encouraged to file their returns in order to claim refunds owed to them as a result of tax changes (Bhutan, Ministry of Finance 2017).

Environmental and green taxes that internalize negative externalities are necessary in the sub-region, but their design needs to accommodate two challenges. One of the challenges is to create adequate national and sub-regional markets for environmental taxation and emissions-type trading systems to allow enterprises to internalize costs for the first time. The other is to maintain good principles of tax design towards universal, simple and transparent rules with a few rates that allow for less discretion but greater accountability. Most countries in the sub-region have yet to develop national carbon accounts or systems of environmental national accounts. Rigor and transparency would be important to avoid rent-seeking behaviours in establishing methods and designing new environmental taxes.

Transparency is vital to stimulate accountability and strengthen the social contract. Despite the complex systems in South and South-West Asia, greater transparency in decisions and processes would encourage greater tax morale when people are confident that there is equity and a level playing field when it comes to paying taxes. Across the sub-region, publishing tax information increases transparency and accountability. Pakistan has set an important good example by becoming the fourth country in the world to introduce a regular complete directory of registered taxpayers and the total amount of tax they paid (Pakistan, Federal Board of Revenue 2017).

Tax reforms, tax policies and changes often differ from their initial proposals before the negotiation and passage of legislation, and this can be confusing if complying with the new rules is not clear and simple for people and businesses to understand. Public information campaigns and education of individuals and businesses will improve transparency, identify any confusion and enable people to anticipate and plan for costs and compliance. In Afghanistan, a new VAT law came into effect eight months after its official publication and included no reactive penalties, which gave time for businesses to check on how to comply with the law and plan for doing so (Grut 2017). However, the same country's 2015 Tax Administration Law came into effect from the date of publication, giving taxpayers no time to prepare how to comply. The publication of the law was delayed and not announced, with many taxpayers subsequently finding out about the bill only after they had received penalties for not complying with it. Information sessions about the tax took an additional year to organize (Grut 2017).

Tax reforms can have unintended consequences and negative results, which policymakers should carefully try to anticipate. For example, to drive up tax filing and non-cash transactions, Pakistan in 2015 imposed a withholding tax on bank transactions targeting both large bank cash transactions (exceeding 50,000 rupees, or approximately $435) and all non-cash transactions at the rate of 0.4%, with tax filers being able to claim refunds for this tax. Instead of encouraging tax filing, the withholding tax has had a negligible effect on revenue but has led to declines in private deposits and a large increase in the amount of currency in circulation, double the annual rate of the last decade (State Bank of Pakistan 2017).

Finally, countries should try to make further progress in adopting measures that address base erosion and profit-shifting (BEPS) strategies (Jun 2017); in this regard, the OECD BEPS Initiative may provide a useful benchmark. An example of ongoing progress is India, which has been active in promoting the OECD BEPS Initiative (KPMG 2017).[8] In following BEPS recommendations, the country passed amendments in its domestic law to be in line with BEPS regulations (Ernst and Young 2018). Several proposals in the Finance Act of 2016 were influenced by OECD recommendations on BEPS, such as implementation of master file and country-by-country reporting (relating to action 13), introduction of an equalization levy which requires withholding on a gross basis for all payments in relation to certain specified digital services (action 1) and a "patent box" tax regime for royalty income (action 5) (Ernst and Young 2018).

It should also be noted that, while BEPS may not be an equally-important issue for all countries, regional coordination and integration can be a useful dimension for learning from each other. The sub-region already has structures for regional cooperation and integration, that is, the South Asian Association for Regional Cooperation (SAARC), which could be more actively used to debate the implementation of measures to tackle BEPS.

13.5 Conclusion

For countries to be able to undertake the investments required towards implementing the 2030 Agenda, a critical condition is their ability to mobilize sufficient financial resources in a stable and predictable manner. To do so, efficiency in mobilizing and administering tax revenues is vital. If tax systems have room for improvement in terms of efficiency, corrective measures need to be undertaken. Of concern is the fact that in South and South-West Asia, tax systems exhibit substantial regressiveness compared with other sub-regions. Thus, efficiency

[8]The master file and Country-by-Country (CbyC) reporting requirements predominantly enforce the principles of BEPS Actions 8 to 10 and Action 13 on transfer pricing.

considerations relating to tax reforms have been explored in the sub-region, which stands out for having very low tax revenues as a percentage of GDP. It has been shown that reforms are needed to simplify tax structures, reduce untargeted exemptions, and make tax administration more effective. The importance of more effective governance will be critical to implement such measures successfully.

Acknowledgements The authors are grateful to Hamza Ali Malik and Aswini Kumar Mishra for useful comments and guidance.

References

Abbasi, A. A. (2017). *A conversation about CPEC*. Online magazine of the Institute of Asia and Pacific Studies, University of Nottingham, UK.

Afghanistan, Ministry of Finance. (2017). *Afghanistan on the road to self-reliance: A year in progress*. Progress report. Kabul, Afghanistan.

Bahl, R., Cyan, M., & Wallace, S. (2015). The potential of provincial taxation. In J. Martinez-Vazquez & M. Cyan (Eds.), *The role of taxation in Pakistan's economic revival* (pp. 488–548). Karachi: Oxford University Press.

Besley, T., & Persson, T. (2014). Why do developing countries tax so little? *Journal of Economic Perspectives, 28*(4), 99–120.

Bhutan, Ministry of Finance. (2017). National Revenue Report 2016-2017. Department of Revenue and Customs.

Byrd, W., & Payenda, M. K. (2017). *Revenue growth in Afghanistan continues strong but future uncertain*. Peace Brief, No. 219. February. Washington, D.C.: United States Institute of Peace.

Deloitte. (2017). Shifting sands: Risk and reform in uncertain times—2017 Asia Pacific tax complexity survey.

Economic Times. (2018). *Confused about revised GST rates? Here's a quick guide*. 19 January 2018.

EIU, Economist Intelligence Unit. (2018a). Bangladesh Country Report, February 2018. New York: EIU.

EIU, Economist Intelligence Unit. (2018b). Afghanistan Country Report, March 2018. New York: EIU.

EIU, Economist Intelligence Unit. (2018c). Sri Lanka Country Report, February 2018. New York: EIU.

Ernst and Young. (2018). *India focus on BEPS—Base erosion and profit shifting*. Available from www.ey.com/in/en/services/tax/ey-india-beps-focus.

Gadenne, L. (2016). *Tax me, but spend wisely?* Source of public finance and government accountability, Warwick Economics Research Papers, No. 1131, October.

GIZ. (2018). *Supporting the tax authorities in Nepal*. Available from www.giz.de/en/worldwide/17876.html. Accessed January 3, 2018.

Grut, C. (2017). *How much do I need to pay? Changes to Afghanistan's tax law cause chaos and confusion*. Afghanistan Analysts Network. 23 March. Available from www.afghanistan-analysts.org/how-much-do-i-need-to-pay-changes-to-afghanistans-tax-law-cause-chaos-and-confusion/.

IMF. (2016). Sri Lanka staff report for the 2016 article IV consultation and request for a three-year extended arrangement under the extended fund facility; staff statement, and statement by the Executive Director for Sri Lanka, IMF Country Report, No. 16/150. Available from www.imf.org/external/pubs/ft/scr/2016/cr16150.pdf.

IMF. (2018). *Government finance statistics*. Database accessed February 14, 2018. Available at: http://data.imf.org.
Jun, J. (2017). *Tax incentives and tax base protection in developing countries*. Working Paper, No. WP/17/07, Macroeconomic Policy and Financing for Development Division, ESCAP.
KPMG Tax Rates Online Tool. (2018). Accessed on January 15, 2018. Available from https://home..com/xx/en/home/services/tax/tax-tools-and-resources/tax-rates-online.html.
KPMG. (2017). *India—Response to BEPS*. Available from https://home.kpmg.com/xx/en/home/insights/2016/06/beps-action-plan-india.html.
Long, C., & Miller, Mark (2017). *Taxation and the Sustainable Development Goals: Do good things come to those who tax more*? ODI Briefing Note, April.
Mansur, A. H., Yunus, M., & Nandi, B. K. (2011). *An evaluation of the tax system in Bangladesh*. Paper presented at the Conference on Linking Research to Policy: Growth and Development Issues in Bangladesh, Dhaka, December 20.
Pakistan, Federal Board of Revenue (FBR). (2017). *Tax directory: For the year ended 30 June 2016*. Tax Directory. Islamabad: Federal Board of Revenue.
Schmidt-Traub, G. (2015). *Investment needs to achieve the sustainable development goals: Understanding the billions and trillions*. SDSN Working Paper, Version 2. Sustainable Development Solutions Network.
State Bank of Pakistan. (2017). *Annual report 2017 (Special Section 1: Impact analysis of withholding taxes on cash withdrawal and banking transactions)*. Islamabad. Available from www.sbp.org.pk/reports/annual/arFY17/Special-Section-1.pdf.
United Nations, Economic and Social Commission for Asia and the Pacific (ESCAP). (2014). *Economic and social survey of Asia and the Pacific 2014: Regional connectivity for shared prosperity*. Available from www.unescap.org.
United Nations, Economic and Social Commission for Asia and the Pacific (ESCAP). (2017a). *Finance for climate action in Asia and the Pacific: A regional action agenda to access debt capital markets*. Publication No. ST/ESCAP/2803.
United Nations, Economic and Social Commission for Asia and the Pacific (ESCAP). (2017b). *Economic and social survey of Asia and the Pacific: Governance and fiscal management*. ISBN: 978-92-1-120780-4. Available from www.unescap.org.
United Nations, Economic and Social Commission for Asia and the Pacific (ESCAP) and Oxfam. (2017c). *Taxing for shared prosperity: Policy options for the Asia-Pacific region*. Briefing Paper. Oxford: Oxfam International and ESCAP. Available from www.unescap.org.
United Nations, Economic and Social Commission for Asia and the Pacific (ESCAP). (2018a). *Financing for development in Asia and the Pacific: Highlights in the context of the Addis Ababa action agenda*. Publication No. ST/ESCAP/2832.
United Nations, Economic and Social Commission for Asia and the Pacific (ESCAP). (2018b). Economic and social survey of Asia and the Pacific: Mobilizing finance for sustained, inclusive and sustainable development. ISBN: 978-92-1-120780-4.
United Nations, Economic and Social Commission for Asia and the Pacific (ESCAP). (2018b). *ESCAP financing for development series no. 2: Tax policy for sustainable development in Asia and the Pacific*. ISBN: 978-92-1-120767-5. Available from www.unescap.org.
World Bank. (2017). *Bangladesh development update: More, better, and inclusive jobs can boost growth*. Bangladesh Development Update, September 27, Dhaka.

Chapter 14
Policy Implications for Financial Inclusion of Unskilled Labor Migrants: Insights from Goa

Mridula Goel and Saurabh Nayak

Abstract With increasing urbanization, India has been witnessing phenomenal domestic migration and the resultant surge in remittances. The paper examines the case of using migrant remittances as one of the key triggers to encourage financial inclusion. It also seeks to initiate a policy debate on the role that the State should be playing towards financial inclusion. The paper echoes the need for a business approach tailored to financial needs and behavior of the end user. In line with this, it attempts to assess the demand side challenges faced by the banking sector in promoting financial services to the poor labor migrants. It also tries to assess their willingness and ability to shift to mobile based platforms of financial inclusion. The paper presents its findings based on a primary survey conducted in the state of Goa which has been witnessing a considerable inflow of labor migrants annually.

Keywords Financial inclusion · Labor migrants · Remittances
Payment banks · *Pradhan Mantri Jan DhanYojna* (Union Government scheme to bank the unbanked)

14.1 Introduction

In spite of the spectacular economic growth witnessed in the last decade, development continues to elude large numbers at the 'bottom of the pyramid' (C.K. Prahalad) in India. The extent of unbanked population has been one of the major impediments in achieving inclusive growth. Low labor productivity, non-wage employment, dependence on unorganized sector further add to the difficulty for families to plan an exit out of poverty, while adverse shocks sink families into spells of extreme duress.

M. Goel (✉)
Department of Economics, BITS Pilani, K K Birla Goa Campus, Goa 403726, India
e-mail: mridula@goa.bits-pilani.ac.in

S. Nayak
BITS Pilani, K K Birla Goa Campus, Goa 403726, India
e-mail: reachsaurabhnayak@gmail.com

A. K. Mishra et al. (eds.), *Current Issues in the Economy and Finance of India*,
Springer Proceedings in Business and Economics,
https://doi.org/10.1007/978-3-319-99555-7_14

Financial services provide tools and mechanisms that help to tackle many of these problems (Mas 2010). Yet, millions still find it difficult to avail the benefits of these services. As opposed to the traditional notion of the poor not wanting banking and other financial services, the success of microfinance in Bangladesh and in other developing countries emphasized the enormous unmet demand for credit that the poor yearned for. It illustrated that the failure of erstwhile business models was due to the high prohibitive costs involved in lending to the poor.

India has been striving for universal financial inclusion since its independence. Although controlling credit through nationalization of banks might have helped successive governments ensure credit flow to the much-deserved priority sectors, the banking 'structure' in India failed to evolve and meet the goal of universal financial inclusion. The financial inclusion efforts in the country have traditionally faced challenges both with regards to the delivery channels on the supply side as well as issues like financial illiteracy, irregular savings patterns, etc. on the demand side (Rangarajan Committee Report 2008). Lack of access to formal channels of finance has been aptly cited as one of the principal reasons for perpetual poverty.

However, this supply side problem is being increasingly addressed by the advancements in mobile and communications technology that have given rise to numerous financial innovations. The UIDAI Aadhar Card scheme too has helped in dealing with the 'Know Your Customer' (KYC) requirements. Such developments, coupled with a growing economy have made it possible for the State to augment its financial inclusion efforts on the supply side. However, the State needs to use its discretion as to the areas where it should directly engage and where it can create a robust policy structure, that can support private sector participation, fostering innovation and competition.

Perhaps we can borrow some lessons from recent experiments in financial inclusion. In the past decade, with a mandate from the Reserve Bank of India (RBI) -the central bank of the country- more than 100 million basic savings accounts or so called 'no frills accounts' were opened in the unbanked villages. Yet, 90% of these had remained inactive (Inter Ministerial Group Report 2010) suggesting a lack of effective design in the financial products and services that were offered to the poor. Perhaps taking a cue from earlier such experiments, RBI warmed up to the idea of creating a framework for issuing licenses to 'differentiated' banks like Payment Banks and Small Finance Banks to meet credit and remittance needs of small businesses, unorganized sector, low income households, farmers and migrant work force (July 17, 2014). This signifies a shift towards a more rational, market driven approach—one that questions a 'one size fits all' approach and seeks to foster business model innovation in response to the demand gaps seen in the economy. The regulatory foresight of the banking regulator needs to be lauded for attempting to create a policy structure of institution-building that is responsive to the economic realities.

It remains to be seen if such a 'demand-driven' economic sense prevails with the current Central Government. Ironically, while the RBI puts in place a structure for 'differentiated' banking, the Government's flagship program of '*Pradhan Mantri*

Jan DhanYojna' (PMJDY) pursues financial inclusion through the existing 'universal' banking structure thereby unduly favoring an existing business model of banking. Under PMJDY some 135 million bank accounts were opened until February 2015. Close to 63% of these however had zero balances in their accounts (source: PMJDY website). While the percentage of zero balance accounts is shown to decrease significantly from last year, it cannot be ascertained if the non-zero bank balances is a result of savings made by the poor or that of government sponsored subsidies routed as direct cash transfers (DCT).

Providing subsidies through the 'targeted' DCT route removes distribution inefficiencies in the subsidy system and in the process government-to-person (G2P) cash transfers also generate demand for banking services for the under-banked. However, it is here, we may argue, that the Government runs the risk of losing its economic sense in its quest for universal financial inclusion. It is necessary to make a distinction with regards to the nature of demand for financial services: one of an unmet but existing demand and the other of government sponsored/created demand. It is the nature of demand in the long run that would help in establishing a sustainable business model for financial services.

The Government sponsored welfare schemes[1] can provide a strong 'pull' factor favorable for the under-banked to use the banking services. However, it is only when the financial services offered are tailored to meet the requirements of the unbanked that such pull factors will succeed in establishing a financial habit. The Government needs to consciously choose the role it wishes to play—whether that of an 'enabler' or that of 'provider'—as this choice has major policy implications on both public expenditure as well as the sustainability of financial inclusion. The authors, therefore, argue the necessity for understanding the financial needs of the under-banked before making policy decisions that involve huge expenditure, lest we misdirect the scarce resources in our pursuit of noble goals.

Sustainable business models grow when they create 'value' for the end customer. There is a need to innovate and customize their products as per the requirements of the end user: the under-banked poor. Through this paper, the authors attempt to channelize the research related to financial inclusion towards a better understanding of the end customers. The paper focuses on studying the financial needs of labor migrants—a demography that has large numbers of the unbanked, that needs to engage with financial flows beyond simple earning and spending, and that is ever expanding in the Indian economy and yet receiving lesser attention in policy matters.

Migration has become an increasingly important phenomenon in the wake of rapid urbanization. The proportion of GDP contributed by migrant workers is estimated to be around 10% in India (Deshingkar and Akter 2009). The urban population is projected to rise from 286 to 575 million by 2030 (UNDP Poverty Report 2009). A substantial portion of the labor flow to urban areas comprises the poor labor migrants who are in search of better avenues of employment to improve

[1]PMJDY, LPG-Subsidies

their quality of life. Majority of these migrants work in the unorganized sector as daily wage earners and contract laborer's, or indulge in street vending activities as a part of the huge casual trade sector in the country (Deshingkar and Akter 2009).

The very nature of casual labor is such that it does not assure the laborer's continuity of job into the next day, week or month. They, therefore, need to insulate their daily expenditures from the inherent income volatility associated with casual labor. Savings can help to provide a buffer and protect against periods of unemployment. If people had secure and efficient savings cushions or insurance mechanisms, they would be able to weather these shocks of joblessness without much setback (Mas 2010). Most of the time, however, informal arrangements like hiding cash at home, buying and holding physical goods, jewelry, loaning out to relatives, participating in rotating savings groups with neighbors etc. cater to the savings needs of these migrants and their families and provide support in times of distress. However, the risky nature of these arrangements, many a time fail to give expected liquidity and often become a source of greater insecurity and stress.

A particular limitation of these informal savings mechanisms is that they operate strictly within the family or community where the saver lives, and thus, require the saver to rely on other 'poor' people in similar circumstances; or worse depend on 'money lenders' and 'loan sharks' type of lenders. This introduces an undesirable direct correlation between a household's condition and its ability to draw value from its savings, rendering the household's savings least effective when they are needed the most. Local informal savings arrangements and networks also tend to be shared, creating social pressure to share any accumulated wealth with family members and friends in times of their distress. This sometimes creates a disincentive to save (Mas 2010). The financial behavior of these millions of migrants also greases the informal value transfer system (Gopinath et al. 2010); and indirectly deepens the parallel cash economy. Too much cash floating in the system helps in laundering money and can thus possibly nurture criminal activities.

The phenomenon of migration results in transfer of income in the form of remittances. This outcome is natural to a society which has close family and village ties. Further, the magnitude of domestic remittances in the future is bound to increase as the labor mobility increases in the wake of economic changes. Domestic remittances in India were estimated to amount to 10 billion USD in 2007–08, of which only 30% was covered by formal sector remitters as compared to 75% in China (Tumbe 2011). This paper proposes to make remittances as an area of focus for engaging labor migrants into the formal channels of finance. The objectives of our study are:

- To examine the financial behaviour of domestic labour migrants
- To assess the extent of financial inclusion of migrants
- To identify the existence of an unmet demand for financial products among these migrants
- To evaluate the readiness of these migrants for adopting mobile based platforms for financial inclusion.

14.2 Financial Inclusion for the Less-Privileged in a Developing Economy

Financial inclusion can be defined as 'providing access to an adequate range of safe, convenient and affordable financial services to the disadvantaged and other vulnerable groups, including low income, rural and undocumented persons, who have been underserved or excluded from the financial sector.' (Financial Action Task Force 2013) This definition, however, calls into question the kind of financial services to be offered so as to bring about an effective financial inclusion. Remittance and Payment Systems, Savings, Credit and Insurance are the four main financial services that can be considered as parameters to measure, develop and channelize the financial inclusion efforts (Kunt and Klapper 2012).

The traditional brick-and-mortar banking model used to depend only on its branches to deliver the banking services. This business model evolved with time as technology got increasingly integrated with banking to enhance the customer experiences and reduce administration costs. Beginning with the ATMs, then the debit and credit cards, internet banking; all of these technology applications which the end consumer interacted with, essentially fulfilled the 'withdrawal' function in one form or another. In this banking model, however, the consumer still has to come to the bank's branch for depositing cash/check in his account.

The depositing function is especially important for the migrant population who need to remit funds often, though not large individual amounts. They also, find it difficult to meet banking compliance norms due to poor identification documents and floating residential status. The cost-revenue considerations of the universal banking model is the primary reason for making the vast under-banked poor an unattractive market, and thus, domestic Indian migrants employed in the unorganized sector remain largely 'unbanked'.

The advent of mobile technology has made it now possible to transcend these limitations and have transformed last mile solutions to reach millions of poor (Mas and Morawczynski 2009). The hugely successful experiments of using mobile technology for finance purposes in Africa like M-pesa (Mbiti and Weil 2011) have provoked interest and have added new dimensions to the financial inclusion efforts in India. Although the Indian and Kenyan economies differ in their endowment, structure and also the approach to financial inclusion, it is interesting to make a note of the conducive factors behind the success of M-pesa in Kenya.

The Kenyan experience suggests that cash transfers are an important need for migrant workers. The fact that M-pesa inculcated in its users an erstwhile almost non-existent habit of saving electronically and was being used as a storage mechanism by both the banked and unbanked populations (Morawczynski and Pickens 2009) suggests that there is unmet need to 'bank' these groups. It is important to understand their preferences in designing the financial product and above all provide ease of access that is suitable to their ability and work-life conditions.

Cognizant of the developments in mobile technology and its applications to finance, RBI devised a new regulatory structure for specialized kind of institutions: Payment Banks, in 2014. The RBI invited applications for banking licenses from entities having existing distribution networks which can serve as a vehicle to channel the financial products and services. From Postal Offices, Telecom Companies to Retailers, these can provide the easy and quick infrastructure to bank the 'unbanked'. Such entities have good distribution networks, and are often frequented by the less advantaged persons for their daily requirements.

In a developing economy, where most people prefer using cash, the network of cash merchants provide people an access to liquid savings and help create faith in the system. Liquidity i.e. availability to deposit and withdraw funds with ease, is especially important to attract the poor into using the service. It is however also necessary to separate the access component from the services component, at least conceptually, because they have different take-up drivers. The access component is driven by customer comfort with the use of the technology platform and related aspects, such as security, privacy, reliability, and convenience. The services component, however, is driven by the relevance and pricing of each service (Mas 2008).

To bank the less advantaged 'unbanked' groups, it necessary to develop attractive products that offer convenience and acceptable risk–return profiles for the poor users. It is therefore, important to identify the critical determinants of demand for the financial products of the economically less privileged class in order to ensure financial inclusion. A clear understanding of both the demand and supply side factors responsible for the limited usage of financial products is necessary to develop this market. Traditional notions and misconceptions have to be dispelled before a suitable mechanism can be worked out and put in place.

The financial institutions need to identify and understand the needs, financial behavior and habits of the poor. For example, in the context of casual labor migrants, remittance is an essential need for most of them. The banking sector can use this inherent need for making safe and secure remittances as the foundation to design suitable products and develop services targeted at migrants and their families. Financial inclusion of migrants, a large and growing populace, can help to create and increase the sustainability of financial models like that of branchless banking.

14.3 Methodology

14.3.1 Sample Area of Study

The findings in the paper are based on a primary survey of domestic migrant workers conducted in Goa, a state on the western coast of India. The state is the richest in India in terms of per capita GDP. The high per capita income coupled with large remittances from abroad contributes in keeping the native Goans out of the labor market in strenuous and hazardous jobs like mining and construction.[2] The high level of economic growth witnessed by the state coupled with the emigration of Goans to other countries has led to an increase in daily wages in the state attracting migrant laborer's from across India.

However, problems related to labor migration have begun to surface after the rapid influx of migrants in the state. Increasing instances of crime and environment pollution have been attributed to such migration by both the locals and the State Government. It has been argued that the scale and kind of labor migration witnessed is not conducive to the 'Goan' identity and also to the local tourism industry which is an important engine of economic growth in the state.[3] The problems faced by the migrants have also, to be dealt with efficiently, more so as the Goan economy thrives on mining and tourism; labor requirements in both sectors are largely supported by domestic migrants. The survey therefore, attempts to study and understand the problems of these migrants as well. It can be argued that a financially included migrant is less likely to create problems in the host economy and therefore, it is in the interests of the host economy to care for the financial well-being of its migrants.

14.3.2 Sample Study Design and Sample Selection

The study primarily focuses on the access and usage of financial services like remittance and payment systems, savings, credit and insurance available to migrants. The survey also, tries to capture the mobile literacy and mobile usage of these migrants to assess if mobile phone can be used as a potential device for increasing financial inclusion.

The sample chosen for the study comprised of migrants that were in the working age group 15–55 years old. 'Migrant', in this study, was defined as any unskilled or semi-skilled person who is originally from a different State in India and who has remitted money back home at least once in the last 12 months. Skilled migrant workers were not included as a large proportion of them already use the organized remittance channels like banks to transfer money.

The respondents in the survey were all male; primarily because most of the women who worked as daily wage earners lived with their husbands in Goa and were not participating much in the remittance mechanism. The sample selection was stylized using these aspects after considering the responses from a pilot survey conducted by the authors themselves.

[2]http://www.business-standard.com/article/news-ians/goa-eyes-rs-25-000-crore-industrial-investment-goa-newsletter-113052400753_1.html.

[3]http://articles.timesofindia.indiatimes.com/2012-09-03/goa/33562112_1_manohar-parrikar-chin chinim-villagers-migrants.

14.3.3 Data Collection and Quality Control

The survey was conducted over 5 months i.e. from January to May 2013. A total of 358 migrants were surveyed during this period. The Field Investigators were accompanied by at least one of the authors on the field trips to monitor the process of data collection.

The survey was administered at different public places, construction sites, slum locations etc. In some places where the laborers could not respond due to lack of time during working hours, their responses were recorded at the place of their residence in migrant settlements. The location of the survey spanned across the districts of North and South Goa to deal with any inherent biases in sample area. The laborers who were interviewed, comprised a random and diverse set of migrants in terms of occupation, state of origin, age, nature of employment etc.

14.4 Results and Findings

14.4.1 Demographic Characteristics

The proportion of migrants from the northern states of India like UP, Bihar, Jharkhand etc. comprised close to two-thirds of the total migrant population surveyed (Tables 14.1, 14.2 and 14.3; Fig. 14.1).

More than 25% respondents had come to Goa in the last one year itself. 50% of the sample belonged to the youngest age group of 15–25 years old; with an increasingly smaller proportion in the higher age groups. This trend just validates the increasing labour migration phenomenon evident in India. As far as schooling is concerned, approximately 60% of the unskilled migrants reported to have either left school after the primary level or have not received any schooling at all. In fact, 67% of all the migrants reported to not being able to read any newspaper.

14.4.2 Access to Financial Products

An analysis of the access to different financial services (Remittances, Savings, Credit, and Insurance) was done using the survey results: (Figs. 14.2, 14.3, 14.4 and 14.5).

Among the migrants surveyed, the remittance systems used included formal channels like banks and the postal system; as well as the cash couriers (physical movement of cash). Nearly two-third of the respondents used banks as channels of remittances, which was surprising, given the popular perception that the labor migrants do not have access to formal financial services. The different savings instruments employed by migrants included savings accounts with banks, savings

Table 14.1 Place of Origin

North count	237
East count	40
South count	61
West count	20
Total	358

Table 14.2 Age group (in years)

16–25	191
26–35	93
36–45	58
46–55	16
Total	358

Table 14.3 Schooling

None	93
Primary	125
Secondary	97
Inter College	35
University	8
Total	358

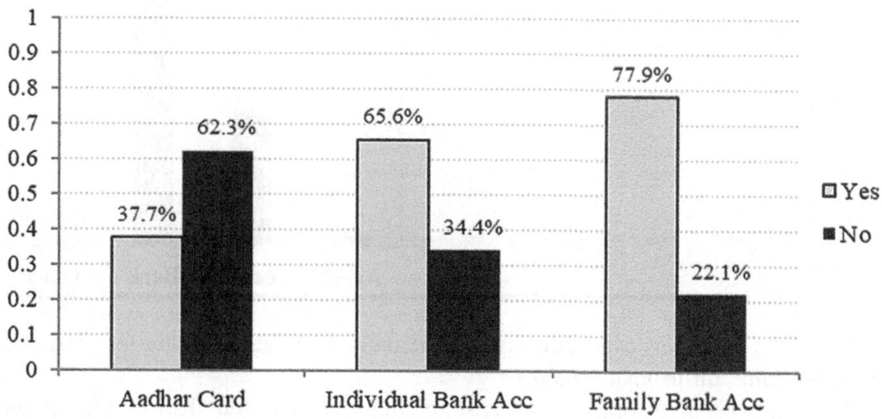

Fig. 14.1 Financial inclusion levels of the migrant population surveyed considering conventional parameters

with the agent/employer and those held as cash. Although, majority of them responded that they had savings with banks; many indicated they had to often wait for some time in spite of the daily nature of payments before they could make a trip

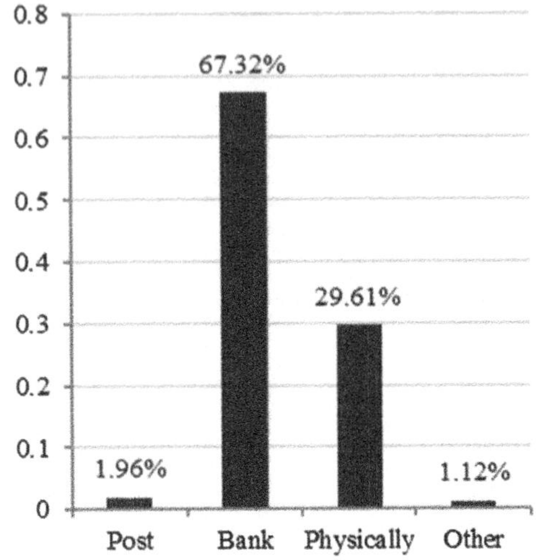

Fig. 14.2 Remittance Instruments

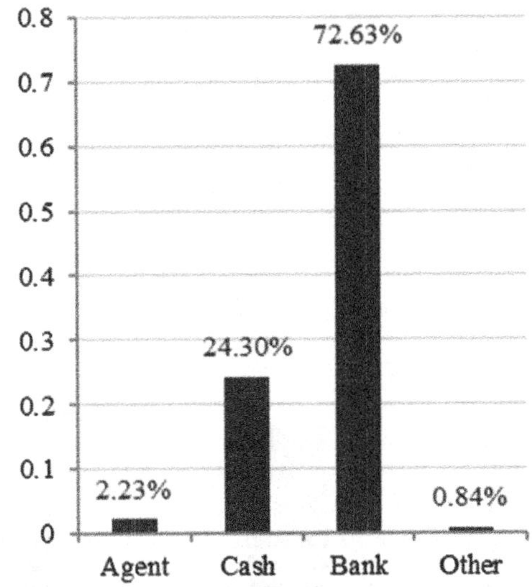

Fig. 14.3 Savings Instruments

to the banks. This was especially true of the daily wage earners who lost wages if they took time off to visit a bank.

The relatively high opportunity cost for migrants was found to be one of the principal deterrents that stop migrants from using formal savings and remittance services. In spite of two thirds of the migrants having bank accounts, only 6% of them had access to credit through formal channels like banks and Micro Finance Institutions (MFIs). This indicated a need for efficient credit channels as also, felt by the surveyed migrants. For the credit instruments available to migrants, formal sources like banks and MFIs as well as informal arrangements in the form of individual lenders and employers were considered. Popularity of life and health insurance services was also considered during the survey. Insurance was found to

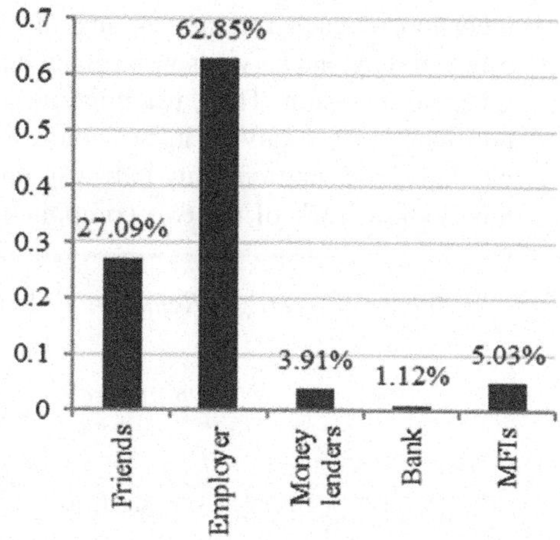

Fig. 14.4 Credit instruments

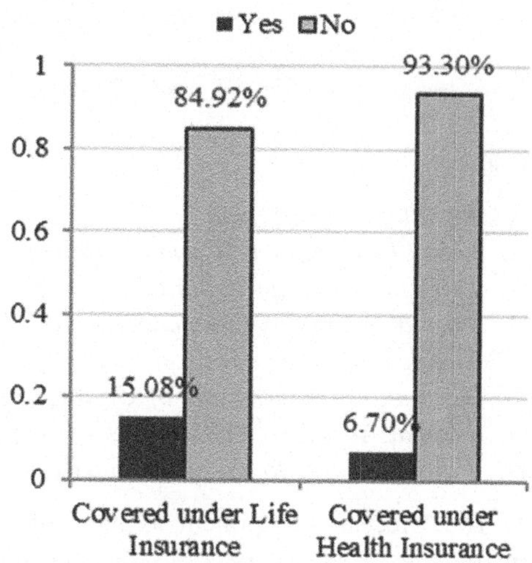

Fig. 14.5 Insurance instruments

be availed by less than 15% of the migrant population and was confined mostly to life insurance products.

14.4.3 Construction and Composition of Indices to Study the Financial Inclusion of Migrants

Financial Inclusion

- We constructed an index that conveys the degree to which a migrant is financially included. The index comprises of access component and usage components of different financial services. It focuses on the degree of financial inclusion of each migrant among the sample surveyed. Both the access and usage of financial services were given equal weights so as to reflect a meaningful financial inclusion. Thus, if a migrant has access to all the financial instruments but does not use any of it, he would have a score of 0.5 instead of 1 and we would call the migrant only half way into the process of financial inclusion. We now look at each of the two components separately

$$Access = Average\,(Remittance,\ Savings,\ Credit,\ Insurance) \tag{14.1}$$

$$Remittance = \frac{1}{3}\left(A - \frac{B}{2} - \frac{C}{2}\right)$$

$$Savings = \frac{1}{3}(D * \mathrm{E})$$

$$Credit = F$$

$$Insurance = \frac{1}{2}(G + H)$$

where,

A. *Remittance instrument*
B. *Cost of Remittance [Commission + Opportunity Cost]*
C. *Days taken by the Remitted amount to reach*
D. *Formal Access to Financial Services [Bank Account]*
E. *Savings Instrument*
F. *Access to formal source of Credit*
G. *Formal Access to Financial Services [Life Insurance]*
H. *Formal Access to Financial Services [Health Insurance]*

The 'Access' component as the name would suggest was with regard to the instruments used to access the financial services. In the case of remittances, where multiple formal channels were available, the parameters were graded favorably according to their degree of institutionalization. Thus, with regards to the parameter of 'remittance instruments', banks got the highest score, followed by post offices and so on. Also, negative weights were attached to the parameters that acted as barriers to the usage of the service. Thus, 'remittance cost' and 'time taken by remittances' were attached with negative weights.

For savings, the weights attached were binary i.e. 0 for informal instruments and 1 for formal instruments. Again, like remittance instruments, savings instruments too were graded favorably depending on the degree of their institutionalization. For credit instruments, loans taken from formal sources like banks and microfinance institutions were scored as 1 while those taken from informal sources was taken as 0. For insurance, the scoring was straightforward: 1 for having an insurance policy and 0 for having none.

Each of the four variables was given equal weight while calculating the Access component. Hence, all the four contributing variables were normalized to have a maximum score (i.e. the best-case scenario) of 1 each. The coefficients attached to various parameters making up a variable were chosen as a part of this normalization. Thus, the maximum value of the Access component which is an average of the four normalized variables comes to 1.

$$Usage = Average\,(Earnings,\ Savings,\ Remittances) \tag{14.2}$$

$$Earnings = \left[\frac{I * 100 * 312}{1000}\right]$$

$$Savings = [J * 12]$$

$$Remittances = [K * L]$$

Where,

I *Daily Wage Rate [in hundreds] †*
J *Monthly Savings [in thousands]*
K *Yearly Frequency of Remittance*
L *Average Amount Remitted [in thousands]*

The Usage component was included to get a sense of meaningful financial inclusion. It was however challenging to capture this component because of the inter-dependence between its determinants. For example, savings and remittances are a function of one's income while credit score is a function of one's payment history. Now, in case of a labor migrant who barely has had access to formal institutions and who generally lives on cash, maintaining a history of payments becomes very difficult. Therefore, remittance and savings history become good indicators of one's discipline and relative stability of income, helping to build a credit score in case of applying for credit.

Group saving schemes have been very successful in empowering financially excluded women and their families in rural India. Lending small amounts to a group has been established as a sustainable business where peer pressure and shared responsibility results in disciplined and timely re-payments. This too, however, is not possible for labor migrants because of the 'mobile' status of their employment.

Therefore, for understanding the usage component we focused on the variables that are relevant to the process of getting financially included. The earnings capability was included as a variable in this component as it directly affects the demand for these services. Thus, financial inclusion of a migrant can be said to have improved with an increase in income. The 'Usage' component also included average annual savings and remittances made by the migrants. All the three variables were then normalized individually by dividing a variable's score by its maximum scores respectively. Each variable was given an equal weight before taking the average to get to the Usage component for a particular migrant. The maximum value for the 'Usage' component therefore comes, to 1.

$$FIScore = Average\,[Access,\ Usage] \tag{14.3}$$

The final FI (Financial Inclusion) Score was then taken as average of the two components: Access and Usage. It was then sorted in an ascending order and plotted as a Financial Inclusion curve. The area under the FI-curve now indicates the level of financial inclusion of the migrant community as a whole. In the case of migrants in Goa, this was found to be only 0.36; indicating that migrants, on an average, were not meaningfully included in over two-thirds of basic financial services.

The FI-Score indicates the degree to which a particular migrant avails the banking services. When applied to demography of people, this approach can be used to compare potential target markets. Just as when a particular product or service is scaled, businesses need to decide on the key target segments which can be captured, the banking sector can use the methodology developed in this paper to define their markets. Financial institutions can use the method developed herein to calculate indices that can be applied on to different demographic profiles or geographic markets. The FI-Score would then help them in making competing choices that involve allocation of limited resources (Fig. 14.6).

Migrant Remittances

Nature and Need of Remittances:

It was discussed earlier that the lower demand for financial services by the poor should not be confused with the poor not being able to afford the services; but that it is the lower value proposition of the services itself that garners lower demand. We also, tested the validity of this argument with regards to the labor migrants in Goa.

The survey revealed two different profiles of labor migrants with respect to remittance behavior: one who is married and stays with his wife in the State itself; and the other who is not married or stays away from his wife and family. This distinction assumes importance as the number of dependents one supports has a direct bearing on the financial behavior of these labor migrants. In the first case it can be argued that when the migrant lives with his wife and family, a major part of their income is spent in the state itself leading to lower savings and also, lesser remittances. On the other hand, a migrant who is not married or is staying away from his wife and family spends less of his income in the host State and therefore, saves and remits more to the place of his origin so as to take care of his dependents. Indeed, among the migrants surveyed, it was found that while the first category remits only 12% of gross annual earnings; the latter remits 25% of his gross annual earnings. Likewise, the first category remits close to 33% of their annual savings while the latter remits more than 42% of their annual savings.

While it is difficult to comment on the remittances of the earlier kind of migrant; it can be argued that the latter kind who is staying alone would most likely be willing to remit all of his savings to his place of origin. However, it was found that although these migrants had earnings on a daily basis, they remitted less frequently primarily because of the high opportunity costs involved in making remittances.

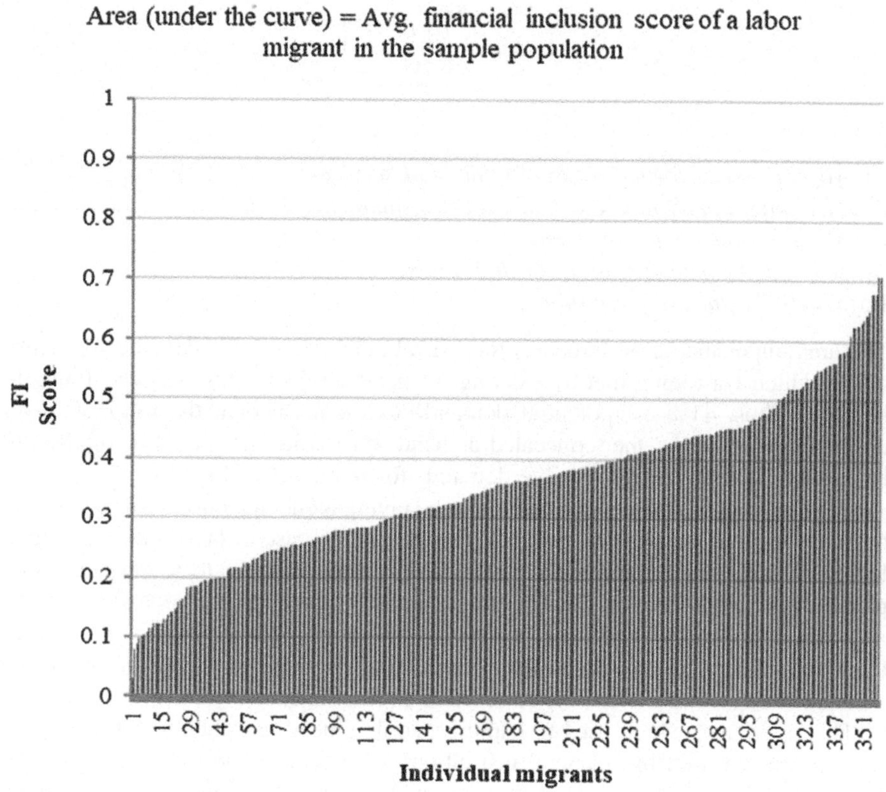

Fig. 14.6 Financial inclusion index for migrants

We therefore, try to assess the concealed demand for remittances which is not directly evident from the actual remittances made.

Measuring 'Concealed' Demand for Remittances:

The assessment was made by constructing a simple index. We attached equal weights to the 'Access' and 'Usage' variables. The 'Access' variable comprised of the parameters like that of migrant and his family having bank accounts; whereas the 'Usage' variable referred to the ratio of remittances to savings. The two respective scores were then normalized individually before taking an average to get a score for 'visible demand' for remittance services. The final score was then sorted in an ascending order to generate a demand curve for remittances.

$$Visible\,Demand\,Score = Average\,(Access, Usage) \tag{14.4}$$

$$Access = \frac{1}{2}\left[\frac{A+B}{2}\right]$$

$$Usage = \frac{1}{2}\left[\frac{D * E}{C * 12}\right]$$

where,

A. *Migrant has a formal access to financial services*
B. *Migrant's family has a formal access to financial services*
C. *Monthly savings [in thousands]*
D. *Average Amount Remitted [in thousands]*
E. *Yearly frequency of remittance*

The area under the curve indicates the 'visible demand' or the demand for remittances which was being met by existing financial services. This area was found to be 59%. Thus, 41% of 'potential demand' was concealed in the form of lower usage. In other words, the 'concealed demand' for remittances could be inferred to be as high as 69%[4] of the 'visible demand' for remittances (Fig. 14.7).

It can be argued that a migrant, although staying alone, may not wish to remit all of his savings to his place of origin. However, in the case of labor migrants, often loans are taken by the migrant's family to send the migrant to work in the first place. Then again there is the important factor of family being dependent on the migrant for its survival and well-being. Such factors indicate that in the case of labor migrants who stay away from their families, there is a case of concealed demand for appropriate remittance services in the State.

This approach, which tries to capture people's need and their satisfactory fulfilment, can be used by financial institutions to evaluate supply-demand gaps for existing products and services. Often, unsatisfactory experiences result in demand becoming dormant although an inherent need still exists. On applying this methodology to a basket of potential services which are to be offered to a target market, one can arrive at demand gaps for the different services. It is then possible for financial institutions to quantify the pain-points faced by potential users and tailor their services accordingly. Addressing a major pain-point would help gain more traction and get the poor to actively use some form of financial services. Other services could then be bundled around the service addressing the main pain-point.

An immediate application of the above argument would be for the soon-to-be active Payment Banks. By virtue of being in the payments business, these Banks could target the labour market for their unmet remittance needs. Payment Banks could use the 'remittance index' to quantify the demand-gaps and choose those geographical markets to roll out their services where there is a strong unmet demand. Choosing the right markets would help the Payment Banks gain easy traction, as also create and sustain a momentum once the services are introduced.

---

[4](1–0.59)/0.59 = 69%

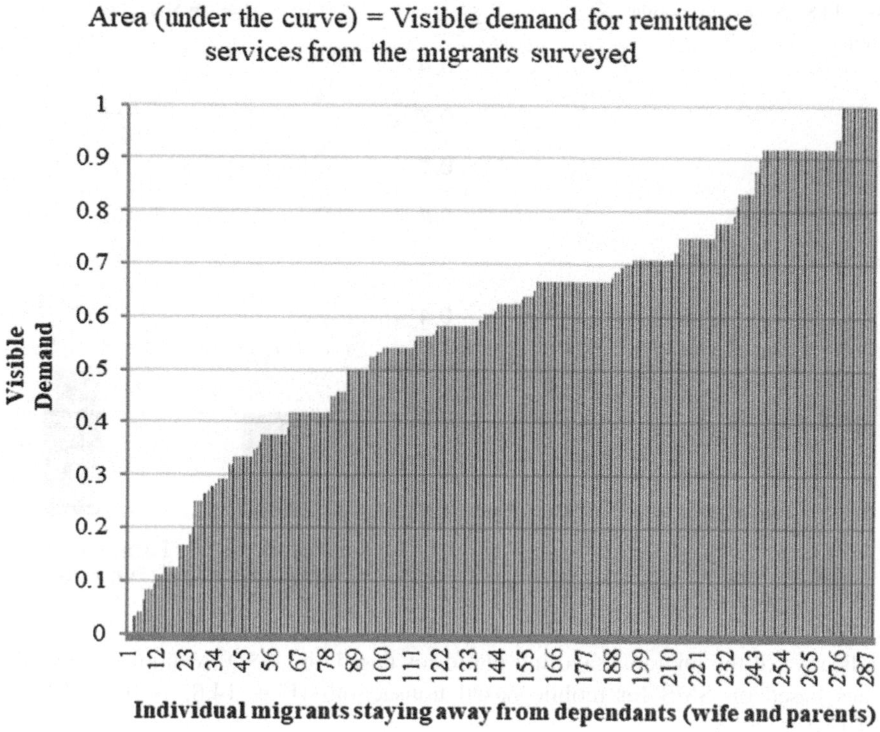

Fig. 14.7 Remittance index

Readiness for Mobile Remittances

As technology plays a key role in deciding the way end users today interact with the financial services, it was felt by the authors that this aspect too needed to be studied. The promising technologies of mobile payments have been around for quite some time but have not really taken off in India. The survey, therefore, made an attempt to study the behavior of migrants with regard to their usage of mobile phones; in order to assess their readiness in using mobiles as a platform for financial inclusion.

It was found that close to 80% migrants had mobile phones while 70% of their families living in their hometown also had one. However, more than one-third of the migrants (34%) did not have the SIM cards issued in their names and were using it by borrowing from someone with better KYC compliance in the State.[5] Another interesting finding was that while close to 68% knew how to check their mobile account balances, only 29% reported to be able to use the SMS facilities. This is

[5]This could be a social concern especially if this practice is creating hindrances in tackling crime in the state.

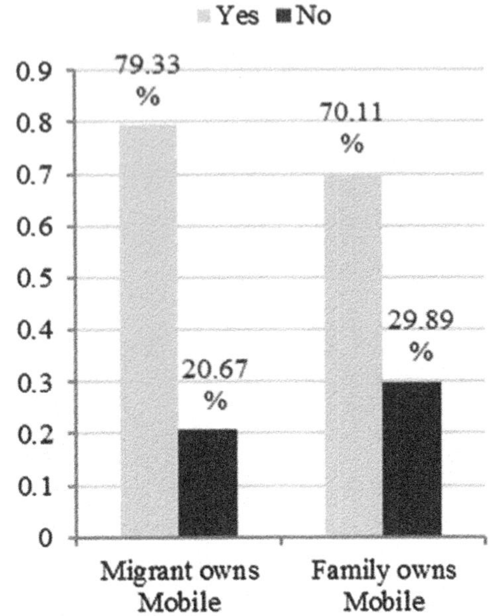

Fig. 14.8 Access to mobile phones

indicative of the migrants favoring platforms based on USSD[6] technology over the ones based on SMS for mobile based transactions (Figs. 14.8, 14.9, 14.10 and 14.11).

The willingness to remit using mobiles, given the choice was assessed by constructing an index based on four variable components: remittance experience, access to mobile finance instruments, mobile usage and mobile literacy.

The first component: remittance experience was selected so as to incorporate the satisfaction levels of migrants with the current remittance instruments. This variable therefore comprised of convenience parameters like the opportunity cost and time taken for the remittance. The access variable included parameters like the migrants having bank accounts and mobile phones. Similarly, the availability of these two instruments with their families back home was also taken into consideration. Mobile usage was included to incorporate migrants' behavior towards mini transactions.[7] The monthly frequency of mobile wallet recharge done by the migrant was considered to be a proxy of his willingness in doing transactions at the retail level. The literacy variable was based on basic reading skills and ability to conduct two mobile functions (viz. checking account balance and sending SMS) that are directly relevant to mobile based remittance platforms as parameters.

[6]Unstructured Supplementary Service Data (USSD) is a protocol used by GSM cellular telephones to communicate with the service provider's computers. It is the USSD protocol that is used to check mobile account balances (example, *123*1#).

[7]Availing products and services multiple times in smaller-valued transactions as and when required.

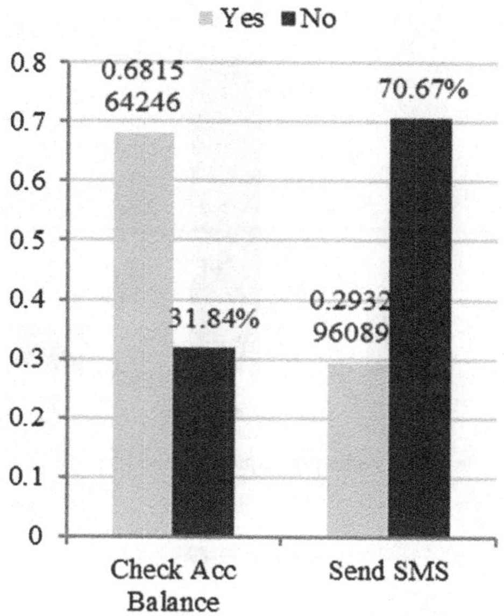

Fig. 14.9 Mobile literacy

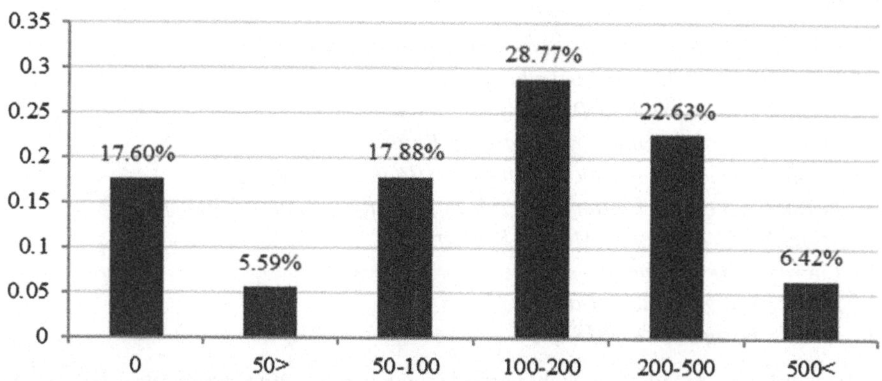

Fig. 14.10 Monthly expenditure on mobiles by migrants

$$Mobile\ Favourability = Average\,(Experience, Access,\ Usage,\ Mobile\ Literacy) \tag{14.5}$$

$$Experience = \frac{4}{3}\left(\frac{A+B}{2}\right)$$

$$Access = C + D + E + F$$

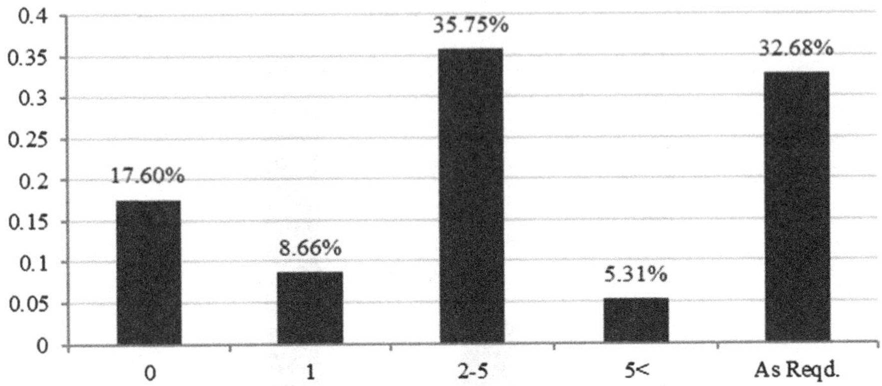

Fig. 14.11 Monthly mobile wallet recharge frequency

$$Usage = G$$

$$Mobile\,Literacy = \frac{4}{3}(H + I + J)$$

where,

A. *Cost of Remittance [Commission + Opportunity Cost]*
B. *Days taken by the remitted amount to reach*
C. *Mobile Usage [Mobile Phone?]*
D. *Mobile Usage [Family owns Mobile Phone?]*
E. *Formal Access to Financial Services [Bank Account]*
F. *Formal Access to Financial Services [Family's Bank Account]*
G. *Monthly Frequency of Mobile Recharge*
H. *Literacy [Newspaper]*
I. *Mobile Usage [Check Balance?]*
J. *Mobile Usage [Use SMS?]*

It should be noted that each variable had a maximum score of 4 (best case scenario); and therefore, the 'ideal score' (maximum), that implies migrant is completely ready for mobile based remittances, was 16. The 'real score' was then divided by 'ideal score' to get a normalized score for each migrant that was later categorized into 10 different groups. The percentage scores in the range 0–10 being least ready to shift to mobile based remittances while those scores in the range 90–100 most likely to make the shift when presented with an option of mobile based remittance payment mechanisms (Fig. 14.12).

It can be argued that if a percentage score is less than 50, the migrant is not yet ready and would exhibit inertia/difficulty when faced with a choice to remit using

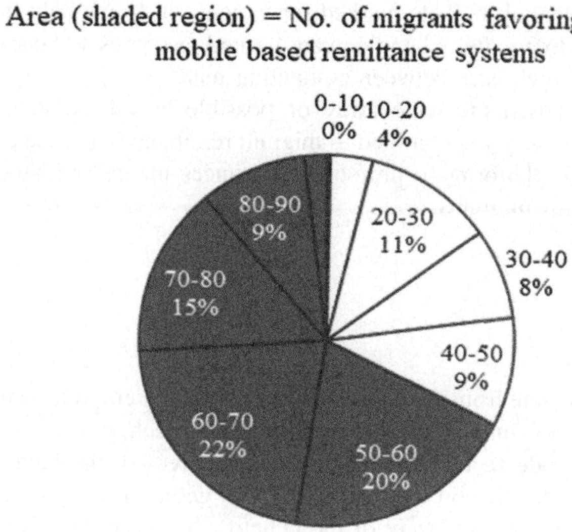

Fig. 14.12 Readiness for mobile remittances

mobiles. On the contrary, a score greater than 50 indicates a willingness and ease to remit using mobiles when faced with a similar choice. Thus, when the scores were grouped into 10 deciles, it became evident that, on the whole, close to two-thirds or 67.6% of the migrants surveyed would be both willing and able to exercise mobile based remittances.

14.5 Scope and Limitations of the Study

The findings in this paper are based on a survey conducted in Goa, a small Indian state with a population of 1.45 million, or 0.12% of the total Indian population. Its per capita state income of Rs. 2, 00,514 in 2012–13 was the highest in the country while the national average is Rs. 67,839. The state of Goa, therefore, may not be a true representation of the national picture. The fact that the per capita GDP of Goa is more than three times that of India as a whole implies that some modifications to our findings would be necessary to suit the state specific scenarios. Any generalization therefore, needs to be exercised with caution.

The authors, recognizing the data limitations, in no way suggest that the paper captures the migrant situation across India. However, it discusses a methodology that can be used by financial institutions to capture economic parameters like degree of financial inclusion, concealed demand for remittances and readiness for mobile remittances in any region or market. These parameters could be helpful in understanding the potential markets marked for expansion. It can help institutions prioritize the markets to go after when there are limited resources and decisions that are to be made involve choices between competing markets.

We have not discussed the wide array of possible benefits that result from financial inclusion. Our study is confined to migrant remittances and the probability of using mobile based platforms to promote remittances for faster financial inclusion of domestic labour migrants.

14.6 Conclusion

In the past, with a mandate from the RBI, banks have been attempting to provide an 'access' to millions of unbanked through different mechanisms and models. Although the supply side factors are being amply addressed, the banking sector seems to be facing challenges on the demand side in getting poor people use their services. The poor are either unaware of the benefits, if indeed there are any, that these financial services have to offer or are simply satisfied with their current financial arrangements. Either argument indicates that the perceived value of the offerings is too low for the poor to change their current financial behavior. It is in this context, that the case of labor migrants, an under-banked section of the population, was considered.

Perhaps, it is the lack of understanding of the problems that has resulted in large scale offering of financial solutions that do not effectively address the needs of the poor. Therefore, the central theme that the paper tries to underline is the necessity to revisit and understand the problems of the poor for whom the financial inclusion is sought. This fundamental approach has its implications on the public policy and business policy towards financial inclusion which are the subject matter of study for this paper.

If the poor do not perceive a value in the financial products and services offered to them, the initial success in on-boarding the poor into the financial system would fizzle out eventually. Having experienced this first hand, the RBI came up with a regulatory structure for issuing licenses to 'differentiated' banks like Payment Banks and Small Finance Banks in 2014. Differentiated banks with their differentiated approach to address the issues of remittances and credit needs would perhaps be better suited to get the poor to actively use formal financial services as compared to the universal or commercial banks, that have so far been using a 'one size fits all' approach to on-board the poor with the existing financial products and services.

It can be worrisome, therefore, when the State pushes for a faster financial inclusion through universal banks -majority of which are state owned entities-under its flagship PMJDY program. Financial inclusion is a noble policy objective but in name of noble policy objectives, hastily carried out big bang reforms could have negative long-term implications. The regulatory frameworks should be technology and business model neutral which allow for both technological and business model innovations. By favoring the existing business model which has time and again been proven to be ineffective for financial inclusion, the public policy of PMJDY appears to discourage business model innovation fostering in the new regulatory structure proposed by the RBI.

The paper discusses financial inclusion opportunity for domestic labor migrants in the wake of increased labor migration. As the people in India become increasingly mobile, the transfer of income in the form of domestic remittances is slated to increase dramatically. Since a substantial section of the labor flow comprises of daily wage earners, majority of who are not meaningfully financially included (as validated in this paper), there exists an inherent demand for safe, secure and efficient remittance systems that can be capitalized by the banking sector to 'pull' these migrants into active financial inclusion.

Our research indicates that current remittance arrangements do not efficiently fulfil the demand and there appears to be a concealed demand for remittances among the unskilled labor migrants. The phenomenon of migration thus spells a splendid opportunity for the banking sector to financially include a sizeable population in the country. To capitalize effectively on this opportunity, banks first need to tailor the products and services according to the convenience of the poor. The convenience and familiarity offered by mobile phones arguably increases the chances of an uptake of the financial services offered to the poor. Our findings with regards to the readiness for mobile remittances demonstrate a willingness on the part of labor migrants to shift to mobile based remittance systems from their current remittance arrangements when faced with such a choice.

As a concluding remark it can be said that while remittances and advances in mobile technology have opened up new avenues for financial inclusion for labor migrants, the success of this endeavor is greatly dependent on the execution by the banking sector and its regulator the RBI, for creating conducive ecosystems in the country. It is high time we design our regulatory structure, products and services keeping in mind the needs of the end consumer.

Acknowledgements This work was supported by the ICSSR, New Delhi under Grant 02-34/2011-RP. The grant was received to conduct research on Tourism in Goa and its Impact on Socio-Economic Conditions and Sustainable Development in the State. At the time of research, crime in the state of Goa due to labor migrants had become a major concern- especially for an economy driven by tourism. The authors felt the need to investigate the systemic reasons for this socio-economic development. Based on the premise that a financially included migrant having a stake in the development of host economy is less likely to be anti-social, the authors narrowed down their focus on studying the financial behavior of labor migrants. In the wake of recent developments in financial inclusion in India, the research eventually came to focus on the policy implications of the financial behavior of migrants

Appendix: Survey Codes

Parameters influencing the variables comprising the 'Access' component	Min value	Max value
A. Remittance instrument	0—Other	3—Banks
B. Cost of remittance [commission + opportunity cost]	1—100 INR	3—>300 INR
C. Days taken by the remitted amount to reach	0—Same day	3—>3 days
D. Formal access to financial services [bank account]	0—No	1—Yes
E. Savings instrument	0—Other	3—Banks
F. Access to formal source of credit	0—No	1—Yes
G. Formal access to financial services [Life insurance]	0—No	1—Yes
H. Formal access to financial services [Health insurance]	0—No	1—Yes

Note All variables were normalized before calculation of the access component

Parameters influencing the variables comprising the 'Usage' component	Min value	Max value
I. Daily wage rate [in hundreds]†	1—	5—
J. Monthly savings [in thousands]	0—<1 k INR	10—>10 k INR
K. Yearly frequency of remittance	1—1	10—>10
L. Average amount remitted [in thousands]	0—<1 k INR	10—>10 k INR

Note All variables were calculated on an annual basis and were then normalized before the final calculation of the usage component

Parameters influencing the variables comprising the remittance demand	Min value	Max value
A. Migrant has a formal access to financial services	0—No	1—Yes
B. Migrant's family has a formal access to financial services	0—No	1—Yes
C. Monthly savings [in thousands]	0—<1 k	10—>9 k
D. Average amount remitted [in thousands]	0—<1 k	10—>9 k
E. Yearly frequency of remittance	0—0	10—>9

Parameters influencing the variables that decide the favorability of mobile based financial inclusion	Min value	Max value
A. Cost of remittance [commission + opportunity cost]	1—100–200 INR	3—>300 INR
B. Days taken by the remitted amount to reach	0—real-time	3—>2 days
C. Mobile usage [mobile phone?]	0—No	1—Yes
D. Mobile usage [family owns mobile phone?]	0—No	1—Yes
E. Formal access to financial services [bank account]	0—No	1—Yes

(continued)

(continued)

Parameters influencing the variables that decide the favorability of mobile based financial inclusion	Min value	Max value
F. Formal access to financial services [family's bank account]	0—No	1—Yes
G. Monthly frequency of mobile recharge	0—rarely	4—weekly
H. Literacy [Newspaper]	0—No	1—Yes
I. Mobile usage [check balance?]	0—No	1—Yes
J. Mobile usage [use SMS?]	0—No	1—Yes

References

Committee on Financial Inclusion. (2008). Dr. C. Rangarajan, Ministry of Finance-India.

Demirguc-Kunt, A., & Klapper, L. (2012). *Measuring financial inclusion: The global findex.* Policy Research Working Paper 6025, World Bank, Washington, D.C.

Deshingkar, P., & Akter, S., Migration and Human Development in India. (April 2009). United Nations Development Programme, Human Development Reports Research Paper 2009/13.

Dror, D.M. (2007). Micro health insurance in India—pointers for progress. *IRDA Journal, 5*, (12) 2007.

Financial Action Task Force [FATF]. (2013). Anti-money laundering and terrorist financing measures and financial inclusion: FATF Guidance.

Framework for Delivery of Basic Financial Services Using Mobile Phones, Report of the Inter-Ministerial Group (2010).

Gopinath, S., Oliver, J., Tannirkulam, A., & Bhattacharya, S. (2010). *Putting money in motion: How much do migrants pay for domestic transfers?* IFMR Research, Centre for Micro Finance.

India: Urban Poverty Report. (2009). *Ministry of Housing and Urban Poverty Alleviation-India, United Nations Development Programme*. Oxford University Press, Incorporated, 9780198060253.

Isern, J., & de Koker, L. (2009). *AML/CFT: Strengthening financial inclusion and integrity. Focus Note 56*. Washington, D.C.: CGAP.

Mas, I. (2008). Realizing the potential of branchless banking: Challenges ahead (2008). CGAP Focus Note, No. 50.

Mas, I. (2009). The economics of branchless banking (April 1, 2009). *Innovations, 4*(2).

Mas, I. (2010). *Savings for the poor: Banking on mobile phones (August 23, 2010)* (Vol. 11, No. 4). World Economics.

Mas, I., & Morawczynski, O. (2009). Designing mobile money services: Lessons from M-PESA (April 1, 2009). *Innovations*, *4*(2).

Mbiti, I., & Weil, D. (2011). *Mobile banking: The impact of M-pesa in Kenya.* National Bureau Of Economic Research Working Paper 17129.

Morawczynski, O., & Pickens, M. (2009). *Poor people using mobile financial services: Observations on customer usage and impact from M-PESA*. © World Bank, Washington, DC.

Prahalad, C. K. (2004). *The fortune at the bottom of the Pyramid.* Wharton School Publishing.

RBI/2010-11/217DBOD.No.BL.BC.43/22.01.009/2010-11. (September 28, 2010). Master Circular on "Financial Inclusion by Extension of Banking Services—Use of Business Correspondents (BCs)".

RBI/2011-12/56DBOD No. Leg.BC.18/09.07.006/2011-12. (July 01, 2011). Master Circular on "Customer Service in Banks".

RBI/2012—13/45DBOD.AML. BC. No. 11/14.01.001/2012-13. (July 02 2012). Master Circular on "Know Your Customer (KYC) norms/Anti-Money Laundering (AML) standards/ Combating of Financing of Terrorism (CFT)/Obligation of banks under Prevention of Money Laundering Act, (PMLA), 2002".

RBI/2012-13/322 DBOD.AML.BC. No. 65/14.01.001/2012-13. (December 10, 2012). Master Circular on "Know Your Customer (KYC) norms/Anti-Money Laundering (AML) standards/ Combating of Financing of Terrorism (CFT)/Obligation of banks under Prevention of Money Laundering Act, (PMLA), 2002".

Tumbe, C. Remittances in India: Facts and Issues. (March 1, 2011). Indian Institute of Management Bangalore Working Paper No. 331.

Chapter 15
Income and Expenditure Mismatch of Poorest of the Poor: An Analysis of Financial Requirement of Slum Dwellers

Firdous Ahmad Malik, D. K. Yadav and Ranu Jain

Abstract Economic and social positioning of individuals are the prime indicators which are directly related to incomes of the households. Income and consumption expenditure determines economic stability and social well-being of the households. Income is used as a display to measure economic deprivations of the households in India. So, both the income and consumption expenditure are used to measure the overall conditioning of the households. Here the question arises weather consumer behaviour is determined more by income or expenditure. Some policy makers and economists believe that poverty can't be displayed by current income and it is not a stable measure to provide an exact description of individuals well-being (Meyer and Sullivan in The American Economic Review, 2221–2241, 2008). Consumption expenditure is not determined by consumers current income, but the measures of consumers "permanent" income are representative by his/her ability to earn income over a longer time period and also Expectations of future earnings and wealth (Friedman in A theory of the consumption function: A study by the National Bureau of Economic Research. Princeton University Press 1957). and the income which Friedman talks about is the annual incomes of consumers expect to earn over the years. It has been observed that income and expenditure didn't remain similar among households. Income is concerned as a good indicator of well-being for various reasons which are Housing, Food, Child care, Health care and other necessities. In low income households there is a possibility of consumption without expenditure and earnings. Income and expenditure are the two key fundamentals by which people make the best efforts to live a good life. Everyone wants to have a handsome income to live in a comfortable way. This study examines the income

F. A. Malik · D. K. Yadav (✉)
Department of Economics, BBAU, Lucknow 226025, Uttar Pradesh, India
e-mail: dev1985icfai@gmail.com

F. A. Malik
e-mail: malikfirdouscrc@gmail.com

R. Jain
SIMSREE, University of Mumbai, Mumbai, India
e-mail: sranujain@yahoo.com

A. K. Mishra et al. (eds.), *Current Issues in the Economy and Finance of India*,
Springer Proceedings in Business and Economics,
https://doi.org/10.1007/978-3-319-99555-7_15

and expenditure pattern of slums dwellers and their financial requirements among the key financial services (i.e. savings, credit, insurance, micro-leasing and pension schemes) of Lucknow city, Findings suggest that poor people can and do save, particularly when institutional barriers to saving are cut off. Institutional polices should target poor people on the bases of poverty so that poor can get an opportunity to promote their poverty into more sustainable and inclusive wealth endorsement policies that will assist them to create own pathways out of poverty.

Keywords Savings · Income · Consumption-expenditure · Financial-services Slums dwellers

15.1 Introduction

Economic and social positioning of individuals are the prime indicators which are directly related to incomes of the households. Income and consumption expenditure determines economic stability and social well-being of the households. Income is used as a display to measure economic deprivations of the households in India. So, both the income and consumption expenditure are used to measure the overall conditioning of the households. Here the question arises weather consumer behaviour is determined more by income or expenditure. Some policy makers and economists believe that poverty can't be displayed by current income and it is not a stable measure to provide an exact description of individuals well-being (Meyer and Sullivan 2008). Consumption expenditure is not determined by consumers current income, but the measures of consumers "permanent" income are representative by his/her ability to earn income over a longer time period and also expectations of future earnings and wealth (Friedman 1957) and the income which Friedman talks about is the annual incomes of consumers expect to earn over the years. It has been observed that income and expenditure didn't remain similar among households. Income is concerned as a good indicator of well-being for various reasons which are Housing, Food, Child care, Health care and other necessities. In low income households there is a possibility of consumption without expenditure and earnings.

The income and expenditure pattern vary from one household to other. Rising inequalities in societies has created larger gaps among rich and poor particularly regional inequalities, social and economic inequalities. Household expenditures remain limited because of household's limited budget but on the other side so many demands, desires, needs, preferences etc. which remain unfulfilled. These unfulfilled essential elements create the problem of inequality which touches social, economic aspects of a household's life. Now the question arises how the poor household fulfils their essential needs of life beyond their limited budget at their disposal.

Economists and policy makers till date remained attached in finding out the reasons of inequalities among communities by analysing income and expenditure pattern of households for social issues only. The importance of this study lies in the use of extensive primary data relating to the poorest sections, to validate the current understanding about how poorer individuals spend on consumption. The study has analysed the poorest of the poor especially Slums and beggars with respect their financial behaviour which one needs after the limits of their income. Study of income and expenditure of household is of long historical origin in economics, (Stigler 1954). Now a day's these areas need greater attention for social well-being of society as a whole.

The following Paper is discussing working conditions and earnings of slums dwellers by analysing demographic variables like education, gender, occupation and income etc. Further expenditure of slums dwellers has been analysed in three sub parts i.e. short run expenditures, Medium run expenditures and long run expenditures. Finally, this paper presents the analyses of income and expenditure mismatch by inflated the income for medium run and long run with addition of saving rates, to predict the working conditions of slum dwellers in India.

15.2 Review of Literature

Globally Poverty is recognised as a big curse on this earth there are several tough challenges for the wellbeing of the marginalised section of the society. It succumbs their free thinking towards the process of growth and development. Which develops the circle under which the section by compulsion of their Socio-economic conditions led them to live with? Now the thing is how to approach the circle of poverty so that to break down it and have prevention from it. Now the question arises who are the poor? Indian planning commissions main thrust was always poverty reduction, variety of methods have been used to measure it. Before 2005 it was measured on the basis of food security and was defined from per capita consumption and ability to pay for essentials of life.

15.3 Income and Expenditure Behaviour of Poor

Katona (1951–1975), posits that both ability to save and willingness to save are important determinants of savings, from this perspective, the low-income individuals may have lower savings rates because they are less to defer consumption.

Birdsall et al. (1996), Bhalla (1980), minimum level of consumption is necessary for survival. Individuals and households with incomes below this minimum cannot afford to save, because survival needs can't be deferred. Access to safe, easy and affordable credit and other financial services by the poor and vulnerable groups, disadvantaged areas and lagging sectors is recognised as a pre-condition for accelerating growth and reducing income disparities and poverty.

Grameen Bank (1998), it is the very poor who suffer most hardship in old age and most need financial protection for the end of their lives and many poor people are excluded from these devices. It again puts question mark how to fulfil the need of savings. It could be approached by two ways i.e. at the time of expenditure and also may be at the time of income received by the individual. So the need arises at the junction of income and expenditure for different purposes i.e. may be for precautionary purposes, transitive purposes and also for speculative purposes, to cope up different emergencies. So how one can determine sufficient level of money income for saving purposes, out of his limited money income by which he/she hardly fulfils their basic amenities to live.

Rutherford (2000) there should be protective needs for poorest of the poor and he argues about whether poor people need "savings" or "loans". Poor people need large sums of money for life cycle needs such as marriages, festivals and old age and also for different emergencies.

Access to a well-functioning financial system, by creating equal opportunities, enables economically and socially excluded people to integrate better into the economy and actively contribute to development and protects them against economic shocks. International consensus, regarding the importance of access to finance is a crucial poverty alleviation tool. The critical importance of micro-finance in achieving the Millennium Development Goals was highlighted at the World Summit, 2005, as well as in the endorsement by the Summit for the Monterrey Consensus of the International Conference on Financing for Development. The final declaration of the Monterrey Consensus put particular emphasis on strengthening domestic financial sectors to include underserved segments, such as rural areas and women. In most developing countries, a large segment of society, particularly low-income people, has very little access to financial services, both formal and semi-formal. As a consequence, many of them have to necessarily depend either on their own or informal sources of finance and generally at an unreasonably high cost. The situation is worse in most least developed countries (LDCs), where more than 90% of the population is excluded from access to the formal financial system (United Nations 2005). In India the basic concept of financial inclusion is having a saving or current account with any bank. In reality it includes loans, insurance services and much more. In an underdeveloped financial system, certain segments of the population experience difficulties in obtaining appropriate access to financial services. As a result, they have to resort to high cost informal sources such as moneylenders. This is particularly true for the sporadic financing requirements of low income households for non-productive consumption purposes and other emergency requirements.

The First-ever Index of Financial Inclusion to find out the extent of reach of banking services among 100 countries, India has been ranked 50. Financial inclusion is delivery of banking services at an affordable cost to the vast sections of disadvantaged and low-income groups. As banking services are in the nature of public good, it is essential that availability of banking and payment services to the entire population without discrimination.

15.4 Significance of the Study

The study mainly takes into account the poorest among the poor. Although almost all the government policies and schemes are formulated taking into account the same. But what is the ground reality being, really horrible and always a question mark for government policies and programmes. The present study represents one vulnerable urban group. Who are facing insecurity, livelihoods vulnerability and more important often outside legal protection from the state. The same group is opting informal banking sector despite availability of formal banking credit at cheap rates. The study will make an attempt to answer all this quire and try to make a policy input for the government.

15.5 Objectives of the Study

- To study the patterns of income flow and expenditure of the poorest of the poor by taking slum dwellers as illustrative case.

15.6 Hypothesis

- There is significant gap between income and expenditure of poorest households.

15.7 Methodology

The study has analysed both the qualitative and quantitative data to examine the research questions and objectives. The quantitative analysis has been done through descriptive statistics. The data was collected with the primary survey of 100 samples of slum households. Stratified simple random sampling has been used in case of slums. A structured questionnaire was used to collect the data which is composite of five parts. The stratification has been done based on the economic activities of the respondents in case of Slums dwellers, to make the population more representative and their economic activities were found to be heterogeneous in nature., the samples were arranged at a proportion of equality. 25 samples were collected from four areas of the Lucknow city, namely (1) RajniKhand (2) Mawaiyya (3) SharamVihar Nagar and (4) Daliganj-Pull.

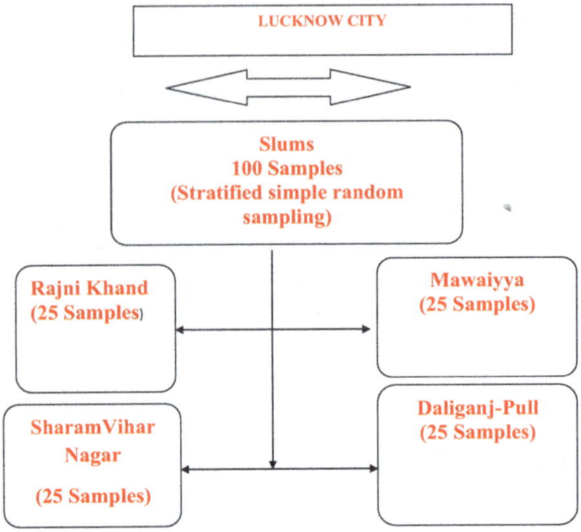

Fig. 15.1 Flow chart of sampling methodology

Fig. 15.2 Map of the study. S4 = Saram Bihar Nagar Mawaiya: S5 = Mawaiya: S6 = Hanuman Setu-Mahanagar: S8 = Daliganj Pull: S9 = Rajni Khand. *Source* PS used at field survey

The study also used secondary data to gain insights from the macro scenario as well as from experiences of other regions. The secondary data was collected from Census of India reports, NSSO, NGO studies, books, journals, magazines (Figs. 15.1 and 15.2).

15.8 Study of Slums

Table 15.1 shows the number of working days per month and number of working hours in day being attended by the slum population. The scaling of working days has been catagorised into three parts in the first part from 1–10 days with 1–8 h of duration, we have only 1 person engaged it this type of working setup. The next scale from 11–20 days in the working hour of 1–8 we have all most 83.33 percent of individuals in this setup, and 16.66% in same working days but with different scale of working hours which is 11–14 h per day. The third category which is from 21–30 days has a maximum distribution of working days against different working hours. From (0–8) h we have 76.47 persons in this particular group, similarly 9–10 h we have the total percentage of 19.85 persons and in 11–14 h we have 3.67% of persons in the vary category and finally the table also shows us the dependent population by the name of no working people who belong to the category of no works and no working hours are in a huge number of 377 persons.

Table 15.2 presents sex wise earnings of slum dwellers, the most important messages that this table gives us is majority of the individuals do not earn regular incomes; and of those who earn an income, of Rs. (200–300 a day) are only 13.84% (Fig. 15.3).

15.8.1 Income Profile of Households

Income plays an important role in determination of socio economic status of a household as well as a particular society. Income is the means of various

Table 15.1 Working days per month with number of working hours attending per day

Number of Working Days in a Month	1–8 h	9–10 h	11–14 h	No work	Total
1–10 days	1 (100.0)	–	–	–	1 (100)
11–20 days	5 (83.33)	–	1 (16.66)	–	6 (100)
21–30 days	104 (76.47)	27 (19.85)	5 (3.67)	–	136 (100)
No working	–	–	–	377 (100.0)	377 (100)
Total	110 (21.15)	27 (5.19)	6 (1.15)	377 (72.6)	520 (100)

Note Figure in parenthesis are percentage of total
Source Estimated from field data

Table 15.2 Sex wise earnings per day

Sex	No earnings	(1–100) rupees	(100–200) rupees	(201–300) rupees	(301–400) rupees	Total
Male	157 (56.90)	5 (1.81)	30 (10.86)	65 (23.55)	19 (6.88)	276 (100)
Female	220 (90.16)	6 (2.45)	5 (2.04)	7 (2.86)	6 (2.45)	244 (100)
Total	377 (72.6)	11 (2.11)	35 (6.73)	72 (13.84)	25 (4.23)	520 (100)

Note Figure in parenthesis are percentage of total
Source Estimated from field data

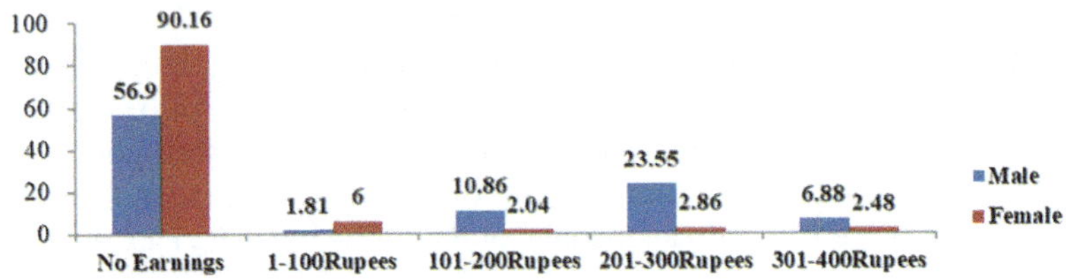

Fig. 15.3 Gender wise earnings per day. *Source* Estimated from field data

necessaries like, food, shelter, and other amenities of life that is health care, education etc. Poor people and their living conditions are highly affected by their lower incomes due to which they couldn't achieve their sustainable life pattern. Lower incomes enforce them into more deprivation time by time but on the other side the richer class due to higher incomes fulfil all important necessities and enjoy their life in a much comfortable way (Adler and Newman 2002).

Table 15.3 presents the income level has been arranged into five sub groups for the facilitation of analysis. The first group includes income levels from (1–5000) rupees in which the percentage of people is (23)%, in second group we have income range from (5001–10,000) rupees in this way (47)% of people. The third group is of

Table 15.3 Distribution of Monthly Household Income

Family income ranges	Frequency	Percent
(1–5000) thousand rupees	23	23.0
(5001–10,000) thousand rupees	47	47.0
(10,001–15,000) thousand rupees	20	20.0
(15,001–20,000) thousand rupees	7	7.0
(Above 20,001) thousand rupees	3	3.0
Total	100	100.0

Note Figure in parenthesis are percentage of total
Source Estimated from field data

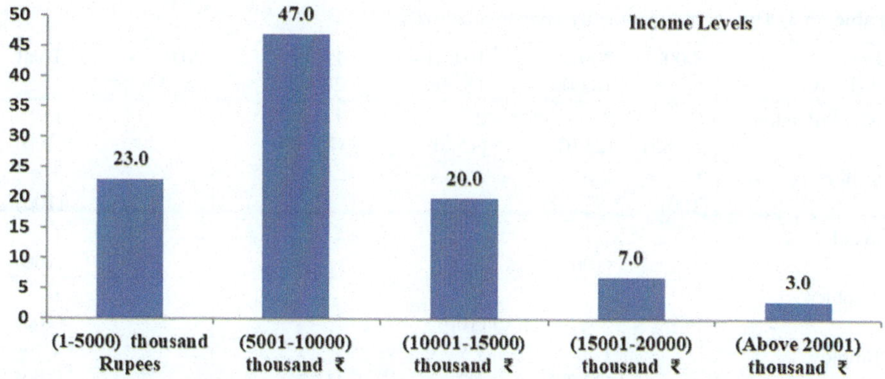

Fig. 15.4 Income distributions among slums. *Source* Estimated from field data

(10001–15000) were we have (20)% and in fourth one from (15,001–20,000) there are (7) of the people and finally from last group (Above 20,001) rupees there is the percentage of (3) people. From above the table the figures gave us the picture of income distribution of these people which shows there is also big gap in the income of poorest of the poor people (Fig. 15.4).

Table 15.4 shows gender wise family income of slums on monthly bases is as follows. From 1–5000 rupees the proposition of male is 22.10% which is the second highest among all income level; following by the second income level from 5001–10,000 rupees the percentage of males is 47.37% the concentration of population is highest within the group.

The third level of income from 10,001–15,000 rupees is 20% and in 15,001–20,000 rupees is 7.36% and the following the last income group from 20,001–25,000 we have 3.15% of male concentration. The story of female group is we have only 40% of women in the first income group and also same 40% in the second group and followed by third group where we have only 20% of women etc. in the rest income groups we have zero concentration of women.

Table 15.4 Household income gender wise

Gender	1–5000	5001–10,000	10,001–15,000	15,001–20,000	20,001–25,000	Total
Male	21 (22.10)	45 (47.37)	19 (20)	7 (7.36)	3 (3.15)	95 (100)
Female	2 (40)	2 (40)	1 (20)	–	–	5 (100)
Total	23 (23)	47 (47)	20 (20)	7 (7)	3 (3)	100 (100)

Note Figure in parenthesis are percentage of total
Source Estimated from field data

Table 15.5 Household income by economic activity

Economic Activity	5000	5001–10,000	10,001–15,000	15,001–20,000	20,001–25,000	Total
KhodaBeedna	7 (53.85)	3 (23.07)	2 (15.38)	1 (7.69)	–	13 (100)
Tailor	2 (100)	–	–	–	–	2 (100)
Welder	–	1 (100)	–	–	–	1 (100)
Cobbler	–	–	1 (100)	–	–	1 (100)
Employ	–	1 (33.33)	1 (33.33)	1 (33.33)	–	3 (100)
Vending	–	–	1 (100)	–	–	1 (100)
Causal Labour	3 (5.89)	32 (62.74)	11 (21.56)	4 (7.84)	1 (1.96)	51 (100)
Driver	–	1 (20)	2 (40)	1 (20)	1 (20)	5 (100)
Rickshaw Puller	2 (28.57)	3 (42.85)	1 (14.29)	–	1 (14.28)	7 (100)
Sales Man	–	2 (100)	–	–	–	2 (100)
No Work	2 (40)	2 (40)	1 (20)	–	–	5 (100)
Bhavsyavani	7 (77.77)	2 (22.23)	–	–	–	9 (100)
Total	23 (23)	47 (47)	20 (20)	7 (7)	3 (3)	100

Note Figure in parenthesis are percentage of total
Source Estimated from field data

Table 15.5 Economic activity and distribution of household income among slums is khodaBeedna, Tailor, Welder, Cobbler, Employ, vending, casual labour, Rickshaw puller, Sales man Bhavsyavani, are the activities in which the slum population is involved. The highest concentration is with casual labour where among the 100 households we have 51 persons in this activity with highest income scale of 5001–10,000 rupees the number of individuals is 32. After casual labour the second highest is the activity of khodaBeedna with number of individuals is 13. With higher concentration of 5000 rupees. Economic activities also determine the level of income of households but the activities the slum population is involved are unskilled and temporary.

15.9 Education and Income of Slums

Education plays an important role in the well-being of the people. It helps in making life better in every aspect. Table 15.6 Shows the educational status with respect to income of slums is that at primary level the number of individuals is only 6 having the highest level of income as 10,001–15,000 with the number of 3 households. The education status shows us that in the first income group we have zero results and the second, third and fourth group we have equal distribution of individual households at different incomes. The total number of individual at middle level is 6 persons. In the higher educational level, we have only three persons we are earning more than 5000 rupees. The illiterate group is the dominated group with 21 persons in the range of 1–5000 rupees, 41 persons in the second income group of 5001–10,000 rupees and 15 persons in the third income group and so on.

15.10 Expenditure Pattern of Slums

Expenditure plays pivotal role in the life structure of households which is fully dependent on income of the households. So, expenditure is directly affected by income constraints of the households. Following are the expenditures on which the slum population has been analysed the first one is expenditure in short run which is a composition of food grains, vegetables, milk products, fuel, egg and related products, health, transport, consumer goods and non-essential food items etc. second expenditure on fuels, third one is expenditure on emergencies, fourth one is the expenditure on services, costumer goods, assets, social expenditures and others.

Table 15.6 Household income by education

Education	1–5000	5001–10,000	10,001–15,000	15,001–20,000	20,001–25,000	Total
Primary	1 (16.66)	2 (33.33)	3 (50)	–	–	6 (100)
Middle	–	2 (33.33)	2 (33.33)	2 (33.33)	–	6 (100)
High	–	3 (100)	–	–	–	3 (100)
Illiterate	21 (24.71)	41 (48.23)	15 (17.64)	5 (5.88)	3 (3.52)	85 (100)
Total	22 (22)	48 (48)	20 (20)	7 (7)	3 (3)	100 (100)

Note Figure in parenthesis are percentage of total
Source Estimated from field data

Every Human being for his/her survival needs consumption of various goods and services to live,

Table 15.7 shows us the short run expenditure of slums dwellers being scaled or categorised on the scales of department of economic advisory. The highest expenditure is on food grains minimum of 360 rupees and the maximum of 4200 hundred rupees per month. The average expenditure on food grains is 1503 rupees and the deviation from the average is 559.28 rupees. The expenditure of vegetables, minimum of 20 rupees and maximum of 3000 rupees, at an average of 279.44 rupees with a higher deviation of 310.51 rupees. The next expenditure on milk products shows a declining participation of households with only 77 members with minimum expenditure of 50 rupees and maximum of 1800 rupees. The average expenditure on milk is 451.30 rupees and a diversion from average is 284.24 rupees. Fuel one of the key expenditures with minimum expenditure of 20 rupees and maximum of 250 rupees with average of 90.63 rupees and the deviation from the average is 40.32 rupees.

Expenditure on egg related products also shows less participation of households but with a very big gap of minimum of 40 rupees and maximum of 3000 rupees. The average expenditure is 648.57 rupees with a lofty deviation of 562.47 rupees. Health among the very important and essential expenditure of human life. The expenses at minimum level are only 20 rupees and the maximum of 1000 rupees shows a wide gap the average expenditures are 170.41 with the deviation of 136.30

Table 15.7 Short run expenditures of slums

Expenditures	N	Minimum	Maximum	Mean	Std. deviation
Food grains (rice, wheat, pulses)	100	360	4200	1503.00	559.281
Vegetables	90	20	3000	279.44	310.514
Milk products (ghee, butter, ice cream, milk powder, dahi, paneer)	77	50	1800	451.30	284.241
Fuel (kerosene etc.)	99	20	250	90.63	40.328
Egg and related products (meat, chicken, fish etc.)	77	40	3000	648.57	562.475
Health	97	20	1000	170.41	136.305
Transport (fare charges)	92	20	1150	171.63	170.895
Consumer goods (Fmcg, other personal goods, expenses on children's pocket money and food items)	96	30	400	467.86	487.739
Non-essential food items (Paan, tobacco, intoxicants, entertainment, liquor/gambling)	92	20	3000	555.92	449.700

Note Figure in parenthesis are percentage of total
Source Estimated from field data

rupees. The average expenditure on transport services is 171.63 rupees and standard deviation of 170.89 rupees.

Consumer goods expenditure also showed a good participation of households with the average expenditure of 467.86 rupees and the deviation of 487.73 rupees. One of the common perceptions that poor people are using their money for ill uses the figures of non-essential expenditures shows us a huge participation of households using their money for non-essential food items with an average of 555.92 rupees and the deviation of 449.70 rupees.

15.11 Medium Term Expenditures

Table 15.8 presents the Medium-term expenditures of slums have been categorised into two broad headings which are social expenditures which consists of minimum 20 rupees and maximum of 200,000 rupees of an average 28,644 rupees and a higher deviation of 3686.55 rupees. Another medium-term expenditure are white goods which shows us the average of 3141.29 rupees and a deviation from mean is 6287.21 rupees.

15.12 Long Term Expenditures

Table 15.9 presents long term expenditure covers all the expenditures which are important as well as very costly the first expenditure which is in the long run is marriages which covers the minimum expenditure of 2500 rupees and maximum of 2,000,000 rupees with a mean of 4984.4 rupees and standard deviation of 36,232.60 rupees. Similarly, the expenditures of assets are which ranges from minimum of 20 rupees and maximum of 31,500 rupees with an average of 434.87 rupees and the deviation of 6151.97 rupees the expenditure on emergencies are 200 hundred as minimum and maximum of 40,300 with an average of 5482.54 and the deviation from average is 7863.16 rupees (Table 15.10).

Table 15.8 Medium term expenses (more than 1 year)

Expenditures	N	Minimum	Maximum	Mean	Std. deviation
Social expenditures (festivals, social events/gifts, expenses on blind beliefs, pilgrimage)	85	20	200,000	28,644	3686.553
White goods (TV, car, refrigerator, fan etc.)	79	30	40,000	3141.29	6287.215

Note Figure in parenthesis are percentage of total
Source Estimated from field data

Table 15.9 Long term expenditures (more than 5 years)

Expenditures	N	Minimum	Maximum	Mean	Std. deviation
Marriages (food preparation, dowry etc.)	48	2500	200,000	4984.4	36232.608
Assets (jewellery and ornaments, shelter own house old age planning, expenses on productive assets, repair and maintains houses)	80	20	31,500	434.87	6151.974
Emergencies (accidents, diseases, unproductive expenses on natural calamities)	59	200	40,300	5482.54	7863.165

Note Figure in parenthesis are percentage of total
Source Estimated from field

Table 15.10 Individual income of slums on average bases

Individual Income daily	Minimum	Maximum	Mean	Std. deviation
Slums	50	600	224.85	96.349
Working days of slums	9	30	27.59	4.124
Working hours of slums	2	14	8.44	2.747

Note Figure in parenthesis are percentage of total
Source Estimated from field data

The individual income of beggars per day at minimum level is 5 rupees and maximum of 300 rupees the average income of beggars is 97.96 rupees per day while the deviation from average income are 73.713 rupees, it shows us very high divergence in the individual incomes. The condition of working days per month is 4 minimum working days and maximum of 30 working days with an average of 27.36 days per month. There is a slight divergence of 6.119 days. Working hours per day with a minimum of 4 and maximum of 16 h a day and the mean of working hours is 8.90 h with a slight lower deviation of 2.301 h per day.

15.13 Mismatch Stories of Income and Expenditure of Slums

$$\textit{Net income Gap of Short Run} = \frac{\textit{Accumulated Savings}}{\textbf{Average Short Run Income Monthly}} * 100$$

$$\textit{Net income Gap of Short Run} = \frac{\mathbf{6530.56}}{\mathbf{9255.55}} * \mathbf{100} = \mathbf{70.56}$$

Table 15.11 Mismatch results of short run (A)

Year	Average short run income	Average short-term expenses of slums	Net position	Saving rate 7.89	Net position monthly
2015	9255.55	3202.57	6052.98	6530.56	70.55831

Note Figure in parenthesis are percentage of total
Source Estimated from field data

Table 15.11 presents average short run income 9255.55 rupees and average short run expenditure is 3202.57 rupees of slums. The net position of slums is 6052.98 rupees with saving rate of (7.89) makes the net savings 6530.56 rupees. The annual Mismatch gap shows surplus of 70.55% in short run. Therefore, the net position of slums in short run is almost positive.

$$\textbf{\textit{Net income Gap of Short Run}} = \frac{\textbf{Accumulated savings}}{\textbf{Average Short run income annually}} *\mathbf{100}$$

$$\textbf{\textit{Net income Gap of Short Run}} = \frac{\mathbf{5730.961}}{\mathbf{111{,}066.6}} *\mathbf{100} = \mathbf{5.45}$$

Table 15.12 shows annual percentage of Mismatch gap which have been estimated by average short run income minus. Net position 7263.76 has been added by saving rate (7.89) which average short run expenditures becomes accumulated saving 5730.76. Hence net income gap of short run has been estimated by the above formula therefore 5.44% is the annual surplus of slums in the short run.

$$\textbf{\textit{Net Mismatch Gap of Medium Run}} = \frac{\textbf{\textit{(Accumulated Savings − Final Value of Medium run)}}}{\textbf{\textit{Accumulated Savings}}} * \mathbf{100}$$

$$\textbf{\textit{Net income Gap of Medium Run}} = \frac{\mathbf{(469{,}506.6 - 38{,}278.22)}}{\mathbf{469{,}506.6}} * \mathbf{100} = \mathbf{91.85}$$

Table 15.13 shows mismatch gap of short run income and short run expenditure. The short run income as well as short run expenditure have been inflated by consumer price index at the rate of 6.09% from 2016–2020. The short run average income in 2015 is (9255.55) as well as short run average expenditure (3202.57) of

Table 15.12 Mismatch results of short run (B)

Slums					
Year	Average short run income annually	Average short-term expenses of slums	Net position	Saving rate 7.89	% of annual miss match gap
2015	111,066.6	38,430.84	72,635.76	5730.961	5.4498652

Table 15.13 Mismatch results of medium run

Slums					
Year	Shortrun average income annually (9255.55)	Short run average expenditures of slums (3202.57)	Net position	Saving rate 7.89	Medium term expenses (28,482.59)
2016	117,830.6	40,771.28	77,059.28	83,139.25	30,217.18
2017	125,006.4	43,254.25	81,752.19	88,202.44	32,057.41
2018	132,619.3	45,888.43	86,730.9	93,573.96	34,009.7
2019	140,695.8	48,683.04	92,012.81	99,272.62	36,080.89
2020	149,264.2	51,647.84	97,616.39	105,318.3	38,278.22
				469,506.6	

Note Figure in parenthesis are percentage of total
Source Estimated from field data

rupees has been converted in annual terms. The net position has been calculated from short run income and short run expenditure and the accumulated savings have been estimated by adding the net savings which are 469,506.6 rupees. Similarly, the medium-term expenses have been inflated from 2016–2020 the final value 38,278.22 have been deducted from accumulated value of net savings. The Medium-term mismatch among slums is 91.84% of rupees.

$$\textbf{\textit{Net Mismatch Gap of Long Run}} = \frac{(\textbf{\textit{Accumulated Savings}} - \textbf{\textit{Final Value of Long expenses}})}{\textbf{\textit{Accumulated Savings}}} * \mathbf{100}$$

$$\textbf{\textit{Net credit Gap of Long Run}} = \frac{(\mathbf{1{,}033{,}832 - 55{,}592})}{\mathbf{1{,}033{,}832}} * \mathbf{100} = \mathbf{94.62}$$

Table 15.14 shows mismatch gap of short run income and Long run expenditure both short run income as well as short run expenditure have been converted annually and have inflated by the inflated rate of 6.09% being calculated by consumer price index from 2016–2025 years to know the actual mismatch gap of slums in the long run. The net position has been calculated by deducting short run average expenses from short run average income. The accumulated savings have been estimated by adding the net position which is 1,033,832 rupees. Similarly, the long run expenses have been inflated from 2016 to 2025 years the final value of 2025 have been deducted from accumulated savings which shows the mismatch gap of slums in the long run of 94.62%. Therefore, the condition of slums in the long run is positive.

Table 15.14 Mismatch results long run

Slums					
Year	Short term average income annually (9255.55)	Short term average expenses of slums (3202.57)	Net positioning	Saving rate 7.89	Long run expenses (30,780.11)
2016	117,830.6	40,771.28	77,059.28	83,139.25	32,654.62
2017	125,006.4	43,254.25	81,752.19	88,202.44	34,643.28
2018	132,619.3	45,888.43	86,730.9	93,573.96	36,753.06
2019	140,695.8	48683.04	92,012.81	99,272.62	38,991.32
2020	149,264.2	51,647.84	97,616.39	105,318.3	41,365.89
2021	158,354.4	54,793.19	103,561.2	111,732.2	43,885.08
2022	167,998.2	58,130.09	109,868.1	118,536.7	46,557.68
2023	178,229.3	61,670.22	116,559.1	125,755.6	49,393.04
2024	189,083.5	65,425.93	123,657.5	133,414.1	52,401.08
2025	200,598.6	667,107.6	69,410.37	74,886.85	55,592.3
				1,033,832	

Note Figure in parenthesis are percentage of total
Source Estimated from field data

15.14 Conclusions

Income and expenditure are the two key fundamentals by which people make the best efforts to live a good life. Everyone wants to have a handsome income to live in a comfortable way. Present study analyses the income and expenditure of two urban "poorest of the poor" sections of society which are slums from Lucknow. The study was examined on the grounds of economic activities of the two sections and their earnings. The income of slums from rupees (1–5000) rupees covers 23% of the slums and from (5001–10,000) rupees 47 persons are in the range. The economic activities in which the slums population is engaged with higher concentration are casual labour 51%, KhodaBeedna 13%, Rick Puller 7% and Bhavsyavani 9% etc. The working days of slums are minimum 9 days and maximum of 30 days per month and the working hours are Minimum of 2 h and maximum of 14 h. The daily income of slums is Minimum of 50 rupees and maximum of 600 rupees. Expenditures of slums on food grains per month by slums is 360 minimum and maximum of 4200 rupees. Similarly, the expenditures on health are 20 at minimum and 1000 maximum per month and the expenditures on non-essential are 20 rupees at minimum and maximum of 3000 rupees respectively.

The net mismatch position of slums in short run monthly is 70.55% and the short run annual mismatch is 5.44% in medium run 91.84% of surplus and in long run 94.62% of surplus. So, the slums are having surplus income in both the three periods. In case of slums they have positive savings but they are compromising all their essential expenditures i.e. Housing, Education of Children, and others day to day things. The surplus income of slums is totally spurious because of small size of sample, seasonal variations in incomes and the reporting problem of the slums etc.

Besides all the "poorest of the poor" tries to earn to make expenses on daily routine things. Their earnings are very low with higher working hours and high problems of insecurity at working places. The psycho economic conditions are very bitter to manage their earnings. Due to which they didn't support their essential of livings of the worrying nature of mentality which keeps them away from regular working days and making ill use of their earnings. The income and expenditure levels of beggars showed us that there is huge and severe gap in short run income and short expenditure but they try to manage their expenses through credit from friends and relatives and having very critical gap in long run expenses which they didn't met same is the cause of slums. Finally, this paper concludes that poor people need credit to full fill their basic needs.

References

Adler, N. E., & Newman, K. (2002). Socioeconomic disparities in health: pathways and policies. *Health Affairs, 21*(2), 60–76.

Atkinson, A. B. (1998). *Poverty in Europe*. Oxford: Blackwell.

Bhalla, S. S. (1980). The measurement of permanent income and its application to savings behavior. *Journal of Political Economy, 88*(4), 722–744.

Ford, J., & Rowlingson, K. (1996). Low-income households and credit: Exclusion, preference and inclusion. *Environment and Planning A, 28,* 1345–1360.

Friedman, M. (1957). *A theory of the consumption function: A study by the National Bureau of Economic Research*. Princeton University Press.

Katona, G. (1951). *Psychological analysis of economic behaviour*. New York: McGraw-Hill.

Katona, G. (1975). *Psychological economics*. New York: Elsevier.

Meyer, B. D., & Sullivan, J. X. (2008). Changes in the consumption, income, and well-being of single mother headed families. *The American Economic Review,* 2221–2241.

Rutherford, S. (2000). *The poor and their money*. New Delhi: Oxford university press.

Stigler, G. J. (1954). The early history of empirical studies of consumer behaviour. *The Journal of Political Economy*, 95–113.

United Nations. (2005). *Microfinance and the millennium development goals: A reader's guide to the millennium project reports and other UN documents*. New York: United Nations.

Chapter 16
Infrastructure Financing in India: At the Crossroads

Bishnu Prasad Mishra

Abstract The spectrum of financing infrastructure in India ranged from complete budgetary support to extensive fund raising in the private space including frantic effort to internationalize the funding Channels. The necessary regulatory changes for varied sources and varied instruments used have culminated over the years in a dynamic construct of funding avenues. The infrastructure engagement over the past years have yielded valuable lessons about project design and appraisal, poverty focus, private sector participation, environmental and social sustainability, the issue of corruption and stakeholders communication apart from supportive funding sources. The experiment of new sources of funding has some extent succeeded in certain cases and some has also floundered to meet the specific needs of the infrastructure. However, it is high time to strengthen the sources where considerable success has been achieved and reappraise the risk and potent deterrent/road blocks where the result has somewhat not up to the expected level. In short, the infrastructure funding space currently looks hazy and badly in need of a relook, if all the announced policy goals have the slender chance of meeting with success in days to come.

Keywords Infrastructure finance · Infra-asset funding · Public private participation

16.1 Introduction

Infrastructure sector is a key driver for the Indian economy. The sector is responsible for propelling India's overall development and enjoys intense focus from the Government for initiating policies that would ensure time-bound creation of world class infrastructure in the country. Infrastructure sector includes Transport of all forms, Energy and Power, Municipal solid waste management, water and waste

B. P. Mishra (✉)
XIMB, Xavier University Bhubaneshwar, Bhubaneshwar 751013, Odisha, India
e-mail: bishnu@ximb.ac.in

A. K. Mishra et al. (eds.), *Current Issues in the Economy and Finance of India*,
Springer Proceedings in Business and Economics,
https://doi.org/10.1007/978-3-319-99555-7_16

water management; social infrastructure and Information and Communication Technology (ICT) development. The infrastructure engagement over the past years have yielded valuable lessons about project design and appraisal, poverty focus, private sector participation, environmental and social sustainability, the issues of corruption and stakeholder communication.

MGI (Mckinsey Global Institute 2016) estimates that infrastructure typically has a socio-economic rate of return of around 20%. In other words, one rupee of infrastructure investment can raise GDP by approximately 20 paise in the long run. These economic effects stem mostly from making a given region more productive through means such as reduced travel time and costs, access to reliable electricity, and broadband connectivity that allows individuals and businesses to plug into the digital global economy. Some infrastructure investments, if well-chosen and well executed, can have benefit-cost ratios of up to 20:1. In addition to the long-term productivity benefits, infrastructure construction immediately creates jobs. Analysis suggests that in the shorter term, increasing infrastructure investment by one percentage point of GDP (Gross Domestic Product) could generate an additional 3.4 million direct and indirect jobs in India.

This paper is structured as follows. The next section presents an over view of infrastructure funding in Indian context. Then the importance of private capital and capital market role in India till date has been reviewed. Next, the assessment is made as regards what can be done to meet the investors need and the complexities of infra asset funding with regard to facilities in terms regulation, market access, funds flow and institutional arrangements. The concluding remarks relates to the options available to be guided for challenging task of reconciling private incentive and government policy for infrastructure asset funding.

16.2 Overview of Infrastructure Funding

16.2.1 Nature of Infrastructure Funding

There is a compelling Indian need for greater infrastructure investment. Well-functioning infrastructure is critical to driving sustainable long-term economic growth. In many countries, it is becoming more challenging to meet funding requirements from traditional sources. Private investors express concerns about regulatory uncertainty, which increases both the risk profile of infrastructure investments and the cost of providing private capital to help fund public infrastructure, despite their long-term strategic interest in infrastructure as an asset class.

Financing a public infrastructure megaproject is highly complex, with multiple financing instruments, various economic and social factors, as well as a range of stakeholders with different and sometimes, conflicting objectives to consider (Henn et al. 2015). Policymakers now recognize that the choice of financing approach not only influences the future stream of financing costs and contingent liabilities that society is burdened with, but also impacts the eventual success of projects. The selection of financing instruments for infrastructure megaprojects also has significant broader economic impacts and unintended consequences, such as the imposition of debt ceilings, credit rating downgrades, infrastructure deficits, and even economic growth (Checherita-Westphal and Rother 2012; Henn et al. 2015).

16.2.2 Funding Paradigm in India

There are four primary pillars of infrastructure funding, namely Governments and other public authorities (ii) Multilateral Institutions (iii) Bank lending and (iv) Capital markets (both domestic as well as international). In recent years, the first two, which are the more traditional pillars of funding, have reduced the amount of capital available to commit to infrastructure investments, though they remain important players.

While most of the earlier infrastructure spending was state funded in India, the Government evinced strong interest in infrastructure only towards the end of the last century. Few designated institutions like IDBI, ICICI, IIBI, and IFCI etc. were created to cater to long term funding of selected category of projects, as decided by the government in power. There were large amount of resource allocation, either from budget sources or through concessional funding. These came to an end due to budgetary constraints and the strong belief that concessional funding for project lending must stop. As a result, these institutions became paralyzed and defunct. For survival, some converted themselves to commercial Banks, while others met with closure.

To fill up the vacuum and to support infrastructure funding in long term, Infrastructure Development and Finance Corporation (IDFC) and India Infrastructure Finance Company Limited (IIFCL) was created in 1997 and 2006 respectively. IDFC's conversion to a Bank was inevitable and the track record of IIFCL did not much reflect its effective role in facilitating infrastructure spending. Hence, Government-led institutions were found to be lacking in fulfilling their intended role and thus, became non-starters.

16.2.3 Multilateral Institutional Funding

Multilateral agencies have played a crucial role in the Indian infrastructure development process. International engagement was quite supportive through the years. World Bank funding, in particular, helped considerably in infrastructure growth, (occasionally even going beyond the country limit). The channelizing agency is

IIFCL which liberally finances PPP projects through funds lent by World Bank. IFC contribution is, however, small. Since 1956, IFC has invested in about 346 companies in India, providing USD 10.3 billion financing from its own account and USD 2.9 billion in mobilization from external resources. From Asian Development Bank (ADB), India has got a cumulative lending grant and cumulative assistance in infrastructure space about USD 27 billion (Dr. H. R. Khan, DG, RBI, Aug 12, 2015). The proposed New Development bank (NDB), popularly known as BRICS Bank, and the Asian Infrastructure Development bank (AIDB) is yet to be fully functional, though it raises great hope to support infrastructure funding as stated in their objectives. However, Foreign Direct Investment (FDI) received in Construction Development sector (townships, housing, built up infrastructure and construction development projects) from April 2000 to March 2017 stood at USD 24.3 billion, according to the Department of Industrial Policy and Promotion (DIPP, July, 2017).

16.2.4 Bank Lending

As infrastructure need was scaled up, Public Sector banks were asked to fund these projects. They had the limitation of insufficient capacity to evaluate these types of projects, particularly debt on the basis of Cash-flow vis-a-vis collateralized ones and structural asset-liability mismatch. Governments from 2000 onwards and the RBI (Reserve Bank of India) encouraged commercial Banking participation in Infrastructure funding. The former by actively pursuing PPP as mode of project execution and later making regulatory changes both accommodating and facilitating Commercial Banks participation in such ventures. The RBI particularly extended numerous concessions and relaxations such as: Raising Group/Individual borrower limit, Guarantee Issuance favoring other lending institutions, asset classification benefits in restructuring guidelines, conditional funding of promoters equity, financing registered SPVs set up for Infra projects and so on.

As a result, the bulk of infrastructure credit came from commercial banking space-major portion being from PSBs. In contrast, private banks were not that interested, except when colluding with large corporates to fund unviable big projects. The rapid scaling up reflects a 39% compound annual growth rate (CAGR) of outstanding bank credit to infrastructure in 15 years (2000–2015) or 104 times (RBI, Deputy Governor N. S. Vishwanatha, November 2016). Percentage share of Infrastructure bank credit rose from 1.6% of Gross bank credit to 13.4% over 2001–2013 (Speech by K. C. Chakrabarty, DG, RBI, August 9, 2013), in spite of the strict exposure norms pursued by the central bank.

Bank loans have some key advantages over bonds or other structured financing solutions in the initial phase of an infrastructure project: (I) Debt holders serve an important monitoring role in the project and banks tend to have the necessary expertise. (II) Infra projects need a gradual disbursement of funds and bank loans are sufficiently flexible. (III) Infra projects are relatively more likely to require debt restructuring in unforeseen events and banks can quickly negotiate restructurings among each other (Ehlers 2014). The jump in NPA level by Indian banks after RBI Asset Quality Review in 2015 (AQR) and the damaging account of loan failures will certainly take a toll on infra financing by these banks. There has been an over-concentration of long-dated infrastructure-related project finance exposure on the Indian banking system rather than it being diversified across banks, bond markets, pension funds and insurance companies. Secondly, banks may have mispriced these loans in the absence of any market-traded credit benchmarks. Cheap long-term loans have the least financial incentive to be paid back. In the "Financial Stability Report" (FSR-17), the RBI has said five sectors—Infrastructure, Steel, Textiles, and Power and Telecom—have contributed to more than 60% of present banking sector stress.

16.2.5 Take-Out Financing by Banks/NBFCs

Takeout financing is a route of refinance wherein new lenders take over project loans of existing lenders and thereby, stretch the loan's repayment over a longer period. Through this route, existing lenders get relief on their capital to pursue new lending opportunities and infrastructure projects get the benefit of a longer repayment period. It allows financing long-term projects with medium-term funds. Despite the obvious advantage, the mechanism has not really emerged as a game changer because this model does not envisage equitable distribution of risk and returns. In this case, the banks bear the initial credit and liquidity risk from the date of inception. Thereafter, the moment the project is economically viable, taking out the loan from book of the banks amounts to loss of opportunity of earning returns on seasoned loans.

RBI allowed non-banking finance companies (NBFCs) to provide takeout financing of projects; an option which was so far available to only banks with the sole purpose to create a level playing field for NBFCs. In a Notification (June 2016), the central bank said. "NBFCs may refinance any existing infrastructure and other project loans by way of take-out financing, without a pre-determined agreement with other lenders, and fix a longer repayment period". The RBI said that refinancing through this route would not be considered as restructured if the loans are classified as standard in the books of all other existing lenders to the project and has not been restructured in the past. Finding such asset is well-nigh impossible in the present context when the banks are in stress for their past lending decisions, mostly in Infrastructure sector.

16.3 The Indian Capital Market and Infrastructure Funding

16.3.1 The Need for Private Capital

The financing requirements are so large that a fundamental shift will be needed in how infrastructure projects are financed in India, where the public sector has, historically, covered over 90% of needs. While banks remain the dominant lenders to infrastructure projects, capital markets investors are starting to make significant inroads into the marketplace.

The deleveraging and shrinking of many banks' balance sheets—together with changes in banks' lending policies as a result of regulations (including the Basel III requirements for increased bank capital and liquidity)—have led most of the banks in India to reduce project finance lending commitments. At the same time, capital market investors such as insurers, specialist fund managers, pension funds and sovereign wealth funds have increased their capacity to invest in project bonds and equity. Insurance companies and pension funds are, in fact, 'natural' investors in infrastructure assets, since the long maturity and fixed rate nature of project bonds are a good match to their long-term liabilities. The different source of funding by a private entity can be summarized as in Table 16.1.

However, private financing is not straightforward and can come across as a multidimensional investment universe; different investors tend to assess the risks and returns of capital-intensive infrastructure investments differently. Infrastructure,

Table 16.1 Sources of funding of infrastructure

	Domestic sources	External sources
Equity	Domestic developers (independently or in collaboration with international developers) Public utilities (taking minority holdings) Other institutional investors (likely to be very limited)	International developers (independently or in collaboration with domestic developers) Equipment suppliers (in collaboration with domestic or international developers) Dedicated infrastructure funds Other international equity investors Multilateral agencies (International Finance Corporation, Asian Development Bank)
Debt	Domestic commercial banks (5–7 years) Domestic term lending institutions (7–10 years) Domestic bond markets (7–10 years) Specialized infrastructure financing institutions	International commercial banks (7–10 years) Export credit agencies (7–10 years) International bond markets (10–30 years) Multilateral agencies (15–20 years) Bilateral aid agencies

Source Ahuliwalia (1999)

as an asset class, provides for portfolio diversification and the potential for stable cash yields. It should therefore, in theory, appear as an attractive investment alternative for institutional investors (pension funds, sovereign wealth funds, insurance companies, etc.) that generally have long-term liabilities and low risk appetites. In reality however, the uptake of the expansive asset class has historically been limited.

"Most institutional investors continue to look for defensive diversification from their infrastructure allocations. In an Asian infrastructure project context, this necessitates effective structuring and risk transfer to high quality counterparties along with feasible options for managing currency exposures." (Toby Buscombe, Partner and Global Head of Infrastructure, Mercer Private Market National Investment and Infrastructure Fund (NIIF) Hong Kong).

For example, infrastructure asset allocation in 2014 only accounted for 0.8% of the USD 50 trillion managed by institutional investors globally. In order to increase institutional investor's commitments to infrastructure asset class, it is important to understand the different investment behaviors and preferences of different investor classes—ranging from duration to return expectations and to type of investment grades.

16.3.2 Indian Capital Market and Infrastructure Funding

However, over a period of time, Indian capital markets, increasingly supported by liberal policies by sector regulators, demonstrated a high level of flexibility for fund raising by Indian corporates as the following table shows year wise project executed by Indian companies (Table 16.2).

Table 16.2 Project commissioned by India Inc.

Year	Rupees in crore
2005–06	109,000
2006–07	191,000
2007–08	224,000
2008–09	305,000
2009–10	393,000
2010–11	347,000
2011–12	412,000
2012–13	366,000
2013–14	329,000
2014–15	397,000
2015–16	458,000

Source CMIE (2018)

Table 16.3 IPOs in the Indian market

Year	No. of IPOs	Amount raised	Top sector	Share(%)
2007	100	34,179	Real estate	38
2008	37	16,904	Power	80
2009	20	19,544	Power	60
2010	64	37,535	Mining	40
2011	37	5966	Financials	55
2012	11	6835	Telecom	61
2013	3	1284	Power	62
2014	5	1201	Infra	27
2015	21	13,614	Aviation	20
2016	26	26,494	Financials	29
2017	54	80,853	Financials	50

Source Prime Data base

To support these projects, Initial Public offers (IPOs) were floated in Indian Capital Market by corporates which were heavily subscribed. Table 16.3 details the share of infrastructure IPO's in total fund-raising efforts over a decade.

In the spectrum of domestic capital market, a lot of flexibility has been provided by the RBI as well as SEBI to increase corporate access to the market for directly mobilizing funds. In this process, new avenues are being opened up with newer instruments so that the funding need of infrastructure can be met. The primary goal is to develop and strengthen the Bond/Debt market so that eligible corporates can have unfettered access to funds directly from varied types of investors, both domestic and external.

16.3.3 Regulatory Facilitation and Instruments for Infra-funding

The form of investment can affect its appeal to investors due to regulatory or commercial restrictions contained in their mandates, regarding for example, listing, credit ratings and security. Project bonds can either be listed on a stock exchange, or issued on an unlisted basis. Listing and public credit ratings have the advantage of potentially expanding a transaction's investor base and enhancing liquidity, but at the cost of requiring the issuer (which may be the project company, or a sister company which issues the bonds and on-lends the proceeds to the project company) to comply with various listing-related regulations and information requirements. That said, this may be seen as an advantage, as the transaction then benefits from the confirmation that the disclosure has complied with the relevant listing rules or rating agency requirements. A 'public' transaction is almost always likely to require a listing and a credit rating, while a privately placed transaction can be listed or unlisted. While a public credit rating is often preferred, it may not always be required.

Masala Bonds are rupee denominated bonds with their coupon rates to be serviced in rupee as well, thereby, bearing no liability in foreign currency. The currency risk is, thus, transferred to investor rather than borrower. Recent Indian issues of Masala Bonds are most innovative financial products bearing their origination to IFC's first Rupee Bond raised internationally in September 2015. Thereafter, various Indian corporates and institutions like HDFC, NTPC and NHAI have further raised around Rs. 12,770/- crore by means of Masala Bonds. Companies have to explore every possibility of using this rupee borrowing option from global investors for bringing cost effective debt fund into India.

Green Bonds typically represents funds raised by the Clean Energy companies from domestic and international investors. Typically, the global climate change and climate control funds as also CSR funds seeking Green (Clean) Energy as a mission destination and generating some returns alongside are clearly allowing the interest tag for Green Bonds. Recent issuances by EXIM Bank, YES Bank and Renew Power are all beads in the same golden thread. The low cost of fund helps achieve lower tariff, thus resulting in a win-win situation for all the stakeholders. Globally, total green bonds issuance stood at USD 21.76 billion during the first quarter of 2017, up nearly 42% from the issuance during the same period last year—according to the Climate Bonds Initiative.

Credit Enhancement has remained as one of the most unique financial products for infrastructure projects seeking access to global money. For example, the Monoline Insurer's stellar role of guaranteeing infrastructure projects in USA and Europe for mobilizing funds from investors is a case in point. The guaranteed support of stronger national and international institutions provided for a fee to any company (which could typically be rated say around BBB or A, A-) would be able to get a rating of around AAA. This shall enable it to seek global money from long term Pension, Sovereign and Insurance Funds (which could otherwise not be able to invest in their lower rated bonds), thus creating a market place enviable for good companies. ShriArunJaitely, Finance Minister in Budget for 2016–17 announced that "A dedicated fund to provide credit enhancement to infrastructure projects will be set up. The fund will help in raising the credit rating of bonds floated by infrastructure companies and facilitate investments from long term investors. As follow up measure, a company named "Indian Infrastructure Company Limited (IIFCL)", having 20% stake in the SPV for credit enhancement purpose is already registered with an initial corpus of INR 500 crore.

Role of InvITs and ReITs InvIT is an acronym for Infrastructure Investment Trust and ReIT is for Real Estate Investment Trust. It represents a Trust, registered with SEBI, formed with an objective to invest in infrastructure/Real Estate projects directly or through their SPVs. It has the potential of emerging as one of the strongest innovative financial products, allowing the unlocking of not only Equity but also Debt. The investment mechanism facilitates capital infusion into the infrastructure/Real Estate sector by providing small sums of money from investors to infrastructure developer to monetize his assets and complete projects that sometimes get stalled mid-way due to lack of funding. This may provide stable cash-flow to Insurance and Mutual Fund entities, given the exemption from dividend distribution tax. In order to restrict the banks in investing, the RBI said banks should not invest more than 10% of the unit capital of a real estate investment trust (ReIT) or an infrastructure investment trust (InvIT), subject to overall ceiling of 20% of its net worth.

There is a debate on whether an InvIT, by its nature of investment, is equity or debt as it has features of both. It is somewhere in between; loosely, debt-plus or equity-minus in terms of risk return profile. The equity-like features are that the units are listed, can change hands like equity stocks; there is periodic valuation of the projects akin to periodic results of companies and economic factors like higher GDP growth or higher inflation would lead to expectation of higher revenue and hence higher price of the units at the Exchange. The debt-like feature is the periodic pay-out of the earnings of the InvIT from the underlying SPVs, which is not exactly like contractual coupon pay-out on bonds but somewhat comparable, as the valuation gives a perspective on how much to expect. It is a hybrid instrument with a somewhat predictable cash flow yield (akin to debt) and potential appreciation with growth of the economy (akin to equity).

Taxation wise, an InvIT is a pass-through vehicle. There is a mandate to distribute at least 90% of net-distributable cash flows. Interest component of income distributed by trust to the unit holders would attract withholding tax @ 10% for resident unit holders. Interest income is taxable in the hands of the unit holder. Dividend income is exempt in the hands of the unit holder and there is no dividend distribution tax.

InvITs have created deleveraging of the balance sheets of infrastructure companies. InvITs are also unlocking equity and causing a return of debt funds borrowed from the bankers. This has not only resulted in healthy situation for banks but also creating capacity for fresh borrowing by infrastructure companies for new projects. Six (6) InvITs have been conceptualized. Two InvITs(India Grid Trust and IRB InvIT Fund) have already raised money aggregating to around INR 7000 Cr. (approx.) from the market and got listed.

Despite attractive yields, InvITs gathered very few fan followers in the secondary market. The first two listed InvITs are currently trading below their respective issue price. What is more, the issuers continue to add more assets in the hope of incentivizing investors. Recently, India Grid Trust, which owns transmission assets, added three new transmission assets valued at INR 1490 crore taking the current AUM (asset under management) to INR 5300 crore. The idea of adding assets at subsequent stages is to improve the overall yields. While companies are adding yield-accretive assets to perk up the overall yield, investors are still not much enthusiastic. Both the listed InvITs offer a yield of about 12%, which is about

526 basis points higher than the 10-year government Gsec yields and 440 basis points higher compared to an "AA" rated three-year corporate bond. Apart from the awareness, what is causing the damage is a perception about the uncertainty of yield. While the yields are calculated more scientifically and independently, they suffer from the estimates and assumptions made for the next 15–20 years. *Transferring assets into the existing portfolio will solve the problems of the parent companies as it will be able to reduce debt. But given the uncertainty of the cash flows, whether InvIT investors make money still needs to be seen.* Cash flow may get impacted based on the revenues and profitability of these assets. But, as pension and insurance monies look for long-dated investments backed by stable cash flow characteristics over time, positive response to this instrument is expected to emerge, giving sponsors a greater diversity of financing sources. But ReIT is yet to take off in the Indian capital market. The Private Equity industry under alternative Investment Fund (AIF), which grew 55% in FY 17, contributed 19% of VC/PE inflows as per the Prequin Report (2017).

16.4 Indian Infra-funding: An Assessment

16.4.1 Infra Asset Delivery so Far

A lot depends on the Government Regulatory framework designed for infrastructure services and the resultant asset structure created thereof. The quality and volume of infrastructure has a positive effect on the attractiveness, competitiveness, sustainability and economic growth. In case of India, the demand for infrastructure investments continue to focus on primary care and utilities, in particular, in the nature of Green field projects. Most of the Brown field Infrastructure facilities must be operated, serviced, maintained, modernized, and adjusted to meet current requirements. Funding for the development and operation of such projects in India has largely been financed with the assistance of development subsidies and multi-lateral sponsor organizations, from budgetary support etc., where private investors rarely got involved up to the last century.

However, when the Government started implementing the mode of delivery of infra services through Public-Private Partnership (PPP) model of different variants, the things changed radically in favor of the private funding initiatives. PPP means an arrangement between Government, statutory entity, or government owned entity on one side and a private sector entity on the other, for the provision of public assets and/or public services, through investment being made and/or management being undertaken by the private sector entity, for a specific period of time, where there is well-defined allocation of risk between the private sector and the public entity, the private entity being chosen on the basis of open competitive bidding receives performance linked payments that conform(or are benchmarked) to specified and pre-determined performance standards and measurable by the public entity or its representative (Public Private Partnership Monitor—ADB 2017).

Table 16.4 Projects granted final approval under VGF Scheme, from Dec 2005 to Aug 2017, as of 19 Sep, 2017

S.No.	Sector	No. of projects	Total project cost (INR crores)	VGF approved (INR crores)
1	Bridge	2	2096	396
2	Metro	1	12,132	1458
3	Power	3	925	162
4	Roads	48	18,595	3537
5	Silos	6	177	15
6	Water supply and sanitation	1	188	38
Total		61	34,113	5606

Source www.pppinindia.gov.in

From the perspective of the number and overall value of projects, India has emerged as one of the major PPP markets. During the period 1990–2016, a total count of 861 projects, with investment worth USD 314 billion, were made in almost all sectors, including Transportation (Roads, Ports, Air-ports and Railways),Energy (Power, Oil and Gas) and Urban Utilities as well as Social sectors. In fact, a lot of projects have got support via "Viability Gap funding" (VGF) from the central Government, as the data shown in Table 16.4.

16.4.2 Investors' Need in Infrastructure Assets

Infrastructure assets offer a wide variety of risk-return cash profiles, theoretically ranging from highly conservative bond/fixed income-style asset profiles through to investment opportunities that are comparable to private equity. Most financing methods employ various financing instruments to ensure an optimal structure. How sponsors or procurement authorities choose the most efficient financing depends on a variety of factors. Deciding whether a bank loan, a debt private placement or a project bond finance in the capital markets is more attractive for a specific project depends on factors such as:

- The size, complexity and the type of the transaction;
- Bank and capital market conditions at the relevant time;
- Issuance and Swap costs;
- The need for special terms such as any non-standard covenants;
- The time available for the marketing and preparation of financial documentation;
- Strategic considerations, such as investor diversification and public visibility;
- Whether staged drawdowns of funds are available and if not, the expected costs of negative carry.

In contrast, all investors in infrastructure generally share certain financial goals (May not form a homogeneous group) and their individual interests may differ when it comes to investing in infrastructure assets. In addition to differing risk-return profiles reflected in selection of certain countries, sectors, stages of entry, currencies and the like, the targeted cash flow profiles, which are most closely linked to the investors investment horizon for such assets, may differ as well (Barbara et al. 2016).

For debt-financed infrastructure assets, Project bankability in emerging markets has been a key concern for investors in infrastructure for many years. Marsh and McLennan Companies' Asia Pacific Risk Center estimates (2017) that between 55 and 65% of projects in Asia are not bankable without support from Government or Multilateral Development Banks. A project is considered to be highly bankable, if it conforms to the following benchmarks:

- Appropriate covenants and funding structure (Potential approval and preparation process enhancements)
- Thorough due diligence
- Proper documentation and deal structure
- Well-structured concession rights
- Presence of legal and economic recourse
- Robust rights to payment
- Ensuring appropriate risk transfer.

"We need to understand why people go through the hassle of doing due diligence, pricing deals, creating covenants and negotiating rights of ways. This is because they need to quantify risk, manage their capital, and ensure efficiency. They are looking for ways to expand the velocity of capital in this sector." (Eric Pascal, Partner, Oliver Wyman, 2014).

16.4.3 The Step Forward

Indian regulatory environment is yet to converge with the fiscal concessions extended by the Government for attracting Infrastructure investments and flexibility shown by SEBI in facilitating and broad basing the infrastructure funding instruments as well as investor profile. However, as pointed out in the recent evaluation report of ADB (2017), the support extended by the Indian Government has to be further enhanced. A few samples are listed below.

(a) With a view to enhance transparency in PPP projects, the Department of Economic Affairs (DEA) proposes setting up of a dedicated dispute resolution mechanism to address issues related to bidding and award of PPP projects. However, this is yet to be implemented.
(b) The approach for Government guarantees varies between central and state sectors. In case of central sectors PPP projects, Government guarantees are part

of risk—mitigation strategy adopted on a project-specific basis and are not defined explicitly.

(c) The Rail Development authority—an entity, as announced in the Railway budget 2016–17 to facilitate fixing of various user charges and to speed up proposed PPP projects, is yet to be established.

(d) In the rail sector, the Central Project Review Board (CPRB) is almost non-functional when the proposed investment is huge (20 projects involving investment of INR 1.4 lakh crore).

(e) Privatization is on full force in the Port sector, but the excess labour issues and related efficiency of labour force are not taken rightly in the absence of data.

(f) Multiple approval agencies are involved in the Aviation sector.

When making infrastructure investments, there are two types of investor class: primarily yield-driven or IRR-driven investors. Yield-driven investors tend to look for a stable, long-term income in order to match the maturities of their assets with the maturities of their liabilities. These include insurance companies, private and corporate pension funds, Sovereign wealth funds, charitable foundations etc. They usually have a buy-and-hold investment horizon for long term and satisfied with the current yield in the form of dividends or interest.

IRR-driven investors have a short to medium-term horizon of approximately two to seven years (an early exit). Such investors include the resale value of the asset at the exit into their return calculation and prepared to forego early and/or current cash flows during the asset holding period. This category of investors includes strategic investors, investment funds managed by professionals as well as institutional investors with similar short-term focus. As a matter of principle, the exit strategies have to be arranged for such investors—sale via the secondary market, a trade sale or an IPO.

Keeping aside the return part in Infrastructure projects, an external investor has to deal with Country level and Project level risks. A key contribution of risk management principle is to allow the bundling and unbundling of various risks to align risk exposures with the ability to bear them. There are three kinds of large scale institutions—MNCs, large commercial banks and multilateral financial institutions (that are capable of generating information and exerting leverage by diversifying their holding)—that are best to bear both the risks. The portfolio investors are strongly advantaged in terms of their ability to diversify country risk, but not the project risk. Hence, their role in the funding space comes when the project cash-flow is stable and project risks are minimized to the extent possible to make it attractive in risk-return spectrum.

The inherent challenges of infrastructure finance call for new types of financing instruments. Infrastructure equity or debt investors face two simultaneous issues: (i) long-term commitments of financial resources to an investment which is typically not liquid, and (ii) an inherent difficulty to price the associated long-term risks. Traditional financing instruments, such as direct equity stakes or bank loans, force investors to deal with these two problems at the same time. In addition, there is a natural tendency for investors to turn to more liquid and short-term instruments in periods of high market uncertainty ("short-termism"). But financial innovation can counter the "short-termism" of investors (Landau 2013).

Financial instruments can help to separate liquidity risks and the pricing of long-term risks. Bonds or infrastructure funds render infrastructure investments tradable, and therefore, help to increase their liquidity. Greater securitization activity for infrastructure loans seems also desirable, as this can help banks to diversify their risks and alleviate large bulk risks of a single project, which are so difficult to quantify. New financial instruments which allow separation of liquidity risks and long-term credit risks would help improve the attractiveness of long-term financing.

Moving beyond the currently prevalent financing instruments of direct equity investments and bank loans has further advantages. As argued above, it can make infrastructure, as an asset class, more accessible to a broader group of investors. In this light, it helps to diversify the large risks of infrastructure projects across many groups of investors. In addition, the vast resources of capital market, which are currently hardly tapped by infrastructure projects, are much more accessible with a broader mix of financial instruments. Infrastructure bonds and infrastructure funds carry a high potential; and other financial instruments, such as collateralized infrastructure loans, for instance, do also attract substantial investor demand. Finally, there also exist other financial instruments that allow a better diversification of risks. This is highly desirable, as infrastructure risks are currently shouldered to a large extent by the banking sector and the public sector through guarantees (Ehlers 2014).

Countries in the emerging markets that want to meet their required investment needs over the next decade and beyond, will have to attract funds from global institutional investors. Till date, they have generally been wary of infrastructure investment in these markets. Innovative ideas to unlock new sources of funding are urgently needed. A good example is the dual-purpose MART storm water tunnel in Kuala Lumpur, Malaysia. In order to generate a return on a major capital investment and attract investors, the central section of the tunnel doubles up as a toll motor way (when it's not raining of course), thus, providing flood protection and alleviating traffic congestion. The world has to find 'smarter' ways like this to manage risks and bridge the substantive funding gap. In reality, however, global investors have global alternatives, and infrastructure projects across much of Asia rarely rank as the most attractive option to deploy capital on a risk adjusted basis—there is simply too much risk and uncertainty over investment returns. The problem is not that these projects represent an acceptable level of return, but are simply beaten by even higher returns in other asset classes elsewhere.

No country presents an ideal combination of circumstances and experience shows that there are many ways of solving problems that constrain such investment—ways that differ from project to project and country to country. Financial markets show great scope for innovation in tailoring financing solutions to financing needs. Policies need to be flexible to allow such innovation to flourish (Ahuliwalia 1999).

16.5 Conclusion

The OECD estimates that USD 70 trillion in infrastructure investment is needed by 2030 to simply maintain the current levels of global GDP growth. Private capital can help bridge the shortfall in infrastructure funding. To promote a greater role for private capital in infrastructure projects, policy makers need to craft a policy framework for infrastructure investing tailored to investors' needs. The infrastructure financing gap is not new, but it continues to grow rapidly. Given this overall boom, it is no surprise that the Asian Development Bank forecasts that the region requires USD 26 trillion of investment in infrastructure over the period 2016–2030. However, this expected demand is tempered by a reality in which there are significant uncertainties over where the money to fund this development will come from. The main reason is that the preconditions for private financing of infrastructure are more difficult to establish than is commonly realized.

India, rightly to date, followed the funding mosaic by graduating from full budgetary support, further led by bank funding through PPP mechanism resulting in islands of successful infrastructure delivery. The much hope for "Sagarmala", "Bharatmala" and other schemes announced for infrastructure sector will only come to fruition, if the Government changes its goal to transit from PPP to PFI (Privately Funded Infrastructure projects) mode. It will help in two ways—The Government Effort will be more concentrated in creating facilitative regulation and Independent Regulators will look after sectorial implementation. Secondly, the direct financing burden will pass on to the private market participants and banks will engage themselves with commercial lending which is their forte.

Encouraging capital markets investment in infrastructure has the potential to bridge the world's infrastructure funding gap, including that of India. A holistic and consistent policy framework is necessary to incentivize greater private capital investment in infrastructure. This framework should provide certainty, transparency, an alignment of public and private interests, and a stable and consistent tax and regulatory environment. Striking the appropriate balance between public policy and investor needs will certainly facilitate and promote greater private infrastructure investment.

References

Ahuliwalia, M. S. (1999). *Financing private infrastructure: Lessons from India*. Planning Commission, Government of India.

Asian Development Bank (ADB). (2017). Public private partnership monitor.

Association for Financial Market for Europe (AFME). (2015). Guide to infrastructure financing.

Ball, R. (2009). Provision of public service infrastructure. *International Journal of Public Sector Management, 24*(1), 5–22.

Barbara, W., Mirjam, S., & Alfen, H. W. (2016). *Infrastructure as an asset class, investment strategy, sustainability, project finance & PPP* (2nd ed.). New York: Wiley.

Black Rock. (2015). Infrastructure investment: Bridging the gap between public and investor need.

Brealey, R., Cooper, I., & Habib, M. (1996). Using project finance to fund infrastructure investments. *Journal of Applied Corporate Finance, 9*(3).

Checherita-Westphal, C., & Rother, P. (2012). The impact of high government debt on economic growth and its channels. *European Economic Review, 56*(7), 1392–1405.

Chkraborty, K. C. (2013, August). Infrastructure financing by banks in India: Myths and realities. *RBI Bulletin*.

Della Croce, R. (2012). *Trends in large pension fund investment in infrastructure*. OECD Working Paper, No. 29.

Ehlers, T. (2014, August). *Understanding the challenges of infrastructure finance*. BIS working Paper No. 454.

Engel, E., Fischer, R., & Galetovic, A. (2010). The economics of infrastructure finance: Public private partnership verses public provision. *EIB Papers, 15*(1).

Finerty. J. D. (2013). *Project financing: Asset based financial engineering*. New York: Wiley.

Hasan, R. (2017). *Meeting Asia's infrastructure needs*. Asian Development Bank.

Henn, L., Charles, M. B., Douglas, N., & Sloan, K. (2015). Multi-criteria framework needed to assess alternative financing methods for large scale projects. *Public Money & Management, 35* (2), 100–102.

HSBC. (2013, March). Infrastructure and PPP bonds: Capital markets and how to access institutional capital.

Inderst, G. (2009, January). *Pension funds investment in infrastructure*. OECD Working Paper No 32.

Khan, H. R. (2015, September). Financing for infrastructure: Current issues and emerging challenges. *RBI Bulletin*.

Laudau, J.-P. (2013, December). Deleveraging, long-term finance and the G20 agenda. BIS Paper No. 75.

Liesel, H., Keith, S., Charles, M. B., & Neil, D. (2016). An appraisal framework for evaluating financing approaches for public infrastructure. *Public Money & Management, 36*(4), 273–280.

Marsh McLennan Asia Pacific Risk Centre. (2017). Closing the financing gap. Infrastructure Project bankability in Asia.

McKinsey Global Institute. (2012, November). *The future of long-term finance: backup material*. Report for Group of Thirty.

McKinsey Global Institute. (2016, June). Bridging global infrastructure gaps.

Meltzer, J. P. (2015). *Financing sustainable infrastructure*. The Brookings Institution. https://www.brookings.edu/wp-content/uploads/2016/08/Global_20160818_financing_sustainable_infrastructure.pdf .

Miller, R., & Lessard, D. (2001, October). *Understanding and managing risks in multilateral development bank*. Working Group on Infrastructure.

Preqin. (2011). *LP views on infrastructure fund management fees*. Preqin Research.

Sorge, M. (2004, December). The nature of credit risk in project finance. *BIS Quarterly Review*.

World Bank. (2006, June). *India, financing infrastructure: Addressing constraints and challenges*.

Yescombe, E. (2007). *Public private partnerships: Principles of policy and finance*. London: Butterworth-Heinemann.

Subject Index

A. K. Mishra et al. (eds.), *Current Issues in the Economy and Finance of India*, Springer Proceedings in Business and Economics,
https://doi.org/10.1007/978-3-319-99555-7